An Inexplicable Attraction:

My Fifty Years of Ocean Sailing

by Eric B. Forsyth

An Inexplicable Attraction: *My Fifty Years of Ocean Sailing*

Cover photo: *Fiona* sails by Greenwich Island, Antarctica

Copyright © 2016

Eric B. Forsyth
Green Ocean Race™ Productions
www.greenoceanrace.com

A Yacht Fiona Book
www.yachtfiona.com

Published by:
Green Ocean Race Productions

Edited by:
Margaret Daisley, Blue Horizon Books, www.bluehorizonbooks.com

Cover and design by:
Jay R. Pizer, Imax Productions, www.imaxproductions.com

Printed in the United States of America

Publisher's Cataloging-in-Publication data:
Forsyth, Eric.
An inexplicable allure: my fifty years at sea / Eric B. Forsyth
ISBN 978-0-692-80681-4

First Edition

DEDICATION

Edith M. Forsyth, M.D., 1933-1991

This book is dedicated to Dr. Edith Forsyth. She was my wonderful wife, a loving mother, and a compassionate physician. For many years she was my shipmate and best friend. I will never know why she married the devil-may-care, flippant young man I was, but I am eternally grateful.

Contents

List of Charts

Sketch charts, not to be used for navigation

Introduction: The Route to Retirement

In 1995, I retired at the age of 63, and within a month I was living on my 42-foot sailboat *Fiona*, starting on a round-the-world circumnavigation. This was clearly a ridiculous thing to do—I could have done it in far more comfort and far less expense by booking first-class on an airliner. But sailing is a curious, inexplicable addiction. A sense of humor helps.

In many ways I have spent much of my life escaping; perhaps the cruise was the latest manifestation. I spent a wartime childhood in industrial Lancashire and escaped the fate of my father and grandfather, both of whom worked in the grimy cotton mills, by going to Manchester University and then flying with the Royal Air Force. Now, flying really is escaping. The first generation of jet fighters which I flew for a few years gave me the keenest pleasure and biggest adrenalin kick I have ever known. But Britain got involved in

Eric at the controls of a Meteor Mark 8, Britain's frontline fighter at the time, 1954

what became known as the Suez Debacle, the RAF shrank, and my squadron, along with many others, was disbanded. I was horrified that the government would so casually jettison thousands of skilled mechanics and hundreds of pilots, including some who had served in the Battle of Britain. Later I was to discover this was not unusual for governments. So I escaped to Canada.

My sweetheart, Edith, whom I had met while at the university, followed me to Canada when I emigrated there in 1957, and we got married at Toronto city hall. We knew nobody; the couple waiting behind us to be married were our witnesses. When the clerk noticed this, he asked us if we knew what we were doing. I picked up a commercial pilot's license, based on a Canadian flying and written test and my RAF experience, but a good job was hard to find, so Edith suggested I enroll in Toronto University's engineering graduate school. Edith had a medical degree from Manchester and set about getting Canadian qualifications.

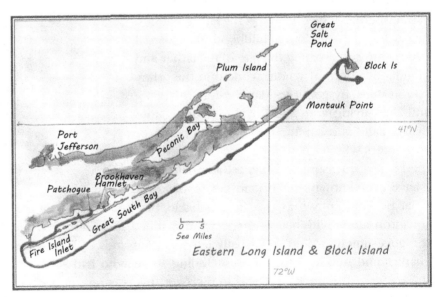

Money was tight and this time I did not escape; we were rescued. By an astonishing series of coincidences after I graduated we were both offered positions on the scientific staff of Brookhaven National Laboratory on Long Island, New York. We drove down in the fall of 1960 in our Morris Minor with our two cats, towing a small canoe. We rented a house on Bellport Bay and the canoe was soon swapped for a 16-foot plywood sailboat. In turn, this boat was exchanged for a 23-foot sailboat with a small cabin and an inboard engine, a True Rocket. Our greatest adventure on that boat was to sail round Montauk Point at the extreme east end of Long Island, a 14- to 17-hour sail.

Eric learning to sail on their 16-foot baby Narrasketuk on the canal behind the house rented in Brookhaven Hamlet, Long Island, New York, 1961

Great Salt Pond

Plum Island

Block Is

Montauk Point

41°N

Port Jefferson

Peconic Bay

Brookhaven Hamlet

Patchogue

Great South Bay

0   5
Sea Miles

Fire Island Inlet

Eastern Long Island & Block Island

72°W

In 1961 we flew to the Caribbean for a winter vacation. We had chartered two bunks for eight days on a 78-foot ketch called *Maverick*, operated by an entrepreneur named Jack Carstarphen who had sailed from San Diego. He was one of the first sailors to offer charters in what were then the unspoiled Virgin Islands. There were no bare boats for charter then and virtually all commercial activity was centered on Charlotte Amalie in St. Thomas. Edith and I were entranced by the tropics; many of the islands were still under British colonial rule and the inhabitants enjoyed a leisurely if somewhat poverty-stricken way of life.

We sailed aboard *Maverick* again a year later, and that time we met a couple who had sailed from South Africa and were en route to England via New York on a home-made 46-foot cutter called *Arvin Court II*. John and Barbara Knight looked us up when they got to New York and we wound up crewing for them in 1964 from Port Jefferson on Long Island to Falmouth, England. It took thirty-three days.

This was the first introduction to deep water sailing for Edith and me, and we were very sea-sick. There were seven of us on the boat, including three women. The men stood watches continuously at the tiller. I learned a great deal from John, including how to navigate by the sun and stars.

Edith at the wheel of Maverick, *British Virgin Islands, 1961*

Once back on land, the sea-sickness was forgotten and we set about trying to find a boat we could sail to the Caribbean. Our son Colin was born in 1965, the same year we acquired *Iona*, a beautiful, Dutch-built sloop, 35 feet long with a steel hull. By 1968, we dug our way out of the financial hole we had created by buying *Iona* and a house, and having a son. We sold the house, and I sailed the boat to the Virgin Islands with four young men for crew. Edith met me in St. Thomas with Colin and the one surviving cat. We all lived on the boat until

Bringing the True Rocket from Quogue to Brookhaven; Edith, Charley Gould, Dave Thomas, Steve Gould, 1963

September of 1969, when we again ran out of money. It had been an escape, but only a temporary one.

I went back to work at the laboratory and Edith started her own family medical practice in 1971 after our daughter Brenda was born. After more cruising between Bermuda and New England, we sold *Iona*. I navigated a 46-foot schooner, *Sea Swan*, from Long Island to St. Thomas, and sailed in half a dozen Newport to Bermuda races as navigator over the next decade as the kids grew up. We also chartered sailboats for a week or two in the Bahamas and Caribbean, but I knew what I wanted.

Sailing Experience Prior to *Fiona*

DATE	BOAT/POSITION	LOCATION	DISTANCE NM
1961-1963	*True Rocket* Captain, with Edith	Long Island	250
1964	*Arvincourt II* Crew, with Edith	Transatlantic Crossing	3,000
1965	*True Rocket, Iona* Captain	Rhode Island, Long Island	250
1966	*Iona* Captain, with Edith	Block Island, Nantucket	340
1967	*Iona* Captain	Nova Scotia, Maine	1,395
1967	*Iona* Captain, with Edith	Newport, Block Island (America's Cup Race)	296
1968-1969	*Iona* Captain, with Edith	Bermuda, Caribbean, Bahamas, Intracoastal	6,607
1969	*Iona* Captain, with Edith	Block Island, Nantucket, Long Island	514
1970	*Iona* Captain, with Edith	Block Island, Nantucket, Long Island	340
1971	*Iona* Captain, with Edith	Bermuda	1,507

DATE	BOAT/POSITION	LOCATION	DISTANCE NM
1971	*Sea Swan* Navigator	Long Island to St. Thomas	2,000
1972-1982	Various Navigator	Newport to Bermuda Race (six times plus one return)	4,800
1972-1982	Various Captain, with Edith	Charters in Bahamas, Caribbean, Florida	500
1983-2012	*Fiona* Captain	*Fiona*'s sailing history follows	247,362
Total:			**269,161**

In 1974, during a visit to California, I found my escape tunnel—a boat being made in Costa Mesa to very high standards, a Westsail 42. She was a classic North Sea design modeled on the double-enders designed by Colin Archer nearly a century earlier. I had been attending a conference in California. Edith came along for a break and I mentioned the Westsail yard was an hour down the road. So we rented a car and drove down to take a look. The first Westsail 42 was on the stocks; Edith took one look and said, "My God, it's another f'ing *Iona!*" Which is why our boat was ultimately named *Fiona*.

Iona and the True Rocket at Eric and Edith's home on a canal in Brookhaven, New York, 1965

I decided to buy the boat as an almost bare hull and finish her myself, which meant that I would not only save a little money, but I could incorporate the lessons I had learned up to then. She was delivered by transcontinental truck to our house in Brookhaven Hamlet in 1975. I worked on the boat most evenings and week-ends. I had no problems with plumbing, electrical systems and mechanical aspects of the construction, but I had no experience with carpentry, especially ship's carpentry, which is difficult because there are virtually no right angles on a boat. I found the wood-working to be very frustrating as I learned on the job.

Fiona in the backyard at Brookhaven during construction

Ironically, to give me a break from the wood work, as relaxation I developed a secondary hobby—restoring an antique Bentley. I found working in metal to be much more satisfying and I was able to get my pre-teen son Colin involved. When the car was road-worthy, Edith and I discovered all the delights of old car rallying with other enthusiasts. Over the years, I accumulated and restored another two old Bentleys.

At the time I had no clear idea of where to escape to, or even when. Edith was very tolerant but she had limits. When my estimated time to complete *Fiona* stretched from three years to an actual eight years, I finally had the boat moved to a boatyard a few miles away. Edith then called in a contractor and had a pool installed at the spot where *Fiona* had lain for so many years. "You're not going to do that again," she said.

Eric and grand-daughter Gabriella in the 1928 Bentley he restored while building Fiona, *1975 to 1983*

Fiona *is ready to be moved to Weeks Yard, 1983.*

Fiona was launched in 1983, and for successive summers until 1989, I made fairly extensive cruises, tweaking the boat and refining my own skills. In 1990 I completed a tough assignment at work that had occupied me for four years and I took a leave of absence for a year with the intention of cruising French Polynesia for the first time. I had equipped *Fiona* with radar and satnav, and Edith had hired a young physician to assist her in her practice. We were ready. The plan was for me to sail the boat through the Panama Canal and meet Edith and our daughter Brenda in Tahiti. Edith would stay six to eight weeks and then return home, and I would then cruise to the Gambier Islands and round Cape Horn about Christmas. I would meet up with Edith again in Uruguay and return home to the Caribbean before the start of the next hurricane season.

At first, everything went according to plan, but on the trip south one of my two crew members became quite seasick. The other missed his girlfriend. But still, I was completely taken aback when they told me they were preparing to leave the boat. They had signed up for the full year, and I had no back-up. I persuaded them to stay on board as far as Panama, which they did, and then fortunately Shoel Cohen, who had sailed with me to Newfoundland in the summer of 1989, decided to join me for the Pacific crossing to French Polynesia.

I remember sitting in the cockpit on a mooring at the Balboa Yacht Club looking at the huge bridge of the Pan American Highway that crosses the canal and thinking that it was a hell of a long way to Tahiti for just the two of us to sail, and Edith would be there in about six weeks. But we pushed on to the Society Islands, of which Tahiti is the largest. We arrived at the capital, Papeete, five days before Edith flew in with Brenda and her friend, both teen-agers at the time.

We spent several weeks of exploring those delightful islands, and when Brenda and her friend returned home, Edith and I sat in our suddenly quiet cockpit as *Fiona* gently rolled on the anchor in the harbor at Huahine, and toasted the start of our gradual retirement. One day we watched from the veranda of the Bali Hai Hotel, sipping on cold beers, as the annual inter-island Hobie Cat racers struggled in to port, having sailed from Tahiti, about 70 miles away. We powered back to Papeete and anchored at Maeva Beach, where a very nice hotel provided all the facilities we needed. We explored the island, and had a funny adventure when we decided to visit the museum dedicated to Gauguin: We took a bus to the museum but discovered we had missed the last bus back to the anchorage. Eventually a charter bus full of tourists saw us sitting disconsolately by the side of the road and stopped to pick us up.

Edith flew home shortly after this, but we planned to rendezvous in Uruguay in early 1991 after I rounded Cape Horn. I set about organizing the return leg and recruited local crew, refueled the boat, re-provisioned, and eventually called Edith to let her know I was ready to leave. It was then that she gave me some staggering news: she had ovarian cancer.

Edith, Eric and Brenda, taken at the start of the Pacific Cruise, 1990

I put the boat on the hard at a small boatyard in one of the Society Islands. Nearby was an American couple who were repairing some serious structural problems on their Taiwanese-built boat. I gave them much of the food I had stored for the trip and bade them farewell and flew home. By then Edith had already been under the knife to remove the tumors which had metastasized. She endured two more operations to remove tissue, and then as a last resort, a bone marrow

An Inexplicable
Attraction:
My Fifty Years of
Ocean Sailing

transplant. But it was of no avail. After an awful year, Edith passed away in September of 1991. She was 58 years old.

1 | About *Fiona*

When we purchased *Fiona*, she had to be shipped from California to our home on Long Island. I already had a cradle sitting in the back yard which I had made to Westsail specification by hiring a welder to fasten together a pile of six-inch I-beams and two-inch steel tubing I had cut up. It was an immensely strong cradle, a feature that saved my life later. *Fiona* had a 13-foot beam and even though the trailer had a slot so that the keel was only inches above the ground, the rig was 14 feet high. To unload I would need a 30-ton crane to lift the boat onto the cradle. The dispatcher estimated it would arrive the following Friday; I was amazed, as it was over 3,000 miles to Long Island. Nevertheless I rented a crane with operator for Friday. If the driver showed up late it would be my loss.

Thursday dawned bright and clear and about 7 am, I heard the rumble of a heavy diesel. Towering above the hedgerow on the quiet lane on which I lived was the outline of *Fiona*. I dashed into the front garden in my shorts, and explained to the driver that the trailer would have to be backed up the driveway. My friend Dick, who was spending the night, and ten-year old Colin joined me. To make the turn, the driver wanted the mailbox on the corner of the drive removed. Dick and I gave the post a vigorous shake so we could lift it out. We were

9

standing right next to the throbbing diesel when, suddenly, I felt a stinging on my torso and for a moment I thought I was being burned by hot particles from the diesel exhaust. Then Colin yelled, "Daddy, Daddy, yellow jackets!" Sure enough, the wasps had a nest under the post and were defending their territory. Dick and I leapt about smacking our bodies and retreated rapidly. Some kerosene fixed the wasps and when the boat was parked just ahead of the cradle, I told the driver, whose name was Wally Wiggins, that the crane wasn't due until the next day. "What?!'" he exploded, "I only make money when dem wheels is turning. I'll take this turkey back to California!" I tried to mollify him and said I would pay for a motel that night. He then spent a couple of hours on the kitchen phone and finally became somewhat happier when he arranged a load to pull back west on Friday afternoon.

Suddenly I had a dreadful thought: Thursday was a working day and I had an appointment to meet some visiting Russian scientists, and I was already late. "Come with me," I told Wally, as I did a quick change into collar and tie and drove furiously to the Laboratory. I strode into the meeting, where they were all waiting, along with an interpreter. I still had Wally with me. "This is Dr. Wiggins," I said. "He's an expert on transportation." Wally loved it.

I built a sturdy set of steps and rigged electric power into the boat. Once I moved all the extra stuff that had been stored in the hull, the interior looked like a vast green cavern. It seemed terribly empty. I had told Edith it would take about three years to complete the construction of the interior furnishings, but I began to have doubts. I had no experience in carpentry, so the first thing I did was to run the DC wiring of the boat. At least I knew how to do that that. I decided to start at the forward end, which consisted of the chain locker, sail bin, and the forward head (toilet). But before I could build the chain locker, I had to decide how the chain would be raised, so I found myself shopping for a substantial anchor windless, which, in turn, required a 100-amp service for the one horsepower motor.

Thus it went. Almost everything on the boat interacted in some way with everything else, and I discovered a cruising sailboat is a very integrated design. When I was building the forward head, I remembered I would have to store the dinghy on the foredeck over the head. The mounting chocks would have to be through-bolted. In order to get those in the right place I had to build a small eight-foot dinghy before installing the overhead panels. (The dinghy can be seen on *Fiona*'s bow in one of the photos on page 5.) It took me a year to build the forward head.

In the spring I started to build the aft cabin. I was concerned that the roof of the cabin was only supported at the sides, so I bought a few lengths of inch-and-a-half diameter stainless steel pipe and installed two as supports between the roof and the hull. They turned out to be very handy for hanging on to when the boat was rolling. Many years later when *Fiona* was "running her easting down" in the Westerlies of the Southern Ocean, we were overwhelmed by a large wave that crashed on the stern of the boat and pushed her deep underwater. (See Chapter 5.) I am sure those extra supports paid off at that moment. To shorten the time spent hurrying from the boat to the basement workshop and back again, I temporarily installed a band saw and large belt sander in the main cabin.

I was very concerned about the noise level when under power—when I built the bulkheads surrounding the engine, I sandwiched a 1/16th- inch-thick lead sheet between plywood. This made a cozy and fairly soundproof engine room. Although it was a tight fit, I also put in a workbench with a vice for repairs at sea.

When the aft end was substantially completed, I started on the forward end of the main cabin. This area contained three bunks and a number of large storage lockers and a hanging locker. When I designed the overhead ("ceiling," in land-going parlance), I used plywood sheets with white Formica glued to one side. Varnished mahogany strips covered the joints. This gave a pleasing nautical look, and it was also very practical, as it was easy to clean and permitted access to the underside of the deck if necessary. The bunk area took another year to complete.

What was left was the galley and dining area. This was quite complicated; the table was mounted on a raised floor ("sole," for the sailors reading this) in the original Westsail design. I decided to keep this feature as it permitted one to look through the main cabin windows when seated at the table. On the starboard side, I had to juggle with the placement of the sink, stove, and refrigerator/ freezer unit. Fortunately, I was diplomatic enough to ask Edith's advice on solving this problem. The stove burned propane gas, so I built a gas-tight locker at the stern, a lazarette, to hold the tank. Before building anything in the galley, I had to secure and plumb the water and fuel storage tanks, which were located underneath. The galley and dinette area took me nearly two years to finish. (A layout sketch is on page 21.)

While building the floor (or sole) over the tanks, I had a nasty accident. Until the companionway steps were finished, almost the last thing I built, I used a temporary ladder made of 2×4 timber studs to get from the cabin into the cockpit. One night while climbing out holding a half-full can of paint, the ladder slipped and I fell back into cabin with the ladder under my body. I broke four ribs, and spilled paint all over the teak frame of the companionway hatch. I got Edith to mop up the paint before she dragged me to the local hospital for an x-ray.

When I recovered sufficiently, I built the freezer using an old compressor off a car air conditioner. Fred Pallas, a sailing friend who was also an engineer at the laboratory, helped me make a fiberglass food storage box for the freezer. During the winters, I made the cabin and locker doors and numerous drawers in the warmth of the basement at home, with forays to the boat to check fit and measurements. The cat we had then, a lovely Himalayan, played an endless game. She would sit at the bottom of the steps and expect to be carried to the cockpit. There she would wait until I carried her down again when I returned to the house. This went on all night.

Eventually in early 1983, I turned my attention to the mast and rigging, painted the bottom, and by April the boat was substantially finished. I then faced the problem of getting it to the sea. I made a contract with the owner of a local boat moving company to haul the boat to Weeks' yard in Patchogue. There were several problems, however. The boat was now higher because I had installed the life-line stanchions and it was sitting on the cradle. I surveyed a route and discovered some electrical lines which posed an interference vertically by about a foot. The contractor suggested that I just get someone with rubber gloves to stand on deck and lift up the offending wires as we passed by them.

Patchogue required a special permit to drive in the village. When I called the contractor a couple of days before the move, he said the company had just gone bankrupt. The move was delayed. This did not endear me to the Weeks brothers, who owned the yard then, and who had a tight schedule for launching boats using their 40-ton travel-lift. My delay would disrupt the schedule, as well as require that I obtain a new permit for transit through the village. Eventually, the contractor called to say he had a trailer and he would drive the rig himself.

One more problem: It was me and not the boat mover who had to crib the boat and cradle 21 inches off the ground so that the trailer could slide underneath. The boat was heavy—even without fuel, water, and supplies it weighed about 37,000 lbs. I rented every 20-ton jack I could find and bought scores of concrete cinder blocks. With the help of Colin and one of his friends, we dug holes under the cradle and put the jacks on pieces of 2×8 timber under the I-beams. It had been a very wet spring and the ground was saturated, so the jacks tended to go down rather than the boat go up. After we had got the boat raised up two courses, or a little less than 16 inches, allowing for subsidence, the ground under the cradle looked like a WWI battlefield, pitted with holes we had dug for the jacks and cribbing. Many blocks cracked and I kept driving to the local mason's supply store for more.

Prior to installing the last round of spacers to get the magic 21 inches' clearance, I was working under the boat operating a jack handle. The cradle was only 6 feet wide, but *Fiona* is 13 feet wide, so I had to crawl right under the boat to get to the jack. Suddenly earth began to spurt horizontally in a hole about two feet from the jack. With a great groan, the jack sank into the ground and the boat began to list to starboard and go down by the bow. I slithered out from underneath as fast as any snake. Fortunately, the motion stopped as all the extra cribbing took up the load. The boat had tilted about 15 degrees, but the cradle held, although the forward supports were no longer just in compression. Nothing bent. Very gingerly, we put more jacks under the list and got the boat horizontal again. Then we finally inserted the last spacers using wooden blocks to achieve the necessary clearance. It had been a long day and I had been nearly squashed flat.

The next day the contractor showed up, and the trailer looked pretty flimsy to me for such a heavy boat. I looked at the beams on each side of the trailer and did a quick calculation; it was definitely overloaded. I mentioned my doubts to the contractor, who pooh-poohed my worries; I was a typical engineer (all theory), he had experience, he said. Slowly the trailer was backed under the cradle and the blocks removed as the load was transferred. As he was organizing this phase, I happened to glance at the tires, which were beginning to look pretty flat. On the wall of each tire it said "max load 4000 lbs." There were six small wheels, so the arithmetic was easy. The rated load was 24,000 lbs., but it was carrying 37,000 lbs.

When *Fiona* was finally loaded, he pulled onto the driveway for the night. Along the main side beams of the trailer I could see a distinct sag. When the contractor returned in the morning I showed him the route I had mapped out and asked him to drive very slowly. I was scared the trailer might collapse and dump *Fiona* on the ground. I also wanted to drive ahead and position myself for a few shots of the trip on my 8mm movie camera. Colin was elected to stand on the deck wearing rubber gloves to lift sagging overhead wires. This worked for a while, but then the idiot driver began to put the pedal to the metal. Eventually, at the crossing of a major highway, Colin had to lift a low-hanging traffic light, which involved running down the deck to lift the heavy light. He was almost left swinging from it as the driver accelerated through the junction. I had little chance to get any movie footage.

Edith launches Fiona, *1983. A unit of the local Revolutionary militia gave a volley.*

By some miracle we all arrived at the yard unharmed. A few days later the boat was lifted from the cradle and put in the water. As *Fiona* swung into the travel-lift straps, Edith properly christened her with a bottle of champagne. Colin belonged to a militia unit of the Revolutionary War, and the whole troop attended. At the launching, at the word of command, a volley was discharged from their muskets. For the launching party, Colin also played tuba with a group that provided Dixie music.

After the running rigging was installed, the sails bent on, and the engine tested, I sailed *Fiona* with some friends to a marina in Greenport at the eastern end of Long Island. I had decided to keep her there for the first summer, as the boat needed a considerable shake-down, and the Great South Bay was too shallow for casual sailing with a boat that drew 6 feet.

In the period 1983 to 1989, Edith and I had some wonderful adventures with *Fiona*. I took all my vacation time, plus unpaid leave, so that

I could sail from July the Fourth to Labor Day. My cruises ranged from Newfoundland in the north, the Azores in the east, and the Grenadines to the south. Because of her busy medical practice Edith often waited until I arrived at some entrancing port and then flew in. On our shakedown cruise to Bermuda in 1983, 'Red' Harting crewed for me and his wife Julie flew down with Edith. While we were anchored at Ely's Harbour on the western reef the propshaft became detached from the transmission when we were leaving and we quietly re-anchored without alerting the ladies to our predicament. On the way home Red's son David crewed and we wound up double-handing to Long Island when 'Red' had severe chest pains and was confined to his bunk. When we got home Edith decided that he had not had a heart attack.

In Lunenburg, Canada, an old fellow who was the harbor master entertained us in the cockpit while he swigged our rum with tales of running booze to New England during Prohibition. On a cruise to the Caribbean one of the crew jumped ship at our first stop at Block Island. Edith persuaded a friend who kept his boat at Weeks Yard to take the ferry to Block. I tied up the boat next to the ferry terminal and 20 minutes after arriving he was on his on his way for a non-stop leg to St. Martin, a modern version of the press gang!

Bob Barta's band playing at a Fiona *farewell party. Eric's son Colin is honking on the tuba*

On another trip to the Caribbean I had Louise, her husband Jon and a friend as crew. Louise had cruised on the west coast while in grad school and became quite addicted to ocean cruising, later crossing the Atlantic aboard *Fiona*. This trip had its share of adventures. On the way south about three hundred miles north of Bermuda I was knocked off the boat by the swinging main boom as I attempted to raise the mainsail by myself, it being one o'clock in the morning and I didn't want to bother the crew. Louise, who was at the wheel, let out a scream that awakened the crew and I think was heard back on Long Island. Edith joined us in St. Martin and we cruised down to the Grenadines. On the return from that cruise a new crew failed to show up in Bermuda and I decided to single-hand to Long Island, a leg which by then I had done a couple of times. Extremely bad weather with winds exceeding a hundred knots caught up with me just near the north wall of the Gulf Stream and blew the mast off the boat when a shroud failed. When things calmed down I had just enough fuel to make it home, Edith was furious that I should be so reckless.

I have always been attracted to cruising the Maine coast, and on a summer cruise there with Edith we decide to explore a small island on foot after landing on a rocky shore with the dinghy. At first we followed a path through the woods, but as time went on I felt we should return to the dinghy before it got too dark. I decided like an idiot that it was a much shorter route by cutting through the woods, bad mistake; we ran into swamps, thick bushes with needles, and clouds of insects. We finally made it back to the dink, which was hard aground because the tide had gone out, muddy, scratched, and in need of a large rum! These adventures could easily fill another book. I have many treasured memories of Maine, sailing with Edith and with friends whose company I enjoyed.

1990 was a watershed year for me. I completed four years as Chair of the Accelerator Development Department at Brookhaven National Laboratory. It had been an intense period; the Department was responsible for many activities including construction of prototype superconducting magnets for the proposed Superconducting Super Collider, construction of a particle accelerator to match the existing Linac to the Alternating Gradient Synchrotron so that very heavy ions could be injected and, most importantly, preparing the design and completing the preconstruction planning for a new accelerator called the Relativistic Heavy Ion Collider (RHIC). I had agreed to assume this responsibility for four years in 1986. RHIC was to be the jewel in the crown of the physics research at Brookhaven. The Department had a personnel roster of about four hundred and fifty souls including over fifty Ph.D. physicists. I sometimes felt that dealing with these highly-strung personalities must have been like trying to run an opera company. Fortunately, the project was funded for construction in 1990 and I stepped down to take a one-year leave of absence and make a long-planned first sail to the South Pacific.

I explained my plans to friends at work, by telling them only half-jokingly that Brookhaven Laboratory was a great hobby but my real avocation was sailing. I had planned to meet Edith and Brenda in Tahiti, as mentioned in the introductory chapter. I would sail with two crew and they would fly. Despite the crew jumping ship in Panama I managed to make it to our rendezvous on time. Edith and I spent a few weeks cruising the lovely French Society Islands and when Edith left, we arranged to meet in Uruguay early in the following year after I sailed *Fiona* round Cape Horn. I signed up a couple of local lads as crew, but when I called Edith to tell her I was set to go, she gave me the dreadful news that she had contracted ovarian cancer. It was the worst year of our lives. Despite the best efforts of her oncologist, Edith passed away in September, 1991.

I had left the boat in the only yard in the Society Islands capable of hauling and storing her, a small operation in Raiatea which serviced the Moorings charter fleet. *Fiona* had been hauled and wedged into place sitting on 55-gallon oil drums. When I returned a year later, the boat was in sad shape. Thieves had broken in and removed many tools, electronics, and booze. Insects had established themselves throughout the interior and small plants were growing on deck. In one locker there was a thriving ant colony, along with the queen at the center of a heaving mass of worker ants. My crew and I buckled down to tidy up and I made a long list of equipment needs to be shipped by air freight to Tahiti. It took us six days to get the boat in the water. For a shake-down, we sailed the boat to Bora Bora. After stops in Huahine and Moorea, we anchored in the old familiar spot at Maeva Beach. Two massive parcels of gear arrived, including a GPS receiver (new at the time) and a stereo for the cabin. I got my boat documents back from French customs—held there during my year-long absence. They suggested we leave as soon as possible, as the cyclone season had already started.

I brought the boat back to Long Island via Cape Horn and worked part-time and sailed widely in summers until I retired in 1995. *Fiona* then became virtually my home for the next 19 years. I returned to Long Island between cruises to fix her up and then left again. The ten cruises I completed are described in the following chapters; they include several trips to the Arctic and Antarctic and two circumnavigations around the world. I posted newsletters on my website during each cruise; these form the basis of each chapter. I have revised each newsletter and sometimes changed names, as I had many crew members and not all of them worked out to our mutual satisfaction.

The psychology of the relationship between crew and captain on a small boat is complicated, particularly when far offshore. Sea-sickness plays a role; it can be very debilitating and the effect on each individual varies widely. Many crew members had never been offshore. As land faded over the horizon, with the prospect of perhaps a few weeks or more before we would see land again, some suffered from an understandable apprehension. They had quite literally put their lives in my hands. I showed the crew how to operate the radios and GPS so they had a good chance of reaching port if something should happen to me. I also gave the crew a thorough safety briefing. It was probably a false sense of security, but that doesn't matter; they felt better.

There is an old epigram: *in vino veritas,* which means that the true character of a person emerges when a little tipsy. The same thing happens at sea, the protective persona people adopt often falls away, and occasionally the person revealed is not as nice as you thought. There is another curious thing about life at sea in cramped quarters; people become extremely sensitive to minor quirks of their companions. Sometimes they explode with irritation but a row is the last thing you want on a small boat. There is nowhere to hide, the residual atmosphere if someone picks a quarrel is very difficult to remove. I have had to tread very carefully with some of my crew if they have sailing experience, especially as captain of their own boat. I try to seek their advice as sailing situations arise and make them seem part of the decision-making process. Sometimes their input is indeed very useful but in the last analysis there can be only one captain.

While I was building *Fiona* I tried to make her as sea-worthy as possible. I added extra bracing and made everything solid with good quality wood. She came in a couple of tons over the designer's weight and the water-line rose. But she turned out to be an excellent sea boat with an easy motion and a wonderful performance downwind, with no tendency to broach. I believe the cutter rig represents the best compromise for a cruising boat in the range 35 to 45 feet.

For several cruises I flew a genoa jib until it finally crossed my mind it usually got torn in the odd squall; the cutter rig using a Yankee jib offers a better choice if stormy weather is in the offing. The jib is carried on a roller furler, but I have had frequent problems with this gear even though I tried two different makers. I have tried several different approaches to the mainsail design. Full-batten sails are nice in many ways, they tend to be quieter and drop neatly into lazy-jacks. But the lower battens often break away from the car at the mast or wear a hole in the batten pocket. If you have to change the mainsail at sea, the battens are a damn nuisance. I have sailed on other boats with in-mast mainsail furling, and they certainly are easy to use, but based on my experience with jib roller furling, I am loath to install a similar system for the mainsail.

So I live with the old-fashioned main with mast slides; more difficult to reef but fairly reliable. My sails usually last only two cruises, typically 40,000 nautical miles, so I got the chance to try many options. The latest mainsail was battenless with a negative roach and performed well when I circumnavigated the North American continent. Since then I have used a battenless mainsail for all subsequent cruises.

Fiona's Vital Statistics

LOA (Not including bow platform)	42' 9"
Measurement Length, Panama Canal	49'
LWL	37'
Beam	13'
Draft	6' 3"
Displacement, empty	37,000 lbs.
Internal ballast (in keel)	11,000 lbs.
USCG Net Tonnage	24 T
USCG Gross Tonnage	25 T
Sail Area, Working Main	470 sq. ft.
Sail Area, Genoa Jib	500 sq. ft.
Sail Area, Staysail	150 sq. ft.
Sail Area, Storm Main	310 sq. ft.
Sail Area, Yankee Jib	280 sq. ft.
Sail Area, Spitfire Jib	40 sq. ft.
Engine	Perkins diesel 85 horsepower
Fuel Capacity	
Center tank	85 gallons
Port tank	50 gallons
Water Capacity	
Port tank	50 gallons
Center tank	100 gallons
Starboard tank	50 gallons
Mast, Aluminum (deck-stepped)	4 x 7.5" x 50 ft.
Air clearance	59 ft.
Rigging	
Headstay and backstay	3/8" 1x19 stainless wire
Forestay and 8 each shrouds	5/16" 1x19 stainless wire
Ground Tackle	
Chain	7/16" x 280 ft.
Fisherman Anchor	65 lbs.
CQR Anchor	45 lbs.
Danforth Anchor	45 lbs.
Danforth Anchor	25 lbs.

Fiona's Internal Layout (not to scale)

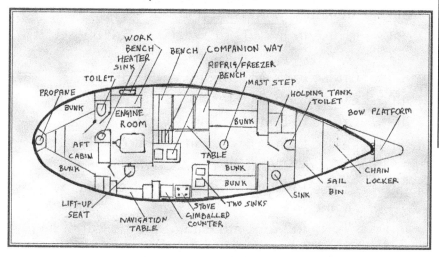

Fiona's Journeys -1995 to 2014

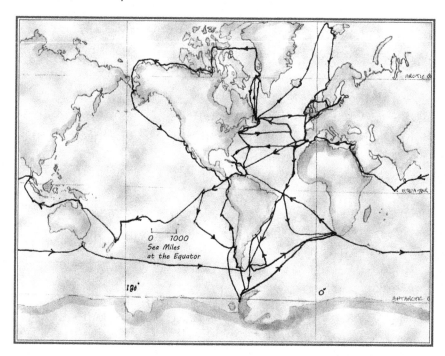

A Brief Summary of *Fiona's* Cruises

1983	Shakedown cruise to Bermuda
1984	Cruise to Bras d'or Lake, Cape Breton Island, Prince Edward Island, and St. Pierre
1985	Cruise to St. Martin and Virgin Islands
1986	Cruise to the Azores and Bermuda
1987	Cruise to Bermuda and Maine
1988	Cruise to St. Martin and Grenadines

Fiona was dismasted between Bermuda and New York

1989	Cruise to Newfoundland, Nova Scotia and Maine
1990	Cruise to the South Pacific via the Caribbean, Panama Canal and Galapagos

Edith flew home from Tahiti and contracted what proved to be a fatal attack of cancer. Fiona *was left on the hard at Raiatea, French Polynesia.*

1991-1992	Eric returned in late October 1991 to sail *Fiona* home via the Gambier Isands, Pitcairn Island, Cape Horn, Brazil, the Cape Verde Islands and Bermuda
1993	Cruise to Newfoundland, the Bras d'or, Nova Scotia and Maine
1994	Cruise to Newfoundland, Labrador and Maine
1995-1997	Circumnavigation of the world via the Panama and Suez Canals
1998-1999	Cruise to Antarctica via Easter Island, the Chilean Canals and Cape Horn. Returned via South Georgia, Tristan da Cunha, Cape Town, St. Helena, Fernando de Noronha and the Caribbean.
1999	Maine
2000-2001	Cruise to Iceland, the Arctic, Spitzbergen, Norway, the British Isles, Portugal, Caribbean, Cuba, Bahamas and Bermuda. Cruise to Maine.

2002-2003	Eastabout circumnavigation following the old clipper ship route around the southern capes
2004-2005	Cruise to Ireland, the Baltic, U.K., Brazil and the Falkland Islands
2005	Six-week Fall cruise to New England and Maine
2006-2007	Cruise to Antarctic Circle
2007	Six-week Fall cruise to New England and Maine
2008	Four-month cruise to Greenland
2009-2010	Circumnavigation of North America via the Northwest Passage
2011-2012	Iceland, Scotland, Portugal, Brazil
2012	Maine
2013-2014	Cape Verdes, Brazil, Falklands, Cape Town
2014	Maine

An Inexplicable Attraction: My Fifty Years of Ocean Sailing

2 | Around the World
via the Suez and Panama Canals
1995-1997

In early July, 1995, I found myself in the cockpit of *Fiona* chugging through Fire Island Inlet, bound for Block Island and then the rest of the world. For crew I had Walter, a local sailor who had made several short trips with me in previous years. He was a qualified millwright (someone who installs machinery), and made a great crew member. The other was a Russian, Yuri, who I recruited from the classifieds of a sailing magazine. Yuri was living in Alaska when he saw my ad. He claimed to be a marine biologist who had sailed on a research schooner in the Bering Sea, but later I came to doubt all his claims. About the only marine biology he knew was what fish were good to eat.

My plan was to sail down the east of Brazil to Cape Horn for an east-to-west rounding and enter the South Pacific. What naïve optimism. We took our departure from Block Island on July 7th and arrived in Bermuda five days later, the only major problem being that I forgot the ship's teapot. Apart from one hideous monstrosity on sale in Block Island I couldn't find a replacement, but we were able to buy a traditional English teapot in Hamilton, Bermuda.

Bermuda was very noisy—two cruise ships pulled into St. George's during the summer weeks and the passengers were wooed to the bars and nightclubs by loud disco music until the small hours. The "White Horse Tavern" used to be a matey, pub-like place that sold drinks and fish and chips. Now the electronic music emanating from the White Horse could be heard a mile away. We anchored on the west side of the islands and did a little skin diving on the old sunken gunboat *Vixen*. We left after five days and dropped anchor in Marigot Bay, St. Martin a week later, experiencing nothing worse than the usual squalls on the way down.

When Edith and I first went there in 1962, it was a typical decrepit West Indian village on a swamp. The French government decided to put in big bucks. They dredged the swamp and put in a marina and now it's a luxury resort. Virtually all the old West Indian shacks have disappeared to be replaced by concrete apartments.

I wanted to see Kay and Dudley Pope again, old friends who lived aboard *Ramage* in the Caribbean for many years. We had become good friends when Edith and I lived on *Iona* in 1968 to 1969. I also wanted to lay in a good stock of Mount Gay rum, as St. Martin had probably the lowest prices in the world for this lubricant of the seven seas. We bought eight cases, two less than when we were here in 1990—we were cutting back on drinking! We did not linger in St. Martin, as I wanted to get further south as soon as possible to clear the hurricane belt. Leaving St. Martin at the end of July, we fueled up on the Dutch side and set sail for Barbados. About two days out we encountered a vicious tropical wave when we were east of St. Lucia. The local radio stations were full of stories of massive flooding; we had winds to 50 knots in gusts and three reefs in the main. We tied up for customs clearance in Bridgetown and discovered the same storm had caused damage there. A popular calypso singer called "the Great Carew" had been swept out to sea sitting on the roof of his house, and later we saw the local coast guard bringing his body back.

We stayed four days in Barbados, one more than planned because August 7th was "Crop Over Day," a traditional date celebrating the completion of harvesting the sugar crop. A main street out of town was full of booths selling everything, especially rum, and there were parades with floats. When I was a young lad I used to read stories of intrepid explorers in the jungle who at some stage usually cried, "The drums, the drums!" Well, only when you have had your brains scrambled by drum music relayed by banks of 20-inch speakers have you heard the drums, the drums! These pockets of sonic energy were spotted all along the road and must have consumed many kilowatts of power.

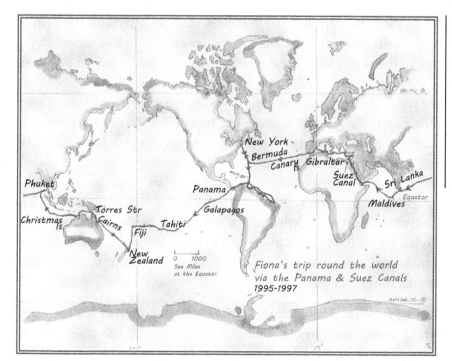

Fiona's trip round the world via the Panama & Suez Canals 1995-1997

Damaged Off the North Coast of Brazil

We left Barbados heading southeast with the intention of rounding the eastern bulge of Brazil. This huge cape sticks out into the Atlantic Ocean to about 35° W, halfway between New York and London. When we left Barbados we were at 12° N and 59½° W, and our destination was Natal, Brazil, at about 6° S and 35° W, a distance of about 2,000 nautical miles (throughout, abbreviated as "nm").

When I planned the trip I knew the wind and current would be against us, but I was obviously suffering from hubris; Mother Nature was about to teach me a lesson. After we left Barbados we had very light and variable winds, mostly from the southeast. Due to the equatorial current, which ran at 3 knots to the northwest, at first we made little progress.

There was a countercurrent which we were able to find with the help of the GPS receiver, which showed course and speed over the bottom. However, during this period, gear began to fail. The jib roller furling stuck and I had to make several trips to the masthead to free it, once in the middle of the night. The jib halyard broke, necessitating another scary trip to the masthead. We got to the equator in late August

27

at 42° W, having crossed the doldrums at about 6° N with the help of the countercurrent, but then it died away. The pilot chart showed it going to the north. After the doldrums we had heavy winds in the 30-40 knot range from ESE. The roller furling was fixed so at least it would furl the sail but the lower bearing was obviously unhappy. Shortly after crossing the equator the mounting bracket of the Aries self-steering broke and we decided we needed a little time in port for repairs. The only nearby port was São Luis, lying 120 nm downwind on the north coast of Brazil. We entered this port using our offshore chart, fortunately in daylight, on August 29th. The currents in São Luis were heavy, due to the tidal range, which is 18 feet when the moon is new or full. In the 1970s it was abandoned as a major port due to shoaling of the bay. At high tide there is a full, wide bay, and at low tide immense sand banks appear with serpentine channels of deep water.

The problem with the roller furling was that one half of a plastic insert forming the lower bearing had disappeared. At this point we met Sami Wassowf, polyglot and local fixer. He suggested a very typically Brazilian solution—use the half bearing that was left as a pattern and have new ones cast in aluminum. Amazingly enough, this worked fine and a day later I had two aluminum bearing inserts at a cost of about ten dollars each.

São Luis is an old colonial city of about one million people. Local fruits were delicious and cheap. However, other things were hard to find. We heard about a person living near our anchorage who did laundry, but it turned out he simply let you use a sink in his garden. So, Walter and I set to using the built-in scrubbing board. All the family thought this was very funny, and brought chairs so they could watch our performance in comfort. In the meanwhile, a large Doberman, which prowled the compound at night, eyed us viciously from his cage and howled continuously in frustration.

With our stores replenished and gear fixed, we left São Luis on September 2nd, and after beating out of the bay headed east. We stayed within 30 miles of the coast, which meant the current against us was a little less, but because it was so shallow the waves were steeper. Typically, the sea was only 100 feet deep 30 miles offshore. The winds were high, 30 to 40 knots, and we had two or three reefs in the main.

At midnight, only two days after we left, I was just entering data in the log prior to changing watches, when there was a loud report like a gunshot, followed by wild flogging of the jib; the headstay had snapped. At the time the jib was fully reefed. We got the mess down to deck level but the roller furling extrusions were either bent or broken. The jib was torn due to the rig swinging violently against the forestay in the heavy seas. I really didn't know why the stay snapped just under the upper tang—it was new in 1993, but when it was repaired later a rigger told me that the stay had been over-swaged, which crushed the individual wires. We braced up the mast with the spare halyard and jib halyard and lashed the headstay, furler, and jib to the port lifeline.

I was reluctant to give up our mileage to windward, so for a day we tried motor sailing in the hope of reaching Fortaleza, the next port east of São Luis. Although we struggled on for 24 hours, it was clear we couldn't make Fortaleza with the fuel on board. Without the jib we couldn't get to windward in the teeth of the heavy winds and seas, so we turned back once again to São Luis.

It was dark when we arrived on September 8th, but this time we had local knowledge. When we anchored, we removed the sail from the shattered Profurl—not as easy as it sounds—and rigged a spare stay. While Yuri stitched a wire rope to the luff of the storm jib so that it could be hanked on, Walter and I rounded up Sami and his battered car. We went on a search for hanks or shackles so we could attach the storm jib to the stay. We eventually located 25 small steel shackles, but when we returned to the boat, *Fiona* was hard aground. It was a spring tide and the current had swept the boat to one side of the channel, which then dried out. The problem came when the tide reversed because a couple of 60-foot ferries moored to the west of *Fiona* swung down in the flood current while *Fiona* was still stuck fast. We had a frantic hour keeping the ferries from damaging the self-steering gear, but we lost a stanchion and damaged the stern pulpit.

The next day, we bent on the storm jib, and reeved a new jib halyard, as the old one had been damaged when the headstay snapped. We tidied up the bent pulpit and celebrated with a few drams of Mount Gay rum. Monday, we left and soon encountered the familiar conditions of heavy winds and seas.

The next day the mainsail, which was double-reefed, began to go. We lowered it and stitched in a patch and redid a seam. But an hour or two later it split from luff to leach. Somehow the cloth just seemed to give up. At this point we had lost our two working sails, we had used all the spare halyards and stays, and we were low on fuel. According to the log we had sailed 3,216 nm since leaving Barbados, most of it to windward, making good about 1,500 miles, but we were still 500 nm from Natal.

With a heavy heart, I realized we had punished the boat enough and we were not going to round the Cape Horn that year. We needed major repairs to the stays, sails, and furling gear.

Return to the Caribbean

I decided to run off downwind and bide our time until the hurricane season was over in the Caribbean, and then return there to make repairs. Georgetown, Guyana, looked like a good spot to head for, so we bent on the storm main—apart from the storm jib the only useful sail left—and slowly made our way back to the west. We pulled into the Demerara River a week after we turned back. In Georgetown we tied up next to a rusting tugboat and the rotting pilings that had been left when the Customs House burnt down 30 years earlier. After the British had pulled out, the place had slowly fallen apart, and there appeared to be a serious racial problem, with the Indians living on one side of the Demerara River, and the Blacks on the other side, with the two not interacting. The Indians were the descendants of indentured laborers brought from India after slavery was abolished in the British Empire in 1835. We were advised to hire a watchman, and he slept on the deck by day and was the watchman by night, but still tools were stolen right off the deck in the blink of an eye. Fortunately, we were able to buy them back through the watchman for $10. Very few yachts call there, only four that year.

The river was very muddy and foul, but there were lots of pretty young women around the dock who smiled a lot, giggled, and suggested they "might be your wife." As you may deduce, people were very poor in Guyana, but there was a festive and exuberant air in the market with lots of smiles and banter. The market was very active with every conceivable item for sale; the local fruit was very cheap. Five-year-old rum was US$2.00 a bottle. The Guyanese had no coins, only paper money, with a Guyanese dollar worth 7/10th of a U.S. cent! The public phones were free for local calls because they had been robbed so frequently in the past.

I was able to get some repairs done, including re-stitching the mainsail. This was done by an old gentleman, entirely by hand, who used to make sails decades ago for the vanished fishing sailboats. But the romance of having a mainsail with the hand-stitched repairs faded somewhat when we set the main for the first time. The old man's sail loft was the street outside his hovel and the sail was crisscrossed with black oily streaks and tire marks. Not only that, the stitches gave way within a few hours after we set the sail.

After picking up the sail, we managed to refill our tanks with diesel fuel, still sold by the imperial gallon, and we were ready to go. I planned to sail to Trinidad and St. Martin for the major repairs and leave for the Panama Canal about February, 1996. I knew St. Martin had been devastated by Hurricane Luis, which struck after we left at the end of July, but I didn't realize the extent of the damage until we returned later. Despite losing the mainsail again, we got to Tobago without further mishap, only to run into a typical bureaucratic problem. According to Tobago's laws of immigration, Russians needed an entry visa and we didn't have one for Yuri. The immigration official said I could buy him a ticket to Moscow or leave immediately. After a reasoned discussion we compromised; Yuri was confined to the boat during our stay and a note to this effect was written on our documents. But this led to a Catch-22 situation, as Yuri was then officially unable to visit the consulates to get visas for other islands when we sailed to Trinidad. At Trinidad we simply ignored the prohibition and we got him a French visa, which covered the French islands, and we hoped that would be good for French Polynesia.

Tobago is one of the last unspoiled Caribbean islands. In the north there is an original rain forest. Anchored off the coast in this area, I was fascinated by the flocks of green parrots that fluttered to the forest each evening to nest, chattering loudly as they flew.

From Tobago we sailed to Chaguaramus Bay in Trinidad, a few miles from Port of Spain. In the past few years there had been intensive development of yacht maintenance facilities and many boats now summered there to avoid the hurricane season in the Caribbean; Trinidad is too far south to experience many hurricanes. My friend, 'Red' Harting, an old shipmate and rally co-driver on Long Island, air-freighted many spare parts and we repaired much of the damage and the mainsail was patched again.

There were close to a thousand yachts at Chaguaramus, more than half on land being stored or repaired. There was an active social life, centered on the bars at the three major boat yards. Food and the necessities of life were very cheap. A bus ride to Port of Spain cost 30 cents. Three dollars got you a fish and chip supper with a beer at the yacht club bar/restaurant. Walter found himself a nice girl friend, originally from Venezuela, who ate supper with us many nights.

'Red' Harting co-driving Eric's 1928 Bentley

When the devastation caused by Hurricane Luis in St. Martin became known, the yachties had a collection and organized a rescue mission. They dispatched a trawler loaded with supplies to the island. On their return, some of the participants gave a talk and video show, including footage taken on yachts during the height of the hurricane. The devastation was heartrending; over a thousand yachts sunk or were driven ashore, with many deaths.

Before we left Trinidad in late November we spent a couple of nights anchored at Chacachacare Island, a deserted island which was formerly a leper colony during British rule. After independence in the 1960s, it was abandoned. Most of the buildings were still in fairly good shape; the church had a curious chute-like structure to the ground, and we figured it was to facilitate getting bodies down to ground level, as the church was on the second floor of the hospital building.

We sailed the 90 miles to Grenada overnight, where prices immediately doubled. In the Grenadines, I had an interesting experience at Mayreau, a small island about four miles from the beautiful Tobago Cays. I first visited Mayreau in the late 1960's when Edith and I cruised the Caribbean on *Iona*, with Colin, then aged three. He used to play on the beach there with a small black child who was deaf. Edith found out from the child's old Auntie (no parents lived on the island due to the absence of work) that he had never seen a doctor about his deafness. We gave her some money so that she could take the child to Barbados on the next schooner going there.

Anyway, 26 years later Mayreau had developed to some extent and now there were several bars, restaurants and small hotels. We were all sitting at a bar sipping on a beer and I asked the bartender if he had always lived here. "Oh, yes," he said. So I told him the story of the little boy on the beach and he immediately said, "That was Phil, the brother of the fellow who owns this bar!" Later on, I spoke to Dennis, his brother, and he said Phil did go to Barbados and was fitted with a hearing aid. This enabled him to get an education, and he became an accountant and lived in the States, married to an American. It was gratifying to hear this news.

Mayreau at the time was visited by a cruise ship, which had rented a section of beach and fenced it off. These ships provoke a great deal of resentment in many islands, as the vacationers buy virtually nothing ashore and can rapidly destroy the local ecosystem. Mayreau had only about 100 residents, while the cruise ship landed a 1,000! In a Grenada newspaper, I read an analysis that claimed 90 percent of the islands' visitors came on cruise ships and brought in 10 percent of the incoming tourist dollar.

This part of the Caribbean, as far north as St. Thomas, was infested with charter boats. They were crewed by folks who just wanted to have a good time for a couple of weeks. If they saw a cruising boat, they always anchored very close. They seemed to assume that we must know something they didn't know. They also didn't use much rope when they anchored. When the wind shifted, they were too close and banged into you. In St. Barts we literally had to fend them off. Of course, everyone on the other boat had gone ashore to tuck into an expensive meal, the price of which went up in proportion to the number of charter boats in the harbor.

Back in St. Martin we completed the repairs and got the bad news from an expert sail maker that the mainsail was kaput. So, we ordered a new one from England in early December and it was promised to be shipped by air before Christmas. We spent the intervening time visiting Anguilla, St. Barts, and Statia. We had Christmas dinner with my old friends Kay and Dudley Pope. They now lived in a condo which had been badly damaged by Hurricane Luis. The local newspaper reported that only 40 percent of the hotels would be open for the winter season, due to storm damage. We left St. Martin in early January, 1996, with a new mainsail and a somewhat depleted cruising kitty. We also put on board another 30 gallons of Mount Gay rum to replace our depleted stock. We had sailed just under 6,000 nm since we left St. Martin in July, or 200 miles per gallon. Of course, we had spent a lot of time in port.

To the South Seas

After a brief stop in Martinique we made a direct sail of about four days to Bonaire in the Netherlands Antilles. Bonaire is famous for its flock of red flamingoes, and a few dozen of these birds flew over the boat as we approached the island on the evening of January 16th. The island also has other kinds of birds, and one of them whispered to Walter, who is very tall and handsome, in a seductive Spanish voice what her address was. The next afternoon, Walter dressed up in his cleanest white ducks and ventured into the town of Kralendijk to find his bird. He returned, chastened, a couple of hours later. The address turned out to be a professional establishment, to put it delicately, complete with price lists and medical certificates. Poor Walter! Nothing seems to have changed for hundreds of years in terms of the dangers awaiting the innocent seafaring man when he sets foot on land.

From Bonaire, we sailed 700 miles to the San Blas Islands, which lie off the Darien coast of Panama. There must be over a hundred islands covering an area of about 2,000 square miles. The islands had lovely beaches and clear water, and the Kuna Indians who lived there had a large degree of autonomy, and so had prevented any large scale development, such as tourist hotels. They still paddled and sailed dug-out canoes, and the natives, mostly women, make a unique embroidered cloth called "molas." Their villages consisted of bamboo huts with palm thatch roofs all crowded close together. When we anchored on the lee of the village we could smell the wood fires they use for cooking.

After ten days we sailed overnight to Colon, the Caribbean entrance point for the Panama Canal. Colon was a very violent town due, I suppose, to the high unemployment rate. All large shops and businesses had guards armed with shotguns at the doors. Visitors were warned to go everywhere by taxi, which we did, but that didn't prevent me from being attacked a few days after we arrived, inside a shop selling electrical parts. Walter and I had gone there to get some bits for the boat. As I stood against the counter, I was suddenly seized from behind. An arm went around my neck and I was being choked. Two confederates darted into the store, one to rifle my pockets, and one to prevent anyone from aiding me. Walter engaged in fisticuffs with him. I had my hand on my wallet, which tore in half in the struggle, but my half had the money in it! And then they were gone, rushing away down the crowded street. It was all over in 20 seconds.

On reflection, I have to admire the precision of this team, for the attack was impeccably choreographed. I never saw the faces of any of them. Fortunately, nobody was seriously hurt, but my throat was sore for a couple of days and I sounded a little scratchy. As the old square rig sailors used to say: There are more sharks on land than there are in the sea. I had lost my original wallet when it was picked out of my pocket in Georgetown, Guyana. This trip was proving to be hard on my wallets!

A mola, an embroidered cloth made by the Kuna Indians of the San Blas Islands

We stocked up with fuel, water and food for the long days coming up in the Pacific, and made it through the Panama Canal in one day, unusual for a southbound yacht, which usually take two days. After last minute shopping in Balboa, we sailed to Taboga Island in the Gulf of Panama for a couple of nights. It was a charming island with a picturesque village.

We then spent three nights at anchorages in the Las Perlas group. At Contradora Island, a blond German lady called Claudia came over in her dinghy from a nearby yacht and offered to bake us some German bread. She had a list of the selections available, with prices—Weissbrot, Dunkelbrot, Muesilibrot, Zwiebeibrot and Schwarzwalderbrot. She must have been a model and was clad only in the skimpiest of bikinis, so of course we enthusiastically ordered a loaf for delivery in the morning.

The Las Perlas seemed idyllic and it was only later that Walter noticed a letter in the Seven Seas Cruising Association Bulletin about a yachting couple whose boat was seized in the Las Perlas area by escaped convicts from the maximum security prison which is located on one of the islands. The couple was forced to take the men to Colombia and the husband was shot for his pains. It's a good thing we read about it after we left on the way to the Galapagos Islands, a leg which took only six days.

It was considerably easier to enter the Galapagos Islands than it was during *Fiona*'s first visit in 1990. Then, you had to bribe the port captain. Now, I still had to fork over about the same amount, but it was all official and we easily got permission to stay for five days. We anchored in Academy Bay where there were a considerable number of boats from a British yacht club who were sailing round the world in 20 months. This enterprise was called the Trade Winds Rally, and it was comprised of over 40 yachts.

In the Galapagos there has been a constant struggle between conservationists, on one hand, and settlers from Ecuador on the other. I think the settlers were winning; sea lions were common in Academy Bay when we anchored there in 1990, but this time I saw only one. We visited the Charles Darwin station where they were breeding the giant Galapagos tortoise and we took a one-day tour of the preserve on Plaza Island.

When we left, most of the Trade Winds Rally yachts were scattered in a thousand-mile-long swathe between the Galapagos and Marquesas Islands. We kept running into them in different ports, as our itineraries were almost identical. It was like a small English village on the move around the world, with its own little melodramas—divorces, romances, and such. This 3,000-mile leg was a three-week downwind run for *Fiona* in 1990, but this time we were unlucky with the winds. For the first ten days, they were mostly light—on the nose, or simply zero. After seven days, we had made good only 380 miles towards the Marquesas and I began to worry about our food supply if the same conditions persisted. We did use the engine a little to edge south, as the meteorologists predicted better winds down there. But I had not refueled in the Galapagos. When I was there in 1990, the fuel was so dirty I had persistent problems with clogged filters for years afterwards.

The rally people had a morning roll call on the SSB radio in which each yacht reported its position and weather conditions. We were not becalmed alone—only the yachts 500 or 600 nm ahead had any wind. Being becalmed on the open sea is not pleasant; there is always swell, which rolls the boat. The sails, which must be set to catch what wind there is, slat violently from side to side. It was a good thing the mainsail was new, for the old one would have surely torn in these conditions. As it was, both upper battens were broken and we also broke half a dozen nylon sail slides.

One morning I was so fed up with the wear and tear, I wrote the following poem in the log book:

BECALMED

The great swells slide across the ocean,

Wind-pecked ripples mottle the sea.

Sullen, the boat rises to the motion

And the sails slat, angrily.

Only when the wind-curved sails fill out

Will she rise and the wheel stiffen.

The captain will scan the rigging and shout,

'Harden sheets — set course again.'

And would you believe a nice breeze came up for a while? Ultimately, it took us 30 days to make the passage, just about all of March. You might think time dragged, but it was surprising how quickly it passed. After breakfast came elevenses—tea and cookies. Then lunch, followed by afternoon tea. Then happy hour with hors d'oeuvres and rum and juice. Supper followed, just before nightfall. After we ran out of the bread we bought in the Galapagos, we baked a loaf every morning.

At 8 pm (ship's time), we went onto two-hour watches, followed by four hours off. All this routine made the time pass very quickly. We had lots of tapes, BBC and VOA on the shortwave, and a couple of dozen trashy paperbacks, traded with other yachts. An odd thing, which I have noticed before on long voyages, is that I became very bothered by the typical modern shoot-em-up violent novel. I could only read a page at a time and I absolutely had to peek at the ending, just to avoid nasty surprises. Modern life, with the constant overwhelming sensory inputs of TV, radio, and other electronic devices leaves one emotionally desensitized. At sea, one's emotional threshold level sinks, and perhaps that's why nothing seems to happen in Victorian novels—the genteel readers would have been shocked if it did.

We also had a good supply of the *Guardian Weeklies*, sent by my daughter Brenda to Panama. We hoarded these and opened them one a week, to be read over again and again. We also did innumerable crossword puzzles, especially Walter, who had several volumes of collected puzzles. Yuri seemed to be writing a book. Finally, each day I usually had a number of maintenance tasks, as it seemed everything on the boat was in the process of corroding, chafing, peeling, cracking, or just plain disintegrating.

We did have contact with the outside world. I was plugged into two radio nets, one operated by other cruising boats, and the other an excellent net run by amateur radio operators. The amateur radio operators had directional antennas and powerful transmitters, and so communication was much more reliable than the cruising net. Each boat registered with the net was called at a specific time each evening. After reporting position and weather, a number of services were available such as a doctor and phone patches to the U.S.

Towards the end of March, we had a glorious view of comet Huakutaki for two evenings, probably better than any other viewers in the world because of the intense darkness at sea, once the moon has set.

The South Pacific

We made our landfall at Hiva Oa in the Marquesas Islands. The village was about a mile and a half from the dinghy dock, but we needed the exercise, as one's legs tend to atrophy on a long passage. We walked up a hill to a cemetery overlooking the beautiful bay. In it was the grave of Paul Gauguin, despised by the French during his life for his loose morals but now revered—he is safely dead—as the original portrayer of Polynesian life.

We then cruised to Fatu Hiva, where I traded some five-minute epoxy for tapa cloth. Then we sailed to Tahuato and to Nuka Hiva, the administrative center of the Marquesas Islands. We were able to get plenty of fresh fruit, especially the delicious pamplemousse, the huge Tahitian grapefruit, which were literally lying on the ground in Nuka Hiva. The bay was full of Trade Winds Rally yachts, and we made a number of friends among them. There was general surprise at the Stars and Stripes on the stern of *Fiona* when they heard my strong Lancashire accent.

Unfortunately, a heavy swell developed due to bad weather to the south and several dinghies were capsized at the dock. Some anchors were lost by several boats, including our stern anchor, on which a shackle worked loose. Despite a search using scuba gear and probing with a long rod we were unable to recover it.

The last island group we visited before arriving in Tahiti was the Tuamotus. This group comprises about forty low-lying coral atolls; we visited three. At Ahe, our anchor got caught on coral, but fortunately a Polynesian with scuba gear was nearby and freed us. The natives use scuba to tend the oysters hanging in long strings below the surface which are used to produce cultivated black pearls. At Apataki, we were able to tie up to the dock, the first time we had been alongside since we were in Martinique in early January. We took the opportunity to take all the chain out of the forward locker and lay it out on the dock. We were then able to repaint the marks at 50, 100 and 150 feet and turn it end for end.

We arrived in Papeete on April 21st, 1995, and within a week, Yuri left the boat and returned to Russia. Unfortunately, I had to buy his ticket, as the French authorities do not permit people to stay unless they have a way of leaving. As captain, I was responsible for Yuri, even though he had assured me earlier he had the money for his ticket. Somehow I wasn't surprised when he told me he was broke.

Walter and I flew back to New York in early May. The boat was left at a mooring in the lovely Maeva Bay, about five miles from Papeete. Since leaving Patchogue in July, 1995, *Fiona* had sailed over 14,000 nm.

The South Seas, Part Two

Walter decided to sign up for another year and we returned in early June. It was not a moment too soon for me. I longed for the peace and quiet of cruising after the crazy traffic and general hurly-burly of Long Island.

We flew back with our luggage crammed with spare parts. A few days after our return to Papeete, the new crew member showed up to replace Yuri. Jaime was a Spaniard who had been working in South Korea for an international business consulting firm. He spoke excellent English and became addicted to crossword puzzles under Walter's tutelage while aboard *Fiona*.

After stocking up at the huge supermarket at Maeva Beach we topped up the fuel and water tanks and headed out. Unfortunately, as we crossed the coral reefs I missed a marker indicating the rather tortuous channel to the pass and the keel bumped heavily on a coral head. At our next anchorage, at Moorea, I swam down with a mask to inspect the damage: a couple of layers of fiberglass at the forward end of the keel had been displaced. As the bottom had not been painted for a year, I decided this was justification for a haul out and I arranged to do this at the Carenage in Raiatea, the same yard at which I left *Fiona* when Edith became sick in 1990.

On the way, we stopped for the weekend at the beautiful island of Huahine. As we came into the anchorage, we passed the most bedraggled boat I had seen in a long time, sailing along the fringing reef. The battered hull had evidently once been painted a vivid orange, the tattered jib trailed in the sea and she only showed about 18 inches of freeboard. Ultimately, this apparition anchored a hundred yards from us and later we rowed over to speak to the sole crew member, a cheerful young man called Steve. We took him back to *Fiona* and, over a glass or two of rum, he told us his story.

The boat was a Bristol Bay cutter, a traditional inshore fishing boat from Alaska. Steve had sailed her to Mexico and then made a single-handed passage of sixty-six days to the Marquesas Islands. He was engineless; the outboard which hung on a stern bracket had given up the ghost long ago. I sincerely advised him not to go to New Zealand where they had a rigorous safety inspection of yachts before a boat was allowed to depart. This was because the New Zealand government had to pay for any possible rescue.

Four days after the haul-out in Riaitea, we were back in the water—keel repaired, bottom painted, a new log fitted, and numerous repairs taken care of. We then sailed to the scenic island of Bora Bora, perhaps the closest one can find to the mythical South Sea Island. In the center is a towering extinct volcano. The white sand beaches are protected by an outlying reef containing small islets called motus.

We had hoped to touch the most westerly of the Society Islands; a small island called Maupiti—rarely visited, but when we got there we found out why. The single passage through the reef was open to the prevailing trade winds. We sailed as close as we dared, but the foaming maelstrom across the entrance looked too dangerous and at the last moment, we turned away and headed instead for Penrhyn Island in the northern Cook group, almost 600 miles away.

When we arrived, we were boarded by a couple of locals in an aluminum runabout. The older man introduced himself as Henry, the customs inspector. The younger fellow was his assistant and also his cousin. After a hint about being thirsty, they gratefully downed a couple of stiff rums. It turns out Penrhyn had been a dry island for the previous two years.

Henry asked if we had any tools on board. This surprised me, as customs officers usually ask about liquor, tobacco, drugs, and guns. When I cautiously said "Yes," he asked me to repair his boat, which desperately needed a few pop rivets! Walter and I did indeed fix up his boat on the shore the next day.

I was fascinated to learn there was the wreck of a WWII American bomber on the island and I went looking. Part of the fuselage had been cut up to create a small hut in the village. Three of the four engines were scattered in a grove of palm trees. It looked to me like the plane was a Liberator. An old man told me the story of how it got there during the war.

Wreck of WWII American bomber plane, Penrhyn Island

An emergency strip had been built on Penrhyn, and one night this plane appeared. (God knows where it came from, as Penrhyn is a long way from anywhere else.) But the generator for the runway light was kaput. So they built two fires of coconut husks at each end of the runway. Unfortunately, the fire at the downwind end went out and the pilot mistook the fire at the other end for the touchdown point. At the last minute he saw the reef at the upwind end in the glare of the landing light, and he managed to pull up, but the undercarriage was damaged. They relit the fires and he crash-landed without loss of life on the strip, and the bits have remained on Penrhyn for more than fifty years.

We had a narrow escape ourselves when we came to leave. A brisk wind had sprung up and the waves were breaking on the rocky shore just 100 yards off the stern. Walter was bringing up the anchor with the electric winch and I was easing *Fiona* ahead to lessen the strain on the winch, when suddenly the wheel became completely frozen—I couldn't turn the rudder left or right! It seemed like the anchor was about ready to break out, not a good situation with the lee shore so close and no steering.

I asked Walter to let out more chain again and we investigated the problem. We found that the stop on the rudder quadrant had come loose and wedged in the mechanism—easily fixed. When we raised the anchor for the second time we found it was jammed in some coral and it took an effort to free it. It was probably a good thing the anchor was jammed, as that stopped the head from paying off when we first tried to raise it.

We left without further incident and headed for American Samoa, 850 miles downwind. This proved to be a sleigh ride, and we arrived after five and a half days of lovely sailing on the Fourth of July. We anchored opposite the Star Kist tuna cannery and waited for customs clearance the next day before going ashore. The main attraction of American Samoa was the ability to stock up with stateside food at a reasonable price.

The harbor of Pago Pago was not very pleasant due to the general pollution, the smell downwind of the cannery and noise from the generating plant. The locals seemed to be imbued with a kind of fundamental Christianity—late one night, Water found himself in a discussion of religious values with a group of young fellows near the dock and when they didn't like his apparently insensitive answer, they started to stone him. He had to make a prudent withdrawal but still got a lump on his head before he made it to the dinghy.

Apia in Western Samoa was our next stop. This was a charming and beautiful island which still retained vestiges of its German colonial past, prior to WWI. Every morning at about 7:30 am, the police brass band marched along the waterfront. The uniform consisted of pith helmets and lava-lavas, and the cheerful tootling and oom-pahs as we ate breakfast were an unforgettable memory of Apia.

We made the mandatory pilgrimage to Robert Louis Stevenson's house, Vailma, a lovely place situated on a hill about two miles out of town. His mother, who appears to have been somewhat of a harridan, didn't like it there because the natives were too noisy! Rugby is taken very seriously in this part of the world and just before we left, I was able to watch the match between West Samoa and Tonga. They played very hard—the first-aid people were kept busy, and as a heritage of their Polynesian ancestry, the teams engaged in a "haka" at the start of the game. In the old days, this was a display of strength and a time for the brandishing of weapons. Now, the teams face each other with aggressive stances and bulging eyes while giving vent to war chants.

From West Samoa we had a fairly short sail to Niuatoputapu at the northern end of the Tonga Islands. When we anchored in the lagoon, I dinghied over to a small dock, but there was nobody around. A board nailed to a coconut tree had a crudely painted arrow pointing west with the terse message, "customs, 3 km." I walked along a sandy path shaded by palm trees until I came to the village—here, I found everybody gathered on the grass between the post office and the police station. A temporary awning had been set up, and under it were gathered some local dignitaries and the Prime Minister of Tonga. As it happened, we had arrived on the very day of the first-ever visit to Tonga by the Prime Minister!

Everyone was dressed in their Sunday best. As I sauntered up in my scruffy shorts and t-shirt, the Prime Minister was handing out long service medals to local officials. Despite my appearance, I was invited to the official luncheon, which was already laid out on the grass, covered with lace to keep the flies off. We ate local delicacies such as crawfish, suckling pig and yams, seated cross-legged on the ground. I discovered the real reason for the flying trip of the Prime Minister was local dissatisfaction over the sparse visits by the supply boat from the capital to the south. It was six weeks since the last visit and supplies of staples such as flour, petrol and toilet paper were scarce. The difficulty of supplying these small islands lying hundreds of miles from the commercial center reminded me of similar problems facing the "outports" of Newfoundland, most of which were eventually abandoned.

While I was clearing in at the desk of the customs officer (which was in the post office), I found out it was Tuesday even though I knew it was Monday. We had crossed the International Date Line after leaving Apia. There is a jog in the date line even though Tonga lies east of 180°. This is so the Tongans can claim "time begins in the Tonga Islands."

There was one other yacht anchored in the lagoon crewed by a Canadian couple who had been cruising the South Pacific for six years. They told us about a beautiful grotto near the village fed by a fresh water spring. And so, the next day we all took our soap and towels and had a fresh water bath!

From Niuatoputapu to Fiji was a five-day sail. Fiji, like many former British colonies has a population comprising the original inhabitants (Melanesians) and descendants of East Indian indentured laborers. I found the capital city, Suva, to be a wonderful place—thriving, exotic, inexpensive, and friendly. The cultural diversity was amazing. Walter and I attended the first night presentation of HMS Pinafore in which Ralph (the poor sailor) was played by a strapping Melanesian and the captain's daughter by a petite Japanese lady who was a little long in the tooth for that role. The usual expat Brits fleshed out the cast and it was all good fun.

While Jaime went on a scuba weekend on Kandavo Island, Walter and I flew to the old capital, Levuka, established by whalers before Suva was founded. The museum there depicted in gory detail the continuous and ferocious wars between Fijian tribes, which eventually died down as Europeans came to dominate the area. The victors invariably abused, tortured and ate the vanquished. I don't mean to imply the Europeans were particularly altruistic; they just wanted the Fijians to work for them and stop killing each other. But the Fijians didn't like work, hence the importation of the East Indians! It does make one ponder the human condition—why did a people unsullied by contact with other races descend to such depths when they were living in a tropical paradise?

After a week tied up at the Royal Suva Yacht Club it was time to go. I had invited my daughter Brenda to meet us in New Zealand and if we were to get there first, we had to leave. Our plans met with raised eyebrows from other yachties on the dock—"Go to New Zealand in winter? Cross the Tasman Sea in winter? You must be crazy!"

New Zealand and Australia

In some ways they were right, although the weather heading south was not so bad. But we did suffer a major equipment failure. About 250 miles from Fiji and 750 miles north of New Zealand we were running with the jib winged out, with a wind of about 30 knots. In the middle of the afternoon the wind began to drop. I was on watch at the time and, as the wind dropped, we suffered a couple of unintentional gybes. I didn't think them too serious as the main boom was vanged down hard, and we had a preventer rigged and two reefs in the mainsail. After the last gybe, I reset the steering and engaged Victor the wind vane, as we call our mechanical helmsman, and left the cockpit to watch the vane in operation. Good job I did. As I stood on the stern I felt a sudden wind shift and the mainsail again gybed, but with great vio-

The broken boom, Tasman Sea, 1996

lence. The boom snapped like a carrot at the vang and the whole mess fell into the cockpit I had just vacated. The boom was foreshortened and no longer fully supported by the sail or topping lift.

The wind continued to fall and fortunately stayed ahead of the beam. We rigged the loose-footed storm mainsail and pressed on. The next day we cut the sail off the boom and tidied up, and we still got to Opua in Northern New Zealand in a little over a week from leaving Fiji. So the Tasman Sea wasn't too bad, although it got its revenge later on the way to Australia. We stayed a week in Opua, a charming spot in the Bay of Islands, where we got a second-hand boom and had the sails repaired. Opua is connected to a small town to the south called KawaKawa by a steam locomotive operated by a gang of enthusiasts. On the Sunday of our stay, we took a jazz excursion on the train accompanied by a Dixie band to a festival in KawaKawa. Jaime left the boat in Opua to go skiing in the South Island; winter still had six weeks to go. When the new boom and sails were ready, Walter and I sailed to Auckland and checked into a huge marina in the downtown area. We beat Brenda to Auckland by two days.

Auckland is a modern, attractive city, Brenda enjoyed the shopping and we did the round of museums, art galleries and the casino. *Fiona* was tied up only a few yards from the Royal New Zealand Yacht Squadron, where we became guest members for a couple of weeks. The America's Cup, which was to be defended at Auckland in the year 2000, was prominently displayed. When I took Brenda to see it, a hush fell on the room when she said she wanted to see it before it went back to New York! We rented a car for a few days and Brenda and I explored the North Island. New Zealand is a charming country with friendly people. In many ways it is more English than present-day England and it strongly reminded me of my youth in the north of England.

We had recruited a wandering South African fellow called Mike as crew for the leg to Australia. He had put a notice up on the local yacht club board, advertising his desire to sign on as crew. When Brenda returned home, Mike moved on board and we worked our way back up the coast, waiting for a good weather window for the departure. While we waited, we cruised the lovely Bay of Islands. Mike was a keen paraglider and one sunny day at the Island of Urapukapuka, he humped his gear up a nice grassy hill and gave us a couple of demonstration flights.

Also on this island there were a number of walking trails to diggings at former Maori villages that had been occupied before the arrival of Europeans. A plaque at the sites showed what the villages must have looked like, and I was struck by the extensive defenses—deep ditches still very much in evidence with palisades (now gone) behind them.

We cruised around and waited for the opportune moment to depart for more than a week. We checked in with marine radio stations and printed numerous weather charts on the fax. The Tasman Sea is notorious for the sudden changes in weather, as it is dominated by high pressure cells moving across the Australian continent and low pressure areas lying to the south. The lows usually lie on fronts stretching north. The best time to leave is after a front has passed and a slow moving high to the north gives southwest winds for a few days. We waited and waited but the southwest winds never came. Finally, the forecasts called for the perpetual northwest winds to give way to westerly winds and so we left.

It was a mistake. We had northwest winds, as the Queensland Coast lies northwest of New Zealand; this gave us a beat. A sailing friend had given me a book during my visit home called *Gentleman Never Sail to Weather* by Denton Moore, the story of a four-year circumnavigation. (It is a good read.). I must say that, after a few days beating in the Tasman Sea, I thoroughly concurred! But we were stuck with it and maybe I'm not a gentleman.

The wind was usually in the 25-knot range, so we had reefed sails. One morning, a squall fell on us that packed 60 knots. The next day, a panel blew out of the jib and it took us seven hours with the sewing machine to put it back together. After six days, we staggered into a bay on Norfolk Island, about 500 miles from New Zealand. The wind was down and we had a good night's sleep.

We called the Australian customs people and they arranged to meet us on a jetty a few miles away. Unfortunately, there was a large swell running. Two of us managed to get ashore but the dinghy was slightly damaged so we went back to *Fiona* to gaze at the island from the relative safety of the cockpit. I can report that Norfolk Island is covered with Norfolk pine trees, but that's about all I saw. A couple of charter fishing boats came close, curious to see a boat from New York, and one of them tossed three fresh fish aboard.

North of Norfolk we were on the Coral Sea, although the weather didn't get significantly better for another week. For the last two days before arriving at Cairns, we had no wind at all and we motored through the Great Barrier Reef under a full moon. With a GPS receiver and radar, it's safe to make approaches at night, which I would never have considered prior to getting these instruments. In fact, before 1990 *Fiona* often spent a night hove-to or ranging back and forth until an approach to land could be made in daylight.

Walter and I put in a heavy week of maintenance at Cairns before Ginny arrived to take Mike's place. Ginny was an old acquaintance who lived in the same hamlet I lived in, Brookhaven, back on Long Island. The weather in the Tasman Sea had left us with a lot to do, including lifting a few teak deck planks and re-caulking underneath. Cairns, which lies about 17° South, turned out to be a lovely up-market touristy town, though years later it was devastated by a hurricane. Whilst in Cairns, I had hoped to get a permit to cruise Indonesia, but I was defeated by the inertia of the Indonesian officials. After wasting $15 on phone cards and mostly being kept on hold, I gave up and decided to visit Thailand instead.

We had strong southeast winds for our trip through the Great Barrier Reef. We anchored every night, usually making good about 55 miles between anchorages. Lizard Island was the best stop and our last chance to go snorkeling, as we were warned to stay out of the water north of Lizard due to the predatory habits of the salt water crocodiles. We spent a couple of days in Cooktown before Lizard—this is the place Captain Cook repaired the *Endeavour* after he crunched on a reef. Following repairs, he sailed to Lizard Island and climbed the hill in order to plot the best way out through the Great Barrier Reef into open water. Cooktown was established many years later as a trading center for the miners heading for the gold fields on the Palmer River—a fascinating story told in a book we got at the Cooktown Museum.

North of Cooktown, the Queensland coast is very desolate. Ginny and I had a curious experience when we dinghied up to a small settlement several hundred miles north of Cooktown. We had anchored *Fiona* and gone ashore to trade paperbacks; we had been told earlier by an Aussie yachtie that this was the place to do it. Instead, we ran into a genuine outback character called Barbara who invited us into her ramshackle abode, amused us with stories of the region, and finally gave us some Holy Heavenly Healing Cloth which she said would cure any ailment, along with typewritten instructions.

We sailed past Cape York into the Torres Strait and spent a couple of days at Thursday Island. At one time this was a great pearling center and we were lucky enough to see one of the old pearling luggers, now sailing as a yacht. From Thursday it was a few days' sail to Darwin, the modern capital of the Northern Territories. Darwin was very hot—in the 90s every day—goodness knows what it was like in summer. We stayed at a new marina, and fortunately, there was lots of fresh water available. We had the anchor chain re-galvanized and took care of other maintenance chores. We rented a car and most days drove down to the yacht club for a beer and a game of pool each afternoon. We also restocked at the last western-style supermarket that we would see for a long time. We then left on the long haul to Thailand, about 3,000 miles, paralleling the coast of Java and Sumatra.

Our one stop was Christmas Island, an Australian possession developed by the British in the late 19th century because of the enormous guano deposits. It was a fascinating place to visit; it had quite a bloody history detailed in a booklet we picked up. The guano was dug up by imported Chinese coolies who sometimes murdered their overseers due to the harsh working conditions. The Japanese invaded in 1942 and the few British soldiers on the island were killed by the Sikh policemen just before the invasion began to prevent any resistance. Every year on Christmas Island, millions of red land crabs migrate to the sea to reproduce. We were there for the tail end—crabs everywhere. Whatever is in their path they climb over, even three-story buildings. We refueled and left, expecting a long, windless, passage through the doldrums as we approached the equator.

The wind dropped the day after Christmas Island disappeared over the stern horizon and we motored over a calm sea for nearly a week. When we crossed the equator, Ginny was truly inducted as a Daughter of Neptune by the old King himself, who climbed over the lifeline to perform the ceremony, fortified by lots of Mount Gay rum.

Apart from the odd encounter with an Indonesian ship, we saw no one. This ship gave us quite a scare, as it pulled alongside just a few feet away and then jogged directly ahead of the bow. We wondered if they were pirates, but there was no sign of hostile intentions. It slowly pulled away, emitting clouds of black smoke from the stack. Later I was told by an old Far East resident that the crew was trying to get the bad luck spirits to leave their ship and jump onto ours.

Above 1° N, the fuel got low and we sailed in very light winds, sometimes tacking to within a few miles of the coast of Sumatra, which looked very green, but with no signs of life.

The Far East

We arrived in Phuket, Thailand, in early December, 31 days after leaving Darwin. Ginny left us here. Her son flew down from Nepal and they went off sightseeing before her return to the U.S. in time for

Christmas. I called my daughter Brenda and she posted a notice on the Internet that produced a new crew member for the leg to the Mediterranean within two days.

While we waited, Walter and I sampled the culinary delights of Thailand, where a dollar or two got you as much tasty food as you can eat in one meal. We also cruised the spectacular bay to the east of Phuket, where islands of volcanic origin with vertical walls tower up hundreds of feet, crowned with dense vegetation. Parts of a James Bond movie (*The Man with the Golden Gun*) were shot here a few years earlier. We wound up at Phi Phi Don, a unique island with no airfield, where visitors arrived by sail or by taking the ferry from Phuket. A few pleasant hotels and guest houses provided accommodation. The village had several streets, each no more than 10 feet wide, absolutely packed with small shops and eating establishments. The place never seemed to close, even in the small hours. We found a pool hall, a game the Thai play very enthusiastically and noisily.

Our latest crew member, Stanley, flew in from Seattle the day after Christmas and, after another brief visit to Phi Phi Don, we sailed to Sri Lanka. This turned out to be a glorious sail, and a wonderful introduction to ocean cruising for Stanley, whose experience had been confined to coastal cruising. We covered the 1,200 miles in just over eight days and, fortunately, arrived in the late afternoon at Galle in time to beat the harbor curfew. The curfew was imposed by the Sri Lanka Navy, who closed the harbor at dusk and then proceeded to discourage Tamil rebels by dropping grenades and sticks of dynamite into the sea near the entrance for the rest of the night. The civil war had clearly had a profound impact on the country, including a severe economic penalty. It was probably the poorest country we had visited since Guyana. The political situation reminded me of Northern Ireland because of the religious disparities between the factions. The Tamils, who originated from India, just across a narrow sea to the north, are Hindu, while the majority of Sri Lankans, called Sinhalese, are Buddhists who are concentrated in the south. In contrast to Ireland, the Tamils are fighting for a separate state of their own.

On our arrival in Galle, the naval officer had noticed from the passports that Walter's birthday was the next day. "Come to the party," we gaily invited him. "I will," he replied, "and I'll bring my boss." Sure enough, a bevy of navy people showed up at sundown the next day and we had quite a party. Several yachties from nearby boats were already aboard, and a couple of bottles of our Caribbean rum were sacrificed to cement Sri Lanka-American relations. I served small snacks with bits of Spam and mustard. The senior naval man had never encountered Spam before and he loved it. He wound up consuming nearly a can of it, sliced on bread. He was also very careful to only drink in the main cabin, so that he could not be seen from the dock.

We made a two-day van ride to Kandy, the old capital which has many beautiful Buddhist shrines. The one we visited was said to hold a tooth of Buddha. The central part of Sri Lanka is lovely, with intensively cultivated hillsides and, of course, lots of tea plantations. Several times we passed through police road blocks. Their job is no sinecure as, on the day we left, 22 policemen were killed by Tamils. Prices were very cheap. Our hotel in Kandy cost $6 per room, with private bath. Expertly made carvings, mostly in teak and ebony, were available for a song.

From Sri Lanka, we sailed few hundred miles southwest to the Maldive Islands. These comprise over a thousand islands grouped in about 18 atolls, spread along several degrees north to the equator. The capital, Male, lies halfway along the chain at about four degrees north. I had expected them to be poor, rather like other atolls we had visited, such as the Tuamotus and the Cook group in the South Pacific. This view was reinforced by an article written by Ginny's son Ian describing a trip he made in the traditional dhow to atolls lying to the south of Male. But I was wrong. The inhabitants were relatively well-off. The Republic of the Maldives was the first Islamic country we visited and unfortunately, we arrived in the middle of Ramadan. Many businesses and government agencies opened only for a few hours in the morning, as Muslims fast during daylight hours and restaurants open only after nightfall, when they are allowed to break their fast. It is considered bad form for Westerners to be seen eating or drinking in public.

Besides these minor problems, Male is one of the worst anchorages we had ever encountered. The water was deep, typically 150 feet, currents were strong, and there were no facilities to handle dinghies. We anchored cheek by jowl with over 20 freighters sharing the harbor. The freighters, however, were the clue to the Maldives amazing prosperity, for they export virtually nothing. The freighters brought only imports. The prosperity had been achieved in the thirty years since independence from Britain by taking a very hard look at what they did have and figuring out how to cash in on it.

What they did have was over a thousand beautiful tropical islands. About 79 were developed exclusively as luxurious beach hotels. A huge airfield, nearly two miles long, funneled dozens of jets in each day, packed with tourists. An infrastructure of ferries, helicopters, and planes dealt with the transportation of the pale, mostly European, tourists to their designated luxury islands. No natives, except staff, lived on the resort island; native villages were to be found on 169 other islands, which had no tourists.

After customs and immigration formalities in Male we sailed to one resort island and anchored off a lovely beach. We were welcome to use the facilities on shore. The hotel there was beautifully designed and landscaped, and prices were out of sight for poor yachties—$30 lunches, but we splurged (once) on $10 cheeseburgers and a beer by the pool.

We returned to Male for outward clearance. On our first visit we had anchored with all our chain, plus 200 feet of rope. It took us two hours to raise it, as the weight of 150 feet of chain hanging straight down was simply beyond the capacity of the anchor winch. On our return, we instead used all rope, with just 30 feet of chain. This was one of the few occasions (perhaps the only time) when I have used rope instead of chain for the anchor.

We ate out in Male after sunset for only a few dollars and I was amazed at how the streets filled with laughing, happy people once the fasting was over for the day. At the restaurant, which was rather dimly lit, I spotted a picture on the wall which looked like a print of a Rembrandt—a girl strumming a lute. When I inspected it closely I found it was an original oil painting. The next day I contacted the artist, who worked at the airport, and negotiated a copy, which was waiting for me when I got home months later.

The Middle East

The two-week sail to Yemen from Male was very pleasant, and there was lots of marine life. At night, the phosphorescence cast almost enough light to read by, and when dolphins swam around the boat, they left greenish-white "contrails" in the water. Every so often there was a slurpy gasp as they sharply inhaled. Walter caught several fish on the trolling line. Most got off the hook, but we did land and eat two.

We gave Somalia a wide berth. Aden was very battered due to a recent civil war. The town was located between harsh, barren mountains. Most women wore long black robes and head veil, the hijab, and their brown eyes peered at you through a little slit in the head-dress. Aden was a grubby, not to say nondescript, town. Trash piles littered the streets, and colored plastic bags blew along the gutters. The peeling buildings had been knocked about a bit in the recent civil war. Furtive feral cats lurked in shadows, scavenging what they could.

But down at Steamer Point there was a wonderful vestige of 130 years of British rule. This was the Customs House, an airy stone building, which long ago greeted passengers arriving by tender from ships anchored out in the deep harbor. The foundation stone proclaimed that it was laid by HRH the Prince of Wales in 1919. One can picture the bustling activity as white-uniformed officials directed the colonials on their way to the Indies or Africa. Aden, of course, was a bunkering port after a transit of the Suez Canal and Red Sea. Bronze plaques were still on the walls to assist the visitors—"Embarking Passengers" it said over the iron-gated portal leading to the dock. The Customs House now provided a meeting place for a few Arabs to gossip the day away and chew kat in the shade.

More visions of this faded outpost of empire were conjured up by an old photograph in the offices of the fuel company. It was entitled "The Union Castle Line" and showed the liner *Windsor Castle* at anchor; "Sailings to East and South Africa" was printed underneath. Ah, those were the days. Now the harbor was only visited by freighters and the odd wandering yacht. There was talk of cruise ships visiting Aden, although what the tourist would do ashore was somewhat of a mystery. There were some very ancient water storage "tanks," actually dammed-up gorges, in the hills behind Aden. An inscribed stone erected in 1895 read that the tanks were discovered in 1854 by a Lt. Playfair. They were built by an unknown ancient people and were full of stones and debris when discovered. The British Army put them back in working order. Altogether, the tanks hold twenty million imperial gallons of water, we were informed. The water was only used now to irrigate a small botanical garden at the base of the hills.

There were only two shops that would be of interest to the casual tourist. One sold Arab curios, Berber jewelry, Indian shawls, and that sort of thing, but the other was a priceless gem, the Aziz Bookshop. It was located about 200 yards from the Customs House, set back under a deep verandah, and it had no windows. The stock consisted of an eclectic collection of second-hand books and old stamps. Most of the books were old paperbacks, lovingly restored and kept until sold. I picked up a copy of *Six Men* by Alistair Cooke. The covers had been reinforced by gluing them to thin cardboard, and all the pages were stitched together with catgut. A yellow Penguin book caught my eye, *While Rome Burns* by Alexander Woollcott, published in 1937. I flipped through it and found that the pages were brown and brittle. On the fly leaf was written, "P. C. Smyth Aden 10.7.38." I read it out loud to the proprietor, an elderly Indian. "Oh yes," he said, "Mr. Smyth, he worked for Cable and Wireless." It seems that in this shop every book had a story besides the one between the covers. He went on to tell me he had worked at the shop since 1946. His great grandfather had come to the Aden Protectorate from India in its British heyday; he was very nostalgic about the old days.

There was a nice display of Aden colonial stamps on the counter, all with the likeness of Edward, George or Elizabeth in one corner. I mentioned to the proprietor that I had been a student when Queen Elizabeth was crowned. I was taking final examinations around about the time of Coronation Day. He immediately fished out a sheet of 15-cent Aden Coronation stamps, dated 2nd June, 1953 and I bought one for the logbook. I dropped into his shop on several evenings and bought a few more books. After we sailed from Aden, I began to imagine that the Aziz Bookshop existed in another time, and if I could go back and step through that dimly-lit door, I could buy a stamp, stick it on an envelope, and when the letter was delivered, it would be franked at a time when the British ran the world and the sun could safely trace its daily path over the Empire on which it never set.

After we left Aden, we sailed directly to Port Suez at the south end of the Canal. This took 16 days. The Trades stayed with us for the first few hundred miles but after that we had persistent northwest winds— dead on the nose with a typical velocity of 25 knots. After a couple of days of beating to windward, the old genoa jib blew to smithereens. I was attached to that sail; we rounded Cape Horn with it in 1992 and it had sailed many tens of thousands of miles.

It took a couple of days before the weather moderated and we could safely lower it and set the Yankee jib. When we got to Port Suez, the log showed we had sailed 2,200 miles to make good a direct passage of 1,300 miles. In Port Suez I got in touch with Jim Meehan of Shore Sails, who built the old jib, and asked him to air freight a new one to Israel, which he did in about a week. Our agent in Egypt was called the Prince of the Red Sea, a charming old man, assisted by his son. He arranged our Canal transit and a tour of the Cairo Museum and the Pyramids at Giza.

The museum with its priceless collection of antiquities was fabulous. The Pyramids were simply impressive—all that labor for the glorification of one man per pyramid. But the touts selling guided tours, camel rides, trinkets, and their sisters were an unremitting nuisance.

Stanley, who had joined us in Thailand, had a silly dispute with me about sharing the cost of our tour van and driver, and left the boat to tour the Med by bus. Stanley was an American from Oregon who had spotted my ad on the internet. He had limited sailing experience and I think manufactured the

Eric and crew, Walter and Stanley, at the Pyramids

row over paying his share for the van in order to give him an excuse to jump ship. Fortunately, we met a Dutch yacht that we had first encountered in Sri Lanka, and the captain was planning to refit in Cyprus. And so one of his crew agreed to take Stanley's place. Our new crew member was young English woman called Celia who had been bumming round the world for the last three years. Celia joined us in Port Said after we made the two-day trip through the Suez Canal. We had to pay baksheesh to the pilots and tender operators, and we had laid in a stock of Marlboro cigarettes just for this purpose. We were greeted off the Israeli coast by a small gunboat as the sun rose. After some questions on the radio they waved us on to Ashkelon. The marina was home to more than a dozen live-a-boards, and we arrived just in time for the weekly barbeque.

Crew member Celia, Aguadulce, Spain

I think there is a general impression held by the non-sailing public that cruising by yacht consists of lounging on palm-fringed beaches and swimming in warm, turquoise waters. Perhaps this is true occasionally, but mostly two activities take a disproportionate time ashore: first, dealing with bureaucrats who treat every visiting yacht as though they are 20,000-ton freighters with paperwork to match; and, secondly, tramping through the hot and dusty streets in some scruffy industrial area of a port looking for an alleged source for a spare part vital to your continued progress.

In Israel, these two activities coalesced when the jib I had ordered was air-freighted to Israel, where I could pick it up. Now, a yacht in transit does not normally pay import duty on parts ordered for the boat, as these are exported when you leave. The procedures to actually accomplish this vary enormously from country to country. In Israel, they achieve a level of complexity, compounded by sheer incompetence, that Kafka would have appreciated. The first step was a phone call from the shipping company to the marina to say the sail had arrived at Ben Gurian Airport, near Tel Aviv. Next morning, bright and early, I was at the car rental agency in town accompanied by Celia—it has been my experience that things go a lot more smoothly when driving a strange car in a strange country to a poorly-defined location if one person drives and the other navigates.

The first part of the 65-kilometer drive went smoothly, but as we got closer to Tel Aviv, the rush hour traffic built up and it started to rain heavily. We jerked along and finally saw the airport turn-off through the steamy windshield. At the airport my navigator's sharp eyes spotted the obscure sign for the cargo area, and at the checkpoint it was so wet they just waved us through. Cars and trucks were parked everywhere, but finally we squeezed in, half on the curb, and rushed through the drenching rain into the customs building. The tiny, cluttered office of the shipping company was easy to find. A man there who spoke a little English explained the procedure after I had drawn a picture of a sail for him. I was to go to customs with the ship's papers, pay a deposit of 25 percent of the value of the sail, get a gate pass and take the sail back to the boat. (Never mind the shipping memo showed that the sailmaker, and indirectly me, had paid for door-to-door delivery.) The sail would then be examined by customs officials when it was on the boat, and with their certificate I could return to Ben Gurian Airport and get my deposit back.

Sometime later we located the appropriate customs agent in the maze of offices who gave me a pile of papers to add to the growing file, after I had drawn a picture of a sail. The official was a young woman who wrote with her right hand and never stopped talking in Hebrew into a cell phone held by her left hand. I took the papers to the bank on the ground floor where they refused to accept a credit card and insisted on cash, 3,000 shekels, no less (about $900) for the deposit. Naturally, I did not have 3,000 shekels, but the teller said I could get the money from the cash machines at the bank in the main passenger terminal.

We dashed back to the car in the rain, parked at the main terminal, found the bank and ran into next snag—the daily limit on the automatic cash machines was 1,500 shekels. So I went to see the bank manager, cap and credit card in hand, and after an hour and some prolonged explaining, I emerged with the money. Then it was back to the cargo area and the bank there. Clutching my receipt, I first stopped by a computer operator, who keyed in a record of the transaction and then returned to customs for the prized gate pass. At the shipping company, after photocopying everything, we were assigned a guide to take us to the warehouse, where I surrendered my passport for a visitor's badge, Celia was sent to wait in the lobby. The man at the office wanted to see a receipt for storage charges. "What charges?" I asked in astonishment. "It only came yesterday!" "You pay for every day," he explained.

After a long phone call to the shipping company, I filled out more forms, and then went back to the bank to pay demurrage, returned with receipt to the warehouse, and finally I was able to totter out with 33 kilos of sail in a large box. I traded my visitor's badge and put the box in the car. It was still raining. By two o'clock we were back on the road heading to the marina, where the manager called the local customs to arrange the on-board inspection.

About five-thirty the next day, two pleasant young men showed up and asked in poor English what was in the box. I drew a picture of a sail, then we emptied the box, they signed the certificate and stamped it. The next day we were back at the airport with all our papers, but discovered my deposits were returned by the fiscal branch of customs, located near the main passenger terminal. It transpired that repayment of the deposit could not be made by the bank that took the money in the first place. Rather, as a non-resident, I was to be given a check cashable only at one particular branch office of the Bank of Israel in Tel Aviv. A young lady laboriously transcribed the name off my passport into Hebrew on a blank check and disappeared to get it signed by someone in authority. "You mean we have to go to Tel Aviv?" I asked, somewhat incredulously. "Yes," she replied, advising us to take a bus. "We have a car," I said, and asked "What time does the bank close?" She glanced at her watch and said, "In about an hour."

After getting vague directions, we rushed back to the parking garage and zipped down the motorway to Tel Aviv. None of the exits corresponded to the fuzzy directions we had and so we found ourselves in a five-lane conveyor belt of steel. In the downtown area, the traffic was too dense to even stop and ask for directions, assuming we were lucky enough to find an English speaker. As the time crept inexorably towards bank closing time, I gave up and decided to head back to the marina. We zigzagged along the crowded streets until we found an entrance ramp back onto the motorway.

Driving back to Ashkelon, I turned over the options. How about just sending the check to my bank at home? No good, as it was written completely in Hebrew. How about simply coming back to Tel Aviv another day? The problem was that the next day was Friday, when many banks and institutions closed early and did not reopen until Sunday. But that week, Sunday was a public holiday, and so they wouldn't be open until Monday. We had planned to leave Israel on Sunday and, of course, the daily rental of the car added to the cost of the whole transaction.

At the marina I laid out my problem to the manager, Armen. He called his bank manager, who had an idea. I could open an account at his bank and deposit the check, then withdraw all but the minimum to keep the account open. That seemed a bit bizarre, but Armen arranged for us to go to the bank later in the afternoon. When we got there, Armen had a long conversation with the manager, who finally agreed to simply cash the check and he initialed it. I stood in line for a teller. When it was my turn I gave her the check and she asked for my passport. When she saw it, her eyebrows elevated and she scuttled back to the manager for a long conversation. They waved me over. The problem, they explained, was that the check was made out in Hebrew to a certain "Eric Patrick" not Eric Forsyth. They would not cash it.

We drove back to the marina in an air of despondency; I could visualize the problems of trying to get customs to issue a new check. I remembered that I had written down the name and telephone number of the official who had written the check, so I went back to the boat to find this information. When I got back to the marina office, a knight in shining armor had appeared. Armen had explained the ridiculous situation to a business associate who had dropped by. He was scandalized by the poor image I was forming of Israel. "Get in the car," he said. "Drive to my bank—I've got a little influence." So off we went, and as we entered he hissed, "You've lost your passport! Don't show it. Just sign the check as 'Eric Patrick'." At an employee's desk, I signed the check as directed, and Armen's friend then cashed it and we left with 3,000 shekels.

The next step was to convert it to dollars, which I did the next day in Jerusalem, where there are still many money-changers near the Temple. After we got my dollars (less a considerable percentage absorbed by exchange rates to and from and commissions), Celia and I had a wonderful day in Jerusalem because the tourists had been scared off by the threats of violence caused by the Jewish plans to build new houses in East Jerusalem. The sites and restaurants were relatively empty. We even visited the tomb of Jesus—actually, the two tombs of Jesus, one inside the walls and one outside. There was a great deal of uncertainty about where things actually happened 2,000 years ago. The next day we drove to the Dead Sea and Masada. The latter was very interesting, particularly as we made our ascent by the ramp erected by the Romans to storm the place, not by the cable car used by most tourists. The region was stark, to say the least, and it was staggering to think of the effort needed to erect the ramp in about three months. It rises several hundred feet from the desert floor and was still useable after 2,000 years.

On the way back to the marina I got caught speeding by the cops, but when they discovered I was a visitor, I was let off with a grudging warning. That was how we spent our time in Israel, and the next day we left in fairly grungy weather for the short hop to Cyprus.

We tied up in Larnaka, on the Greek side, Cyprus being an island divided between peoples of Turkish and Greek ethnic origin. When we arrived, it was a public holiday celebrating mainland Greece's Independence Day. This may help explain the enmity on the island; the

Greeks were celebrating independence from Turkey. We stayed three days, during which time I got lots of photocopies of charts for the trip west. (Note that in Cyprus, "copyright" means it's alright to copy!)

From Cyprus we sailed to Antalya, on the Anatolian coast of Turkey—another hop of three days but with its share of heavy weather. We sheltered for the night in Limassol Harbor before we could weather the western end of Cyprus. The marina at Antalya was about five miles from the old town. A cosmopolitan collection of cruising boats wintered there and we arrived in time for the wind-up party of the social club. When a couple from New England discovered Walter and I lived on Long Island, the wife confessed to having attended Patchogue High School, just a few miles from my home—small world!

Eric in the amphitheater, Aspendos, Turkey

A few days later we went to a dinner party at the jazzy restaurant on the marina site and I wore a tie and blazer for the first time since the circumnavigation began. The archeological sites in the vicinity of Antalya are fantastic; most of the ruins are of Roman origin. We rented a car for a day and visited three sites. Perges covers an extensive area, and much of the public baths with its complicated heating system remain. Fragments of statues, columns and mosaics literally lie under your feet as you walk among the ruins. At Aspendos the amphitheater looks much as it did in Roman times—they could put on a play tomorrow with seating for about 10,000 people. Side is a seaside resort full of restaurants and souvenir shops, but the remains of an old temple are next to the shore on a beautiful cape. The place was swarming with tourists, mostly German, and I imagined it was chaos at the height of the season.

From Turkey, we faced a thousand-mile leg to the island of Malta. This took us eight days. Much of the wind was on the nose with gusts as high as 40 knots, and we were reefed most of the time. Occasionally, the wind dropped to nothing and we had to power. As someone remarked in one of our cruising guides, "In the Med you power from gale to gale." On moonless nights, the fiery comet Hale-Bopp hung over our starboard bow.

When we got to Malta we noticed several strands had broken on the bobstay (7/16" diameter wire rope) and we had to have a rigger make us a new one. Malta has been a fortress for centuries. As you approach the harbor, vast sand-colored stone walls loom up on every shore. Behind the ramparts one can see the dome of the cathedral and the towers of numerous churches. We went for lunch at the yacht club, which is housed in one of the old forts on Manoel Island. The walls penetrated by the narrow windows that overlook the water are five feet thick.

From our berth on Msida creek to Valletta, the capital, it was a short bus ride or a 45-minute walk. The old, narrow, streets are crowded with shops and restaurants punctuated here and there with graceful plazas. We visited museums, the fine arts gallery and the underground labyrinth which comprised the military control center in WWII. The rooms have been restored and filled with period equipment, complete with mannequins dressed in uniforms of the day. The island and its defenders were awarded the George Cross, Britain's highest civilian award for valor, after the intense German and Italian bombing during the war. The story of the blockade and the ships that ran supplies to Malta was a central theme of several exhibitions.

The day before we left was another of my 39th birthdays. Celia and Walter planned a surprise party by inviting several couples we had gotten to know on adjacent boats. Unfortunately, I spotted the cake they had bought when our agent came to get paid. Celia and Walter watched with trepidation as I cut it up into large slices and suggested with the agent should eat it with us, accompanied by the usual rum. The invited guests showed up a little later, and fortunately, there was enough cake and rum left to get the party going.

After we cleared Malta we ran into a northeast gale which whisked us to Bizerte in Tunisia in a couple of days; it was downwind sailing for a change. Bizerte is a small, pleasant town with an old walled section containing the Kasbah. The highlight was a one-hour bus ride to visit Tunis, where the Bardo museum had the most amazing collection of mosaic I had ever seen; they were from the Carthaginian and Roman periods. Many of them were huge, forty feet square, and they were often mounted vertically so they could be viewed easily and were virtually complete. The subjects were mostly Gods and their associated legends, or local scenes showing people at work or fishing. Many incorporated such small fine stones to form the picture that I was reminded of the pointillism style of French impressionistic painting. I was also struck by the thought that the scenes were so pastoral for an era one thinks of as fairly brutal.

In contrast, the Fine Arts Museum in Valletta had had a good collection of Italian classical paintings, many of them depicting in gory detail martyrs dying in every imaginable manner and, of course, numerous versions of Jesus Christ hanging on the cross. The Bardo also had some rooms from old Islamic mosques containing the most elaborate stone carvings.

After the Bardo and lunch in Tunis it was a short taxi ride to Carthage; the center of the empire that was ultimately conquered by Rome about 200 BC. The place was sprinkled with ruins, including the old circus where, according to the guide, the still-visible tunnels were the ones used to let lions loose in the ring where they ate Christian captives. There was a plaque celebrating two Christian lady saints that the lions refused to eat in 203 AD, thus convincing the frustrated spectators that maybe their religion had something after all.

Ancient mosaic, Bardo Museum, Tunis

Back at sea, our six-day trip to Almeria in Spain was plagued by long calm spells under engine and occasional head winds. Ironically, we had waited an extra day in port for a forecast gale to clear the area. After clearing with the authorities in Almeria, we moved down the coast to a charming marina in Aguadulce, where the boat stayed for four weeks under the care of Celia while Walter and I flew to New York. Fortunately, Walter was able to get a good job for three weeks to replenish his cruising kitty. I had a large number of repairs to electronic equipment to take care of, and I also squeezed in the annual vintage Bentley rally.

When we returned, the willowy Celia announced she had got a job modeling swimsuits, leaving Walter and I to sail the boat to Gibraltar. We jogged down the coast in easy stages, but each afternoon we had strong winds—on the nose, of course. Most nights we tied up in marinas, where we usually enjoyed sunset rum and exchanged yarns with other cruisers. The numerous restaurants in this part of the world are quite inexpensive and we were able to take a break from the Spam and beans suppers on board. We also ran into old friends of the British Trade Winds Rally whom we had seen periodically since we were in the Caribbean. Unfortunately, the marinas were littered with flotsam and jetsam, and at Fuengirola I had to don scuba gear to clear a rope which had wrapped itself around the prop shaft. In the process, I discovered that the forces generated on the cutlass bearing had been so high the cotter pin had sheared, and the nuts holding the propeller had worked loose; we were lucky not to have shed the propeller.

The Last Leg

We sailed to Gibraltar to stock up for the transatlantic leg and to pick up our new crew member, Derek. Derek and I had both served as pilots in the RAF and had briefly been stationed at Gibraltar more than forty years earlier; this was my first return visit since then. It was massively changed. The military presence was gone and huge buildings dominated the limited level land. One afternoon, I climbed to the top of the Rock. I got the adrenalin pumping by negotiating a narrow path up the cliffs on the east side. At the top I ran into a family of the famous Barbary apes, and later explored one of the tunnels driven into the rock by military engineers in the 18th and 19th centuries. By the time the British Army left, they had drilled over 33 miles of tunnels—the famous "solid as the Rock" is really Swiss cheese!

Walter and I took the ferry to Tangiers one day, but this turned out to be rather a bust. We were the targets of relentless touts everywhere we went. When Derek showed up, we beat it out of the Med through the legendary Pillars of Hercules against a stiff wind and current. Once into the Atlantic, conditions eased and we had some lovely sailing to Tenerife in the Canary Islands.

As usually happens, it was the middle of the night when we arrived at Santa Cruz. This is a very pleasant town with many sidewalk cafes and we stayed three days before leaving for Bermuda, 2,500 miles away. By this time it was well into the hurricane season. Cyclonic activity was low, although I carefully monitored weather forecasts on short wave, and printed weather faxes as soon as we got within range of the U.S. stations. We had a very easy passage, with winds rarely over 20 knots, and for four days we used the engine to push us over a wind-less sea. When the wind dropped, we often took the opportunity for a swim, as it's always fun to swim in blue, warm water going down two and a half miles under the boat. On one occasion, we found the propeller had become fouled by a piece of fishing net and it took Walter and I in turns some time to cut it free.

Derek had a birthday during the trip. We baked a cake and gave him a card on which we inscribed:

ON REACHING 65

Congrats on reaching sixty-five.

Tho' your eyes may be dim

And you're not quite so slim

It certainly beats the alternative!

In reply Derek wrote in the log book:

THANKS FOR THE PARTY

Though birthdays are by custom only annually repeating

With increasing age, the time between them seems more fleeting

But should I make another ten

And reflect on all this, then

My 65th on board this ship will certainly take some beating!

The muse, of course, was inspired by liberal swigging of our Mount Gay rum. About half-way across the Atlantic I succeeded in rising two friends on Long Island on the ham radio with the help of an amateur operator in Barbados. From that point on, our friends and relatives at home had some knowledge of our progress. With winds that were usually in the 10- to 12-knot range, we had a leisurely sail and sighted Bermuda just over 20 days after leaving Tenerife. We finally tied up at St. George's in the middle of the night. Bermuda marked the completion of the circumnavigation. We had left from there in July, 1995, for the Caribbean. I was apparently in such a rush to touch land, I dented the pulpit on a post at the customs dock. There is lovely cruising in Bermuda and we sailed *Fiona* to a few of my favorite anchorages so Derek could see some of it before he flew out to rejoin his family who were vacationing in Florida. Isn't modern technology wonderful? In a few hours, Derek was transported from the idyllic, tranquil life aboard the boat to the frenetic madness of Disney World!

Just before Derek left, we were joined by Walter's older sister Del who flew down for a few days, and a couple of days later his sister Debbie dropped in. When they left, Walter and I took the boat over to Castle Harbor, the only anchorage in Bermuda which, over the years, I had not explored. There are interesting ruins on Castle Island, which was fortified in 1612 by the first English settlers. We also did the last in a series of noon sights which we started in mid-Atlantic to see how accurately we could measure longitude by knowing the time of the sight, all this inspired by Dava Sobel's interesting book on the development of the marine chronometer. This was a crucial test of Harrison's chronometer when he invented it in the 18th century. The Royal Navy, who desperately wanted the chronometer put into production, used a prototype to measure the longitude of Jamaica after a voyage from England. I had always suspected the results were too good to be true, and on our trip from Gibraltar to Bermuda, we could not duplicate the accuracy the Navy had achieved. Perhaps a little fudging went on back then.

For the third crew member of the leg from Bermuda to Newport, Rhode Island, I recruited Ginny, who had already sailed with us from Australia to Thailand. The day after Ginny flew in, we refueled and left. We had an easy sail. The sea was quite placid when we crossed the spot where *Fiona* lost the mast in 1988, and it was within a day of the same date, so I was pleased when we got north of the Gulf Stream with its potential for violent weather.

We arrived in Rhode Island in the middle of the night (as usual) and anchored in Mackerel Cove on Jamestown Island. In the morning, we entered Newport Harbor and cleared customs. Ginny took a bus back to Maine where she was supervising extensive alterations to her new house on Peaks Island. A day later, Walter left to attend a wedding on Long Island, and I was left alone for a short while.

I sailed *Fiona* to Block Island so we would be positioned for the final leg to Patchogue, the idea being to arrive 800 days after we left. We actually left earlier than planned because the wind was forecast to be from the very desirable southeast, changing to southwest. We left as soon as Walter and his friend Tim arrived on the ferry from Montauk, Tim being the last in a long line of third crew members.

The trip along the Long Island coast turned out to be a great sail, but once we were through the Fire Island Inlet we had to anchor for over twelve hours before traversing the shoals of Great South Bay.

Walter combed through the log books and came up with these statistics:

Total Distance logged:	34,360 nm
Number of days at sea:	298
Average sailing day:	115 nm
Total diesel consumption:	1900 gallons
Total rum consumption:	70 gallons
Number of novels read:	≈250 (and ≈113 Weekly Manchester Guardians)
Number of countries visited:	34

It had been quite an experience. I greatly enjoyed visiting the many countries, but usually after a week or two I was ready to move on because I also liked the challenge of ocean sailing. I have fond memories of lying in my bunk reading a Patrick O'Brian novel, with the sounds of the wind and creak of the main sheet blocks in the background—this greatly added verisimilitude to his stories.

The social side of cruising was great fun. There were a lot of interesting folks out there and there was a strong camaraderie among cruisers. We had about 180 guests on board at various times for happy hour (so that's where the rum went!), representing 18 countries in addition to those we visited.

Walter thoroughly enjoyed the trip and developed into an excellent sailor. On the way back from Bermuda we discussed the possibility of another cruise and decided Antarctica looked interesting.

3 *Fiona's* First Cruise to the Antarctic
1998-1999

I had a busy winter reading all I could about other small boat sailors who had cruised in Antarctica, and laying in a large collection of charts. I decided to sail down the Chilean Canals to get to Antarctica. For a cruise destination in Antarctica itself I consulted an old friend, Dennis Puleston, who had sailed there many times as the resident naturalist aboard small expedition liners.

Things seemed to conspire to keep the cruise from getting off the ground, literally. While the boat was still on the cradle several time-consuming problems developed. During winter I had decided to replace the teak deck. It was 23 years old, and dealing with leaks was getting to be too much. With the help of friends, I ripped out the teak planks and plugged over a thousand screw holes. Weeks' Yacht Yard then started to put down a fiberglass deck with a non-skid surface. A wet spring seriously hampered and delayed work.

Then when I started the engine for the first time after the winter lay-up, a fault with the starter switch caused the starter motor to over-speed, a cast iron bracket broke, and bits fell into the bell housing. These had to be cleaned out before we could start the engine. While I was off on the annual vintage car rally, Walter rigged a frame so that we could lift out the engine. When I returned, less than two weeks before the scheduled departure, we dropped the transmission and bell housing in and cleaned out the debris.

We put it all back together, got the boat in the water, rigged the sails, loaded provisions and we were ready to go. Mike flew in from South Africa; he had crewed in 1996 from New Zealand to Australia. Our route would take us through the Panama Canal to Easter Island, down the west coast of Chile and across the Drake Passage to the Antarctic Peninsula. I hoped that the crew for the whole trip would consist of Walter and Mike.

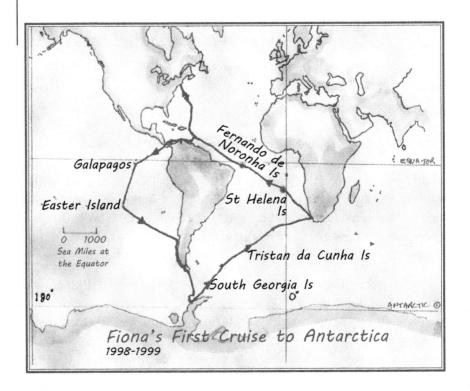

To The Panama Canal

We left on July 9, three days later than planned, and, in fact, we ran behind schedule for this whole phase of the cruise. In each port I felt a little like the White Rabbit—"I'm late, I'm late!" Sticking to the time-table was important so that we got a good weather window at Cape Horn. We skipped our traditional one-night layover in Block Island, heading straight to Bermuda.

For the first two days the winds were light and variable, but then we picked up good northeast winds and romped to Bermuda in a little over five days after leaving Fire Island Inlet. The shock I encountered on this leg was not caused by the weather or some problem with the boat: sitting comfortably in the cockpit at happy hour with a glass of rum in our hands the day before landfall, Walter announced, out of the blue, that he was getting off in Bermuda and flying home. He felt he just was not ready for the trip.

I must say this was a blow, as Walter was a veteran of *Fiona*'s 1995-97 circumnavigation and had become a very competent sailor. Mike, on the other hand, had only a month or two of blue water experience under his belt and we were heading for some of the roughest sailing grounds in the world. I think Walter had fallen in love, always a problem for skippers when they have a young crew. Once in Bermuda, Mike called friends in Africa who might want to join the cruise and my long-suffering daughter, Brenda, posted "crew wanted" messages on internet notice boards. Finally, we left—late again, with the search for crew being the delaying factor this time—with a Bermudian crew member who had once sailed across the Atlantic and had several good references from yacht skippers.

We had wonderful winds and made the 900-mile passage to St. Martin in a little over six days. We had a very near-miss with a freighter one night a few hundred miles from St. Martin. Despite prolonged discussion about collision avoidance with the captain on the VHF radio, the clown put his helm over when just yards away and barely cleared our stern.

When we got to the French side of St. Martin, the immigration officials refused to admit Mike, because South Africans needed a special visa. So we puttered round to the Dutch side and cleared in there. As there is no border control between the French and Dutch parts of the island, this is a perfect example of mindless bureaucracy.

In St. Martin we parted company with our Bermudian crew; he just wasn't working out, considering what lay ahead. I got him a ticket home and, after stocking up with duty-free rum, Mike and I sailed the boat to Bequia, the start of a leisurely cruise of the Grenadine Islands. Wandering about the small island of Mayreau, we came across the gravestone of Margaret Alexander, born in 1837, who died on the 31st of January, 1950, aged 113! It is staggering to think that this lady, who died well after WWII, as a child might have seen British men-of-war at Antigua whch could have been in the Battle of Trafalgar. Her parents were probably slaves, but she was born just as the British Empire renounced slavery. Later on we talked to a local who was her great-great grandson.

We also dived on a sunken gunboat on a reef west of Mayreau, but the boat was from a later era; it had a boiler. And, at each island I bombarded Brenda with phone calls concerning possible crew replacement. She had flushed out on the internet a Frenchmen called Bruno who was very interested and I finally managed to talk to him myself—a not inconsiderable feat, considering the phones on most West Indian islands. He seemed okay and we agreed to rendezvous at Curacao, our next stopover with decent air connections.

We had a great down-wind sail to Curacao, arriving in the middle of the night, as usual. We made it to an inner lagoon by means of a winding channel with a rock-bound narrow entrance. It was quite hair-raising in the dark and we went very slowly. Unfortunately, Bruno had not contacted Brenda to give her a flight number and date and, after waiting a few days we gave up on him. However, the island did hold a pleasant surprise.

During my vintage auto rallies I had come to know a Danish couple, Birte and Nic, who owned a hotel on the island. I gave them a call and they insisted Mike and I stay with them for a couple of days. Nic was previously a diamond merchant, but got fed up with that line of work and decided to go into the hotel business, with no previous experience. But he was a very good businessman, and over the years he expanded the hotel until it became one of the most luxurious hotels on the island. For two nights we enjoyed a sybaritic existence, particularly enjoyable after the semi-Spartan life on a cruising sailboat. Ultimately, however, we tore ourselves away and sailed for the San Blas Islands, the beautiful archipelago of tropical islands off the Darien coast of Panama.

At the San Blas Islands, things seemed little changed compared with our visit in 1996. The Indian ladies came alongside in dugout canoes to sell embroidered cloth molas, which unfortunately for them they had been over-produced; prices were down from our last visit.

The crew situation was now getting really worrisome, as the Panama Canal was about 100 miles away, and once through it we were committed to some very long distance sailing that could be strenuous for a crew of only two. There was a solitary phone booth outside the customs house on Porvenir Island, a rare symbol of civilization in these islands, and I thanked my lucky stars I could raise the AT&T operator on it, so calling home was not a problem. I got Brenda to call several of my old sailing chums in a vague hope they might have a few months to spare that they could spend getting cold and wet off Tierra del Fuego. Meanwhile, Mike recalled an old colleague of his from Zimbabwe, Bruce, who was presently on a walk-about (an Australian term for a vacation) in England. The only point of contact was a secretary at his old firm in South Africa who, we hoped, would have a number for him in London. All Brenda got was the phone number of a pub in London, but with this slim lead she managed to track him down, sell him on the idea of an adventurous cruise, and he agreed to join us in Panama!

When we tied up at the Panama Canal Yacht Club in Colon I found the city had improved considerably since our last visit in 1996. Many decrepit buildings had been knocked down and people on the street seemed happier and better dressed. Most importantly, nobody mugged me this time! We stayed a few days in order to complete the formalities of transiting the canal and made final arrangements to meet Bruce when we got to Balboa, on the Pacific side. I had to hire three Panamanian youths as line handlers, as the commission rules require four people on board as well as the skipper and commission pilot. We stopped for the night in the Gatun Lake, between the Atlantic and Pacific locks. We were definitely discouraged from swimming when we noticed an alligator casing the boat.

Bruce arrived on schedule at the Panama City Airport, and we left within a couple days and anchored for the night at an island in the Las Perlas group, so that Bruce was not thrust immediately into an ocean passage. He had no deep water experience.

The Galapagos Islands

After a day in the Las Perlas Islands we left for the Galapagos Islands. On my previous two trips there, we had encountered light and variable winds and we motored a lot. This time we had a steady head wind. Although we did not have to use the engine, we had to tack and tack, making the 900-mile trip in 11 ½ days, during which we logged just over 1,400 miles.

We spent a few days at Santa Cruz Island. Mike and Bruce went on a tour of the unique wildlife, while I was rather blasé and said I had seen them all before in 1990 and 1996. "Once you've seen one blue-footed boobie you've see 'em all," I told them, facetiously.

We left Santa Cruz just at nightfall so we could motor over to Santa Maria and anchor for the night. We arrived at midnight. Santa Maria was famous among sailors for being the place where the old whalers left letters for homeward-bound ships to collect. A barrel was attached to pole at what became known as Post Office Bay. As the outward-bound ships were often away for several years, this was their last chance to send mail home for some time. Strictly speaking, yachts are no longer allowed to cruise to individual islands in the Galapagos, but I felt tradition demanded that we stop at Post Office Bay. When we dinghied to the beach early in the morning we were met by a National Park ranger who was escorting a gaggle of tourists. We had seen the mail barrel through binoculars, so we pleaded to be allowed to walk over to it, but we were firmly ejected. I wondered if the tourists appreciated the irony—we were just the kind of sailors the barrel was set up for; we were bound for a 4,000 nm trip to Easter Island.

"Lonesome George," a tortoise, Galapagos Islands

Easter Island

The trip to Easter Island was a delight, as we had strong southeast trade winds on the beam the whole way. We reeled off 170 miles a day and made the 1,900-mile leg in less than 12 days. At one stage the boisterous winds tore the mainsail, which we removed and repaired using the old Read sewing machine. We approached the island just at sunrise with some trepidation, as there was no proper harbor and many sailors had told of the difficulty of getting ashore in their dinghy through the pounding surf. We anchored well clear of the surf line and saw local boats using a gap between the breaking waves. We inflated the 10-foot rubber dinghy and attached the 8hp outboard. Without an engine of that size, we would not have been able to get ashore.

Just inside the surf was a small breakwater with a thick hawser hanging six feet above the water. The idea was to tie the stern of the dinghy to this as we shot by and then fasten the bow to the dock wall. Once ashore, we went through the arrival formalities at the port captain's office and then treated ourselves to a good lunch at one of the restaurants in the small village of Hanga Roa. The owner was a very helpful Frenchman, and through him we arranged to rent a jeep the next day so we could tour the island.

The island has a fascinating history. Polynesians from the islands to the west (probably the Australs or Gambiers) arrived by ocean-going catamarans about the 7th century AD. It must have been a shock after the lush islands they left—although Easter Island is sub-tropical (it lies near 27°S) only the occasional palm tree on the shore can be seen. Perhaps the interior was more thickly treed at one time but now it is fairly desolate and wind-swept—you could as well be in Labrador or the highlands of Scotland. The early settlers apparently cut down most of the trees, and ate most of the native birds and animals.

A scientist who had been investigating old middens told me that it appeared there had been some contact with South America. Thor Heyerdahl had tried to prove with his famous Kon Tiki expedition that Polynesia was populated from South America, but modern scientific opinion is that contact was sporadic and the islands were populated from west to east by people from southeast Asia. A long period of hardship began, which they dealt with by carving huge statues of former chiefs (Moai, pronounced Mo-eyes) who were associated with the Good Times. When a statue was erected and mother of pearl and obsidian eyes inserted, its spirit (Mana) guarded the land. The statues always had their backs to the sea.

As times got tougher the Moais got bigger, finally achieving over 30 feet in height. Ultimately, the Polynesians descended into cannibalism and fierce fighting between factions led to the destruction of many Moais. This period began just as Europeans discovered Easter Island; their diseases and slaving raids completed the annihilation of the Rapa Nui culture. There were hundreds of the big statues; some had been restored like the ones we saw on the northeast coast at Anakena. Further south was the quarry where most were made from the soft pumice-like rock. It lies on the side of a huge volcanic crater, where many half-finished statues abounded.

Finally, we drove to the huge crater on the southeast corner of the island called Rano Kau. At a high point, right on the precipitous cliffs, was an amazing collection of stone dwellings made from flat basalt rock. Each hut had one small opening for ingress, perhaps two feet square. Why on earth people chose to live at this exposed spot, with winds howling in, I don't know. Perhaps it was where they kept the lepers.

Immediately south of this small community were a couple of very small rocky islands about three-quarters of a mile offshore. Legend

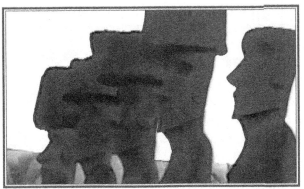

has it that in the heyday of the Rapa Nui civilization, a young man was chosen each year as the bird king. To achieve this honor, the youths climbed down the cliff, swam to the larger island (Motu Nui), found a bird's egg, and raced back with the egg unbroken in a box tied to his head. The winner was crowned and received many honors for the year. I don't know what happened to him after that—a sacrifice was called for, I suspect.

Moais, Easter Island

To Chile

When we left Easter Island, we sailed in a big arc round the permanent high pressure zone centered on 30° S. Apart from the first couple of days, we had good winds on the stern and we ran day after day for the South American coast with the jib set wing and wing, a leg of about 2,000 miles.

As we drove south the temperature fell, and our t-shirts gave way to pullovers. Our only companions on this lonely stretch of ocean were the sea birds, including the graceful albatross. Some evenings we showed a video using the camcorder as a VCR; we had a small black-and-white TV set. Perhaps it is a sign of the generation gap that when I screened the Astaire/Rogers comedy *The Gay Divorcee*, I had to explain to the crew that nobody was getting divorced because they were gay; in 1934, it meant Ginger was happy and carefree. Then I had to explain what a co-respondent was (a common way of divorce in England in the 20's through the 50's was to use a professional co-respondent to imply infidelity, the basis of the plot). I guess some films don't age well, but the dancing was wonderful.

We anchored south of the lighthouse at Punta Corona 14 ½ days out of Easter Island. The canals (Spanish for channels) have fierce currents and we waited for the flood to take us in—it ran over 8 knots! We tied up at an excellent marina in Puerto Montt, having logged 8,637 nm since leaving Long Island.

I flew home for two weeks from Puerto Montt, coming to considerable grief by carrying a fuel pump from the diesel engine in my backpack. It was regarded with deep suspicion by security and the plane's crew on the leg to the U.S. When I changed planes in Dallas, I was escorted off the plane by security men. I was made to ship the pump in a special box as hazardous freight and, of course, I missed my connection to New York. Eventually, I caught up with the pump two days later at JFK Airport. I had the pump overhauled and when I returned, I shipped it in my checked baggage, without problems.

When I got back to the boat, I found two charming young ladies, one Peruvian and one Israeli, living on the boat with Mike and Bruce. They had met when the boys toured the scenic Lake District to the north of Puerto Montt. They were both backpacking to tour the beautiful countryside of Chile at minimum cost and I didn't begrudge free lodging on the boat, but we had to move on if we were to make the good weather window at Cape Horn.

The Chilean Canals provide some of the finest cruising in the world. However, it was fairly tough cruising with little in the way of navigational aids—few ports, and weather that can turn nasty very quickly. Limited fuel was available in isolated ports by jerry jug. But in the major ports at either end, Puerto Montt in the north and Puerto Williams in the south, one can find experienced skippers who have often traversed the route and are only too willing to offer advice to the neophyte visitor. I searched them out.

We took four weeks to reach Puerto Williams, probably the minimum time required to make the passage while still providing some opportunity to make side trips. I believe the north-to-south passage was easier than the other way; we were able to sail for about two-thirds of the distance with northerly or westerly winds predominating. A Belgian skipper I talked to in Puerto Montt before departure told me he had powered almost all the way north from Puerto Williams—this requires careful consideration of your powering range and refueling

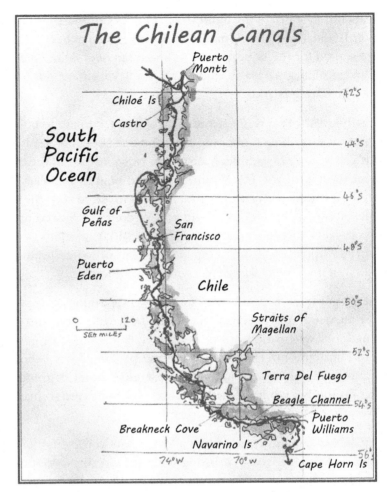

options. Other cruisers I talked to when we got Puerto Williams, and who were planning to sail north, assumed it would take at least two months, so that they had time to wait for favorable winds.

I found the Chiloé region to be very pleasant cruising, reminiscent of eastern Maine and Nova Scotia. When we were there, the weather was relatively warm (50's F) and dry. An open-sea passage is required across the Gulf of Peñas (Spanish for penance—that says something about this leg). South of the Gulf the country changed dramatically; grassy fields gave way to forbidding rocky shores, and it got colder. This was like Newfoundland. When we finally reached the Patagonian Channels the scenery was starkly beautiful, similar to Labrador. Glaciers abounded, and we learned something about sailing in water studded with floating ice.

Finally, heading east along the Beagle Channel there was a gentler region, sheltered by mountains to the west. I was lucky that Mike and Bruce were young and enthusiastic and accepted some hardship as part of the fun. In many ways the sense of accomplishment on reaching some remote anchorage was augmented by the struggle to get there. On average, on the way south we experienced about 19 hours of daylight, so we were able to cover a considerable mileage in a day's sailing.

The Chilean Navy took a paternal interest in all visiting yachts, requiring authorization at major ports and attempting to maintain radio contact. I found them to be very professional and helpful, but an English-speaking person was rare. Still, time and again, at each major port, they told us not to eat or gather mussels or clams, which they said had been contaminated by the "Red Tide." Red tide is a common name for a phenomenon known as an algal bloom which takes on a red or brown color. The red tide algae deplete oxygen in the waters and/or release toxins that may cause illness in humans and other animals. This was a great shame, as succulent-looking mussels abounded at every anchorage.

Fiona *in the Chilean Canals*

Heading south, on our left we had the magnificent snow-covered Andes towering above us. At first, in the vicinity of Chiloé, the countryside was pastoral with farms and small fishing villages. Within a week, however, this changed, when even to the west the islands were steep and forbidding. There was almost no habitation. In fact, we found only two isolated small communities after we left Chiloé.

Perhaps you can get a feel for the people and places if I tell you about one of them—Puerto Eden, or the Port of Eden. The port was obviously named in the same spirit that led Eric the Red to call Greenland "green" land (although on a later cruise, I gave him the benefit of the doubt; see Chapter 8). It was hardly a Garden of Eden. A community of about three hundred souls lived clustered on the side of a steep hill around a small bay. There were no vehicles; there was nowhere else to drive to. A mile or so of boardwalk connected the houses at either end of the village. There were two or three tiny shops. When we dropped anchor opposite the small school it was late afternoon.

We rowed ashore, where it was rocky and covered with weeds. Some men were repairing a small wooden boat, beached at low tide. With our poor Spanish we asked them if there was a restaurant—they were baffled. Later, when we discovered how poor the village was, and we realized the question had been ridiculous. Nevertheless, somehow we were directed to a small house a few yards away, nothing more than a two-room hut really, where a sprightly and rather plump middle-aged woman agreed to make us dinner. We sat in the kitchen cum dining room, where a large wood-fired stove kept the place cozy. The planks forming the outside wall were ill-fitting and I could see daylight through the cracks. Cloth tacked over the gaps kept out the draught. Through a curtained doorway I could see into the other room, a sort of living room/bedroom combination. Despite the basic nature of the house the family had a TV, VCR and "hi-fi" system.

She fed us a good meal of salad (onions and tomatoes), potato and fish and a curious sweet, followed by coffee. We also had a glass of wine. Not bad for $6 each! We arranged for her to bake four loaves of bread in the morning.

The first thing we had to do in the morning, however, was replenish our fuel. Puerto Eden was our last chance to get diesel before we arrived in Puerto Williams, near Cape Horn. The fuel was kept in drums near a small, run-down jetty. We had to pump it by hand into our jerry jugs and schlep them out to the boat in the dinghy. After that, we tried to buy fresh vegetables or fruit, but the small shops were shut. When I went to pick up the bread, another lady was there with a large purple bag. In it was a selection of new clothes she was peddling. I looked at them in a perfunctory way, but I wasn't buying—I had spent all my pesos on diesel fuel. At this she made a moué and in voluble Spanish wanted to know how an honest woman could make a living if rich gringos didn't buy her stuff. Guilt-stricken, I offered to pay in U.S. dollars. She rushed off for a consultation with someone in the village about the worth of a dollar, and upon her return I bought an insulated plaid shirt, which was actually a good value.

After that we all took a walk along the shore and returned to the boat to await the Port Captain, who had promised to bring over the papers authorizing us to proceed to Puerto Williams. It was happy hour when he showed up; he really enjoyed our rum. He wanted to know if he could help us further in any way, so I asked him to get us a few onions and some fruit. As incentive, I gave him a bottle of Mount Gay rum from our cache. He returned a couple of hours later with a large plastic bag that heaved and bulged in a funny way. What on earth was inside? The answer was four king crabs, all alive-o, that's what. The seaman he brought with him rapidly dispatched two to crab heaven by ripping their bodies apart. I shuddered, and we boiled the legs in our biggest pan.

It was incredibly dramatic sailing up a fjord to our first glacier, the Pio XI glacier, which was about three miles wide. It was a river of ice snaking down between two mountains whose snowy tops were lost in clouds. As we got close, we had to pick our way through myriad floating ice pieces that had broken off the glacier. We put our bowsprit up against one medium-sized 'berg and chipped some antique ice for our happy hour drinks.

Chipping ice from an iceberg for our happy hour drinks

As we got further south, the days lengthened and got colder. I was amazed at how old the towering rocks on either side looked. They were grey and scarred but smooth, as though they had spent a million years being ground down by ice. Hardy vegetation clung to the lower slopes and in crevasses. The trunks of the small trees were bowed horizontal by the almost continuous gales. Our anchorage each night was usually a small, deserted, cove in which we could tuck ourselves out of the wind. Usually, pristine streams emptied onto the sea. Bruce often went fly fishing and once caught several trout.

In one narrow pass, we were caught by a williwaw, a strong gusty wind, that knocked us over and put the whisker pole in the water, but *Fiona* was a tough old lady and no damage resulted. But as we traversed the western reaches of the Magellan Strait the weather was, quite frankly, terrible—frequent rain, hail and sleet with strong winds and temperatures in the 30's were our lot. We wore heavy clothing and our foul weather gear all the time on deck. In the narrow channels we usually hand-steered, as we could not trust the self-steerer in the gusty winds. The guy at the wheel got frequent infusions of hot drinks and soup passed up from the cabin, where the heater ran most of the time.

We had an interesting, if not unique, experience in the Cockburn channel, which runs southwest from the Magellan Strait to the south side of Tierra del Fuego. After a rough day, which began very early when we were literally blown out of our anchorage by 45-knot winds—the anchor dragged, so rather than reset it, we just left—we finished with a hard beat against wind and current up to a large bay called Niemann Harbour. Once inside the bay, conditions were much more moderate and we searched for a suitable spot to spend the night.

To our amazement we found the best little sheltered cove had been annexed by another yacht, which was lying with four lines ashore. It was an American boat and we gave them a call on the radio. A middle-aged couple came out into the cockpit, as amazed to see *Fiona* bobbing a few feet away as we were to see them. They had been there three or four days, waiting for a break in the weather. We found another cove about a mile away and secured ourselves with the anchor and three lines to trees on shore, and then we talked to the Americans on the VHF radio. They were in contact with a large yacht they had met further north, which belonged to a wealthy New Zealander. A professional captain, his wife and a crew member were bringing the boat to Ushuaia (near Puerto Williams, on the Argentinian side of the Beagle channel), so that the owner could board her for a trip to Antarctica.

The next day it was arranged that all three of us would meet at an anchorage on the southwest side of Tierra del Fuego. It was a spectacular setting—the anchorage was a huge natural amphitheater forming almost a complete bowl. Vast mountains soared above on three sides. Lakes above the bowl fed sparkling waterfalls. All three yachts rafted together with a dozen lines ashore. The other American boat spaced themselves a few feet away to prevent their cat from jumping ship. That evening we had a potluck dinner on the luxurious New Zealand boat (70 feet long) and screened a video of Hal Roth and his wife negotiating these same Chilean canals 25 years earlier. As it was very rare to see another boat, let alone another yacht, it was hard to imagine that three yachts had ever rafted up before in this lonely spot. We decided to call ourselves the Tierra del Fuego Yacht Club. At the western end of the Beagle Channel, I noticed the character of the mountains had changed. They were no longer smooth and scarred; they were now sharper with a jagged skyline. These mountains, however, protected the eastern end of the channel from the fierce Westerlies that sweep across the Pacific Ocean (the Beagle is about 55° S). The countryside took on a softer appearance; a little grass showed on the shore.

Puerto Williams was on Navarino Island, which lies south of Tierra del Fuego. On a nice day it was very pleasant, and so we took several walks through the woods. Beavers were introduced in the 1940's and their dams were everywhere. The port was run by the Chilean navy, and basic supplies were available.

The yacht club must be one of the most exotic in the world. It was housed in an old freighter, grounded and sunk in a small creek off the Beagle Channel. There was a wonderful bar in the old wheel house with a roaring fire every night, and souvenirs on the bulkheads from the many visiting yachts and expeditions. The port had an interesting museum dedicated to the extinct Yaghan Indians, who inhabited this region for millennia before the arrival of Europeans, after which, unfortunately, disease and deliberate extermination finished them off within a century.

Eric in the Museum of Yaghan Indians, Puerto Williams, 1992

A fascinating souvenir for those interested in Antarctic exploration was the bow of a ship cemented to a wall rather like a huge elephant head. It was from the *Yelcho*, the Chilean tug that rescued the remnants of Shackleton's expedition off Elephant Island in 1916. The Chileans were so proud of their part in rescuing the men that when the *Yelcho* became too rusty to safely sail anymore the bow was cut off and erected as a permanent monument.

Antarctica

From Puerto Williams we headed south, leaving on Christmas Day. We anchored for the night at a small island in the Beagle Channel between Argentina on the north, and Chile to the south. In the 1970's this island and several nearby were the subject of a territorial dispute, over which the two countries nearly went to war. I believe the territorial dispute was adjudicated by Britain's Queen Elizabeth. And in fact, these countries still have a very chilly relationship.

To maintain their claim, the Chilean Navy stationed a man in a house on shore. We rowed over to show our papers. He was delighted to see us, and his wife made tea and gave us home-made cake. The officer had his wife and two children with him, but otherwise they were alone. The posting was for a period of a year—I didn't envy them.

The next day we were trapped by a 45-knot gale which blew out after 24 hours and then we left to sail past Cape Horn and out into the Drake Passage. As we sailed south, the short nights faded entirely, and below 60° S it was light all day. My first glimpse of Antarctica was Smith Island, part of the South Shetland group, which fringe the western side of the Antarctic Peninsula. It rose vertically out of the sea, the top shrouded in cloud and the sides a stark study in black and white. There was no vegetation whatsoever in Antarctica that I could see.

We threaded our way in the strait between the Shetlands and the mainland under powerful easterly winds, a feature of Antarctic summer I hadn't appreciated before. Later, when I understood the meteorology, I used this knowledge in planning a circumnavigation of Antarctica. The sea was dotted with icebergs. As we approached Port Lockroy, the ice became quite dense in places and we finally dropped the sails and motored slowly through the ice, jinking from side to side to avoid striking any large pieces.

Port Lockroy consisted of a few huts on a small island in a bay, which is part of Wiencke Island. Activity began here in the 1940's when the British started a secret radio station to relay weather information during WWII. After that it became a scientific research base with emphasis on ionospheric investigation. In the 1960s, it was abandoned. Following an Antarctic Treaty that required countries to operate or remove the detritus of their activity, the Brits restored a couple of huts and made them a live-in museum of 1950s scientific work. During the summer (November to March), two men occupied the huts, living just as they did 50 years ago—lots of canned food and kerosene lanterns. They operated a small post office and rooms were set up with scientific gear of the era.

Port Lockroy was frequently visited by the small cruise liners that bring the more adventuresome tourists to Antarctica. We arrived on

New Year's Eve and were invited ashore by the residents. We took some rum and champagne, and it was quite a night in their little hut, eating cottage pie and swigging our Caribbean rum in front of the wood-fired stove. I shall remember the start of 1999 for a long time.

But there was a consequence. We lay abed on New Year's morning and it was 24 hours before I ran the engine again. When I turned the key, the engine groaned but did not turn over. This shouldn't really have been a surprise; the boat was sitting in 32°F seawater and the oil was like molasses. However, when building the boat, I had allowed for this kind of contingency. In the engine room was a brass link that connected all the ship's batteries in parallel when screwed into place. I bolted on the link and poured a little gasoline from the outboard into the air intake. I turned the key and to my relief, the engine slowly cranked over and then thundered into life. Life without it in the Antarctic would have been very difficult. From then on, I started the engine every twelve hours.

The Brits shared the small island they live on with a penguin rookery. This had its drawbacks, which you will appreciate if you have ever smelled one. Another problem for them was fresh water. When the ice was firm they could walk to Wiencke Island for pieces of ice to melt. But when we arrived, the so-called "fast" ice that is firmly fastened to land was melting, and large pieces kept bumping into *Fiona* as they drifted down the bay. This made it impossible for the residents to find ice that was uncontaminated by penguin droppings. The resident scientists had no boat, so one afternoon we gave one of them a lift to a nearby island in our inflatable to search for a skua's nest that he had roughly located using binoculars.

Penguin and chick, Port Lockroy, Antarctica

Besides all the nesting penguins, skuas, terns and cormorants, there was a complete whale skeleton on the shore, a relic of the old whaling days. Further onshore were dozens of staves off old wooden barrels from the same era. When we left via the Peltier channel, it was like sailing down a canyon of ice. At the Bismarck Strait we reached our furthest point south—64° 53' S. We had heard reports of thick ice just a few miles further south in the Lemaire Passage from the cruise liners. If they couldn't make it, I wasn't going to risk *Fiona*'s fragile glass hull. The U.S. maintained a research station on Palmer Island run by the National Science Foundation. As we sailed by on our way back north, I gave them a call on VHF. After a delay, I got a very guarded reply. I told them the boat's position and reassured them we were not planning to stop by. The operator seemed relieved, but his attitude changed when I asked for a weather forecast. After a long pause, he came back with a statement that it was not policy to issue forecasts. I got the impression that the long arm of the lawyers in Washington, DC, was reaching out to avoid any possible grounds for a suit even at this distance.

The northeast wind died as we headed into the Bransfield Strait and we powered to Deception Island. This was an ancient volcanic crater several miles across. The entrance was through a break in the crater wall called, dramatically, by the old whalers, "Neptune's Bellows," due to the erratic winds that funneled in and out. Once inside there were the remains of an old whaling station, inundated by a volcanic eruption many years before. The buildings and machinery were half-buried in ash. You could still find coal, old cans, and all the junk abandoned by the whalers. There was also a small hangar containing the wings and fuselage of a plane.

Fiona *sailing reefed in the Gerlache Strait, Antarctica*

At low tide, hot streams reeking of sulfur ran into the sea, causing a mist of steam to rise. The bottom of the bay was extremely irregular, with ridges almost up to the surface, but 20 feet deep a few yards away. The rapidly falling tide caught me unawares, and *Fiona* grounded fast, lying on her bilge as the tide went out. We were in this embarrassing position when a small Russian cruise liner entered the harbor and called on the radio to see if we needed help. I assured them that we were simply taking advantage of the large tidal range to change the zincs on the propeller shaft and that we would refloat with the rising tide. The captain invited us over for lunch when we had finished. We were very fortunate that there was no wind when we were in such a vulnerable position. I read later of another cruising yacht that was blown onshore under the same circumstances and ultimately spent the winter there.

The ship was a former Russian ice breaker called the *Professor Malcanov*; it was under charter to an Australian company. While the Australian tourists wandered through the buildings on shore, we changed the zincs on the propeller shaft, which became accessible as *Fiona* settled on her side at low water. Then we went over to the Russian ship. I am afraid we were obviously regarded as part of the local entertainment put on for the tourist's benefit, as Mike, Bruce, and I were divided up to sit at different lunch tables and invited to spin our yarns.

When we returned, the tide was making up and *Fiona* was soon free. The captain was nice enough to give us 100 liters of diesel fuel. From Deception we sailed along the north side of the South Shetland group, past the last island, Elephant Island, and into the Scotia Sea, heading for South Georgia. In 1916 Ernest Shackleton and five companions made the same passage in a 22-foot ship's whale boat, the *James Caird*, and entered into Antarctic folklore. Their ship, *Endurance*, had been crushed in the ice further south months earlier. They floated north living on ice floes and finally sailed to Elephant Island in three small boats. They had no radio, and their only hope of a rescue was for someone to make it to the whaling station on South Georgia, about 700 nm away. Shackleton left most of his men on Elephant Island to make the small boat trip. Conditions were horrible for them, and as we sailed along the same route I could only wonder at their stamina. We had a comfortable, heated, boat almost twice as long as theirs, but still, it was not a joy-ride. The water temperature was a freezing 32°F. We endured heavy swells that broke the shaft of the servo blade on the self-steerer. The winds reached gale force several times. Ultimately, Shackleton made it, organized a rescue expedition for the men left behind, and got them all home without loss of life.

We sailed along the north coast of South Georgia with a strong wind behind us. On our right, the rugged outline of the high mountains was sharply etched in black and white against a deep blue sky. It looked like a painted backdrop. South Georgia was about the same size as Long Island, New York, but instead of millions of people, there were millions of penguins.

We headed for Grytviken, the site of the largest whaling station, founded by Norwegians in 1906, and operated for nearly 60 years. As we sailed into Cumberland Bay, the scenery was magnificent. Several glaciers emptied into the bay—ahead was the 9,000-foot-plus white edifice of Mount Sugartop, slashed with jet black. When we approached the settlement, scores of birds wheeled overhead with shrill cries. Fur seals gamboled in the water, and on shore, crowds of King Penguins eyed us nervously.

The base at Grytviken was extensive; nearly a thousand people worked there at its peak, but most buildings were now in ruins. Half-sunken whale catchers lay at crumbling jetties. At King Edward Point, about half-mile to seaward, were some well-maintained buildings, initially built to house scientists, but now occupied by a score of British soldiers and the harbor master. South Georgia was briefly occupied by Argentina in 1982 and the troops were there to prevent a repeat.

We dropped anchor near the shore. Ahead of us was a sailboat famous to a generation that learned to sail in the 1950's and 60's—Eric Hiscock's *Wanderer III*, now belonging to a young Danish couple. More surprisingly, they had got married just the day before in the restored whaler's chapel. Tied up to one of the derelict whale catchers was *Curlew*, an engineless 28-foot boat, over a hundred years old, that was sailed to South Georgia eight years before by Tim and Pauline Carr. The Carrs ran a great museum in a renovated building. There were sections on the natural history of the island, the Shackleton expedition, whales and the operation and life at the Grytviken whaling station in its heyday. Apart from the early years, the factory was designed to use every part of the whale, including the bones.

Wandering through the buildings, I was extraordinarily impressed by the difficulty they must have experienced in erecting and operating the complex boilers, generators, cutters, centrifuges, and other machinery in such a harsh climate. All this effort, and it resulted in the virtual extermination of the whale species; about 175,000 whales were killed at Grytviken during its working life—500,000 whales were killed in the Antarctic as a whole. A holocaust indeed. Quite early on, scientists warned of this likely outcome and government regulations were put into effect to limit the yearly catch. They were circumvented by the whalers who built factory ships that operated on the high seas out of reach of the regulators.

In the end, Grytviken closed simply because it became unfeasible, economically, to pursue the few remaining whales. Some types, the Blue whale for example, may be so few in number that they will die out. An optimistic note, however, is that fur seals, also hunted to the brink of extinction, were now making a spectacular come back. These seals were quite aggressive on land, in fact, and I was chased by two of them along the beach while they made blood-curdling barks.

One night, Pauline and Tim gave a little party at the museum and showed over a hundred slides of expeditions they had made on skis to the interior. We were also invited to the mess at the army base and the harbor master let us use the shower in his cozy living quarters. Everyone was very hospitable.

Under sail on the evening of the day we left Grytviken, a huge iceberg materialized out of the gloom. On the radar it was a mile across, with an absolutely flat top and vertical sides; it had obviously calved from the ice shelves in the Weddell Sea to our south. It was our last glimpse of Antarctica.

On the way to Tristan da Cunha the nights got longer, the sea water got warmer, and the wind howled, at least for the first part. The usual gear failures followed, but we kept the boat sailing and we arrived off this lonely island early in the morning of the tenth day out. The settlement of about 300 people was nestled on a small plateau under a brooding volcano. It was founded in the early 1800's when a few British soldiers, who had been stationed there to prevent any rescue of Napoleon from St. Helena, got permission to stay after he died. In 1961 the volcano erupted and all the islanders were evacuated to England for a couple of years. They were largely self-sufficient, growing vegetables and fishing. We were cleared in by Sergeant Glass, a descendent of the original leader of the community, Corporal Glass.

We only managed to stay a few hours, as the anchorage was an open roadstead and *Fiona* rolled violently in the ocean swell. But we did manage to launch the inflatable and get ashore. We bought a few supplies at the small supermarket, visited the museum and post office, and sent e-mail messages from the administrator's office. He gave us some mail to be sent from Cape Town when we got there, as another boat was not expected for weeks. About a dozen small, graceful sailboats were parked on the shore; the islanders sailed them to two nearby islands for guano which was used as fertilizer. Like Pitcairn Island, which I had visited a few years earlier, I got the feeling on Tristan that the people lived an intense, closed life which outsiders simply cannot penetrate, especially in a few hours. We had mostly light winds and calms on the way to Cape Town—typical of the high pressure cells that move across the South Atlantic in those latitudes. We made contact with an amateur radio net in South Africa run by a friend of Mike's father. As a consequence, Mike's parents drove down to meet us in Cape Town. The 1,500-mile leg took us 11 and a half days. As dawn broke, Table Mountain was silhouetted against the pink sky. It was a dramatic welcome to Africa.

The South Atlantic, and Then Home

Mike's parents gave us a quick tour of the Cape of Good Hope region south of Cape Town and the new waterfront development in the city itself, and then Mike left with them to spend nearly two weeks at their farm. The remaining crew member, Bruce, looked up some of his old pals from the time he was a student and after a couple of days became so nostalgic for his homeland in Zimbabwe that he decided to stay. And so once again I was looking for crew.

Fortunately, finding replacement proved easy. Bill Steenberg, a retired engineer, had just spent a year working as a volunteer on a housing project in Zimbabwe and decided it would be neat to sail home to the U.S. We linked up at the yacht club and he signed on. Bill was a few years older than me and had an adventurous time in WWII as a U.S. Navy pilot. He was shot down in the Sea of Japan and picked up by a U.S. submarine. He was on board when the atomic bomb ended the war. Bill owned a small sailboat and turned out to be excellent crew. We have stayed friends since this trip and he crewed for me again on a later trip.

There was a fair amount of maintenance needed to repair the ravages of our Antarctic cruise. Each day Bill and I worked on those in the mornings and behaved like typical tourists in the afternoon. A complication was the heavy wind—it howled every day. When a large oil drilling platform that was undergoing repairs broke loose at a dock about a mile away, the local paper reported the wind at 65 knots, the highest we experienced during the voyage. The oil rig sank several small ships as it ricocheted down Cape Town Harbor. The wind rapidly shredded flags, burgees and halyards, anything that was free to flap. Worse, the covers blew off some railway cars upwind and distributed the contents, copper ore, over all the boats at the yacht club.

Cape Town far exceeded my expectations, as it turned out to be a clean, modern city with pleasant streets, parks and museums. I never felt threatened and met nothing but courtesy from the locals of all colors. A bonus, thanks to the ludicrously under-valued rand, was the low prices for anyone with dollars. Bill and I ate out on the last night in Cape Town at a nice restaurant for a total bill of $8, including beer. He had rented a car during his stay for $17 a day, which we used to restock the galley in several heavily-loaded trips from the local supermarket. When Mike returned, we left for St. Helena.

Jamestown, the capital of St. Helena, lies on the west coast in a steep valley. Apart from this rather dramatic setting, it reminded me of a small English village of the 1950's. There was no airfield and contact with the outside world was maintained by infrequent ships. This led to a leisurely pace of life and a feeling of timelessness. The shops had heavy wooden counters that smelled of furniture polish. When I bought some onions, they were weighed on a scale with iron weights in one pan. There was a sunken steamer in the harbor (it caught fire and sank in 1911), which provided great snorkeling.

We ate out each night in a beautiful open-air restaurant surrounded by tropical shrubs and flowers, and rented a car and toured the sights, of which the most famous was Longwood, Napoleon's place of exile after he was defeated at Waterloo in 1815. It is quite a modest house for a man who was once an emperor. He lived there with a few aides and servants until he died in 1821. During the tour we saw huge fields of flax left to grow wild. Apparently, some years ago the British Post Office decided to switch from string to elastic bands and that killed the market for St. Helena flax. When we left, we had the south equatorial current under us, which added about 20 miles a day to our progress. The days and evenings were warm, and at night the stars shone with great brilliance. Each morning we had a crop of flying fish to consign to the deep. Dolphins cavorted alongside and sometimes birds would alight on the whisker pole or radar post and hitch a ride. Mike and Bill honed their skill at celestial navigation, and the sun sights got pretty good, within a few miles, but their one starsight that gave a credible fix was 20 miles off—good job the GPS receiver was working.

The 1,900-mile leg to Fernando de Noronha took two weeks under winds that hovered around 15 knots most of the time. Fernando was a small island about 250 miles off the northeast coast of Brazil. It had lush vegetation and startling, steep, pinnacles of volcanic origin. There was a runway, built by the Allies in WWII, and a small tourist economy based on modest hotels and restaurants. The locals all drive dune buggy versions of the VW beetle, which was still produced in Brazil.

We took a tour in one and discovered that most of the roads were awful, just dirt tracks with lots of muddy puddles. Still, Fernando made a very pleasant interlude, especially the change from boat cooking. Unfortunately, there was a dark side to the island's past. When Brazil was a Portuguese colony, Fernando was a prison. The ruins of the grim fort we explored witnessed a couple of centuries of cruelty to the unfortunate inmates.

Almost as soon as we left Fernando de Noronha we ran into the doldrums, a region several hundred miles wide of calms, fickle winds, and intense squalls. We slowly worked our way through and once we were far enough north, we picked up the northeast trade winds. Now we started to move, past São Luis of so many memories from the 1995-97 cruise, and past the Amazon delta where the sea was muddy even a hundred miles to seaward.

Passing the coast of French Guiana, we enjoyed a spectacular sight. Just after sunset a large rocket, launched by the European Space Agency, blasted into the sky on our bow. When it was overhead, it separated with a huge smoke ring and the booster fell into the sea on our starboard, trailing sparks.

When we crossed the equator, Bill was inducted as a son of Neptune, which we sealed with a toast of Umzumbe Dew, a potent liqueur made from sugar cane. By coincidence, we held the ceremony on the second full moon in March, the "Blue Moon." A few nights later, we had a brilliant stellar display after moonset—the Pole Star and the Big Dipper on the starboard, Orion overhead, and the Southern Cross on the port quarter. A few hundred miles from Barbados we experienced a light countercurrent instead of the steady push we had before from the equatorial current. This, combined with a drop in the Trades, slowed us down, but we made it to Barbados in two weeks from Fernando de Noronha.

Eric poses as Father Neptune; many "pollywog" crews were welcomed by him as Sons of Neptune on numerous crossings of the equator over the years.

My main reason for choosing Barbados as our Caribbean landfall was to find the grave of my great-grandmother Susannah, who was buried there in 1882. She was the wife of my great-grandfather, who was the Regimental Sergeant Major of a British regiment stationed in Barbados, the main British military base in the Caribbean by then. She had died in childbirth, and I found the grave of Susannah and her baby in the neatly-kept military cemetery.

After that we went on a tour of the island in a taxi driven by a man named Dwight. We wound up at the Mount Gay Rum Distillery. Dwight said it was his birthday, and what with the sample rum and the toasts to Dwight's birthday, we all got pretty merry. We planned to sail to a beach for the afternoon and considering Dwight's condition, we thought he would be safer off the road, and so we invited him along. Unfortunately, poor Dwight got as sick as a dog in the brief two-mile sail from our anchorage to the beach.

Eric's great-grandmother Susannah's grave, Barbados

When we were leaving Barbados I went to the customs officer for outward clearance. As he was completing the forms, the official asked where we had come from. I mentioned Cape Town, but said before that we had been in Tristan da Cunha, South Georgia, and Antarctica. He didn't know where they were, but there was a large world map on the wall of the office. So, ever helpful, I sprang up to point out these places. Unfortunately, the map's border was drawn a little south of Cape Horn, so I pointed vaguely below the edge of the map and said, "Down there!" He was profoundly impressed—his jaw literally fell and he repeated, "You sailed off the edge of the map!" I felt like the ancient mariners who feared they would sail off the edge of the world.

Our next stop was St. Martin, partly to restock our vital Mount Gay rum supply, and also to see my old friend Kay. Sadly, her husband Dudley had died since we last passed their way. After a day of visiting, we sailed for Bermuda, where the highlight was a fly-in visit to the boat by my daughter Brenda. Fortunately, the weather cooperated as we cruised the beautiful western shore.

As soon as Brenda left, we sailed for Newport, Rhode Island, despite gloomy weather predictions. The forecasters were right, and we had northeasterly winds the whole way, usually 20 to 30 knots, which certainly kicked up a rumpus in the vicinity of the Gulf Stream. Although it was a wet sail, we set a record for *Fiona*—three and three-quarters days from the Mills buoy off St. George's to Brenton Reef buoy off Newport. In contrast to the South Atlantic, we had two reefs in the main nearly all the way.

After clearing customs, Mike and Bill toured historic Newport and I attended a meeting of the Cruising Club of America which, coincidentally, was held in Newport at the same time. We spent a night at Wickford visiting old friends and then sailed home in thick, thick fog via Block Island.

We sailed up the Patchogue River at high tide on the evening of May 9th (a day later than the cruise timetable) and tied up at Weeks Yacht Yard. We had logged 21,784 nm since leaving.

Postscript

In the year 2000, I was very pleased and honored to be awarded the Blue Water Medal by the Cruising Club of America in recognition of the cruise to Antarctica. To quote from the club rules: "The Blue Water Medal shall be awarded annually for a most meritorious example of seamanship, the recipient to be selected from among the amateurs of all nations." I am sure there were many amateur sailors deserving of the award that year, and so perhaps I was just lucky. The success of the cruise certainly owed a lot to the crew, particularly Mike and Bruce for enduring the toughest leg in the Chilean Canals.

The citation reads:

For a remarkable voyage in his 42-foot sloop to Antarctica from Patchogue, Long Island, via the Panama Canal, Galapagos, Chile, Port Lockroy on the Antarctic Peninsula, South Georgia Island, Cape Town, and home by way of St. Martin and Bermuda, 21,784 miles, 10 months with a crew of 1 or 2 young men. Wrote copious descriptions of his cruise and produced a special guide to the Patagonian passages.

The Cruising Club of America Blue Water Medal, awarded to one amateur sailor annually. Eric received it in 2000 for his cruise to Chile and the Antarctic, 1998 to 1999.

Log of Anchorages in the Chilean Canals

DAY	GPS POS	LOG (NM)	COMMENT
Start		0	Marina del Sur, Pto. Montt, left early morning with high tide at 0316 hr. local. This gave favorable currents for much of the first week as far as the Gulf of Corcovado.
1	Not recorded	41	Los Banos Cove, Llancahué Is. Anchored in 25'. Bathed in thermal spring water ($4) at the white building.
2	41°19.45' S 73°15.27' W	33	Anchored E of Mechuque Is. Salmon farm nearby.
3	42°28.69'S 73°45.47' W	45	Castro, Chiloé' Is. Nice place, many shops and restaurants. Checked in at the Naval HQ. Anchored in 50'.
4&5	44°44.14' S 73°21.54' W	154	Good N wind so we crossed the Gulf of Corcovado at night. Anchored Pangalillo Bay in 50'.
6	45°09.52' S 73°31.15' W	25	Anchored Pto Agiurre, 30' plus 2 lines ashore, just north of the port. Checked into the naval HQ, plus bought 106 ltr of diesel in jugs. Limited supplies available.
7	45°27.61' S 73°56.85' W	32	Small cove on W side of Empedrado Strait (Darwin Channel). Anchored in 55' + 2 lines ashore.
8,9 &10	47°45.09' S 74°33.87' W	212	Beat out of the Darwin Channel. Contacted Cape Raper lighthouse. Reach across Gulf of Penas. Contacted San Pedro lighthouse. Tricky entrance to Pto Francisco in the dark. Anchored in 80'.
11		0	Heavy rain. Explored Pto Francisco by dinghy, did some fishing in the streams.
12	48°29.64' S 74°23.57' W	46	Anchored in Connor Cove plus 1 line ashore, 25'. Famous tree with a dozen boat plaques nailed on it, caught some trout in the stream.
13	49°07.64' S 74°24.82' W	35	Anchored first opposite the naval HQ at Pto Eden, then moved to the inner harbor. Anchored in 30' opposite the school.
14		0	Bought 180 ltr of diesel fuel. Limited supplies. A lady baked us 4 loaves and made supper for a modest fee. Nice shore walks.
15	49°14.00' S 74°06.67' W	61	Visited the fabulous Pio XI glacier in Eyre Sound. Anchored nearby in an unnamed cove on S. side of Elizabeth Bay, 35'. Be aware that if you anchor near a glacier you may be surrounded by ice in the morning.
16	50°10.89' S 74°48.99' W	68	Anchored in Tom Bay, W of Bond Point. One line ashore.
17	50°59.27' S 74°12.98' W	56	Anchored in Pto Bueno, 70'. Lovely stream and lake to explore in fine weather.

DAY	GPS POS	LOG (NM)	COMMENT
18	51°18.71' S 74°04.31' W	18	Anchored in 50', Pto Mayne.
19	52°09.67' S 73°35.58' W	61	Anchored in Isthmus Bay, 18'. Lots of kelp around. Watch for the rocks - not shown in Mantellero sketch chart.
20	52°37.60' S 73°38.92' W	27	Anchored in Burgoyne cove (40') with 2 lines ashore.
21	53°13.18' S 73°22.24' W	46	Called Fairway Is radio en route. Entered Strait of Magellan. Weather miserable. Anchored Pto Angosto, 75'. Lots of williwaws. Lake is a nice climb.
22	53°41.44' S 71°59.41' W	50	Anchored in 30', Gallant Cove, Fortesque Bay. Strong wind in the early morning caused us to drag near the sandbar at the river mouth. The only time we experienced dragging - used plenty of scope, but the holding was not too good.
23	54°19.19' S 71°54.75' W	56	Short cut to the Cockburn Channel via Pedro Sound. 20' near the island at O'Ryan Pass. Anchored Pto Niemann. Required 3 lines ashore.
24	54°32.68' S 71°54.62' W	18	Three yacht raft at Breckneck Cove. Wonderful, scenic anchorage. Great walk to lakes above. Anchor with lines ashore.
25	54°53.24' S 71°00.41' W	50	Anchored Fanny Cove, Stewart Is, 60', gusty winds, 2 lines ashore.
26	54°47.75' S 69°37.78' W	48	Explored the Pia glacier formation. Enter at 54° 50.49'S, 69°40.98' W. Take first channel on right. Anchored in cove E of small peninsula. Anchor in 50' plus 2 lines ashore. Small bergey bits surrounded us in the morning. Visited the glacier using the inflatable.
27	54°55.39' S 68°19.37'W	54	The Beagle Channel. Picked mooring at Naval HQ, Pto Navarino
28	Not recorded	29	Tied up to the ship "Micalvi"; the YC at Pto Williams.
	Total mileage	1,287	
	Fuel Use		500ltr (130 gal)

An Inexplicable
Attraction:
My Fifty Years of
Ocean Sailing

4
The Arctic, Norway, Scotland, Ireland, Portugal, the Caribbean and Cuba
2000-2001

I had sailed to the Antarctic, so what next but the Arctic? The problem was that it took half a year to get to the Antarctic, but the Arctic was only a few sailing weeks away from Long Island. What to do with the rest of the year?

Well, wintering in the Caribbean didn't seem like such a bad idea. My crew for the first part of this cruise consisted of John Magraw, an English sailing instructor, and Chris, a scientist from Brookhaven National Laboratory who was squeezing a month's vacation to sample the real world. John was about my age. He'd responded to the crew call on my web site. Besides serving as a part-time instructor for the U.K. Royal Yachting Association (RYA), John had worked at a laboratory in England similar to where I worked in the U.S. (Brookhaven National Laboratory). So, we had a lot in common. Chris was German and serving a post-doctoral appointment at the same laboratory. He had little sailing experience, but was keen to learn.

We should have stayed in port—as John, Chris, and I sailed out of Fire Island Inlet we encountered a stiff easterly wind that did not let up for a couple of days as we clawed our way to Block Island. Normally, this leg takes about 20 hours from Patchogue, but this time it took 40 hours. It was midnight when we picked up a mooring in the Great Salt Pond, Block Island.

A good night's sleep combined with a brisk walk to the southeast lighthouse and supper at Ballards restored our good spirits. We left the next morning, bright and early, for a sail to the Cape Cod Canal and a mooring at Provincetown, on the top of Cape Cod. Here the best entertainment was to sit on a bench in front of the Town Hall and watch the throng passing by. The prize went to a creature on six-inch platform shoes dressed in gauzy pink, of indeterminate gender.

Probably there was no greater contrast to Provincetown than Lunenburg in Nova Scotia. We tied up there after a three-day trip across the Gulf of Maine, mostly in foggy, windless conditions. Lunenburg was one of the leading fishery and shipbuilding ports on the Nova Scotia coast, but the collapse of the cod fishing has had a dramatic impact. There is an interesting museum devoted to the Atlantic fishing business, including a genuine Grand Banks schooner.

Moored at the Scotia Trawler dock, we encountered a fascinating yachtie, Bill Butler. He and his wife survived 66 days in a life raft in the Pacific after their sailboat was sunk by a whale (they think it was a whale that did it). He wrote a book about the experience (*66 Days Adrift*). Bill now has a new boat and a new wife.

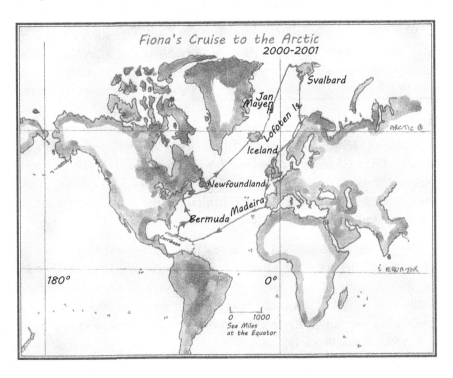

Into the Fog

Our next stop was in St. John's, Newfoundland. St. John's was England's first colony, a tribute to the enormous value of the cod fisheries, now fished out. It is the capital of Newfoundland, and an impoverished town. The Newfies were extremely pleasant, and one cruising couple invited us over to their apartment for supper. It was unnerving for a New Yorker to step into the street and find all the traffic grinding to a halt, crosswalk or not. The residents complained a lot about the weather. The passage to Iceland took 11 days. The logbook was full of the word "foggy." The Labrador Current, coming down the Davis Strait on our port side produced damp, chilly conditions with, yes, plenty of fog. Sometimes it was calm, sometimes we had winds to 25 knots. The period of darkness fell to three or four hours as we gained northing. The boom and sail dripped and condensation appeared in the cabin. The seawater temperature fell into the 40's. Chris was not impressed. It reminded me of my first transatlantic passage with John and Barbara Knight aboard *Arvin Court II*.

When we entered the snug harbor at Reykjavik we found a NATO exercise in full swing with six frigates tied up. The public telephones in the town were very busy with crews calling home. Reykjavik is a pleasant town with striking architecture. Virtually all the buildings were heated by geothermal springs, as Iceland lies on a major fault line in the earth's crust. These springs also provide electric power in such abundance that Iceland is a smelter of aluminum, using bauxite transported from half way around the world. The thought crossed my mind that when our planet runs out of fossil fuel the Icelanders will still be warm and probably running cars using hydrogen obtained by electrolysis.

In Iceland, a young man who had spent a year at a local school on Long Island had arranged to meet us. Eli Erlingsson was waiting on the dock when we tied up. He was a treasure. We had a great supper with him and his partner, Hildur, in their modern apartment. On the day Chris flew home, Eli gave us a tour of the southwestern corner of Iceland. Near the coast the terrain is barren, jumbled rock with little vegetation. Crossing this barren place, we were attacked by hundreds of terns protecting their nesting area. Inland it was a little greener. We walked through the rift which is slowly tearing Iceland in half. It was a dramatic setting and was the site of the first parliament when the

Vikings settled Iceland in the 9th century. It was a society ridden with blood feuds—parliament was a neutral place with weapons laid aside.

We had an elegant meal with Eli and Hildur in a small restaurant one evening; it was astonishingly expensive by American standards. Perhaps it was the fare: smoked puffin for appetizer. One can only wonder at the energy and productivity of the Icelanders—it is a fully functioning democratic society with good social services, international and national airlines, ferries, and a fishing fleet, and virtually free energy—though imported fuel was very expensive—all with a population of about 320,000 souls.

Eric bridges the geological fault dividing Iceland

When Chris left we were joined by Doug, a recently-retired professor of oceanography who flew in after just completing a field trip to the Great Barrier Reef. He liked his life to be full of contrast, obviously.

After leaving Reykjavik we sailed by Surtsey, an island formed in the 1960s by a volcanic eruption off the south coast. Landing was forbidden, and scientists were eagerly observing how quickly plants, and ultimately, animals established themselves on this brand-new land. Later in the day, we tied up next to a trawler in the Vestmann Islands. Legend has it that these islands were first inhabited by escaped Irish slaves during the Viking period, as they figured no one would venture to such a wild place. But the Vikings tracked them down and killed them anyway.

The main island, Heimaey, was imperiled by an eruption in 1973 when a river of lava threatened to close off the harbor. They imported dozens of big diesel-powered pumps and cooled down the flow with sea water, so now the lava forms a nice breakwater; the harbor was actually improved. We climbed to the top of the volcano, Eldfel, which was still gently steaming and warm underfoot. Halfway up we found a monument to the occasion when the harbor and town were saved—a rusting diesel engine and pump!

The Arctic

Our next landfall was Jan Mayen Island, north of the Arctic Circle. We were not sure if we would be able to land, as there was no harbor. Thus, one must get ashore by dinghy and, perhaps more of an obstacle, prior permission was required from a Norwegian government office in Europe. The passage was a study in contrasts: high winds, then calm, fog, then sunshine.

The nights grew shorter. A day before we arrived, engine trouble surfaced, and it would plague us for the first part of the trip. Early in the morning the smoke detector in the engine room clanged away. There was steam everywhere; the engine had lost its cooling water. The leak was in the fresh water pump, and the problem was not finally solved until we got to Norway.

Jan Mayen is dominated by a 9,000-foot-high volcano, Beerenberg, which is permanently covered with snow. When we had it in sight we called on the radio and were directed to anchor in Walrus Bay on the west side of the island. It was late afternoon when we arrived; conditions were calm. We were given permission to land "for two hours"; a knot of people met us on the rocky beach, including the station commander. I think the two-hour limit was to meet an official directive about admitting strangers to the island; we wound up staying for over five hours.

Beerenberg, a 9,000-feet-high volcano on Jan Mayen

A jeep-like vehicle transported us to the main base 18 km away, dubbed "Aluminum City" because of the style of the clustered buildings there. Twenty-six people lived on the island manning radio transmitters and a meteorological station. There was a sprinkling of women; we met a couple in the cozy lounge while being served tea and cake.

First, our guide insisted we take a shower—towels and soap were ready. Was that for our benefit or theirs? After visiting most of the facilities and a small museum, we returned to the beach. Even though it was after midnight it was quite light; a pale sun hung low on the northern horizon. In the museum were some pieces of a German Kondor that had crashed on Jan Mayen during WWII. It was probably damaged while spotting Allied convoys that were often routed this far north. The pilot obviously hoped for a successful crash landing on this rocky island, but all six aboard were killed. The full story we will probably never learn.

It was still clear when we left and we got several snaps of the volcano as we departed. According to the guide book we carried, the peak of Beerenberg can only be seen one day in a hundred, so we were very lucky. We got good ice charts from the meteorological office in Jan Mayen. The pack ice was a little further south than usual this year, we discovered. The last tendril of the Gulf Steam was deflected along the west coast of Svalbard, causing the pack ice to be further north closer to the coast. As we sailed northeast from Jan Mayen, we encountered northerly winds which pushed the sea ice to the south. We finally encountered ice at 78° 37'N, about 10 percent sea coverage. Some of the floes were 100 feet long and perhaps 10 feet high. John spotted a dark object on one but it slid into the sea on our approach—probably a seal.

We started the engine to keep maneuverability and took lots of photos, and we had no difficulties working free of the ice as we sailed east. A day later we reached Ny Alesund, on the north coast of the largest island of the archipelago, Spitsbergen. At 79° N, it claimed to be the world's most northerly settled town. It was founded in the 1920s as a coal mining village, but a series of explosions, culminating in a shocker in the 1960s, shut down mining operations. For a couple of decades, it has been the home of a number of teams interested in High Arctic scientific research. It was very busy in summer with visiting investigators; a few hardy ones winter over.

I talked to one British scientist who knew Dave Burkett, the chief at Port Lockeroy, who I had met in 1999 during the Antarctic cruise—small world. (See Chapter 3) A museum full of mining artifacts and photos testified to the hard life the miners and their families led. Some coal mines (mostly operated by Russians) were still in business in other parts of Spitzbergen. Both Norway and Russia claimed Svalbard, but in 1925 a treaty gave control to Norway, although it allowed existing Russian activities to continue.

Ny Alesund must be one of the few places on earth where you are not allowed ashore without a gun. Doug had put his 12-gauge shotgun aboard before we left New York and it was checked by a policeman on our arrival. The danger was polar bears, which in summer move north with the receding pack ice, looking for seals to eat. For some reason, a few forget to go north and then they hang around the coast looking for something else to eat—you, for instance!

This was an historic spot in the story of Arctic exploration. Many expeditions had left from Ny Alesund. For example, the tower for mooring Nobile's dirigible, in which he flew over the North Pole in the 1920s, was still there, about half a mile from the dock. We tied up next to a very interesting fellow, Hans, who had built his own steel sailboat, which he chartered each summer to scientists going further north. The same length as *Fiona*, she weighed 50 percent more, as the bottom and bow were made of steel plate over an inch thick. I asked how far north he had sailed and he replied 83° N in a good year. This must be a record for a yacht—only 420 miles from the Pole.

One afternoon as John and I walked to the research base, an Arctic fox raised havoc among the nesting terns by searching for eggs. Ultimately, it found one despite the distracting attacks by the terns, and then scampered away.

After a couple of days, we sailed down the scenic Forelandsundet, a spectacular 90-mile journey past high mountains and wide glaciers to Longyearbyen, the capital of Svalbard. This, too, was a coal mining village and overhead cables and supports dotted the rugged terrain. Although the population is under 2,000, the village boasts "the second-best restaurant in Norway," to quote a guidebook. Doug felt a trip there for the crew, after all our hardships, ought to be his treat, and so one evening, we trooped off together for dinner.

The room was impressive: gleaming glasses and plates on snowy table cloths. Each setting had four knives and forks, not counting the little fork for dessert. Now, it has always been my maxim that the bill is proportional (not necessarily linearly) to the number of forks, and in the past I have steered the guys away from places with only two forks. Four forks would be a new point on the curve. The meal was indeed sumptuous, and the wine list ran to about six pages. The waitress was disappointed that we only ordered one bottle, but as each course appeared, she suggested the appropriate bottle, which we declined.

103

Doug did pay the bill, for which we duly thanked him. It was in the stratosphere.

On the day we arrived, as we walked past the police station on the way into town, we noticed the police unloading three dead polar bears from a trailer. Apparently, they were a mother and two two-year old cubs. The mother was shot by a Polish scientist at a base out of town when it destroyed some equipment. The police shot the cubs, which appeared fully grown to me, as a precaution based on past experience. It was tragic to see these wonderful animals lying supine and bloodied.

Alcoholism is a problem in these northern communities, we discovered. Residents are rationed as to how much they can buy and they are given a ration card. Unfortunately, visitors don't get a ration, and we had hoped to add a couple of cases of beer to our dwindling stock. Fortunately, Hans showed up and when he learned of our plight, got himself a card (he resided permanently in Svalbard) and went with me to a store to get a case.

One evening, we went to a pub in town for a quiet drink before returning to the boat. When the owner heard our accents, he insisted on setting up tots of vodka on the house, to be downed in one gulp, Russian style. He had the brilliant idea of calling his wife who was visiting New York City at the time. Goodness knows what the poor lady thought of our rambling discussion of the Big Apple. After the fifth round we staggered home in the light of midnight sun.

While in Ny Alesund I called my old shipmate, 'Red,' in Bellport and asked him to mail a new water pump for the engine to my English friend Derek who was planning to join *Fiona* in Scotland at the end of August. Since Jan Mayen, it had been necessary to add fresh water to the system whenever we ran the engine, but I felt we could live with that for a few weeks. This turned out to be a miscalculation.

Norway

Shortly after we left Svalbard, while still under power, there was a loud shriek from the engine room, followed by the now familiar clamor of the smoke detector. This time it really had detected smoke; the pump had seized up solid and the slipping fan belt had caught fire.

Our destination was the Lofoten Islands, about 600 miles to the south, but still above the Arctic Circle. After I removed the pump, it was clearly past fixing on board—broken ball bearings fell into my hand as I pulled it apart. Thus, we decided to head for Bødø (pronounced Buddha), a fairly large town just south of the Lofotens. One problem was that, without the engine, we only had the generator running off the propeller shaft to keep the batteries charged. This provided a few amps only, so we instituted rigorous electrical economy: no heater and only one side of a tape for music at happy hour.

As we sailed south, Murphy struck again: the jib fairlead came loose, the sheet chaffed on the aft turning block and broke. The subsequent flogging of the jib caused the roller furler foils to separate and the jib got ripped. This left us with only the main and staysail as a means of propulsion. Over the next few days we rigged a spare bilge pump to pump fresh water round the engine and we stitched the jib so it could be hanked onto a temporary stay. We crossed the south end of the Lofotens near the infamous Maelstrom whirlpool and tied up at Bødø eight days out from Svalbard.

We were able to contact a charming lady sailmaker who bore away the jib for some TLC. Next to us was a 103-year-old Colin Archer sailboat owned by an interesting character called Steinar. When we said we needed a new water pump, he cell-phoned an acquaintance on a nearby island who ran a diesel repair business, and arranged to have a new one shipped to the airport by the local SAS carrier that afternoon. By half-past five on the day we arrived, I had the new pump in my hands. I was deeply impressed by this demonstration of Nordic efficiency. Not only did I have the pump, I had also paid for it at a bank on the waterfront, which transferred the money electronically to the vendor's account. The next day I installed the pump while Doug and John took a bus ride to some of the local scenic spots, including Saltstraumen, the fastest flowing tidal stream in the world (20 knots). A couple of days later our sail was delivered and we left for an abbreviated cruise to the Lofoten Islands. These islands, lying about 30 miles off the Norwegian coast, were famous for their mountainous beauty and rugged coast line. The night we crossed over, the wind piped up and we ducked into the old whaling port of Skrova for shelter. Later in the day, we ran downwind to Stamsund, which was Steinar's home port. He was nice enough to pick us up at the boat that evening and gave us a tour of Vestervagen Island in his van.

On the morrow, we caught a bus to the interior to visit a reconstructed Viking long house and ship. Although the coasts of these islands were forbidding and looked like the homes of trolls, the interiors were quite gentle, with fertile valleys, farms, and grassy meadows—a veritable northern Shangri-La. We visited two quite charming fishing villages. One of them, Nusfjord, was a World Heritage Site. We liked the pub there, where two interior walls were chiseled out of solid rock.

Then we left the islands from Reine for the 400-mile leg to Alesund on the Norwegian mainland, crossing the Arctic Circle on our way south. It was a mild, three-day sail. We refueled and left after 24 hours. The town was pristine, though the center had been burnt to the ground in disastrous fire in 1905. The place had been rebuilt to reflect the best of Norwegian architecture.

Scotland

Up to this point we had not seen the Northern Lights because usually the sky was too light at night. But the apple green curtain appeared in the northern sky after sunset as we ploughed our way to the Shetland Islands. We also sailed through the North Sea oil field—one evening we had twenty rigs in sight at the same time. As we approached the islands, the wind piped up on the nose and we gave up the idea of making the capital, Lerwick, by nightfall. Instead, we tacked into a wide bay on the southeast side of Fetlar Island. With gale force 7 winds forecast, we gratefully dropped the hook before dark and contemplated the barren landscape, which was almost treeless, with a few isolated farms.

The next day was an easy sail to Lerwick. This old town of sturdy, stone buildings was a great introduction to what would be a dominant motif of this part of the cruise—European history. Lerwick is so picturesque, with twisting quaint streets that scarcely run 20 yards before disappearing round a corner, that it could form a set for Brigadoon. Doug was delighted to be re-acquainted with the typical highland pub. An overnight sail brought us to Kirkwall, the principle town of the Orkneys. We tied up next to several rather dirty and smelly fishing boats, and then toured the island by bus, stopping off in Stromness. We were just in time to visit the beer festival held at a Victorian edifice called the Stromness Hotel. We also visited the Stromness museum, which had a section devoted to the Hudson's Bay Company. Many of their factors (supervisors of the trading post) came from the Orkneys. It was in Stromness that half-Indian children were sent to school—the offspring of the Orkney men and their (temporary) Indian wives.

There was also an exhibit about one of my favorite Arctic explorers, Dr. John Rae. In Chapter 9, I describe sailing through the strait he discovered, which was the key to opening the Northwest Passage. In the cathedral, we found his impressively-carved marble tomb, depicting him on a sled. At Kirkwall itself there were the wonderful ruins of Patrick Stewart's Palace, a magnificent 16th-century building next to the cathedral.

South of Kirkwall lies Scapa Flow, the deep-water harbor used by the British Royal Navy North Sea fleet for many years. In 1918, the German fleet surrendered here at the conclusion of WWI—nearly 70 ships. A year later, the commanding admiral, Von Reuter, convinced the Versailles peace talks were going badly for Germany, ordered all the ships scuttled. On receiving the secret pre-arranged signal, the skeleton crews on every ship simultaneously sank them. At the same time, a party of school children was touring the impressive sight in a launch. Goodness knows what they thought as each mighty

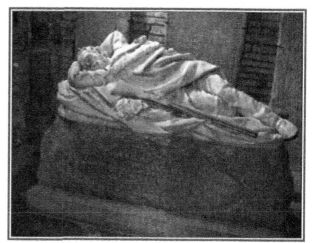

The tomb of Dr. Rae, Eric's favorite Arctic explorer. He is lying on a sled.

battleship began to sink and turn turtle. ("It wasn't my fault, Miss, honestly, I didn't touch anything!") Salvaging the wrecks provided work in the Orkneys for years. There is some suspicion that the Brits colored the reports of the treaty negotiations received by the German admiral, as they did not really want a competitive battle fleet left in Europe in the post-war years.

We powered overnight to Inverness across a calm sea full of coastal traffic. At Inverness, John signed off and we were joined by Colin, a serious Englishman who was studying for his Royal Yachting Association (RYA) skipper's ticket. I had known him many years before when he spent a sabbatical leave at my laboratory on Long Island. In addition, my old friend Derek and his wife, Hilary, joined us briefly for the passage through the Caledonian Canal to the Atlantic Ocean. Derek had served with me in the RAF and crewed for me in 1996 from Gibraltar to Bermuda.

The passage was a lot of fun. There are lunchtime and evening tie-ups, often near castle ruins or charming Scottish pubs. The highlight was a traversal of Loch Ness, of Monster fame. Heading west, I was delighted to see an ancient "Puffer" coming the other way. For many years prior to the 1950s, these small sturdy steam freighters served the Scottish islands. There are now few left, and these are operated by enthusiasts.

An ancient "Puffer" in the Caledonian Canal, Scotland

The highland scenery is magnificent the whole way. There are a couple dozen locks and *Fiona* was raised to over a hundred feet above sea level. When Derek and Hilary left us at Fort William, we sailed to Tobermory on the island of Mull. We took a bus ride to Craignur, where a gimmicky narrow gauge steam railway transported tourists to a restored family castle and garden called Torosay. By sheer chance the late owner, David James, was in the Royal Navy in 1944 when he helped build the base at Port Lockroy in Antarctica, the southerly destination of *Fiona*'s 1998-99 cruise. Before that, he had served on Motor Torpedo Boats in the Channel, got captured, busted out of the POW camp, and was subsequently posted to the Antarctic to keep him out of more trouble.

From Tobermory, our destination was Coll, a remote island on the western fringes of Scotland, with a population of 140 hardy souls. The forecast was not good—gales, gales, gales, and our anchorage was open to the south. The next day we left with the hope of sailing to Ireland, but wind and seas were against us. The forecast was force 8, perhaps 9, and so with rare prudence, we altered course for a cove on the southwest corner of Mull. We sailed past Staffa on the way, with Fingal's Cave on the south side.

On entering the cove, the engine refused to start and we anchored under sail. The problem lay with the starter motor, discovered after a couple of greasy hours in the engine room. I changed the starter for the spare which *Fiona* had carried on all her previous voyages without it ever being needed. The southwest gales persisted but never mind—we were only four miles from Iona, so a bus ride and a trip on the ferry landed us there for a tour of the famous abbey. By the 6th century A.D., monks were discovering the western islands and establishing themselves there, goodness knows why. The living must have been terribly hard. Later the Vikings made life even tougher. The abbey has been restored and is now used as a religious retreat. The museum contained some great 12th and 13th century effigies of dead knights displaying the Norse influence. The nunnery, established in the 12th century, lay in ruins.

A westerly wind gave us hard sail past Bloody Foreland, the northwest corner of Ireland and, in view of the time lost at Mull, we sailed right past the mouth of Donegal Bay without stopping and anchored at Clifden, in County Galway, two days out from Mull.

Ireland

Clifden was an interesting town. It was about as far west as you can get in the British Islands. For years, Marconi maintained a radio transmitting station nearby in the early part of the century. When Alcock and Brown made the first non-stop flight across the Atlantic, in a war-surplus Vickers Vimy bomber in 1922, they crash-landed at Clifden. The mayor at the time, bedeviled by the poverty of the area, envisaged a great airport because of the proximity to the American continent.

We took a bus ride to Galway, the nearest city. As the bus trundled along the coast road I was struck by the harshness of the country-side—vast gray-green rocky outcroppings interspersed with bogs. Here and there stood the gable ends of small, ruined cottages, probably abandoned in the Great Famine of the 1850s. While anchored in Galway Bay, I ran into a young Irish sailor called Damian who needed ocean time for a license. He agreed to join the boat later at Lisbon for the transatlantic leg to St. Martin. On leaving Clifden, we beat past Slyne Head with a moderate wind and headed for the Aran Islands. We moored in Kilronan harbor, on the largest of the islands, Inishmore. Until recently, life was very hard on those islands, located on the fringes of the Atlantic Ocean west of Galway. A famous documentary, "Man of Aran" made by Robert Flaherty in the 1930s, was shown several times daily at the visitor center. In order to grow anything, the islanders had to scrounge soil from cracks in the rocks and mix it with seaweed. Now they just go to the supermarket.

There was a fantastic Iron Age fort on the west side of Aran overlooking a 300-foot vertical cliff. In some ways it reminded me of the defensive Maori settlements I saw in New Zealand in 1996. Apparently, in all primitive societies there were always people who found it easier to kill and steal, rather than toil to produce food. Have we changed much?

When we returned to the boat, we found the wind was forecast to be northwest for the night, so we slipped the mooring for an overnight sail to Dingle. Any help in sailing round the prominent capes, which jut out to the southwest, was welcome. This part of Ireland is full of pre-Viking monasteries, and on a tour, our guide claimed 440 AD for the founding of the earliest, which I felt was a little fishy as this was about the time St. Patrick arrived in Ireland, and he lived in the north. Still, the ruins were obviously very ancient. One small building, possibly 8th century, known as the Gallarus Oratory, was still in perfect condition and quite watertight. It was constructed of dry stone; no mortar was used, even for the roof. The ruins of many churches in the area contained graves from the 12th century and again reflected the enormous Viking influence after about 1000 AD. It seemed to rain continuously during our stay in Dingle.

From Dingle we sailed, again with a northwest wind, to Sneem Harbor, which was a very pleasant, wooded anchorage. It was a two-mile walk to the village itself, a picture-perfect Irish village with a rustic bridge over a gurgling river. As we were leaving to walk back to the boat, a van in the small market area was displaying antiques for sale. There were several small oil paintings in heavy, old-fashioned gilt frames. The owner said he had got them from a nunnery which was being closed. One of small fishing boats clawing off a stormy coast caught my eye and I hesitantly asked the price. When he quoted forty pounds (about $50), I could not resist buying it. At that price, Colin also bought a still life of flowers. It left us with the problem of getting them back on board via the dinghy and then protecting them until we could get them home. When Colin examined his painting more closely at home he found our "paintings" were actually varnished prints—but they looked nice! We sailed from Sneem to Dursey Sound, a turbulent, tide-wracked strait, and then to an anchorage at Castletown, where we refueled at the fishing boat dock in the morning. We were now on the south coast of Ireland and were finished with beating past rocky capes sticking out in the Atlantic. On the way to Kinsale, we sailed past the imposing edifice of Fastnet Rock lighthouse. We passed right over the spot where the *Lusitania* was sunk in WWI. From Kinsale, we had a relatively short sail in heavy weather to Crosshaven. We tied up at the Royal Cork Yacht Club (RCYC), our final port in Ireland, where we planned to rest up for week before leaving for Portugal.

In fact, there was not a lot of resting achieved. Apart from a few repairs to the boat, it had to be restocked for the next leg. In addition, my Aunt May flew in from London with her sons, and we had a couple of days in their rented car seeing the sights and chasing down a little family history in Cork. In Chapter 3, I mentioned visiting my great-grandmother's grave on Barbados in 1999 on the return trip from Antarctica. When she died in 1880, her husband returned to Cork and married her sister, Margaret. Their house was listed in a 1900 census. In the pouring rain, May, my cousins, and I tramped through some fairly mean streets looking for my great-grandfather's old addresses. We did find one, and perhaps two—streets have changed so much in a hundred years. The house had been greatly gentrified and looked like it was worth a million dollars.

We also visited Cobh (pronounced "Cove"), which is perhaps better known as "Queenstown" when it was the last European port for many transatlantic liners heading west. In the old railway station, now no longer used for trains, there was an Irish Heritage center. Naturally, it featured much of the story of the great emigration from Ireland in the 19th century. Many left from Queenstown and probably arrived there at that very station. I was surprised at the different emphasis on the tragedy of the Great Famine and subsequent emigration by the Irish, as opposed to the Irish-American view. In the latter, the villains are the English, who allegedly refused to provide aid and encouraged emigration to clear the land. The Irish view was more balanced, I thought. In this view, the land was too poor to support so many peasants and well-meaning people in Ireland and England tried to help. When the potato blight occurred the problem became overwhelming. The same benefactors provided money for emigration because it was genuinely felt that the only chance for the poor peasants (who generally agreed) to lead better life was in the New World.

The Arctic, Norway, Scotland, Ireland, Portugal, the Caribbean and Cuba 2000-2001

111

When we arrived at the RCYC (still "Royal" after nearly 80 years of home rule,) I renewed my friendship with Barbara and Frank Fitzgibbon, who lived nearby. We first met in Thailand during the circumnavigation, 1995-97, described in Chapter 2. Barbara and Frank had a lovely house overlooking the approach to Crosshaven. They invited me and the crew to dinner and later sponsored a cruising evening at the yacht club, where we showed the video of the Antarctic cruise of 1998-99.

Portugal

When we left Ireland, we had a stiff northwest gale behind us that pushed us more than 180 nm in the first 24 hours, but then the wind switched to southwest and we sailed close-hauled, sometimes in gale strength. Poor Colin, who had not experienced open ocean conditions, was very seasick as we left the Irish coast. He was contemplating buying a cruising sailboat, but this leg gave him second thoughts. Near 44° N, we sailed into a high pressure zone that produced lighter winds. These finally backed and died out, and we motored the last 80 miles to Viana do Castelo in Portugal. The swell from the remains of Hurricane Isaac a few hundred miles to the northwest caused impressive surf at the stone breakwater guarding the entrance to the harbor. It had taken us five days from Ireland.

As soon as we got to Portugal, there was a noticeable improvement in the weather and Doug was moved to put on shorts for the first time this cruise. However, he enjoyed only a day in Viana before leaving for the U.S. His place was taken by Bill Steenberg, who was actually waiting on the dock at the marina as we pulled in. Bill had sailed on *Fiona* in 1997 on the Cape Town to New York leg (Chapter 3) and had signed up for the transatlantic run to St. Martin. Viana do Castelo turned out to be a lovely town with pleasant plazas, restaurants, and pastelerias. Bill and I greatly enjoyed a ramble each morning into the town square to sample the variety of cakes and tarts with coffee. There was an imposing church on a hill overlooking the town, which was reached by means of the elevador, or funicular.

We took a bus to Porto when we tied up in Leixoes, which gave us a chance to see the countryside. Many of the harbors on the coast were about 35 miles apart, and so sailing from one to the other was quite feasible during a daylight run. This set the pattern of our Portuguese cruise—a day sail, followed by one or two days in port to allow exploration of nearby attractions. Porto is not recommended for yachts, due to heavy seas that frequently break on the bar of the River Douro. We bussed to it. It was a fascinating town, almost vertical in places, with red-roofed houses crammed into the slopes. The Portuguese are a lovely people, but they do love their dogs, so when walking in town it pays to do so penitently, with head bowed. On the south bank were the famous port wine cellars, from which all port is shipped after it has aged. A tour of the Sandeman cellars revealed why I am quite partial to port: it is 20 percent brandy, which is added to "fortify" it.

From Leixoes we sailed to Aveiro, just an overnight anchorage on the river, and then we headed for Figueira da Foz, a nice seaside resort. We took a bus to Leiria to inspect the old castle and the next day a train ride to Coimbra. There was an amazing miniature village, which predates Disney World by about 50 years. But the main point of interest was the site of the country estate where Inez de Castro was murdered in the 14th century. Now, it is a very up-market hotel but they have preserved a small building called the "Font d'Amores."

The story of Inez was fascinating. Prince Pedro, the son of King Afonso IV of Portugal, was forced into an arranged marriage with a noble lady. Although they had three children, the marriage was loveless, typical of the political maneuvering of the period. Pedro fell in love with a lady-in-waiting called Inez and moved her onto an estate at Coimbra. Inez was Spanish and the King was very concerned that Portugal would become embroiled in the feuding between Aragon and Castile. When Pedro's wife died during the birth of her third child, the king decided Inez was too much of a threat and sent three knights to kill her. They tracked her down to Coimbra and stabbed the defenseless lady to death—so much for chivalry.

It was at the Font d'Amores, close to the scene of her death, that Pedro and Inez first made love, according to the legend and the tourist bureau. A year later, Afonso died and Pedro assumed the throne. He had been distraught over the death of his beloved Inez and now he had his revenge of sorts. He caught two of the three knights, who died rather cruelly. He then had Inez disinterred from the Monastery of St. Clara and the body moved to Alcobaca. Before reburial, Inez was cleaned up and sat on a throne wearing the crown of Portugal. Pedro made his nobles kneel before her and swear allegiance while kissing her boney hand. Pretty macabre. When we were tied up at Nazaré we took a bus to Alcobaca, where Pedro and Inez still lie near each other under elaborate marble effigies in the vast monastery. They are positioned feet to feet, so that when they wake up on Judgment Day, the first thing they will see will be each other.

From Nazaré, we sailed to Cascais near Estoril, and then I arranged to spend a month at the Expo 98 marina on the River Tagus in Lisbon. The Expo was still going strong with crowds on the weekends. The aquarium was fantastic; it is one of the largest in the world. The buildings were most imaginative and interesting.

Bill left for a couple of weeks with friends in Zimbabwe and I flew to New York. Colin went home, having accumulated enough sea miles to get his RYA skipper's license, and having learned how to plot running fixes from sun sights. But he changed his mind about buying a sailboat and retiring on it.

The Atlantic Crossing

After a hectic two weeks in New York, I returned to Lisbon in mid-November. Bill had already returned to *Fiona* after his brief trip to Zimbabwe. A third crew member, Damian, whom we had met in Ireland, had arranged to join the boat after crewing on a trip to the Canaries. In fact, he got on board just a few hours before I did. The next day, we did the final shopping for fresh provisions in preparation for our transatlantic departure on the morrow. In the afternoon, Damian checked his e-mail. I don't know what it said, but after reading it, he returned to the boat with a taxi, loaded his gear, and hightailed it to the airport.

Bill and I looked at each other after Damian's departure in some consternation. During my trip to New York, I had had a hernia patched up and I had promised the doctor to take it easy. Bill was a very active 76-year-old, but I was not too sanguine about a two-man 3,000-mile transatlantic crossing. Nevertheless, the next day we sailed down the Tagus River past the Lisbon waterfront in mist and rain and set sail in light winds for Madeira. When we arrived, the small inner harbor at Funchal was crowded, but we managed to raft up to another boat tied to the wall. We enjoyed our brief stay and took the new teleferique to the top of the hill. A traditional way down, now enjoyed by tourists, was to shoot down the hill on a wicker toboggan, guided by two locals in straw hats. We took the cable car.

We checked our e-mail, bought some Madeira wine, refueled and left. Two days out, a vast low pressure system over the English Channel well to our north gave us some heavy weather, with gusts to 30 knots. We reefed in driving rain, and later, on my watch, the cumbersome whisker pole came loose from its lashings and nearly went over the side. I managed to catch it and tie it down again. Somehow I wasn't having the kind of restful recuperation envisaged by my surgeon. Fortunately, the weather moderated and we had fairly light winds as we plowed south and west to a point not too far from the Cape Verde Islands. Then the idea was to turn west and pick up the trade winds, but we had to push on a little further south.

We finally did get the Trades at 23° N and we headed for St. Martin. Each evening at happy hour we listened to the tape of a book entitled *The Heart of the Sea*, the true story of the sinking of the whale ship *Essex*. The ship was rammed and sunk by a maddened whale in 1821. The story tells of the subsequent survival of the crew in small boats as they sailed thousands of miles to windward across the Pacific. Ultimately, they were reduced to cannibalism. I eyed Bill, but he looked like tough eating to me. I hoped we wouldn't meet any aggressive whales.

During the trip I had almost daily radio contact with my friend Mike McKeown on the 21 MHz ham band. Mike lived a few hundred yards from my house in Brookhaven.

As we approached the Caribbean, the swells grew larger and *Fiona* began to surf down the slopes. This had the effect of momentarily backing the mainsail, which filled with a crack as we lost speed on the next back slope. Finally, very early one morning, the sail split from luff to leech from so much slatting and we doused it. As we were only a couple of days from St. Martin by then, we

Eric checking in with a ham network, using a single-side band radio

sailed under the jib alone and dropped our anchor at the usual spot in Marigot Bay without further difficulty.

The trip from Lisbon had taken us 30 days. It was my tenth Atlantic crossing, ninth as captain.

The Caribbean

Things started happening after our arrival—Bill flew home for a Christmas in California, and my daughter Brenda flew in for a Christmas with me. We all had Christmas dinner with my old friend Kay and her daughter Victoria, our usual shore-side contact in St. Martin. A highlight of the holiday season was a visit to the Chinese circus. I was struck by the thought that Marco Polo probably saw a similar circus 700 years ago, as the acrobats and jugglers used minimal props, mostly chairs and umbrellas.

After Brenda flew home, two new crew members joined the boat— Teresa, an Italian lady living in Switzerland who sailed with me in Maine in 1999, and Deborah (known as "Dee") who crossed the Atlantic on another boat at the same time as Bill and me. I had visited St. Martin on many occasions but this year, I was a little disappointed. When Edith and I first came to Marigot in 1963, it was a typical West Indian village of shacks on the seashore, with a swamp behind. Now there was traffic gridlock, the swamp had been converted to the Port Royale marina, and the shacks have given way to boutiques and fancy shops. No doubt everyone was much more prosperous, but the price of it was dirt, noise and crime. Perhaps I was soured by the theft of items from the dinghy almost as soon as we arrived. Also, after a month on the (mostly) quiet Atlantic, I found the noise almost unbearable. Jet skis in the harbor, powerful motorbikes on the roads, blaring loudspeakers from the restaurants and bars and the jackhammers of endless construction all added to the cacophony. On the good side were morning coffee and croissants in the Port Royale complex and those wonderful French baguettes, not to mention cheap Mount Gay rum.

After a few minor repairs and refueling, we pushed off early in the New Year for a crossing of the Anegada Passage to the British Virgin Islands. We cleared in at Virgin Gorda early in the morning and visited the Baths during the afternoon—a crowded anchorage now, compared to my visits in the 1960s.

The next day we sailed to Anegada Island. Located in the middle of a reef, it used to be considered a dangerous place to visit. Now there was a buoyed channel to the anchorage, one advantage of the bareboat chartering, I guess. The miles of white sand beaches, the clear green water, and a friendly bar on the shore made Anegada the epitome of the perfect tropical anchorage. The ladies were entranced and went for long walks collecting shells, driftwood, and other flotsam.

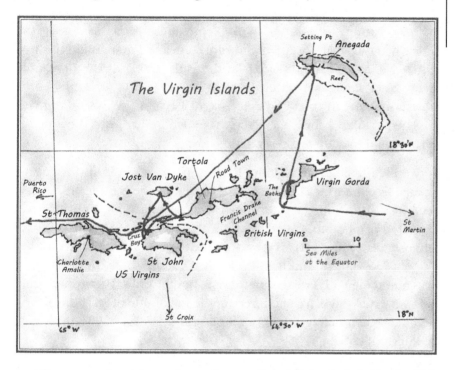

After a couple of days of paradise, we headed for St. John in the U.S. Virgin Islands. Here we ran into a bureaucratic problem: Teresa and Dee were Italian and British, respectively. Normally, both would be given temporary visas on arrival in the U.S. But when I took the ship's papers and our passports to the customs and immigration office in Cruz Bay, they wanted to know where the visas were. "Don't you issue them?" I asked. "Oh no," was the reply, "That only applies to arrivals on a scheduled carrier. A foreigner on a private yacht must get a visa first." I must have looked dumbfounded, for the officer quickly said, "But there is a loophole. You can take your boat back to the British Virgin Islands and return on the ferry. That counts as a scheduled carrier and we can issue a visa. Then you can return with the yacht." Ah! The bureaucratic mind. But that is just what we did. We anchored at West End,

Tortola, and took the ferry to St. John and back—a beaten-up steel boat that got to Cruz Bay in 20 minutes.

Actually, I was quite pleased to see West End again. Edith and I had often anchored there during *Iona*'s 1968/69 cruise. It is, of course, greatly expanded with jazzy restaurants, a big marina and even a Pusser's Rum bar.

From there we sailed to Jost Van Dyke and had a drink at Foxy's Bar before returning to St. John. No problem with the visa this time, as the ladies had the all-important green slip. Edith and I first visited the area when we cruised on *Maverick* in the early 1960s. At the time, only a few black families lived on Jost Van Dyke. After 1970, the bareboat chartering fleet in the U.S. Virgin Islands began to grow and the visitors began to look for a bar when they anchored at Jost. Foxy saw his chance, and the famous "Foxy's" was born.

We greatly enjoyed St. John. It was not crowded, and there were several free moorings in nice bays provided by the National Park Service. The visit included a tour of an old sugar mill, typical of the slave-operated plantations. One day, we took the ferry to St. Thomas, an act of nostalgia on my part, as it was our base for several months during the 1968/69 cruise, and many years had passed since my last visit. It was humming with cruise-ship tourists, but the old Yachthaven marina was very run-down. We anchored on the north side of St. Thomas for a night and then sailed to Culebra, a pleasant island about 15 miles east of Puerto Rico.

From there we sailed to Vieques, an island mostly owned by the U.S. Navy, which used it as a weapons range and for amphibious training. The Puerto Ricans would like them to go away and there was considerable animosity on the issue. When we landed at a small village on the south shore, we found dozens of signs hanging in the street demanding a "free" Vieques. The local paper carried stories of hotels in dire straits because the navy had restricted beach access.

It was time to think about a short trip to the States, as I had been told I was about to receive the Cruising Club of America (CCA) Blue Water Medal and the award dinner was in mid-January. Teresa decided to visit New York at the same time. Unfortunately, however, Dee and I had had some disagreements about the way I captained the boat, as she had recently received an English skipper's license, and obviously felt she was an equal. I had no problem with that, but when she walked away from the wheel in a huff while we were negotiating a reef passage and told me to steer, something had to be done. Sadly for Dee, there can only be one captain. So I bought her a ticket to England via New York.

While in New York I left *Fiona* at a sumptuous, and expensive, marina near Fajardo. Before we left, I rented a car and we drove to San Juan for an interesting day in the old part of town. It was many years since I had first visited El Morro, the massive fort guarding the entrance to San Juan harbor. On my first visit, there had been an old execution chair in the courtyard; in years past prisoners were garroted by a metal band attached to the back of the chair. Now it is gone—the National Park Service wants a family-type experience. No mention either, as there used to be, of the thousands of slaves who died of exhaustion and disease building the massive structure for the Spanish.

On the last day before departure for the mainland, Teresa and I drove into the rain forest which covers the slopes of a high mountain called "El Yunque"—the rain-maker. When we stopped to ask directions, a lady invited us into her house, which had a wonderful view of the valley below. After coffee, I asked if I could take a shot of the panorama from her patio. Returning with a camera, I petted a large dog and then, perhaps out of jealousy, a small dog, almost unnoticed in the corner, shot across and sank its teeth in my calf. I popped in to see a doctor when I was back in New York with visions of rabies, but she was reassuring and told me not to worry.

The week at home was as frantic as usual. 'Red' and his wife Julie, my daughter Brenda, and Teresa all went with me to the CCA ceremony at the New York Yacht Club.

I recruited the son of a friend, Chris, to replace Dee. Chris met us at JFK Airport and we flew to San Juan, took a taxi to the marina and shoved off the next day. What a nice change it was to be back to the peaceful cruising life. We jogged along the south coast of Puerto Rico, anchoring every night.

Eric receiving the CCA Blue Water Medal in 2000 at the New York Yacht Club

At one stopover, there was a spectacular modern development built to look like one of those vertical villages on the Mediterranean coast.

The problem was that there were no people in this village. It was like walking through an empty movie set.

The Ponce Yacht Club used to be very exclusive. It was built on a small cay connected to the mainland by a man-made causeway, so access was very controlled. However, in recent years, a vast parking field was built at the end of the causeway and a boardwalk along the shore sported dozens of bars, snack stands, and even small dance halls. At weekends, the whole of Ponce seemed to come down for a good time, so the exclusivity of the club was somewhat degraded by the loud Latin music emanating from the area.

The city of Ponce itself is located a few miles from the beach. It is quite a pleasant city with a very impressive municipal art gallery. The old Parque de Bomberos, a wonderful Victorian firehouse, was moved to the center of the city for the benefit of tourists and converted into a museum.

We left Puerto Rico from Boqueron and crossed the Mona Passage to Samana in the Dominican Republic. I'm afraid the officials there, and the water taxi man, were quite corrupt and avaricious. The place had a bad reputation for dinghy theft too. Nevertheless, after we got through the thicket of waterfront thieves, some uniformed and some not, we found it interesting. We had a very reasonably priced lunch at a "French" restaurant which featured linen napkins, a pleasant change. We took a ride in a motorized rickshaw to a waterfall which was a 15-minute walk from the road through a beautiful wood. An old man attached himself to our party and proceeded to name all the trees and bushes. He found us some grapefruit and gave us aniseed, oregano, cacao, tamarind, piña de Colada, and other flora to taste or smell.

The south end of the harbor at Samana had a solitary cay with nothing on it, but it was connected to the mainland by an impressive bridge supported by a series of arches—a bridge to nowhere. We were told the story: When Trujillo was dictator, he and some cronies bought the cay intending to build a fancy hotel and restaurant. Of course, people had to be able to get there and so the government built the bridge. The hotel was never built, but now residents can take a nice stroll to the cay on Sunday afternoons, though there was nothing to do there except turn back.

Our next anchorage in the Dominican Republic was Luperon on the north coast. Luperon is a good example of the tendency of yachties to nucleate—there were over forty boats there when we arrived, despite the relatively small size of the bay. The officials were pleasant and not very corrupt. A small contribution was asked for, but it was purely voluntary, it was emphasized. Shortly after we arrived, a familiar face looked up at us from a dinghy. A fellow boater from Weeks Yacht Yard in Patchogue had spotted *Fiona*—Pete Hansen was on a long winter cruise to the Caribbean and had sailed as far as Luperon single-handed.

Off to one side from the village was a small marina with a very active bar. In the village a new generation had discovered wheels; young men roared up and down on large motorbikes, mostly modified by removing the insides of the muffler. Many of the older buildings were typically West Indian—weathered planks with corrugated iron roofs. Chickens scratched away in the debris, roosters crowed their presence.

Decrepit shack at Luperon, Dominican Republic

Chris and I took the publico to Puerto Plata; there were seven of us squeezed into a medium-sized car. I sat on the transmission hump at the front, and every time I eased my leg a little, I inadvertently shifted gear and the driver patiently reselected. The ten-mile ride cost about two dollars. We visited the old fort and the unique amber museum. For some reason, there are extensive amber deposits in the Dominican Republic and it is mined. The most impressive pieces have an encapsulated insect inside. We saw a very rare piece with a captive 50 million years-old lizard trapped inside.

When it came time to return we couldn't figure out where to catch the proper publico. Suddenly a young man seemed to understand, gestured for us both to mount his motorbike and we careened off through the crowded streets. I had joked about the locals riding three to a bike (without crash-helmets) and now, here I was doing it. He dropped us off next to the Luperon publico, all for 65 cents. Teresa took a bus to Santo Domingo on the south coast, leaving at 6 am and getting back rather exhausted at 10 pm. I asked her what she thought of Santo Domingo. "Dirty!" was the short reply.

Soon it was time to leave. Our destination was the forbidden worker's paradise of Cuba.

Cuba

Due to the embargo, U.S. citizens were not allowed to spend dollars in Cuba, but nothing prevented them from visiting there if the trip was sponsored, i.e. someone else picked up the tab. In our case, Teresa wanted to visit a professor she was acquainted with at the University of Santiago and she agreed to sponsor *Fiona*'s trip. We left Luperon with a brisk easterly wind and enjoyed a great two-day run past the coast of Haiti, across the Windward Passage and along the north coast of Cuba to a port of entry called Puerto de Vita. It was a new marina built specifically to lure yachtsmen and foreign fishermen to Cuba.

The marina was obviously laid out by some anonymous planning committee. There was a large parking lot, properly striped and sign-posted, but no cars. There were slips for about thirty boats, but very few yachts. During our stay, the number varied between five and ten. The bathrooms for each sex were sparkling clean, each with five hot showers. It was all very luxurious compared to Luperon, where one rather dirty cold water shower at the marina served the needs of over 40 yachts. The resident facilitator, Ernestina, worked in an air-conditioned office, spoke good English, and was our point of contact. She greeted us on the dock when we arrived and told us not to leave the boat until cleared by customs, immigration, police, and health authorities. She was horrified when Chris jumped on the dock to adjust the mooring lines. Quite literally, we had to stay on the boat.

The relevant officials showed up shortly afterwards. Two customs officers roamed around the boat opening drawers and lockers, and they even brought a sniffer dog. However, I have to say in their defense that although the search was quite intrusive by the standards of most ports I have visited, Cuba was, by and large, drug-free. Throughout our stay, I struck by the contradictory aims of the two branches of the Cuban government we encountered. On one hand, the tourism people had provided an excellent marina, obviously at great expense, and on the other hand, the Guarda Frontera were very concerned at the freedom of yachties to move at will. The compromise was to restrict the yachts to selected marinas and to make it difficult to anchor anywhere else.

On our first afternoon we took a walk down the road outside the marina. The entrance gate was guarded day and night to keep out the great unwashed. Cubans were obviously very poor but the fields were cultivated and neatly tended. There was absolutely no litter by the roadside. I'm afraid the average Cuban was too poor to buy goods packaged in plastic. Most people walked or pedaled. A few drove by on small mopeds—one even had a live pig tied on the back! Very few private cars passed us. There were quite a few buses, all crowded. Now and again, vast trucks roared by crowded with workers standing in the back. Cuba has a two-tier economic system; the peso was officially priced at one to the dollar. They would solemnly give you a peso for a dollar at any bank, but don't expect to get a dollar for a peso. Outside, on the street, touts offered about 20 pesos to the dollar. However, pesos were not much use to tourists, as shopkeepers and restaurants would only accept dollars. Most items were priced in dollars, even in shops patronized only by Cubans.

We rented a car and drove it to Santiago de Cuba—the cost was $60 a day. The drive to Santiago was quite an adventure, as roads in Cuba were not numbered and signs of any kind were rare. We got hopelessly lost and wound up driving down rutted roads in the middle of extensive sugar cane fields. Some were being harvested and the workers looked at this apparition emerging from the dust with amazement. Teresa's friend at the university had arranged a bed and breakfast place for us. Chris and I shared a room for $20 per night. Many homeowners rent rooms in order to get some dollars.

Most of the buildings in Santiago were very shabby with peeling paint and rotted timber. The Casa Granda Hotel was an exception and we greatly enjoyed our first evening in town there. We were entertained by an eclectic Cuban band and a magician who wandered among the tables performing for the tourists. The streets were crowded, but fortunately cars with tourist plates get reserved parking places. They really want your money. Teresa's friend Lionel arranged a little party at his house the next night, and we showed a sailing video and met several of his English students. Lionel said his pay as a professor was 500 pesos a month, which illustrates how important dollars are to every Cuban. At the unofficial exchange rate (but one on which prices are based) he was making $25 a month.

Television was everywhere, but there weren't many channels. An old lady living at the B&B where we stayed watched continuously, although much of the content seemed to be government-controlled news. I was fascinated by the shower in the bathroom. Warm water was produced by flowing water through a small electric heater next to the shower head, about the size of a large mug. To turn it on, the 230-volt switch was conveniently placed next to it on the wall, so you could reach it standing in the bathtub. Any building inspector in the States would have had a fit seeing this set-up.

There was no doubt that Cuba is a controlled society. In Santiago, policemen were ubiquitous, frequently checking the Cubans' IDs. On the open road, control check points stopped all civilian traffic, except tourists. We were able to use a computer terminal at a ritzy hotel to check our e-mail. The average Cuban can send and receive e-mail but cannot plug into the internet, and was not allowed to use terminals in tourist hotels. Political posters are the only ones in good shape; almost everything else needed a coat of paint.

The Cubans I met were well-educated, intelligent, and very pleasant. Our landlady, for example, had written a book. As I said earlier, Cubans were very poor. The famous 1950s cars, acquired prior to the revolution, are fairly common in Santiago, but were mostly in sad shape. My simple-minded impression of the U.S. embargo was that it was counterproductive. Posters urged unity at this special time, and explained the failures of the government could be attributed to the embargo, not internal problems. The Cubans are a proud nation, I felt, and change would only come slowly, even if Castro stepped down. There must have been some terrible diplomatic failures on both sides in the early '60s to produce this situation. However, Americans should be thankful the Mafia was still not running Cuba as it did; the drug problem in Florida would have been worse. The Seven Seas Cruising Association (SSCA) had a guide for us yachties wanting to visit Cuba. No U.S. currency could be used. Teresa signed an affidavit that she paid for dockage, petrol, and etc. We had to have receipts for all the food used on the boat from outside Cuba. We had stocked up in Puerto Rico. All this paperwork had to be mailed to the U.S. State Department, which I did.

Nothing more was heard.

Teresa decided to stay in Santiago for a few weeks to improve her Spanish. Chris and I drove back to the marina with the idea of heading to the Bahamas the next day. When we left, we got the same going-over by customs, except they left the dog at home. What they were looking for remained a mystery. Stowaways?

A curious incident occurred just before we shoved off. Chris took a video of the marina from the boat, and it included a uniformed officer coming down to the dock. He came to the boat and got Chris to erase that section of the video, as he didn't want his picture taken. We left as the sun set with a Norther' brewing up, much to the amazement of the more staid cruisers at the marina.

The Bahamas

Despite heavy weather we made it to the Jumentos Cays in the Bahamas by lunch the next day. These islands were some of the least visited in the Bahamas, and in fact we encountered only two other cruisers in the three places we dropped our anchor.

Our first stop was the south end of Ragged Island. A local entrepreneur, Percy, had salvaged a wrecked DC-3 and turned it into a restaurant/bar right on the beach. It was closed when we were there, which wasn't surprising, as hardly anyone ever goes to Ragged Island, let alone the lonely south end. Our next stop was Raccoon Cay, which was, in Chris' opinion, the loveliest of all the anchorages he had encountered so far. A sheltered bay, white sand, crystal clear water—what else do you need? From there we went to Jamaica Cay, where we discovered two very lonely men slowly building a holiday resort for the ever-enterprising Percy of Ragged Cay. When Chris and I showed up, we got a royal welcome and a tour of the simple foundations they were making from coral blocks, which would perhaps someday support small cottages. There was no runway on Jamaica Cay, so Percy would be dependent on seaplanes to deliver his potential customers. He supported the workers by sending a boat twice a week with some fish and basic supplies. I went back to the boat to get them some smokes (Cuban cigars) and rum to cheer them up.

At Jamaica Cay I studied the charts carefully and found there was no exit across the sand banks to the north for a boat of *Fiona*'s draft. Consequently, we sailed east overnight to the south cape of Long Island and anchored a day later at Clarence Town. Edith and I had sailed into the harbor in 1969, when there seemed to be fewer residents. A curious feature of Clarence Town was two magnificent churches. The first, St. Paul's was built by a young Anglican missionary called Jerome Hawes, who had studied architecture. He then left, converted to Roman Catholicism, and returned as Father Jerome, determined to build a new church to outclass St. Paul's. The result was the impressive Saints Peter and Paul. Now Clarence Town has two great churches to save the few hundred souls who live there.

We spent a couple of nights at George Town in the Exumas. This has become a major nucleation center for yachties. Several hundred boats were anchored there when we arrived. When Edith and I visited in 1969 there were two, ourselves and a Canadian yacht. Most of the yachts stay there for weeks, snowbirds escaping winter but not willing to go too far. They hold regattas and play lots of volleyball on the beach at Stocking Island. We refueled and moved up the Exuma chain.

At Norman Cay there was another wrecked plane lying half-submerged in the anchorage. It looked like a C-46. During our visit there in 1969, we found a small hotel at the south end with a few yachts that stayed a couple of nights. A few years later, a developer built some private homes towards the north end, mostly for wealthy Americans attracted by the lovely surroundings and the convenience of a 3,000-foot runway not too far from Nassau. In the late 1970s, a gentleman with a Colombian mother and German father and connections to the Medellín drug cartel bought out the hotel, imported some heavily armed thugs who vandalized the private homes, shot at yachties (it is rumored some were killed but the bodies never found), and soon became the undisputed king of Norman Cay. His name was Carlos Lehder. For several years, Lehder ran a drug-running operation centered on Norman Cay. Ultimately, I believe he was jailed in the U.S. Now there was a very quaint bar/restaurant just north of the runway called MacDuffs. A few vacation cottages were for rent.

From Norman Cay, we had a great sail to Rock Sound at the south end of Eleuthera. Chris called his parents from there and discovered they had booked him a ticket home from Marsh Harbour in the Abacos five days hence. From the weather forecast, we learned a cold front was due to cross the area in a couple of days, thus the logical thing was to get to the Abacos asap. The next day we left bright and early, aiming to be at a pass in northern Eleuthera called Current Cut by slack high tide in the late afternoon. From there, it would be an overnight sail to the Abacos.

However, as we got within a few hundred yards of the cut, we had a series of small rocks on our left and a shallow sand bank on the right. The depth of water under the keel slowly fell to a foot. Which way to turn? From the sketch chart in the cruising guide it appeared deeper water was on the right, so we turned that way. Wrong! We bumped and were hard aground. I quickly rowed a kedge out in the dinghy but we couldn't get off. The tide fell and we were firmly stuck. That night, the bad weather ahead of the front arrived. As poor *Fiona* creaked and groaned on her sandy bed, the wind increased to 25 knots with driving rain and lightning. It was a long night.

Just after 4 am there were signs she was coming free. The compass began to swing and soon we were able to kedge her off and stay in deeper water until it was light enough to traverse the cut. In full accordance with Murphy's Law, the wind fell and we had to power to the Abacos in heavy swells. We anchored behind the reef with little protection from the stiff northwesterly wind that sprang up behind the front. To cap it all, the anchor winch made loud noises when we shifted our anchor to just north of Little Harbour. Investigation showed a thrust bearing had fractured. We fixed it temporarily and then took advantage of an invitation to a delicious lunch by two friends belonging to the CCA who had a charming cottage on Little Harbour. The next day we moved to Man o' War Cay, 15 miles to the north, for a CCA cocktail party, part of the Abacos 2001 Cruise. The next day we anchored in Marsh Harbour for the final party at Mangoes.

When Chris flew to Florida, I was left with a few days to kill at Marsh Harbour before the arrival of Chip and Al, two Long Island sailors who were joining for the final push to Bermuda and home. During the wait I had two amazing coincidences. The first occurred when I saw another Westsail 42 dropping anchor nearby. The boat was called *Consort*, and she was crewed by Russ and Pat. I soon discovered over a couple of rums that she was hull Number 1, the very Westsail Edith and I saw on the stocks at the Westsail yard back in 1974. The very one, indeed, that inspired Edith to call our own boat *Fiona*.

The second coincidence involved a small ketch anchored in the harbor called *Arvin Court III*. Now, *Arvin Court II* was the boat Edith and I first sailed across the Atlantic in 1964 when she was captained by John Knight. It turns out that John sold the boat to Gillian and Tom, who sailed her for many years before reluctantly selling her. But they loved her so much that they named their subsequent boat Arvin Court also.

When Chip and Al arrived, we cruised the Bahamas for a few days before leaving for Bermuda. Our first night out of Marsh Harbour was spent at Guana Cay, where unfortunately, the wind sprang up from the west, which put us on a lee shore. We had had difficulty getting the anchor to set, but after three tries it finally dug in. Good job too—during the night the wind piped up enough to cause the anchor chain to jump over the cogs on the gypsy, link by link. The racket soon brought us all on deck, and we let out more scope and slept soundly after that.

In the morning we crossed over to the west side of Abaco Sound to get some protection. We anchored at Treasure Cay, where there was a very ritzy hotel and marina complex. However, as we wandered around it seemed almost deserted; probably only about 20 percent of the slips contained boats. The beach there was quite fantastic.

Our next stop was New Plymouth, on Green Turtle Cay. This is a quaint village that was a center for Loyalists after the American Revolution (or the "Rebellion," as it is called there). We spent some time at an interesting museum which was located in a house owned by a family that could trace its roots to those turbulent days.

The Last Leg to Long Island

We left the Bahamas for Bermuda with a stationary high pressure system in place and experienced light winds all the way except for the last day. On that day, about 40 miles from Bermuda, when we were sailing on a nice reach with Victor the Vane in control, we espied a large red sailboat rapidly overhauling us from astern. It turned out to be an 80-foot Norwegian maxi, returning home from the round-the-world Whitbread Race. As they came alongside they eased up to within a couple of feet on our starboard and started tossing freeze-dried food packages on the boat. Apparently, they were heartily sick of them after weeks at sea!

Within a few hours, we tied up at the customs dock at St. George's. Standing on the dock waiting to greet us was Selena, a friend of Chip's. I expressed surprise at seeing her and she said, "Well, your schedule called for an arrival in Bermuda on April 10th, so here I am." It was indeed the 10th. I forbore from pointing out that sailboats do not behave exactly like airlines. Chip and Al had never visited Bermuda and so had a wonderful time exploring the island on the pink and blue buses. I looked up an old friend, Bernie, who has been greeting yachts there for years. We managed to squeeze in some cruising to the lovely anchorages at the west end of Bermuda and spent a night at the impressive old naval dockyard.

As we rounded Daniel's Head, formerly an unspoiled pristine beach, I was horrified to see dozens of tacky huts built on stilts over the beach. Apparently, this was Bermuda's latest attempt to entice the dwindling hotel tourists: an eco-resort. It is a paradox—for years Bermudians complained about falling tourist numbers, and yet they built more hotels, thus slowly destroying the very beauty that makes the place so attractive in the first place. Although violent crime is relatively rare in Bermuda, there seemed to be a lot of petty theft. The local daily, *The Royal Gazette*, featured a column, "Around the Courts," which made interesting reading. I was amused by a story about two young men who stole a few thousand dollars from a store and went on a binge at a fancy hotel. They purchased drinks and drugs and hired some professional ladies. They both had lengthy records; one covered 17 pages going back to 1982. The poor defending attorney was hard pressed to think of any mitigating circumstances, but finally pleaded (and I quote), "… my client had not really benefited from the activity with the ladies of the night. They weren't up to the quality that one would expect from ladies that professional," said their lawyer. One got three years and the other five years. Perhaps if the ladies had been better, the thieves would have got more time to reflect on their misdeeds.

We attended the annual Agricultural Fair and the Peppercorn Ceremony, at which the Masons pay a nominal rent to the government with great pomp and ceremony for the use of their headquarters in St. George's. One day, Princess Anne showed up to grant St. George's UNESCO World Heritage status.

When we left, another high pressure system had settled in. This produced record-breaking temperatures in New England and gave us five days of northwest winds on the nose. We were pushed east and crossed the Gulf Stream with light winds most of the time, but we had strong currents on the day we crossed the eddies on the north edge of the stream. At one time we were sailing with a good wind and the log read about 7 knots. The GPS, which showed speed over the bottom, indicated we were making good only 2 knots. Finally, as we got to the south of Cape Cod, the wind veered to the north and then northeast, and we had a nice sail past Nantucket, Martha's Vineyard, Block Island and the south shore of Long Island.

We entered Fire Island Inlet in the dark and anchored east of the bridge until the morning. We then threaded our way through the shallow channels of Great South Bay and came up the Patchogue River to Weeks Yard at high tide on May 7th, 2001, (a day early, Selena!). The mileage logged for this cruise since June, 2000, was 14,832 nm.

5 | Circumnavigating the World Eastabout
2002-2003

The great clipper ships reached their apogee in the late 19th century. They were extraordinarily efficient, carrying thousands of tons of cargo with crews of 30 men or fewer. There was no fuel cost, of course, apart from what the cook used. But being so heavily laden, they were slow, and because they did not sail too well to windward, the captains sought routes that kept the wind behind the beam, on average. This often made the sea miles between ports much longer than the direct path.

Over the years these routes between major ports became formalized and were published as sailing directions. Typical was the route from New York to Cape Town. First, the ship sailed east across the Atlantic, keeping north of the permanent Azores-Bermuda high. When the wind shifted, they would sail south into the prevailing northeast trade winds. Near the equator lie the doldrums, an area of calms and fickle winds. Working their way through this region, usually with some difficulty, the ship would pick up the steady southeast trade winds, and sail south for nearly two thousand sea miles. Finally, the captain would work through variable winds to reach the boisterous westerlies and then run before them for thousands of miles to Cape Town, Australia, New Zealand, and home via Cape Horn.

The Southern Ocean was notorious for heavy winds and huge swells. Such a trip may well have lasted a year, depending on the time to unload and load in port. We found out what it was like because,

apart from a few diversions to interesting islands that lie near the
route, this was the plan for *Fiona*'s next cruise.

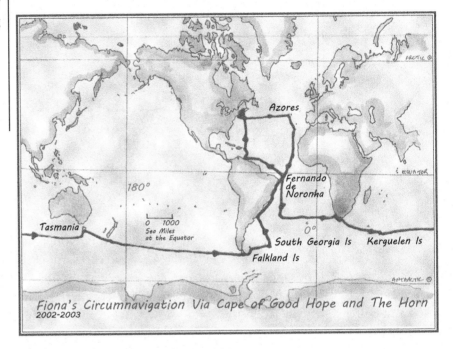

Fiona's Circumnavigation Via Cape of Good Hope and The Horn
2002-2003

The Atlantic Leg to Cape Town

My crew for almost all the trip consisted of Bob Bennett, a computer programmer in his forties, and David Pontieri, a young man who
had just finished college. Bob had about ten years of coastal sailing
under his belt on his own boat. He had taken a year's leave of absence
to tackle the Southern Ocean before he became too old. David had
never sailed before and, although he was quite athletic, he obviously
had some learning to do before we reached Cape Town.

Quite a few friends and relatives came to see us off when we left
Weeks Yacht Yard on schedule, June 10th, 2002. We were escorted
down the Patchogue River by Bob Lyons' classic power boat *Fireplace*,
in case we got stuck. To avoid that embarrassment, our water tanks
were empty, which saved nearly a ton of weight. I don't know if that
did the trick, but we did not touch bottom all the way to the inlet. In
order to water and refuel we stopped at Block Island for a couple of
days. We walked to both the southeast and north lighthouses and had
our last shoreside meals for a few weeks.

Fully loaded, we left for the Canaries. Northeast winds in the vicinity of Georges Bank drove *Fiona* a little more south than I wanted and we did not get a significant boost from the Gulf Stream current. Rather, for several days, we had to fight an unexpected west-going countercurrent. Sometimes the GPS receiver tells you more than you really want to know—ignorance is bliss. We experienced mostly light winds, although we did have a spell when it gusted to 30 knots, necessitating a double-reefed mainsail. Thus, it was a complete surprise on the twelfth day after leaving Block that David discovered, when he went forward to check the roller furling gear, that the bobstay had snapped. This heavy, 3/8-inch chain (listed breaking load 7 tons) attaches the bowsprit to the hull at the waterline and resists the upward force of the headstay. With this restraint missing, the jib pulled up the bowsprit and allowed the stay to bend.

Bob Lyons' vintage power boat Fireplace, *which accompanied* Fiona's *many transits of the shallow Patchogue River*

However, the aluminum tubes around the stay do not like to bend too much and the lower piece cracked at the furling drum. Temporary repairs had to be made. Fortunately, if I can use that word, the break occurred in the middle of the chain, so we were able to snag the bottom bit with the gaff, pull it up and attach it to the upper piece with a shackle. A break near the bottom would have been much more difficult to deal with, as we would not have been able to reach it from the bowsprit. We were able to turn the furling gear with a useful tool called a chain wrench, so that within a day or two we were sailing quite nicely again. However, permanent repairs were needed and I decided to make for the Azores where there were reasonable facilities. On the way across the Atlantic I used the ham radio and, on one or two occasions, even managed a contact with Mike, who lives just down the street in Brookhaven. We also had on board for the first time a satellite Iridium telephone that I used to call my daughter Brenda, who made sure the latest information about our progress would be posted on my web site (www.yachtfiona.com). Bob also called his partner Sue Montana on a weekly basis, and she kept all our friends in the South Bay Cruising Club (SBCC) up to date. *Fiona* communications had joined the 21st century!

Shortly after we fixed the bobstay we sailed into the Azores-Bermuda high, which extended much further north than usual. The pressure rose to 1040 mb (30.7 inches), higher than I could remember experiencing before, with light or zero winds. But we slowly made it to the most western island of the Azores, Flores. Here we hoped to pick up a little fuel so that if the calm conditions persisted we could motor to Horta, about 120 nm further east, where we planned to make our repairs. I had last visited Flores on the 1986 cruise, and I had vowed never to go there again. Although it is one of the most beautiful islands in the world, the harbor at Santa Cruz was incredibly dangerous. A narrow rock-strewn passage led to a small cut swept by Atlantic swells. Once inside you had to tie the boat to a thick hawser stretching from a rock to the harbor wall. We had nearly come to grief on a previous trip. However, the latest guide said that a new harbor at Lajes had been built at the southeast corner with room for a couple of dozen yachts.

And sure enough, there was a solid, large jetty that provided a dock for the ferry and shelter behind it, probably built with EU funds. We dropped our anchor near a few other boats, launched the rigid dinghy with its antique Seagull engine (the one I used during *Iona*'s 1968-69 cruise), and treated ourselves to a beer and pizza at the Beira-Mar café, handy to the dock. Entry was very informal. The marine policeman drove down to the port a couple of times a day, and I spoke to him the next day. We trudged up a long hill with our jerry jugs, but the gas station was out of diesel. However, the market next door was nice enough to phone for a taxi from Santa Cruz and we enjoyed a perfectly breath-taking ride through the green hills and valleys. The driver gave us a short tour of Santa Cruz after we filled our jugs. I gazed at the old harbor and wondered how we ever squeezed *Fiona* in there.

We left in the late afternoon and, sure enough, found ourselves motoring across a mirror-like sea. In the small hours during Bob's watch, he picked up a distress call from a yacht that had developed engine trouble. They were not too far away, so we motored over to them. In the absence of wind, they asked for a tow to Horta. Normally, it would have been quite impossible for *Fiona* to tow a 39-foot boat on the open sea, but conditions were so calm we gave it a shot. We were slowed down, of course, but by the late afternoon we had covered the 60 nm to Horta. The boat was a Canadian yacht called *Tuaq*, under delivery from the Caribbean by two British lads.

The harbor was very crowded, but we were given a berth rafted up to other boats. The next day we replaced the broken bobstay with a piece of our own anchor chain. We also cleaned up the bottom end of the jib furler and got that working again. We had lunch at the famous Peter's Café Sport and repainted *Fiona*'s sign on the jetty wall. The seawall at Horta is a veritable art gallery with hundreds of pictures in every style painted by cruising yachties. *Fiona*'s original sign, painted during the 1986 cruise, had long weathered and been painted over by later visiting yachts.

Besides repairs and painting, the hectic four-day layover included a taxi tour of the island, re-provisioning at the supermarket, checking our e-mail, sampling the local restaurants, and chatting with other visiting crews. It was a nice break after the ocean passage, but it was not on the original schedule and set us back a few days we never regained.

Eric with Fiona's *sign on the breakwater at Horta, Azores*

The one-week passage to Santa Cruz, Tenerife was quiet and brought no surprises. It is quite an elegant city with many outdoor cafes and a pleasant climate. On the evening after we arrived, we witnessed a traditional ceremony in which a statue of the sailor's patron saint, Virgen del Carmen, was paraded round the harbor with a vast flotilla of local boats hooting away. There were lots of fireworks almost until midnight. It was all very Spanish. On the way to and from the boat we passed a large memorial to the siege of Santa Cruz by Admiral Nelson. The Admiral had failed to take the city and lost an arm in the bargain, it gleefully noted. At the local chandlery I was amused to see a Seagull outboard just like mine on sale as a collectible antique. We could not linger, as we were pushed for time, and so left after a couple of days for Mindelo, on St. Vincent Island, the second largest city of the Cabo Verde group, and almost on our direct route to Fernando de Noronha, Brazil.

We were now well into the tropics and picked up strong northeast trade winds. Each morning we found a crop of half a dozen flying fish that had been unfortunate enough to crash onto the deck during the night. We planned only a brief stop at Mindelo, as much as anything so that Bob and David could experience a genuine third-world African country, and we needed to pick up fresh fruit and vegetables. I had visited Praia, the capital, in 1992, on the way back to the U.S. from Tahiti. I had been rather horrified at the dire poverty then, but this time things seemed a little better. At least young women weren't blatantly soliciting at the cafes. But unemployment was still rife, and a bunch of men clustered at the dinghy dock, offering to be guides or to take care of your dinghy.

A young man called Orlando had approached us in a dinghy as we were anchoring and I hired him to help us get through entrance formalities. When I got some escudos at the bank, I gave him a couple of days' pay to get it out of the way, but that turned out to be a tactical error. This windfall went to his head and the next day he was so hung over, he showed up very late and we had to get someone else to help do the fresh food shopping. When we left the next day, Orlando chased us out of the harbor in a borrowed dinghy demanding to be paid. When I pointed out I had paid him up front, he turned shorewards, looking very puzzled. We were not sorry to get on the open sea.

That afternoon, with St. Vincent still in sight, I was below when we felt a slight bump. I rushed up the companionway just in time to see a vast iron-gray, corrugated wall slide past the stern. We had grazed a whale. A whole pod of them surrounded the boat, serenely gliding to the east and paying not the slightest attention to us.

The sailing direction for sail ships give very specific instructions on crossing the doldrums, which lie a little to the north of the equator. Two strong currents must be crossed and near the equator the voyager runs into the edge of the southeast trade winds belt. The first current sets to the east, and square-rigger captains were advised to sail southeast while they could, so that when they encountered the west-setting equatorial current and the Trades, they would be as far to windward as possible. The danger was that they may not have been able to weather the great bulge of South America poking into the South Atlantic at Cabo Branco. As *Fiona* has a diesel engine with about a 500 nm range in calm conditions, to assist with crossing the doldrums, I felt it was safe to ignore that injunction and head directly for Fernando de Noronha. In fact, we were able to sail close-hauled to the southeast trades and made it to the Baia de St. Antonio in one tack from the equator. When we crossed the equator we were honored by a visit from old

Father Neptune himself, who inducted our two pollywogs, Bob and David, as true sons of Neptune.

Fernando de Noronha is a volcanic, lushly tropical island lying about 200 miles south of the equator. For about 200 years, until early in the 20th century, it was a prison for Brazil's most incorrigible political dissidents. When I walked to the fort down a path through the jungle, the cobblestones underfoot had the look of a make-work project for the prisoners. Now the government of the Pernambuco State was trying very hard to make it an attractive but low-key tourist resort.

No officials seemed interested in our arrival. (How things changed in later years! See Chapter 10.) There was only one small hotel but many homes functioned as posadas, or B&B's. A couple of dozen small charter boats operated sight-seeing trips or scuba diving. David had his first underwater scuba experience on one of them. We sampled the many restaurants and bars, restocked the fresh food and shuttled a few jugs of fuel out to the boat. Also anchored was a 39-foot South African yacht run by a retired surgeon. On board were his wife, two children and two crew—goodness knows where they all slept. His wife was kind enough to bake us four loaves the morning we left for the long

Eric with Elda, Trinity Bay, Fernando de Noronha, 2002. She ran a bar on the beach for many years.

haul to Cape Town. The 4,100 nm leg to Cape Town is basically a beat with very long tacks; the southeast trades blow directly from South Africa. For about 1,600 nm we sailed due south, as the wind varied in strength. At one point, we furled the jib entirely and set the staysail. After a few hours we found the forestay turnbuckle had snapped like a carrot—5/8-inch diameter stainless. Fortunately, I had a spare.

Near 30° S the wind became variable and we were finally able to sail east. The boat settled down into a daily routine: stand watch, eat, sleep. After we crossed the Greenwich Meridian, the weather deteriorated and instead of the westerly winds we expected, we often had easterly winds. Twice we hove-to in winds that reached 45 knots. We tore the genoa jib, so took it down when the wind moderated and set the Yankee jib. However, we slowly gained and on the last day, almost within sight of Table Mountain, we had a great day of sailing. Sea otters basked on the surface of the sea.

When we pulled into the Royal Cape Yacht Club, Bob's partner Sue was waiting on the dock. The leg from Fernando de Noronha had taken five weeks. The next few days were hectic—sail repairs, stainless welding, airline tickets, laundry, and so on all had to be organized. We were a week late on the original schedule, due to extra days spent in Horta and the Cabo Verde Islands. When we had made a dent in the accumulated maintenance, Bob and Sue moved into an apartment, David flew to visit relatives living in Botswana, and I flew to New York.

The flight from Cape Town to New York took a little over 24 hours. First I flew to Johannesburg for the international connection. When I got there, I had never seen such chaos in my life. The departure lounge was a mass of humanity, pushing carts, trying to clear security, trying to get a boarding pass. Obviously, I was not going to make it. I appealed to a porter, telling him that I had an hour to make the New York plane. "You won't make it, mon," he said. I looked desperate. "I can help, but it will cost," he proffered. I took his bait. "How much?" "$20 U.S.," he said, and I replied, "Okay. Let's go." He led me to a corner and told me to wait. After a few minutes, a South African Airways rep appeared and led me to a ticket agent. Within minutes, I had the boarding pass and passed through security. Then the rep intercepted me, as he wanted $20 as well. Clearly, the people at Johannesburg International Airport have worked out a solution to the endemic unemployment of the area. Twenty minutes after strapping myself in, we taxied away. Once airborne, I had double rum and felt much better.

Back in Brookhaven I had a busy two weeks. I sent the SSB radio I had carried home for repair, winterized the house, and bought a lot of spare parts. On my return, we re-provisioned for the leg to New Zealand. We found time to squeeze in a tour of the South African wine-making region at Stellenbosch. A full day tour cost $24, including lunch. Such was the ludicrously favorable exchange rate for the Yankee dollar at that time.

The Southern Ocean

We left Cape Town on October 15th with a fair wind and sailed south to clear Cape Agulhas, which is the southernmost cape of the continent, not the Cape of Good Hope as many think. Once clear of the Cape, the weather deteriorated and almost before we knew it, we were dealing with heavy seas and winds up to 60 knots. After a couple of days, the whisker pole broke into two pieces, and a little later, the staysail halyard block disintegrated. This allowed the sail to flog itself to bits before we could furl it. I surveyed the damage and decided to return for repairs to Cape Town, which lay 400 miles astern. Just a week after leaving, we pulled into our old slip at the Royal Cape Yacht Club. The riggers and sailmakers were wonderful and we left again shipshape after only four days.

This time we had a hard beat to weather to clear Cape Agulhas. Once clear, we had to decide on the route to New Zealand. The world is a globe, and the shortest path is to sail south east, but it gets windy and cold and Antarctica is in the way. Sailing directions issued by the British Admiralty recommend sailing east at a latitude of 40° S, claiming the weather is better than further south. But by sailing at 50° S, the distance shrinks by about a thousand miles, and we would pass close to the mysterious island of Kerguelen, one of the most remote in the world. Naturally, we opted for the higher latitude, though the weather was indeed grungy. A little over a week after clearing the Cape, the wind swung to the east and increased to 60 knots. We set the double-reefed mainsail, reefed staysail and hove to. In 36 hours, we drifted backwards by over 25 miles; it was very frustrating.

While working on the foredeck, David was struck on the head by the staysail boom, which laid him out cold. He was bleeding copiously as Bob and I carried him into the main cabin. The boat was rolling badly, so we wedged David on the bench seat of the dinette and Bob grasped a pole with each hand so that he could press against me to hold me steady while I shaved away the hair around David's scalp wound. I applied plenty of antiseptic and pulled the edges of the wound together with butterfly strips. After a few hours, David seemed little the worse and resumed his watches.

Conditions were miserable. The boat interior was wet and chilly, and we were usually on deck several hours a day shifting the jib on and off the whisker pole, or reefing the mainsail. Finally, we devised a method of rigging two whisker poles at the same time so that it alleviated some work on the foredeck. As we approached the Crozet Islands, the boat was overwhelmed by a huge wave that literally buried the vessel.

David's scalp wound, received in the South Indian Ocean; he was struck by the staysail boom.

The cabin darkened for a moment and seawater poured in through the slides of the main hatch. Some equipment on deck was broken or washed away, but for the time being, the ocean had spent itself and after that, the weather improved.

Three weeks after leaving Cape Town for the second time, we approached Kerguelen. The coast was covered by a thick fog. We got good radar contact and headed down the coast for the French research station at Port aux Français. As the long sub-Antarctic twilight faded, the fog lifted to expose the stark, snow-covered mountains of Kerguelen. By morning we were near the base. The weather turned sunny and a call on the VHF radio brought out an inflatable to guide us to an anchorage that was free of kelp. The station is home to about 100 people, all scientists and support personnel. They were very hospitable, and we were assigned a guide, a Scottish scientist based in Australia. We were told only one or two yachts sail to Kerguelen every year. We had a shower, did some laundry, and met the station chief, who extracted a stiff fee for our visit. In return, we ate wonderfully in the base canteen. We found the post office, which was apparently famous throughout the world to collectors who mail envelopes there so that they can be returned with the rare Kerguelen stamp and frank. To my surprise, they wanted to borrow *Fiona*'s rubber stamp, so some lucky collectors would get a bonus—all the envelopes awaiting the next supply ship would carry our stamp as well as the Kerguelen frank. Several years later, Bob spotted one of these envelopes with the both the Kerguelen frank and the *Fiona* stamp for sale on eBay, and he bought it for me as a souvenir.

We took a walk along the beach to inspect the many elephant seals and king penguins and let them inspect us. We bummed some fresh veggies off the chef, got our jerry jugs refilled with diesel, and prepared to leave. By late afternoon we weighed anchor so that we would be clear of the coast by nightfall. The meteorological office gave us a five-page forecast of westerly winds, but we had easterly winds for 12 hours. Our destination was Wellington, New Zealand. We stayed near 49° S latitude for over 1,000 miles, a region of the Roaring Forties characterized in a recent book as "Godforsaken." In fact, the weather wasn't too bad—it was better than the stretch of ocean near South Africa that we had experienced, though we had our share of gear failures, of course, mostly chafed lines and a few stainless fittings that cracked.

Each day we checked in with ham operators in South Africa or Australia, and each week we called Brenda and Sue on the Iridium satellite phone. Watch succeeded watch; on average, we spent a couple of hours each day on deck, reefing or shifting sails. We cooked and baked bread, and every few days we opened fresh *Guardian Weeklies* from the stack my daughter Brenda had accumulated for us. The time passed quickly. Once a week when the weather wasn't too bad, we had a movie show, either black and white on my old 5" TV, or in color on Bob's laptop. We tried to educate young David to appreciate the classic movies, such as *Lawrence of Arabia*, *Casablanca*, and *The Maltese Falcon*. Nearly two weeks after leaving Kerguelen, we were 800 miles south of Cape Leeuwin, one of the famous capes rounded by the square riggers. They usually passed the cape closer than we did, as they favored latitude 40° S. We saw the solar eclipse on December 4th. A few days later, in the middle of the night, the Aries self-steerer failed, due to a structural collapse of the support assembly. We had to steer by hand most of the time, a tedious and chilly experience. As Hobart was a thousand miles closer than Wellington, we decided to switch our destination to Tasmania. We only had a one-in-a-million chart of Tasmania, but we managed to contact the Royal Yacht Club of Tasmania on the radio and got a promise of help as we got closer.

Our last night at sea produced the heaviest weather we had experienced since leaving Kerguelen, full storm conditions. We sailed up the Derwent River in the morning and a member of the club, John, paralleled us in a car and guided us on the VHF radio to a slip he had arranged right in downtown Hobart.

Two days after we arrived, Bob's partner, Sue, flew in via New Zealand. She brought with her some new DVDs for our weekly movie show and spare parts sent by 'Red,' our "ship's wife" back in Bellport. A couple of days later, David's sister, Lindsay, flew into Hobart. We got our repairs organized and Helen Franklin in England shipped in spare parts for the Aries via DHL.

Hobart proved to be a great stop-over. The city itself had a population of about 45,000. It was founded as a prison colony in the early nineteenth century, and there were many very fine examples of Victorian architecture still remaining. Several downtown blocks were now a pedestrian precinct with malls and outdoor restaurants. As we were there during the Christmas holiday season, we experienced many festive activities, such as a food-tasting fair on one of the harbor piers. Despite it being Christmas, we were in the Southern Hemisphere—summer started a week after we arrived.

The five of us took a tour of the Tahune Forest, a surviving bit of original rain forest on the west coast of Tasmania. On the way there, the countryside reminded me of England. The lower level of the forest was full of huge, impressive ferns. The upper level canopy could be viewed by means of an "Air Walk," which in one spot was cantilevered out 60 feet over the trees. The sight of these massive, tall Huan pine trees with the wild river beyond was unforgettable. The tour ended with an ascent of the 4,000- foot Mount Wellington, which overlooks Hobart and Storm Bay.

I enjoyed pottering round the city. When I went for a beard trim, I found the barber was quite an accomplished amateur artist. I bought a painting of a cricket match right off the wall of his shop. I found several used-book stores to browse in, and visited the many museums and art galleries. The old prison church, built by convict labor, was fascinating. The bricks were handmade by the prisoners, and on many their thumb prints were still visible, left there when the bricks were pressed from the mold. The tiny, dark cells for solitary confinement were built directly under the pews, presumably so the unfortunate inmate could hear the service in a muffled kind of way. It was an interesting aspect of the Victorian psyche that, by 1840, even the Governor said the cells were not fit for animals, let alone humans. The church was converted to a courthouse and used until the 1970's, which is why it survived. The original Victorian prison—with cells, workshops and treadmill—was knocked down as late as the 1960s, sadly enough. It was huge—the 20-foot high wall covered two city blocks, and held 1,500 prisoners.

David and Lindsey rented a car for island sightseeing over Christmas. While they were away, Sue, Bob and I took another organized tour to see Field Mountain and a game farm. On the mountain, we saw wallabies in the wild, and at the game farm, we inspected Tasmanian Devils, wombats, Koala bears and kangaroos, the latter two of which are not native to Tasmania. The other animals were mostly orphans of road-killed parents and would be released when they were older. The "Devil" was so named because they are nocturnal and their howls at night convinced the original settlers, who could find no source, that the countryside was haunted by devils. They are scavengers and are not a danger to humans unless you stick your hand in their hole.

In Hobart, I had curry almost every night at one of the numerous Indian restaurants. I often ate lunch in a pub, accompanied by a glass of good but inexpensive Australian Chardonnay. I saw a couple of movies, and most days I spent an hour checking e-mail at a friendly internet café. It all seemed very civilized, after our few weeks in the Roaring Forties.

On Christmas Day, we moved the boat to the Royal Yacht Club of Tasmania, about a mile out of town, as our slip at the downtown pier was needed by early arrivals in the annual Sydney-to-Hobart Race. I usually picked a different route for the walk into town from the club each day through the suburbs of the city. Generally speaking, the houses were small, often with corrugated tin roofs, and the ramble was great fun. One day Sue, Bob, and I went on a massive shopping spree at the local supermarket and packed enough food in the boat to get us to Brazil, which would be our next chance to restock.

An old cruising friend, Pauline Chapman, noticed while checking the *Fiona* website that I had fetched up in Hobart and she contacted a friend of hers who lived nearby. He arranged to pick up David and I for lunch at his farm on New Year's Eve. He farmed alpacas, a very superior-looking animal. We had a very interesting stay and a pleasant meal with him and his wife before he dropped us back at the boat in time for the evening's festivities.

I also had a date that afternoon with the Australian Quarantine Service, which had sealed all our canned meat when we arrived. They checked the seals and gave us permission to leave the next day. When it dawned, Sue started her long trek back to New York at 4 am and we cleared for Stanley in the Falkland Islands just before 10 am. The controller manning the harbor radio did not know where Stanley was and seemed mildly surprised at our destination.

To Cape Horn

An enthusiastic member of the local yacht club insisted that we visit Auckland Island, lying about 300 nm south of New Zealand at 51° S. He said it was on the way, it was unique, and he even gave us photocopies of detailed charts. It was a World Heritage Site and prior permission was needed for a visit, so we decided to sail by without landing. It took us a week to get there. We arrived at the south coast just as dawn was breaking and were greeted by thousands of seabirds that wheeled and screamed overhead. It appeared to be typical sub-Antarctica tundra, with no trees and no high mountains. Our friend had pressed us to visit a particularly scenic bay on the east side, but it was beset by turbulent winds and choppy seas. I was not keen to get too close to shore, but we got within a quarter mile. The chart copy we had was dated 1883, and it was entirely likely that things had changed since then. We took the mandatory photos and hung a right. Ahead lay Cape Horn and Stanley, 5,000 nm downwind in the Furious Fifties.

On January 12th, we crossed the international date line. It was a Sunday, so we had two of them—the first when ship's time was 12 hours ahead of Greenwich, and the second when we were 12 hours behind. The next day the weather deteriorated, and eventually we had

to hove-to, just holding our position until the storm blew itself out. Unfortunately, a heavy wave broke onto the boat and burst the stay-sail, which was sheeted to windward. This was a very useful sail for windy conditions, so we carried it below to repair it with the old Reads sewing machine I keep on board. We suspended watches and all worked full-time to stitch two patches on the T-shaped tear. One person was needed just to stop the machine from sliding about as *Fiona* rolled furiously in the storm. We had the job done in about five hours and we were able to set the sail again.

David and Eric man the sewing machine to repair a sail, South Indian Ocean

A few days later, we entered a region of very high humidity and the boat was plagued by heavy condensation. Water dripped copiously off the bulkheads and hatches. It played havoc with the electronics, most of which we were able to dry out, but the radar didn't work again. Perhaps the condensation was associated with the presence of icebergs, which also appeared about this time. They were huge, and probably originated at the Ross Ice Shelf that lay a thousand miles to our south. Even though we kept a good look-out, it was a little scary at night, as we were without radar. We hoped one of these 'bergs would not get in the way.

After a few days we failed to see any more, but then came a period of intense squalls with wind shifts and cold rain. At one time when Bob was on watch, he counted six, scattered about from horizon to horizon. Even without the transient effect of the squalls, we were finding the weather down in the Fifties was never constant for long. There were frequent shifts of wind direction and speed which had us on deck several times a day, reefing or jibing so that we could hold the course. While we were furling the jib on January 23rd, we noticed the Profurl was not working correctly. Inspection revealed that the lower drum mechanism had split into two pieces. The upper piece carried the drum, and the lower piece carried the bearing, which was visible as the parts separated. I called the Profurl company on the Iridium satellite phone for advice, but they were pessimistic; the unit could only be repaired at a service center, they said.

We winched David to the masthead so he could relocate the stop and thus limit movement of the foils, and this enabled us to use the jib in light winds. A day later the wind increased to gale force, and we reached under reefed staysail and reefed main. At the height of the storm, I was working in the cockpit when I noticed a pod of pilot whales surfing through the waves next to the boat. They seemed to be enjoying the storm; their shiny black skin glowed.

It was still blowing hard when David reported the toilet in the forward head had blocked up. As we pitched and rolled, I pulled the plumbing to pieces looking for the stoppage. This is when you find out if you are really cut out to enjoy ocean cruising. January 26th was David's birthday. I baked a cake to have with our happy hour rum. As it lay on the counter awaiting the addition of a few candles, a large wave dolloped on the main hatch and sea-water spurted under the slides, splashing part of the cake. We took this as a hint that Father Neptune wanted some, so we cut a soggy slice and tossed it over the side as a peace offering. We were running under reefed main and boomed-out jib, and the wind was hovering between 45 and 55 knots (relative). Victor the Vane seemed to be handling the wheel quite competently; Bob was on watch and came into the cabin in foul weather gear for his rum and slice of cake. Curiously enough, after that we had an unusual spell of very calm weather. For six days we never even reefed the mainsail. Can it be that there is something in the old sailor's superstitions?

Our daily mileage dropped, and we were frustrated, especially as we were below 54° S, where the wind is supposed to blow all the time. Eventually, near 100° W, the wind came back and our daily rate picked up dramatically. Cape Horn was now a little more than a thousand miles away. One day the pressure fell by 17 mb in 12 hours, and when it bottomed out we got a gale. About midnight, a steering line on Victor chafed through and we all spent a couple of hours on deck repairing it. When we finally got back in the cabin out of the noise and spray, we had a stiff tot of rum. Two nights later we again had gale force winds and we spent two hours on deck reefing and shifting sails. More rum!

Bob and David, celebrating David's 23rd birthday, Southern Indian Ocean, 2002. The curtains are drawn because the ports have deadlights mounted.

We arrived in the vicinity of Cape Horn as dawn was breaking on a rainy, misty day. The wind was piping up to 30 knots from the north. Just as I cracked the old joke to David and Bob, "There's Cape Stiff, if you're lucky you won't see it again," things began to go wrong. We were working forward to clear a fouled halyard when I noticed Victor's vane seemed rather wobbly. Walking over to the stern for a look, I saw that the support strut had broken again. This was the same failure that forced us into Hobart, but this time it was the starboard strut. I had replaced both struts the previous winter before we left because they were worn, so clearly the manufacturer had a quality control problem.

Eric on Fiona *off Cape Horn*

Unfortunately, we would have to hand-steer until we got to Stanley, 400 nm away. Shortly after Victor's demise, the starboard jib sheet parted with a bang. We passed about three miles south of the Horn and gave the Chilean navy people a call on the radio. After recording details of the boat and voyage, they wished us luck. The Cape was only intermittently visible in the driving rain and fog; I think they were being more than just polite.

Later that day the wind picked up to about 50 knots, so we furled the mainsail, and as we adjusted the boom, the topping lift broke, permitting the boom to fall with a crash. David was lucky to escape being brained. As it was, the force bent a stanchion. We ran at over 6 knots with just a small spitfire jib of only about 40 square feet hanked on the forestay. Despite all our problems, there was one good thing: we picked up a three-knot current that whisked *Fiona* past the Horn and Staten Island and ejected us into the Atlantic Ocean like a cork out of a champagne bottle. We made it to Stanley three days later, arriving in the late afternoon of Valentine's Day, 46 days after leaving Hobart.

The Falklands and South Georgia Island

You may recall at the start of this chapter that one objective of the cruise was to duplicate a typical clipper ship voyage around the world. Putting into Stanley needing repairs after rounding the Horn was very typical. In fact, there are a number of hulks of old square-riggers still littering the harbor that made it to Stanley but were too battered ever to leave. That was not to be our fate, as we soon got our repairs in hand, but other similarities are worth a comment.

I cannot properly compare our experiences as sailors with those of the old salts that manned the clippers. Theirs was a brutal existence, man-hauling heavy ropes and gear on a ship that weighed several thousand tons. Frequently, lives were lost on a rounding of the Horn, often by falling from the rigging as they worked as much as a hundred feet above the pitching deck. Though for every watch we donned our foul weather gear and sea boots, once we were soaked by a wave, or our boots were full of seawater, we were just as wet and cold as they were. Below, the boat was damp from leaks and condensation, which made me appreciate a remark often seen in the memoirs of old seamen—namely that they went to sleep "all standing," that is, in their wet clothes. The continuous exposure to salt water means that the minor cuts on one's hands never heal. You accept the bruises and bangs inflicted as the boat rolls unexpectedly as normal. Although we were not working a hundred feet in the air like the sailors of centuries ago, it was often pitch dark and slippery as we worked on deck to reef or furl a sail at the onset of a gale.

And there was no let-up. We had to stand watch after watch, day after day, week after week. There were frequent gear failures that had to be dealt with immediately with all of us on deck, regardless of who was on watch. When we got the chance, we slept and ate, and got through one day at a time. We had one advantage the seamen of old did not enjoy—we knew where we were. They depended on scuttlebutt, usually passed on by the cook. We plotted our position every day and watched it creep slowly across the chart of the featureless South Pacific Ocean. One question I had, however, was how on earth did they manage without flashlights in the old days? We all worked at night with our small Maglites, often clenched between our teeth.

Stanley itself had changed considerably since I was last there in 1992, a reflection of the affluence brought by selling licenses to foreign companies to fish their waters. Quite a modern-looking suburbia was growing on the east side of the town. One development we really came to appreciate was a new Seamen's Centre built adjacent to the floating dock where we tied up the boat. It provided toilets, showers, laundry, e-mail, a snack bar, and many home comforts for visiting fishermen. I was a little hesitant at first that we dilettante yachtsman would be able to use it, but they treated us as real seamen. It functioned under the auspices of the U.K.-based Royal National Mission to Seamen, who described themselves as Christians with their sleeves rolled up, and that seemed apt.

The Globe Tavern, Port Stanley, South Georgia

The social center of Stanley was still the Globe Tavern. David and Bob soon discovered it, along with its attractive barmaids. We mostly ate our lunches at the Seamen's Centre but we tried just about every eatery in the place for our suppers during our one-week stay. These ranged from the up-market Upland Goose hotel, to a fish and chip shop on wheels. It was a pleasant 30-minute walk along the shore into town, unless it was raining, which it did most days. I talked to the administrator of South Georgia, who is based in Stanley, and he told me that plans were under way to remove most of the old whaling station at Grytviken because of asbestos contamination. I also talked to the Fisheries Department people about the ice conditions for our trip. They predicted plenty. For openers, there was a 35-mile-long iceberg aground off the northwest of South Georgia. For this reason, combined with our lack of radar, we decided to skip a visit to the South Orkney Islands as originally planned, and go directly to South Georgia.

We were a little pushed for time anyway. When I talked about our trip to the British Antarctic Survey, which has a summer base at King Edward Point, they suggested taking the mail, as few ships call there. The post office put together a 20-pound bag of accumulated mail in a sack with the imposing label "Royal Mail." We refueled, restocked our fruit and veggies, and we left a week after we arrived.

At first the wind was fairly light, and then it died altogether, and for about a day we ran the engine. With the lack of wind, the fog descended on us. It was a little scary peering ahead, while hoping an iceberg would not emerge out of the gloom. The visibility dropped to a hundred yards or so. I had looked at our defunct radar when we were tied up in Stanley, and found that the problem seemed to be a defective integrated circuit chip, which was impossible to fix without a direct replacement.

The Seaman's Center in Port Stanley, South Georgia

When the wind came back, the fog dispersed and within a few hours we found ourselves surrounded by icebergs. We sailed through them for over a hundred miles. They came in all shapes and sizes, but many were flat, suggesting they had broken away from an ice shelf. We maintained a constant cockpit look-out, and at night we slowed the boat down by reefing the mainsail. The big 'bergs were easy to spot, at least in daylight, so the real danger was the small pieces, called "growlers," which had broken off the big ones; though they weighed many tons, they showed little surface above the sea. As we sailed past the 'bergs, seals popped their heads out of the water to get a look at us. Dolphins frequently gamboled across our bow; the vicinity of the ice must have been rich in fish.

Large iceberg several miles in extent in the Southern Ocean. Because it is flat it must have broken off a shelf.

149

For the last night of that leg we sailed along the coast of South Georgia, invisible in the inky night. We set a double-reefed main to both slow us down and to allow us to arrive off the land at daybreak. As the sky lightened, the fantastic, jagged black and white outline of South Georgia appeared before our eyes. As the sun rose, the white mountain peaks were bathed in pink. We tied up temporarily at the government jetty at King Edward Point. The resident Fishery Department Officer, who was also customs, immigration, magistrate officer, and the wearer of many other hats, briefed us on the current conditions and the care we had to take to avoid damaging the environment. The old Norwegian whaling station at Grytviken, across the bay, was then in such dangerous shape that it was off limits. The museum, church, and the whaler's cemetery were still open, however.

Norwegian church at the Grytviken whaling station

After a shower and a cup of tea at the resident's apartment (which, by the way, must have one of the most spectacular vistas in the world through a picture window), we motored across to Grytviken and tied up to the rotting dock. This was the chance to renew my friendship with Pauline and Tim Carr; the Carrs still ran the museum as they did when I stopped by in 1999.

The next day we walked to the cemetery that holds the grave of Sir Ernest Shackleton. Numerous fur seals barked at us as we passed. Then we hiked a few miles to see the dammed lake above Grytviken, built by the whalers to get hydroelectricity. After that, we walked on to the site of a helicopter wreck, a victim of the fighting when the Argentineans invaded in 1982. In the evening, we staged a movie using a DVD on Bob's laptop—*It's a Mad, Mad, Mad, Mad World.* The next day we trudged past hundreds more fur seals to King Edward Point and the Shackleton memorial, erected by his shipmates when he died in Grytviken in 1922. We were just in time to see the Royal Navy patrol boat *Leed's Castle* tie up, carrying the Governor of the Falkland Islands on an inspection tour. The next morning, he stopped by the boat for a few minutes to chat. I think he made the visit because almost any decision about the future of the old whaling factories at Grytviken and other sites along the coast will cost big bucks.

Another sailboat tied up next to us, carrying a group of mountaineers who planned to climb the formidable peaks for the next month. We had quite a party on board their boat that evening. We left the next morning and powered over to Stromness. This was where Shackleton wound up at the end of the epic journey over the mountains and glaciers of South Georgia after his whaleboat, *James Caird*, had made a landfall on the west side of the island in 1916. We did not land, as the dangerous condition of the dock and buildings has caused the authorities to put it off limits to visitors. We could see the manager's house where the three men first made contact with civilization again after two years, and we saw the stream they splashed down on their way out of the mountains. After a brief look at the remains of the whaling station at Leith, we put out to sea. Our destination was tropical Brazil.

Sir Ernest Shackleton's grave, Grytviken, South Georgia

Destination: The Tropics!

Once clear of the coast we again encountered the field of icebergs that had plagued us on the way down. There was no moon, and as night fell we decided to lie a-hull for the night—that is, take the sails down and drift for the night. The wind was blowing up to gale force.

Just after Bob came on watch at 10 pm he was horrified to see a growler close to the bow on the port side. Bob's growler was about the same size as *Fiona* but, of course, weighed much more, as most of its mass was under water. He gave me a call to start the engine, and just as I came on deck we grazed the thing, but by then the engine was running and we backed away without damage. I shall not easily forget the sight of its tortured outline in the beam of our flashlights as the storm tossed spray over it and it faded from view into the darkness.

When the sky lightened in the morning we counted 13 large icebergs in sight. We set sail and zigzagged through the field all that day and again lay a-hull the following night. By the next day the iceberg count had thinned, although we still spotted a few. But it seemed safe enough to sail through the night with a look-out in the cockpit. The starlight gave just enough visibility to see an obstruction ahead.

The next day we were clear of the ice, but by then the clouds rolled in and the wind increased to strong gale force on the nose. As we got into the Roaring Forties, the wind strengthened to 50 knots, but that is an estimate based on the sea surface condition—the wind had blown away our anemometer and its masthead mounting bracket. Mother Nature was making us fight to leave the Antarctic and get to the tropics.

We slowly worked our way north to the Horse Latitudes, a band of variable weather lying above 39° S, allegedly so-named because the old clippers had to abandon their cargos of horses and dump them in the sea when they ran out of fresh water. "Variable" is certainly the right word. On the 16th of March, we enjoyed happy hour in the cockpit for the first time in months. A few hours later, just after midnight on the 17th, we had to fight to furl the reefed mainsail in a wind that increased to over 60 knots and was shrieking across a foaming sea. But by late in the day, we were jogging over a calm sea under a full moon, listening to President Bush on shortwave as he announced the attack on Iraq.

The weather continued to be fluky with head winds, calms, and occasionally a nice reach. But it was much warmer. On the 18th, we saw some flying fish. The next day we dropped the mainsail in a calm period to make a minor repair and decided to take a swim while the boat was stationary. The water was wonderful. Then, we slowly fought our way towards Santos, also bucking the strong current that flows south from the equator. It took us three weeks to make good the 1,860 nm distance from South Georgia. We had logged 2,448 nm to do it.

Celebrating Happy Hour: Bob, Eric and David

I had visited Santos 11 years previously when I was sailing home on *Fiona* from Tahiti after Edith had passed away. I had two strong recollections of the place. First was the memory of the luxurious yacht club at which, as a foreign yacht, we got to stay for eight days free. Secondly, I still remembered the bureaucratic nightmare I got involved in because my American crew did not have Brazilian visas. To sort out the mess I had to hire an agent. I was hauled up before an administrative judge and fined $30 for illegally bringing aliens into Brazil. I pleaded that failure of the ship's transmitter had forced me into Santos for repairs. The judge asked to see a letter from a repair shop before I could leave. The agent connived with a technician to get the letter, which cost me $200 and he did not even bother to fix the radio.

This time I was ready. Bob and David had got their visas from the consulate in New York before we left. After we had tied up at the yacht club, which seemed little changed, I took a bus into the center of Santos to start the dreary round of official approvals needed to enter the country by boat. At Customs, after a couple hours, I was told that the only man who knew the correct procedures was away that day and I should return in the morning. I still had time to make it to Immigration before dark.

I took a taxi along the miles of decaying waterfront warehouses to the station of the Federal Police, which deal with matters of immigration. It was a dingy office. Three or four fellows in black uniforms with side arms were lounging about, mostly watching a very loud TV. I gave my little pile of papers to a balding man with a mustache at a desk. He riffled through them and seized the passports. "Visas?" he asked. I pointed to the large stamps in the passports. He shook his head and scowled. He said something I didn't catch over the noise of the TV and put a beefy finger on the date—May, 2002, just before we left.

I finally got the message that they were only good for 90 days. I explained we had been in the Southern Ocean and Antarctica for the past few months, areas notably deficient in Brazilian Consulates, and that we had got them when we could. We had paid the $45 fee, wasn't that the important thing? By this time, the other fellows had smelled some fun and gathered round the desk. There was a long conversation in incomprehensible Portuguese. Finally, a woman was produced from a back room who spoke a little English. She told me the visas were no good, and Bob and David would have to leave Brazil immediately. I was exempted because I showed them my British passport. I put my case again that they had visas. But she was adamant. "Go to Argentina," she said. "Visas can only be issued outside the country." That didn't seem like good idea, as Argentina lay well to our south. I was shown the door and told to come back in the morning, and told that in the meanwhile, Bob and David must not leave the boat.

I returned to the Yacht Club feeling disgusted. A few weeks earlier I had been battling 'bergs, and now I was battling bureaucrats. I think I preferred the 'bergs. When I got to the boat, I found that Sue had flown in from New York and that she and Bob had booked themselves into a nice hotel on the beach. It didn't seem like a good time to tell him to stay on the boat. I poured a stiff Mount Gay rum instead.

Later, one of the club security guards came by to say they had a fax from the Feds and I was to meet them at 8 am next morning. The next day, I also discovered the fax had instructed the club not to let Bob and David off the premises, but fortunately, nobody paid any attention. I guess the Brazilians are used to their overblown officialdom.

Before Bob and Sue and David retired to the beach we discussed strategy. Just in case we were forced out, we decided that the three of them would go to a supermarket in the morning and restock the boat while I was at police (I nearly typed "Gestapo") headquarters. I got up bright and early, as I had no idea how bad the morning rush would be. In fact, it was light at that hour and I arrived back at the same dingy office by 7:20 am. The night shift was just getting ready to clock out. The captain spoke a little English, so I explained that I had just arrived from Antarctica on a yacht and that yesterday, I had been told to come back because the visas were dated. "Antarctica," he mused. "Show me the papers." He looked at the clearance manifest from South Georgia to Santos. "It's no problem," he said, and promptly made out and stamped the form I needed for the Port Captain's office. I grabbed it, thanked him, and scooted out before my nemesis showed up at 8 am. I completed the clearing-in procedures, got my beard trimmed, and returned to the club.

David, Bob and Sue had done the shopping and loaded the food aboard *Fiona*. One of the uncooperative policemen from the dingy office was standing on the dock watching, but he said nothing. For the next couple of days, we did boat maintenance in the mornings and explored the region in the afternoons. I was lucky enough to run into a Brazilian yachtsman, Dancini, who spoke good English. He helped me get repairs done that required local experts. He took the jib furler to a rigger and came back a few days later with it rebuilt. David took the bus for a long weekend in Rio de Janeiro.

One evening on the way back to the boat from supper, I noticed a circus had pitched its tent in a large lot, and the show was due to start in 20 minutes. So I treated myself to a night at the Circus Stangowich, which had one ring, two clowns, some dancing horses, and a rather moth-eaten camel. The Brazilian children loved it. On Sunday afternoon, I walked over to the beautiful beach on the seaward side of Santos in a very upmarket area called Gonzaga. The seafront consisted of a park behind the beach and then a wide boulevard in front of tall apartment blocks. In the park, local artists exhibited their paintings, and one showed an Arabian scene with camels. I bought it as a reminder of my night at the circus.

Soon it was time to go. David returned from Rio, suitably exhausted, and Sue flew home. On our last evening, Dancini took us to a small factory belonging to a friend of his that made surfboards. David knew a bargain when he saw one and bought a nine-foot board on the spot.

I steeled myself and went into Santos to repeat the clearance procedure so that we could leave. Unfortunately, my cooperative captain was not on duty at the Federal Police office and my documents were heavily annotated to state the crew must not leave the boat in Brazil, thus making sure I had problems in the future at other ports. Our first stop was the beautiful cruising area near Ilha Grande; it took us a little over a day to get there under power. We anchored in a pretty bay with a bar on the beach, and cooked some Brazilian sausages after a few beers at the bar. Dancini had given me a cruising guide to the Brazilian coast that mentioned another anchorage not far away, which had access to a beach on the seaward side with good surfing. Naturally, David had to try his new toy and so the next day that is where we went. We took a jungle path over a hill and emerged on the beach that had huge waves rolling in.

After a while, Bob and I walked back to a small restaurant and had a few beers while we absorbed the local color. Rio was only about 60 miles away and several ferries had disgorged a bevy of bikini-clad beauties who frolicked in the water. It was all quite a change from our ocean cruising regimen.

During the night it poured, the first rain we had seen in a while. The next morning, we powered over to a charming fishing village and anchored. There were no vehicles in the village, and we tried to do e-mail without much success. After lunch, we left for the long haul north. Dancini's guide mentioned that the coast in this region was notoriously windless, and we found this to be true. After using the engine for two days, I decided to refuel at a city a couple of hundred miles up the coast from Rio called Vitória. The guide mentioned that the fuel dock at the local yacht club was quite shallow. I wanted to sneak in and refuel without attracting the attention of the Port Captain who might look askance at our clearance papers from Santos. Fortunately, as we got close we found a Swedish cruising yacht anchored near the club who was also refueling by using his dinghy to transport jerry jugs. The captain very kindly offered to take me in, and while Bob and David circled outside, I went in with the Swede and sounded out the depths. We could just fit. I went back to the boat and we cautiously crept up to the fuel dock with only one minor bump from the keel on a launching ramp and tied up. Within 20 minutes we had a full load of diesel and we were away.

It took us eight days from Vitória to make the leg of slightly over a thousand miles to Cabedelo, located at Cabo Branco, the easternmost tip of the South American continent. Although we were well inside the region of southeast trade winds, they did not materialize and we sailed with light winds or powered in the calm spells. On the way we celebrated my 39th birthday—again!

We arrived a couple of hours after nightfall on Good Friday. Our guidebook recommended anchoring just south of the main wharf if arriving at night and proceeding up the Paraiba River to the yachties' hangout at Jacare in daylight. We anchored in the designated spot and were just enjoying a well-earned rum and apple juice, when a huge car ferry emerged out of the gloom and passed us with a few feet to spare, the captain hooting his displeasure as he left us rocking in his wake. It seemed like a good idea to move a half-mile further down the river. Later, we discovered the ferry service had been instituted since the guide was published.

In the morning, we negotiated the river sandbars and dropped anchor near several other yachts at a marina that was famous in cruising circles. It was run by an expat Englishman called Brian. One reason it was famous is that the local officials are fairly relaxed. Considering it was a holiday weekend, I decided it would be unkind to burden them with extra paperwork so we did not check in at all. The day after Easter Monday, we quietly glided down the river and left for the offshore island of Fernando de Noronha.

Talk about a small world—while we were at Jacare we had a cup of coffee on an American yacht belonging to a single-hander called Alec. He mulled over the name *Fiona* and said it rang a bell. Finally, we discovered he had known Barbara and John Knight in St. John, USVI for years. Edith and I had made our first transatlantic crossing as crew for John aboard *Arvin Court II*.

Just south of Brian's marina were a number of bars and restaurants that were very popular with the locals. This holiday weekend they were very busy, and the whole area throbbed with Brazilian music. One evening there was a dance with live bands that changed every hour as they exhausted themselves, such was the energy they put into it. We bought tickets and jostled our way in. On the way to the dance floor we were frisked for weapons. Ah, Brazil!

Fernando de Noronha had a special significance for us. We left this island on August 13th, 2002, for Cape Town. Thus, we completed a circumnavigation, albeit in the southern hemisphere, when we returned on April 24th, 2003. There were two other yachts at anchor, and so we invited the crews over for a party to celebrate the evening after we arrived. The captain of one boat, a Swiss, brought over an imaginatively decorated bottle of champagne titled "The Jules Verne Trophy—Round the World in Eight Months."

"Jules Verne Trophy," given by the captain of another boat after Fiona *had completed a circumnavigation*

Later, we all adjourned to Elda's restaurant overlooking the harbor for supper. Most of the die-hards then went on to a dance in the village, but I must confess I took the dinghy back to *Fiona* and fell fast asleep. We did a little maintenance and boat clean-up, and on two afternoons David surfed with his new board. We left after three days for the final leg, with the original crew, across the equator to Barbados. A complete circumnavigation would not be officially completed until we crossed the equator again a couple of hundred miles north of Fernando de Noronha.

The leg to Barbados had two distinct parts. The first, from Fernando de Noronha to about 3° N, was across the equator through the doldrums. The wind was fickle and light, and the current was often against us. There were frequent squalls, some with strong wind gusts, and heavy rain. This was frustrating sailing. Then we ran into the northeast trade winds, and they were steady and strong. We tied two reefs in the mainsail and flew. Victor the Vane handled the steering as we made tremendous time to the island. The speed over the bottom shown on the GPS was often over 8 knots, due to the boost from the Brazilian Equatorial Current.

We sailed the last thousand miles in six days—great sailing for an old cruising boat. We arrived about 11 pm local time and anchored in Carlisle Bay, Bridgetown. We cleared customs and immigration in the morning, hassle-free compared to Brazil.

As we stepped ashore David spotted his father, who had flown in the day before. Bob and David planned to leave *Fiona* in Barbados after completing their Southern Ocean circumnavigation. Before he left, Bob trolled the logbook for some unusual statistics of the cruise to that point:

Days at sea:	184
Days in port:	72
Total days:	256
Total mileage logged:	21,828 nm
Average:	119 nm/day
Number of times mainsail was reefed:	54
Number of times staysail was reefed:	4
Number of times spitfire jib rigged:	4
Total time under power:	492 hrs (20.5 days)
Max continuous run:	62 hrs
Total fuel added:	
Diesel:	495 gal
Propane:	86 lbs
Lowest pressure recorded:	981 mbar (Feb 7th, 2003)
Number of times we replaced steering lines on the Aries:	15
Number of ships logged:	Approx 78
Number of icebergs logged:	127
Number of icebergs hit:	1

The Caribbean

I flew home from Barbados for a couple of weeks, mainly to partici-pate in the annual vintage Bentley meet. When I returned, I brought back two duffel bags packed with spares, including the radar, depth finder, newly-machined support tube for the Aries self-steerer, and a new lower unit for the jib furler. American Airlines was nice enough not to charge for excess baggage.

I had left *Fiona* at a very odd marina called Port St. Charles, which consisted of luxury condos costing half a million dollars and up, with slips for the owners' yachts. The marina was a small addition to the de-velopment, but unfortunately, the builders apparently ran out of mon-ey before they completed the toilets, showers, and any social ameni-ties such as a bar. It was like living on a film set.

The character of the cruise changed radically after I returned to Bar-bados in early June. No more long hauls across thousands of miles of open ocean. What I envisaged were leisurely sails in the islands of the Caribbean, Bermuda, and the coast of Maine. The longest legs would be Puerto Rico to Bermuda, and Bermuda to Maine, each about 800 nm. It did not quite work out that way.

The day after I got back, I moved the boat to Carlisle Bay near Bridg-etown, completed a few repairs and waited for the new crew, Stella, to fly in. I had not been able to persuade anyone else to sign on for the last leg. But while sinking a Heineken at the bar on the beach, I got talking to an Australian, Andrew, who was taking a scuba diving course. He decided to meet me a little later in Puerto Rico for the leg to Maine.

Stella was a young English woman I had met in Bermuda a few years before and she had kept in touch, as she wanted to taste the cruising life. As it turned out, she didn't enjoy it that much, which might have been related to the fact that the refrigerator would not work. In the 90° F heat this was a serious problem. It had to be fixed—I was expect-ing my daughter Brenda and her husband to spend a week on the boat when we got the Virgin Islands. When Stella showed up, we lugged the refrigerator out of the galley, into the dinghy, and took it to a repair shop. Fruitlessly, as it turned out. It still didn't work.

One day we took a bus along the winding lanes of the Barbados back country to an old slave plantation that had been restored for the tourists. The bus, on the way home, filled up with chattering school children and the driver turned up the volume of the rock music on the radio. He drove faster and faster, screeching the old bus round the tight bends. Suddenly he stopped at a gas station. The driver dashed inside for a bottle, which I assumed was to drink. Wrong—it was brake fluid! He poured the fluid down a hole in the dash, pumped vigorously on the pedal for a couple of minutes and, satisfied with the pedal pressure, resumed his mad ride to the center of Bridgetown.

About a week after Stella joined the boat, we sailed overnight to Union Island in the Grenadines. As we were checking in with the customs and immigration officials at the airport, a yachtie came up to me and said, "Eric, remember me?" I confessed to a senior moment. "Rich and Nancy," he replied. "We met at the marina in Portland, oh, about four years ago." It slowly came back to me. I had been on the way to Maine after the cruise to Antarctica in 1999. Such is the small world of the cruising fraternity. We agreed to meet at a bar on the shore for a sundowner, but we never made it. Why? Because about an hour before our rendezvous, we dinghied to a tiny island in the harbor called the "Happy Hour Bar." We had a very acceptable rum punch and then I hauled the inflatable dinghy alongside for the ride to shore. I then discovered the dock was made of conch shells set in concrete.

As Stella and I climbed in, the dinghy rubbed against the shells, which tore a one-inch gash in the rubber. The dinghy began to deflate very quickly. We made a dash to the boat as it settled lower and lower in the water and stepped aboard just as the dinghy sank. Fortunately, one pontoon was still intact and we were able to hook up a halyard just as the outboard motor was about to disappear under the waves. Rich and Nancy finally came looking for us, only to find me gluing a patch on the remains and muttering about idiots and conch shells. We had our sundowner on *Fiona*—in fact, we had several.

From there we sailed to Mayreau, a small island that was a favorite anchorage of Edith's and mine when we cruised the Caribbean aboard *Iona* in the late 1960s. Progress had come to Mayreau—they now had a central generator and the village had sprouted poles festooned with street lights and electric distribution wires. We climbed to the top of the hill for a breathtaking view of the islets and reefs forming Tobago Cays lying to the east, as they were to be our next stop.

Unfortunately, the next day it was very windy as we edged our way through the shallows and dropped the hook in company with about 20 other boats behind Horseshoe Reef. Snorkeling in half-gale winds wasn't much fun and the wind was too strong for us to rig the awning to keep off the sun.

The next day we sailed to Bequia, and discovered Rich and Nancy anchored off the village. We dined with them a couple of times, hiked over to the south shore where there was a very friendly bar, and got our laundry done. The plan was to sail to Martinique next, but fate intervened. As we sailed out of the lee on the west side of St. Vincent, we encountered a notorious wind acceleration zone. Although we only had a reefed jib set, *Fiona* heeled in the gusts. Suddenly, there was a loud bang, I made a quick trip forward to confirm my fear, and yes, the bobstay had snapped, again. It had broken before on the transatlantic leg of the cruise. We had then replaced it with a piece of anchor chain which had seemed thick enough to last the remainder of the trip. When I examined it after this failure, I found deep corrosion on the link attached to the hull at the waterline. The loss of tension on the bobstay caused the bow platform to move up and this, in turn, jammed the jib furler. I could not roll the jib in or out. The flogging sail made a tremendous racket and the slack headstay snapped viciously in the wind gusts. Poor Stella, who did not have much sailing experience, was clearly very frightened, but she managed to steer the boat downwind to keep the tension off the sail while I worked with a chain wrench to slowly roll in the jib, inch by inch.

Then I had to brace the headstay. I also noticed a heavy stainless steel bracket which attached the bow platform to the hull had cracked. Obviously, I was in for some heavy maintenance again. I decided the only practical solution was to sail directly to St. Martin, more than 400 nm to the north. All the facilities I needed could be found there. We set a reefed mainsail and, with an assist from the engine, made the trip in two and a half days. We were both heartily thankful that the hot, refrigerator-less trip was over when we dropped anchor into 10 feet of clear water in Marigot Bay. Kay Pope immediately invited us to dinner at her apartment, preceded by a shower. The next week was mostly devoted to fixing the boat, although every morning we started the day with a delicious breakfast ashore featuring French croissants. We usually picked up a delicious baguette at the same time for our lunch—no one makes baguettes like the French.

I installed a new refrigerator, bobstay, and jib furler. One day, Stella and I powered *Fiona* over to the Dutch side of St. Martin for a visit to the welder. The next day we started to bend on the jib, but the sail caught on a protruding cotter pin and tore. When I went to inspect the offending pin, the boat gave a roll in the wind and I gashed my leg badly on the same pin! Kay ran me over the emergency room of the local hospital where a doctor put in five stitches. Total cost: $23. When I took the sail for repair it cost $40, but after all, the sailmaker put in more stitches.

When the sail was returned we were ready to leave, but Stella had had enough of the continuous maintenance. It certainly had not been the kind of cruise she had hoped for. I was sorry it hadn't worked out. Tension had increased between us, and at our last supper ashore, we wound up having a silly quarrel. The next day Kay ran her to the airport and she left for London via New York, at my expense, of course. Under international law the captain is responsible for making sure any crew member brought into a foreign country also leaves. I sailed the boat single-handed to Tortola in the British Virgin Islands just in time to meet my daughter Brenda and her husband Rich, who were, incidentally, the mistress and master of the yachtfiona.com website. Rich brought a new laptop, as my old one was never the same after the rigors and dampness of Cape Horn. We sailed from Trellis Bay to the beautiful and relatively unspoiled island of Anegada, where we hiked along the sandy beach, stopping for refreshment at convenient small hotels.

From there we sailed to West End, Tortola, and the next day we took the ferry to St. John in the U.S. Virgin Islands. After this brief taste of the U.S., we made the short sail to Great Harbour and the famous Foxy's Bar on Jost Van Dyke. The next day, we re-entered the U.S. at Culebra and then sailed to the huge marina just south Fajardo in Puerto Rico. Brenda and Rich liked the showers. We rented a car and drove to the old part of San Juan for a day. While Brenda and Rich explored the casino, I scouted for a doctor to take the stitches out of my leg, which had become swollen and red. We finally wound up at the emergency room of the local hospital, where a very nice young physician snipped away. Total cost: $106.

Brenda and Rich flew home the next day, and the day after that, I picked up the first of my new crew, William, who ran his own computer company. He brought along his laptop so that he could do some work while sailing. Combined with my new computer, I suspected we had more computing power on board than was possessed by the Pentagon ten years earlier.

While waiting for the arrival of the second crew member, we drove to the Caribbean National Forest, a wonderfully scenic rain forest on the slopes of El Yunque, the Rainmaker. We parked the rental car and climbed the last 1,000 feet in the trees to the summit. It was shrouded in cloud, so we did not get a view, and the top was cluttered with antennas, transmitting equipment, and a diesel generator.

The next day my Barbados recruit, Andrew, showed up to sign on the crew list. He was a young Australian on a six-month walkabout. We left the marina almost immediately for the 850 nm leg to Bermuda. We enjoyed great beam winds for the first four days, then we ran into a windless high pressure ridge lying over Bermuda and had to fire up the old Perkins, but we still managed to tie up at St. George's a little over six days from leaving Puerto Rico.

Bermuda seemed much the same. We arrived at the peak of the cruise ship season—during the week there were usually two in St. George's. The locals appreciated the week-ends when the hordes of pale, often overweight tourists were briefly gone.

Several days after we arrived, Bermuda held a general election, and the ruling Progressive Labour Party was returned to power, but scandal came a couple of days later when the party fired the leader, who is automatically the premier, in an internal coup. The new deputy premier was quite frank that this change was in the works before the election but they kept it quiet so as not to affect the outcome. I was amazed at the passivity with which the voters and the opposition party accepted this bit of double-dealing. We stayed over a week in St. George's tied up to Somers Wharf. We got the mainsail repaired and did other maintenance chores, but it was about 90°F each day, so we didn't push it.

The next big event was the annual cricket match between St. George's representing the east end, and Somerset the west end. The two-day affair ended in a draw, but nobody minded, as it was the festivity that everyone enjoyed. William and I went to the first day, and Andrew saw the match through to the end. Visitors were able to sit on benches in a shaded stand. Free drinks and fresh fruit were frequently passed out to counteract the heat.

After the match, we moved the boat to Mangrove Bay, just in time for another big party, this time on the water, the annual Non-Mariners Race. Spoof boats were specially built to take part; none were expected to finish, as it is a non-race. The event was attended by literally hundreds of boats, with many of the spectators jumping in the water and swimming over for a better view—this was no hardship; the water temperature was 85°F at that time of the year. We anchored near the head of the bay early in the morning, but by lunchtime we were hemmed in by dozens of boats that came within a few inches of us, as the rafted clusters swung in the light breeze. It was all very noisy and jolly and a great deal of beer was swigged.

From there we sailed to another favorite anchorage, Ely's Harbour. This was a beautiful spot with small beaches, clear water and great snorkeling. Andrew had bought a disposable underwater camera he was eager to try. We visited the massive fortifications of the old naval dockyard by bus and then sailed in Great Sound to anchor in Paradise Cove. Bermuda's Long Island lies on the north side of the cove. During the Boer War, the most obstreperous Boer prisoners of war were sent to Bermuda, as escape was virtually impossible from there. A few dozen died, and they are buried on Long Island. For some reason the gravestones are identified only by a number, but at some stage the Boers themselves erected a memorial which named each numbered grave. We landed by dinghy and wandered through the lonely cemetery, and it was impossible not to feel sorry for these men dying so far from home. When the war was over the men were repatriated if they signed a promise not to fight against the British. I believe at least one hold-out never did sign.

The next day we picked up a mooring at Hinson Island belonging to Tony Jones, the Rear Commodore of the Bermuda Station of the Cruising Club of America. He and his wife Liz treated us to a memorable supper in a gazebo on the lawn overlooking Hamilton harbor. Then it was time to return to St. George's and get our clearance for the leg to Maine. As summer still had six weeks to run I had decided we would visit one of all my all-time favorite cruising grounds, Maine, before returning to Long Island, New York.

The Completion of the Circumnavigation

We experienced mostly fair winds for the trip. We encountered some adverse currents in the Gulf Stream, but we sailed out of them in a day or so. As we sailed north, we finally encountered cooler weather. Near 40° N *Fiona* crossed her outward track and thus completed her second circumnavigation. A day later, we picked up a mooring in Bar Harbor, Maine, a week after leaving Bermuda.

During this leg William assiduously practiced celestial navigation; he was planning to buy a sailboat of his own and the trip aboard *Fiona* was a way of getting back in the swim after a long break. He left us at Bar Harbor, and his place was taken by Lew, an old friend who is a professional video editor. We anchored or moored at several lovely islands as we slowly made our way through Penobscot Bay.

In Stonington, we ran into a young woman at the old opera house who was working on its restoration, and she gave us a guided tour of the dark interior. Many Maine towns had an opera house during the late 19th century. The one at Stonington is quite large; it is listed on the National Register of Historic Buildings. After a night at Belfast, we spent two nights at Rockland, a small town with two great museums—the Farnsworth and the Owl's Head Transportation Museum. The Farnsworth always has a number of Andrew Wyeth paintings on view, as he spent his summers nearby where he often painted members of the Olson family. From there we explored Hurricane Island, where the Outward Bound School was located.

We watched the students learning rope climbing at an abandoned granite quarry, and when I stepped off the trail to inspect an old, rusting steam engine, I nearly poked my eye out on a tree branch, and sported a black eye for my pains. I had arranged to meet a fellow vintage car enthusiast at her summer cottage on Muscongus Bay. Sarah Rheault is a Buggati fan, and several other Buggati drivers were staying with her before attending a meet in Connecticut. We all went out for a sail aboard the boat to give them a taste of Maine cruising. Unfortunately, I made it too realistic by running the boat onto a ledge as we entered the anchorage at Harbor Island for lunch. In my defense, I had expected Sarah to supply local knowledge and I was only casually checking the chart. Andrew and Lew got a lift to Brunswick from Sarah's place and departed on the daily bus to Portland and points south. I was joined by Malcolm, who is a friend from vintage Bentley rallies. We sailed west at a leisurely pace.

One day we sailed to Damariscove Island for lunch and anchored in the narrow harbor. It is a small island about a quarter-mile wide and a mile and a half long. It lies five miles south of Boothbay Harbor in the Atlantic Ocean. Despite its small size and remoteness, it has a turbulent history. It was visited by the Mayflower in 1620 and frequently used by ships from Europe in the 17th century for the transshipment of cargo, so they avoided running closer to the coast. In the late 17th century, hundreds of colonists fled to the island during the Indian wars. Much later, a farmer kept cows and delivered milk to nearby islands by row boat, winter and summer. It is now a Nature Conservancy, and as we walked along one of the trails, scattered foundations and dry stone walls were testimony to its past.

Ding in Fiona's *keel after striking a rock in Maine*

In the late afternoon we sailed to Monhegan Island, about 12 miles to the east. We arrived an hour before sunset so that we could use one of the moorings of the charter vessels that make daily visits to the island. This was perfectly acceptable, provided you leave before 10 am the next morning. As the sun sank, we sat in the cockpit with our rum cocktails and witnessed a strange sight. A lobster boat circled the harbor with a knot of people standing at the stern. A small crowd gathered on the wharf. Then the boat launched something on the sea that blazed with crimson flames and sent a plume of black smoke into the sky. Looking through the binoculars, I saw it was a miniature Viking ship. We found out the next morning when we went ashore that we had witnessed the Viking funeral of a local resident whose ashes were in the little ship. They do things differently at Monhegan.

At Five Island Harbor on the Sheepscot River, we collected mussels off the rocks and put them in a bucket to clear the sand. We ate them for happy hour at Seguin Island the next afternoon. This remote offshore island has one of the first lighthouses to be built in the United States, authorized by George Washington himself. We spent a night at Sebacus, where Malcolm and I contacted some friends who live locally and we had dinner together.

The next day we sailed to a yacht club on Orr's Island where we made contact with the family of a CCA member I had met in the Azores in 2002 at the start of the cruise. His mother arranged for the commodore of the CCA to visit the boat the next day, and he and his wife came for happy hour. They were very interested in the trip and it turned out that they and Malcolm, my crew, had mutual friends—small world, indeed.

The next day we sailed to Eagle Island, the retirement home of Admiral Peary, but the house was closed. We sailed on in thick fog to Jewel Island for the night. The island has WWII fortifications, and so we climbed to the top of the old watch tower and then squelched our way through the thick undergrowth to the rocky south side. From Jewel, we sailed to South Freeport and then Portland where Mike came up from Long Island to join us for the jaunt home down the coast of New England. I was sorry to leave the wonderful coast of Maine, as we had enjoyed warm wonderful weather even though we could have used more wind.

We were delayed a day by a gloomy weather forecast caused by Hurricane Isabel. There was no wind as we left Portland, and so we powered to Isles of Shoals and stopped for supper. There we met another CCA member and his wife, Skip and Ilze, who lived on their boat and had completed a circumnavigation of several years. I decided not to waste the night sleeping so we cranked up the engine and powered overnight to Provincetown on the tip of Cape Cod. Compared to my previous visits there, it seemed very quiet, a situation attributed equally to the economy and Hurricane Isabel, the locals said.

The next day we had a wonderful sail across Cape Cod Bay to the canal, but when we emerged into Buzzards Bay we encountered steep, unpleasant seas kicked up by a southerly wind blowing down the bay at up to 30 knots. We sought a sheltered bay for a quiet night on the anchor. The following day, we had great sailing conditions for a sail to Newport, a charming town. We were just in time for a party at the Ida Lewis Yacht Club, where we picked up a mooring. After exploring the town in the morning we sailed to Block Island, but head winds delayed us and we arrived after dark.

In the old tradition of the square riggers we spruced up the ship the next day and then left for the drag down the south shore of Long

Island, which we did under power. After entering the inlet, we had a tense time sailing the shallows of Great South Bay in a thick fog. When we tied up at Weeks Yacht Yard it was a year and fifteen weeks since we had departed, with 32,869 nm logged. The condition of *Fiona* certainly reflected this high mileage, about half of it in the Southern Ocean. It took many months to get her shipshape again.

In retrospect this was the most satisfying retirement cruise up till then. I was fortunate in having good crew, especially David and Bob in the grueling Cape Town to Brazil leg. The conditions in the Southern Ocean tried my seamanship to the limit. They also pushed our stamina to the limit—from Australia to the Falklands we sailed for 46 days without let-up, and almost every day we dealt with heavy seas, high winds, and frequent gear failure. When we got through that we really felt we had accomplished something. Later on, Bob and Sue wrote a book about the experience (*Two Sailboats, One Moon*) based on the logs each kept that year while they were apart except for the infrequent rendezvous at distant ports.

6

Cruise to Ireland, the Baltic, England, Portugal, Brazil and the Falklands
2004-2005

This cruise was preceded by a very busy winter of maintenance. Returning from Maine in 2003, I smelled fuel in the bilge which, after exhaustive elimination of all possible leaks, I decided must be coming from the fuel tanks. They were made of black iron and were originally supplied by Westsail when I bought the hull, and they were shaped to fit exactly to the turn of the bilge. Removing them meant that the aft end of the main cabin had to be completely disassembled. The job lasted several months. When they came out I found pin-hole leaks along the bottom corner of one tank.

The tanks were 28 years old and goodness knows what kind of junk had been pumped into them in the four corners of the world! I guess that is all the life I could expect from them. I replaced them with aluminum tanks, as the U.S. Coast Guard does not allow stainless steel tanks, probably due the tendency of that material to crack.

Numerous problems were dealt with both big and small—a new stove, mast rewired, and new halyard winch mounting plates welded on. I replaced the halyard winches, re-bedded the chain plates, and replaced the propeller shaft and cutlass bearing. The bow platform was straightened out, a new freezer built using R154 refrigerant, a new ½" chain bobstay installed, the Espar heater

Walter assists in removing a leaking fuel tank, 2004

rebuilt, a new prop shaft generator installed, and on and on. Walter rehabilitated himself by helping with many of the heavy jobs. 'Red' was with me almost every day and was invaluable, as the work goes not twice but thrice faster when there are two people on the job.

I envisioned that the southernmost point of this cruise would be somewhere in Antarctica. But the first order of business was to attend a CCA rally in Ireland, followed by a cruise to the Baltic and on to London. The start of the cruise was a couple of days late (June 12th), as last-minute problems with the new prop shaft generator required some machine shop work, ably performed by Bob Berg. The generator worked very well during the trip, so the delay was worth it.

'Red' repairing Fiona's mast at Weeks Yard

The crew for the first leg consisted of Shoel and Joe. Shoel was a veteran of several cruises aboard *Fiona*, including Canada and Tahiti, but it was Joe's first trip. Shoel is a clinical psychologist; Joe runs his own electrical contracting business in Massachusetts. Shoel lived in the same hamlet as myself; he and his wife Nancy were family friends. He had made several trips aboard *Fiona*, including the 4,000-mile leg from Panama to Tahiti. Joe was a wannabe ocean cruiser and seized the chance when he saw on my web site that I had an opening for the transatlantic leg.

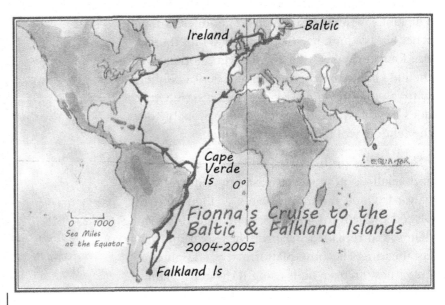

We had a short stay in Newport, Rhode Island, to attend a cocktail party at the New York Yacht Club for members of the CCA who were sailing across the pond to participate in a rally. The rally was planned to start at Kinsale in mid-July, to celebrate the 75th anniversary of the founding of the Irish Cruising Club. Most of the other boats intended to stop at the Azores; we were the only boat heading for a northern route.

After a transit of the Cape Cod Canal we stopped at Provincetown, and compared to some of my previous visits it was very quiet, as the tourist season had not cranked up that early. Our trip across the Gulf of Maine was without incident and we pulled into Lunenburg in the dark in order to clear into Canada.

Canada and the Transatlantic Crossing

In the morning I phoned Canadian customs in Halifax. To my surprise, they said they would make the one-hour drive to the dock to inspect the boat. Sure enough, just before lunchtime a small car pulled onto the old wooden pier and disgorged four burly customs officers. They inspected the boat, including separate questioning of the crew. Fortunately, I had declared my stash of rum, stored aboard from last year to lubricate this trip. Rather reluctantly, I thought, they agreed my three cases could be bonded, but told me customs at St. John's, Newfoundland, our departure point, would confirm we had not broached our cargo, and thus threaten the economic stability of Canada. I rather suspected that they drove all the way to Lunenburg to enjoy a traditional mug-up for lunch. Naturally, customs at St. John's evinced not the slightest interest in us, coming or going.

A highlight of the trip from Lunenburg to St. John's was an amazing aquatic display as we crossed the edge of the Grand Banks. For nearly an hour, pilot whales, dolphins, and unidentified large whales cavorted at the sea surface—broaching, leaping and darting in a frenzy of eating. At lunchtime on June 27th, the narrow rockbound entrance to St. John's loomed out of the fog and we entered the impressive natural harbor. I have always enjoyed my visits to St. John's, as the town is unpretentious, the inhabitants very friendly, and it has a number of old book shops and cozy coffee bars. We visited a few bars that dispensed the local rum, Screech, reportedly first discovered when they steam-cleaned used barrels of Jamaica rum and sampled the run-off.

We rented a car and treated ourselves to lunch at the Royal Newfound-land Yacht Club on Conception Bay.

On the way home, we stopped at Brigus, a small village on the west side of the bay which was the home of Bob Bartlett. Like the man himself, his grave, which we found after some searching, was very modest. Bartlett was Peary's captain on the North Pole expeditions. In 1913, he captained the *Karluk*, a research ship that got trapped in the ice north of Siberia and sank. Bartlett trekked hundreds miles across the pack ice and then through Siberia to get help, a feat that compares with Shackleton's amazing rescue of the crew of *Endurance*. On our last evening we were invited to a cozy club near the waterfront called the Crow's Nest. An unusual feature mounted near the bar was a fully-functioning periscope that was liberated from a German U-Boat which surrendered at the end of WWII.

The Atlantic crossing, my thirteenth, was the quietest, least trying passage I have made across that ocean. There were no storms, we only reefed once, and we had winds that rarely exceeded 10 to 12 knots. In the vicinity of the Labrador Current, we experienced rather damp, chilly conditions, of course, but we saw no icebergs, much to the disappointment of the crew, who wanted a story to tell. When the occasional sun appeared, Joe took the opportunity to brush up his celestial navigation. One day an errant line fell over the side and wrapped itself round the prop. On the next really calm day, Joe slipped over the side with a mask and wet suit to untangle it.

About once a week, we continued an old *Fiona* tradition of watching a movie. But we had upgraded to showing DVDs on the laptop, and some were even in color. Most days I talked to Trudi, who ran the amateur radio Transatlantic Net. During the previous cruise, I visited her house when we anchored in Barbados.

On the July 15th, we spotted Dursey Head, Ireland, and the next day we tied up at the Kinsale Yacht Club, a 15-day passage from St. John's, and almost exactly forty years since Edith and I had made our first Atlantic crossing as crew for Barbara and John Knight aboard *Arvin Court II*. The light average winds for our trip resulted in a slow passage and our arrival was actually a day behind schedule. Shoel had arranged to meet his wife Nancy in Northern Ireland for a short vacation to recover from the rigors of the trip, and so he left the boat the same day.

That evening there was a reception for the participants in the Irish Cruising Club rally and the crew for the next leg turned up: David, who sailed around the world with me in 2002-2003, and Frank, an old cruising friend I first met during the 1995-1997 circumnavigation. After a couple of days, Joe caught the train to Dublin and a flight home. The rally kicked off with a wine reception at the Royal Cork Yacht Club in Crosshaven, and then we were bused to a full-blown dinner at the Cork City Hall. This set the tone for the one-week shindig, which consisted of beating to windward for 20 or so miles each day, followed by a social event. As there were nearly 180 yachts in the rally, the social gatherings were crowded, noisy and great fun. The small coastal villages on the south side of Ireland were uniformly charming and they enjoy a very temperate climate, due the impinging Gulf Stream.

On the third day, a photographer was stationed off Fastnet Rock lighthouse, a huge structure that signals the westerly presence of the British Islands. The poor photographer had to endure several hours in his pitching and rolling vessel south of the light as the rally yachts beat out and sailed past for a souvenir snap with the lighthouse.

Fastnet Lighthouse

While at Glengarriff we tied the dinghy near the ferry dock and walked into the village for a drink and a meal, incidentally using the rigid dinghy with its old Seagull engine I had bought in 1968 for the Caribbean cruise I made with Edith aboard *Iona*. We got quite a few stares and comments as we chugged past sleek modern yachts with the Seagull exuding copious oil and smoke—we were a relic of a prior sailing era. On returning from our walk in Glengarriff, we noticed a sign indicating a short cut to the jetty through an area of trees and thick bushes. The foliage blotted out the sky and at several points the path came to "Y" junctions. None were signposted, but we chose the direction that appeared to lead to the water. After 20 minutes, with the light fading, we realized we were lost. We pressed on and shortly after came across a small creek that seemed familiar. A hundred yards away was the original sign to the jetty—we had made a complete circuit. From there we stuck to the main road.

One objective of the visit to Glengarriff was to form a "Sunflower Raft" in the large, protected harbor. The raft master with his minions in inflatable dinghies tried to organize all the rally yachts into a circular raft but a high wind defeated him, and after a morning that had the appearance of a Chinese fire drill, the effort was abandoned. We had dinner that evening with Frank's wife, Barbara, who had driven up from their house near Crosshaven and the next day David, Frank, and I left for Scotland.

Scotland and the Baltics

At the start, we had head winds as we beat our way past the headlands that jut southwest into the Atlantic. But after a couple of days, the wind shifted to give us fair sailing and we arrived at Corpach, the western end of the Caledonian Canal, just after sunrise, four days after leaving Glengarriff. The Canal is an amazing piece of pre-Victorian engineering. It was completed in 1822 to provide a passage from the North Sea to the Atlantic, and thus permit sailors to by-pass the stormy Cape Wrath at the northern tip of Scotland. It is just over 60 miles in length, about 20 miles consisting of man-made canals connecting natural lochs along a rift, of which Loch Ness is the largest. The canal has twelve locks up and twelve down. This was my second transit of the canal.

For our first evening's mooring on the Canal, we rendezvoused with my cousin Philip and his friend Mary; Philip lived in Pitlochry, about an hour's drive from the Canal. We had dinner at a small hotel that advertised itself as the "Forsyth Family Hotel." I asked the landlord if Forsyths got a discount, and he replied with a heavy accent that "Forrrsyths pay a prrremium."

Our next stopover was the attractive town of Fort Augustus. From the earliest days of the Canal, it had been a tourist center, where specially-designed elegant steam ships used to take Victorian tourists to view Loch Ness and Ben Nevis. But now, sadly, the ships are diesel-propelled and ugly. While tied up we got to meet a Danish sailor with whom we discussed our plans for the Baltic. He strongly recommended a transit of the Limfjord Canal rather than entering the Skagerrak strait from Scotland, as we had planned. The Limfjord Canal is a mostly-natural waterway in northern Denmark, which avoids the notoriously stormy seas of the Skagerrak between Denmark and Norway.

We made the transit of Loch Ness in one day—we had intended to take two, but the intermediate harbor we had chosen was crowded and we barely made the last lock-down of the day into the Canal terminus at Inverness. At Inverness, Philip's daughter Sheena met us and we used her car to do some re-stocking at a supermarket. I was able to buy such British goodies as Marmite, Branston Pickles, and mushy peas. While Sheena cooked a delicious supper at her apartment, we toured the ancient village she lived in and its ruined abbey. At Inverness, we linked up again with our Danish friend and made a photocopy of his charts, which showed the entrance to the Limfjord at Thyboron on the Danish west coast. After refueling, we passed through the last lock and started our passage across the North Sea to Denmark.

The North Sea has a grim reputation for storms and heavy seas, but our three-and-a-half-day passage was made mostly under engine, as the sea was mirror-like. We tied up at Thyboron at midnight, a port that clearly declaimed its industry by the fishy smell we detected several miles offshore. In the morning, we paid our dockage dues and bought four detailed Danish charts of the Limfjord Canal. We refueled from an extremely battered diesel scow in the commercial harbor; the operator was very reluctant to sell a mere 272 liters to a yacht, when he had a large trawler waiting for 15,000 liters. But fortunately, we had tied up to the scow before the operator arrived. And so, with bad grace, he pumped our diesel. And then came the shock—I didn't have enough money to pay! Welcome to Scandinavia, where fuel ran to nearly $6 a gallon. Fortunately, David and Frank had been to the ATM that morning and, by dredging up every krona we had between us, we just had enough to pay the bill.

The Canal wound a leisurely way through flat countryside that was dotted with literally scores of huge wind generators. There were no locks, as curiously enough there is no tide in the Baltic. We tied up at two small towns. The temperature was very mild, about 75° F by day, surprisingly warm considering we were near 57° N. From the Canal we sailed south to Thuro Island, where I had arranged to pick up some detailed charts of the central Baltic from a fellow Cruising Club member who kept his boat there.

After getting the charts at Walsted's Boatyard we sailed directly to Bornholm Island against an easterly wind. This turned out to be a three-day beat, unusual as it turned out, as the wind was supposed

175

to be predominately southwest. There was an astonishing volume of sea traffic in the narrow sea between Denmark and Germany—at one time on a night watch I counted the lights of twenty ships in sight. We tied up at Ronne, a very pleasant town with a supermarket, e-mail, and a reasonably-priced restaurant within a few minutes of the marina. Cycle paths are a feature of most of the roads in Denmark, and on our second day, Frank and I rented bicycles and pedaled about six miles to a small village down the coast, the first time I had been on a bike in more than 20 years.

The next leg took us to Visby on Gotland Island, Sweden, and the southwest wind returned to waft us northeast. On the way, the topping lift broke and when it fell into the sea, it too was attracted to the prop. Fortunately, the shaft continued to turn, and when we got into port, Frank went for a swim and freed the prop of the trailing rope.

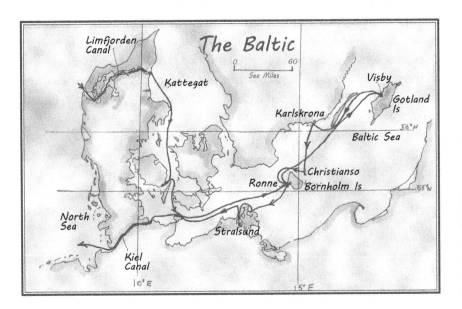

David flew to Stockholm the day after we arrived, and then Frank also decided to leave the boat earlier than planned, due to problems with some medical tests he had taken before we left Ireland. He caught the huge ferry that plies daily between Gotland and the Swedish mainland.

I spent the time after the crew had left touring the stunning city of Visby. It was a major element in the medieval Hanseatic League, a network of trading ports. The old town was completely walled-in. Every corner of the twisting cobbled lanes presented a photo opportunity. My mind was blown away by an exhibit at the museum. After wandering by early stone-age artifacts and the Viking-era relics, I came across items excavated from a mass grave dug just outside the city wall during a civil war in the 13th century. Apparently, about 1,200 bodies had been tipped into a massive trench just as they lay, and were covered up for the next 700 years. Eyeless skulls peered through the slots in the armor helmets and shattered bones protruded from iron gauntlets. One skull had three iron arrowheads embedded in it. Many of the bodies were not soldiers, however—old folks and children had died; their bones exhibited signs of rickets and arthritis.

In the late afternoon, I walked to the airport to meet the 5 pm flight from Stockholm. Teresa and Catherine disembarked and thus became the third crew for this trip. Teresa has sailed aboard *Fiona* twice before in the Caribbean, but this was to be Catherine's first trip. She worked for the British Hydrographic Office and was editor of the *Nautical Almanac*.

By this time, the southwest wind had hardened and, as our route lay back to the southwest, we were trapped in Visby for a couple of days until the wind let up. One afternoon, we took a bus ride to a nearby village to inspect a ruined medieval abbey. On our return, we found the wind was piping up to 40 knots outside the harbor and I thanked my lucky stars that we were safely tucked up. But Fate was not going to let me off so easily.

The captain of a German power boat also tied up in Visby decided to shift his berth for one that was more protected, and as he sailed past *Fiona*, his wife signaled me to take a line. I stood on the concrete wharf as they approached against the wind, took the line and passed a full turn 'round a steel ring in the dock. It was a heavy rope with a large knot on the end. But the captain then panicked, reversed hard, and pulled the rope through the ring. I let go, but the rope whipped through the ring and the knot struck me a blow on the top of my left hand—so hard that it knocked me to ground, and my hand opened up like a squashed tomato and spattered copious blood on my favorite Falkland Islands sweater. To make a long story short, I then experienced the excellence of the emergency room of the local hospital, where a Greek lady physician chatted with me in English and with the nurses in Swedish while she stitched my hand back together.

The next day the wind had dropped and veered a little to the west, so we left and set full sail. It became clear that with two ladies on board and me with only one usable hand that we were a little short of muscle power. Later in the day the wind died and we started the engine. By the next morning we cleared the southern tip of Oland Island and were able to change course for Karlskrona and set some sail again. We tied up in the old Swedish naval center just after happy hour.

We spent two days at Karlskrona, doing a little shopping to get rid of our Swedish money and exploring the wonderful maritime museum. Each day, Teresa re-bandaged my hand, which was very swollen and black and blue.

Eric displays his hand damaged at Gotland, Sweden, 2004

Our next destination was Christianso, a small fortified island just off the coast of Bornholm, so we were back in Denmark. We arrived rather late in the evening, but the one and only inn was able to lay on an elegant, albeit expensive, dinner for us. After a walk round the island the next morning, we left for the short leg to Allinge, on Bornholm. On the way over we took some sights on the sun and plotted our position using a new program Catherine had installed on the laptop computer. Besides being the editor of the British *Nautical Almanac*, she had co-authored a book on computer methods of celestial navigation.

Allinge turned out to be a pleasant tourist town, located on the north end of Bornholm. The next day we powered around the north cape and then had a nice sail under the jib to Ronne. We stayed two nights and then left for Rugen Island in Germany. The wind was persistently southwest, on the nose, but we motor-sailed and covered the 53-mile leg in 11 hours, dropping anchor in a quiet bay on the northeast side of the island. The next day we moved along the coast and anchored about a half-mile from the beach at Dornbusch Island, which put us within striking distance of Stralsund, our destination for a crew change. This was an area of the north German coast characterized by wide, shallow lagoons known as "Bodden." The Boddens teemed with wildlife and were protected as a Nature Reserve. There was a very active sailing and chartering fleet visiting these lagoons.

Our plans were put on hold by high southwest winds and a warning on the Navtex weather forecast of "near gale force" winds. I elected to stay just where we were, even though the bay was rather wide and did not provide much of a lee if the wind shifted to north. So we hunkered down, and in the evening watched a movie on the laptop. The next day we had no problems getting to Stralsund. When we docked, I walked to the local hospital where a nurse snipped out the stitches in my hand at no charge. In the evening, Catherine treated us to a sumptuous dinner at one of the better restaurants, a complete contrast to a steady diet of our Spam-and-beans yacht meals, and the next day the ladies left early by train.

Stralsund was another city that was a member of the old Hanseatic League. The port was lined with traditional narrow buildings with high-pitched roofs and small, square windows in the Baltic style. Besides a fleet of modern yachts at the marina on the north wharf, there were a number of wooden Baltic schooners in the port and two large square-riggers. The marine museum was mostly devoted to fishing in the Baltic and had a truly impressive aquarium. As I waited for the next crew to show up, I did a little maintenance and some food shopping. On Saturday morning, there was a band in the main square and later several choirs and bands gathered on the waterfront for a musical evening.

As I ate my supper at an Italian restaurant, entertained by the nearby singers and musicians, I pondered how such a clever and cultivated country as Germany could have descended into the nightmare of the 1930s and 1940s. I decided that, under some circumstances, it could probably happen anywhere. I hoped our political leaders pondered the same question occasionally.

The next day my fourth crew showed up—David and John, my first father and son combo. David was a very experienced seaman who was coxswain of a lifeboat for many years. John had been following the cruise using the web site updates. When he saw the crew vacancy, he persuaded his father to join him.

We had very pleasant conditions for visits to several ports on the German Baltic coast. Besides the wind, the prices were down too, compared to Scandinavia. In one small port, we happened on a festival of sea chanties, and most of the singers arrived in traditional wooden

Baltic schooners and gaff-rigged "baders" with huge lee boards. On the way to our last port in the Baltic, we were intercepted by a German Coast Guard vessel and asked to change course five miles to the north, as we were entering a live firing range.

Our fourth canal of the trip was the Kiel, opened in 1895 to provide access to the North Sea for the German Naval Fleet, without the necessity of traversing the Kattegat. There was a lock at either end, and in-between, the canal wanders for nearly 60 miles through attractive flat land, with the occasional small town. The canal was inhabited by a large number of commercial ships of all kinds and there were ducks, swans, and fishermen on the banks. We spent our last night in Germany at Brunsbuttel, the western terminal of the canal and then transited the last lock to enter the Elbe River.

The forecast was for gales the next day, but as most sailors know, if you wait for a perfect forecast you will never leave. However, this time perhaps I should have waited. We had strong gale force winds on the nose, combined with steep breaking seas and heavy currents caused by the spring tides. We reefed *Fiona* down and pushed on, driven north until it seemed we might sail over the notorious Dogger Bank, a graveyard of ships. The genoa jib blew out a panel, and we clawed down the wreckage off the headstay and bent on the Yankee jib when we got a chance. The tremendous pounding seas dislodged the counter in the forward head, tipped drawers off their slides, and forced water through every crack on the boat. Then a miracle—the wind shifted to northwest. With three reefs in the mainsail, a reefed staysail and reefed Yankee, we flew south, making 7-plus knots.

By midnight on our fifth day in the North Sea, the wind dropped and we started the engine. We faced a tricky navigational problem: our arrival at the Thames Estuary had to be timed exactly to match the start of the flood tide. Compounding the problem were the presence of many ships, seemingly going in all directions, and the shallow sand bars formed by the scouring currents. We powered through the night, fighting a stiff southwest wind that had come back and created a nasty chop. We all stayed on watch, monitoring the radar, GPS readout, helming the wheel in 30 minute spells, and keeping an eye on the shipping. As the sun rose on the sixth day, we were two hours late. We were running the engine much harder than usual, but a leak developed in the rubber exhaust hose and we had to cut back the rpm. A quick calculation showed we were not going to make the lock opening at our destination at the slower speed. At a quiet stretch of the channel, free of commercial traffic for a while, we shut down the engine, and I fastened a rubber patch on the hose with a couple of clamps. This worked and, with the engine roaring away at nearly 2,000 rpm, we entered the Thames River, where the flood tide grabbed the boat, and to our relief, we soon saw the GPS indicating 9-plus knots over the ground.

In a few hours the majestic Tower Bridge hove into view and we entered the lock into St. Katharine's Dock, London, with time to spare. The North Sea had certainly taken its revenge for the calm passage to Denmark in August, but in the end it let us off and we thankfully watched the lock gate close behind us as *Fiona* entered the tranquil haven. We were just a few yards from Tower Bridge. We arrived on September 17th, two days behind schedule. David and John returned home the next day after a sound night's sleep. I arranged for the jib to be repaired and booked a flight to New York.

To the Tropics

When I returned to London from New York I was preceded by a few hours by Sean, a 19-year old who worked at Weeks Yacht Yard. He had signed up to complete the rest of the cruise, and with the arrival of Andrew a few days later, I imagined I had solved the crewing problem at least until March of 2005, when Andrew planned to leave in South America. Andrew, an Aussie, was an old *Fiona* hand, having sailed from Puerto Rico to Maine with me in 2003. We were running about two weeks behind schedule, and if we were to make the summer window in the Antarctic we would have to push.

Before Andrew showed up, Sean and I completed a few repairs and bent on the sails, which had been repaired during my trip home. Sean got a chance to see something of London. I introduced him to a typical pub one evening, and later we had a curry at one of the ubiquitous Indian restaurants, another first for him. Somehow, I found time to visit my aunt May in Swanley, and one afternoon I took the train to Didcot, near Abingdon, where I was met by Catherine, who had crewed earlier when we were in the Baltic. That evening I showed the video of the previous cruise to her local yacht club, an event organized by John Magraw, who had crewed on the 2000 trip to the Arctic.

We left London on the ebb on the afternoon of October 13th and tied up in the dark at a strange little dock that seemed to be in the middle of a swamp in Queen Borough. I had been tipped off by a member of the Little Ship Club that this was the only refuge to make for before the tide turned foul. Our next stop was Ramsgate, where we tied up at the local marina at dead low water and briefly touched bottom as we made our way up the harbor channel. After some shopping in the morning, we left for the slog down the English Channel where I planned to put into Falmouth at the western end of the Cornish peninsula. This leg took two days and was complicated by the fierce tides in the Channel and brisk southwest winds on the nose. Sean was seasick, but I assured him that was fairly normal and would pass. Apparently he did not believe me, for as soon as we touched dry land at Falmouth he booked himself a flight home and by the next evening he was gone. I e-mailed Rich, who put a crew call on the web site, and Andrew and I sounded out the local sailing clubs for someone who might sail as far as Lisbon. Andrew also alerted the Aussie "mafia" in London, but we had no success.

Curiously, the next day a policeman stopped by the boat and asked if we knew where Sean was. I was amazed—apparently his mother back on Long Island had reported him missing. The policeman was a pleasant young fellow who hailed from my own home part of the U.K., Lancashire. He was fascinated by the boat and my cruising life. We enjoyed a chat in the main cabin while he drank a cup of tea.

We carried out a few repairs and bent a new storm mainsail on the boom. This sail had been copied from my old storm mainsail, which had propelled the boat round Cape Horn three times, but finally gave up the ghost after the 2002-2003 circumnavigation. We waited in Falmouth for a good weather opportunity to sail across the Bay of Biscay, but day after day the forecast was for strong or even gale force winds from the southwest. While waiting, I linked up with Helen Franklin, who lived in the nearby town of Penryn; she was the daughter of Nick Franklin who designed the Aries self-steerer, aka Victor the Vane. The waiting was not unpleasant, as Falmouth is an attractive port with good pubs, teashops, and a nice library. One night, Andrew and I went to an excellent play put on by local amateurs.

Finally, after a week of waiting, it looked like a window—northerly winds for a couple of days, but then an intense low was forecast to hit the area. I was probably too eager to get away. I figured we might get far enough to the west that we could ride the counterclockwise winds to the south, but instead we were trapped to the east of the low and Andrew got his first taste of heavy weather as we lay hove-to in a force 10 storm. To make matters worse, the low pressure center stalled off the coast of Ireland and then made a turn southeast, thus heading straight for *Fiona*. Apart from getting thoroughly soaked, we suffered no real damage until the jib tore. We furled it, but a remnant of cloth gave the wind something to grab onto and over the next few days the wind reduced the sail to tatters. At the height of the storm, with *Fiona* hove-to in the Bay of Biscay, a French maritime reconnaissance plane emerged from the low cloud and called up on VHF. They wanted to know if we were okay, and I assured them that we were. I didn't bother telling them we were wet, cold, and fed-up with the weather. I imagined them landing an hour or two later and heading for a cup of coffee in a nice, warm, dry lounge.

We made Lisbon in eight days after leaving Falmouth, and as we powered up the Tagus River, a police launch approached, observing the shreds of sail hanging from the headstay. They asked us if we needed help. Then it turned out the marina we were heading for at the Expo had been closed due to shoaling, and they guided us to another marina near the center of Lisbon. We were fortunate they encountered us, as we would never have been able to find the marina by ourselves. It was a pitch black night and the marina was hidden in the depths of the commercial dock area.

Our first priority was to get the jib repaired, but when the sailmakers inspected it a day later they suggested a new sail. In the end, we ordered one from a sailmaker in England and had it shipped by air. This took time and we wound up spending two weeks we could ill afford in Lisbon. Andrew tried to get a Brazilian visa while in Lisbon, but was frustrated by the bureaucracy. After filling out a comprehensive form, he went back after a statutory five days to pick it up and found they had done nothing with it, because the photo he had supplied was an eighth of an inch too small. By then it was too late to start over, so he arrived in Brazil without one, leading to more problems.

A bit of good news was that we found an enthusiastic South African yachtsman to take Sean's place once we got to Brazil. He had seen the crew call on the website and arranged to take a couple of months off from his work in Cape Town. That left us with the problem of finding someone for the leg to Brazil. Enter Celeste. Celeste was one of those characters that one tends to meet in the strange life of world-wide cruising. She wanted to go somewhere warm for winter, and Brazil seemed as good a place as any. She had no sailing experience but was wildly keen on any project that caught her fancy.

Celeste spoke five languages fluently, so I signed her up for the trip. She was very helpful when I had my own brush with Portuguese bureaucracy—I tried to reclaim the 19 percent VAT that was extracted when I paid for the new sail. First, we were directed to several offices of the customs, and in each they claimed ignorance of the procedure but sent us to another office. Finally, we discovered the number of the form we had to complete, but first we had to buy the form itself from the government printing office. We chased around Lisbon by taxi trying to get one before everything shut on a Friday afternoon. In the end we just made it, and Celeste and I completed the form over the weekend. On Monday morning, we made another dreary round of office visits. Finally, we wound up in the office of a chief poohbah who determined that VAT refunds applied only to commercial ships and that decadent, supposedly rich, yachtsmen were not entitled to get the money back.

The three of us made a sightseeing trip to Sintra, a wonderfully scenic town near the coast west of Lisbon where the ancient royalty had a summer palace. Before them it had been occupied by the Moors, who built a castle in the 8th century. Lisbon has excellent public transportation, including a subway and streetcars. A couple of routes have very quaint, cast-off, English trams, some of which Celeste claimed were a hundred years old. But there are hazards. On one of the new, jazzy streetcars I was jostled by a bunch of professional pickpockets who neatly abstracted my old video camera from my backpack. Fortunately, I had changed the cassette just the day before so I did not lose any precious footage.

The new sail was shipped from England on a Thursday but got trapped at the airport by the weekend, and so it was not finally delivered until late Monday afternoon. We ran it up the stay, saw that it looked fine, and so we cast off and headed down the river for Brazil. Celeste picked up the elements of watch-keeping easily enough but she had a prickly personality, perhaps due to her upbringing. She said it had been difficult with a white mother and black father. She claimed to be a lesbian, a vegetarian, an artist, a musician, and all around free-thinker. I would add a touch of paranoia to the list, and so I was not surprised when she decided during our brief stop-over at Santa Cruz, Tenerife, that it was warm enough, and she abruptly left the boat. On leaving, she staged quite a scene at the dock, claiming in a voice loud enough to get all the nearby yachties out of their cabins, that I was an inconsiderate pig who made slaves of the crew. Worse, she said I was an American capitalist bastard, and was responsible for the attack on Iraq, and that she would not set foot on the boat again. Andrew had to dump her kit on the dock.

That left another long leg of over 2,000 nm for Andrew and me to sail by ourselves. We restocked the fresh food, refueled, and left after two days. I had not intended to put into the Cape Verde Islands, which lay almost directly on our route, but prolonged calms and heavy engine use dictated full fuel tanks before we crossed the doldrums. We anchored at Mindelo, a port we had visited on the 2002-2003 cruise. I went to the immigration office three times to check in, but it was always closed. We refueled, spent the night at anchor, and left the next day without ever officially having been there. Diesel cost twice as much as it did on my last visit, but otherwise the place seemed little changed.

As soon as we left the island, we picked up good trade winds and *Fiona* surged along, often accompanied by dolphins that gamboled around the boat. I started to grow a beard. After a few days we ran into squalls and calm patches. George, the autopilot used when we were under power, started to give us trouble. I traced the problem to faulty connections on a printed circuit board. The unit was 25 years old, and like its captain, was getting creaky joints.

Later, other problems developed with some of the chips used on the boards, but fortunately, I carried a few spares. The days flew by as Andrew and I stood watch after watch. We frequently found flying fish on deck. Although the wind became erratic and stalled at times, we never encountered the flat calm I had experienced on previous crossings of the doldrums. And so, by the time we crossed the equator at 31° 31'W on December 10th, we were once again sailing well with southeast trade winds. Our old friend Father Neptune showed up the next day to induct Andrew, always an excuse for a little extra rum at happy hour.

Each day I checked in with a ham radio net, and they plotted our daily position on a website. This was a great help to Gary, our new crew, who was planning to arrive in Brazil on December 10th, and naturally was hoping we would arrive about the same time. The 10th, of course, was the day we crossed the equator, but the winds were strong, so we reefed the mainsail and flew towards Cabedelo, our landfall on the northeast coast of Brazil. We arrived at the river mouth in the late afternoon of the 13th and got the anchor down at Jacare before the sun set. Gary was staying at a pousada (Brazilian B&B) and was sipping a beer at a waterfront café when he saw us arrive. The 2,281-mile leg from Tenerife had taken us 23 days, including our stop at Mindelo. Jacare is a small village on the Paraiba River, half-way between Cabedelo and the city of João Pessoa. It was the home of a boat yard called Cabedelo Nautico, which I first visited on the return leg of the west-to-east circumnavigation. Run by an expat Brit called Brian Stevens, it was a well-known hang-out for yachties. There were four other cruisers anchored in the river when we arrived.

Every evening a local band practiced at the restaurant/bar next to the marina. For some reason, they always played Ravel's "Bolero" as the sun set, and they played excruciatingly badly. Our first order of business the next morning was to sort out the paperwork with the federal police, a battle I usually lose every time I arrive in Brazil. This was to be no exception.

Gary and I went to the police office in the dock area at Cabedelo and I presented our passports. Consternation reigned when they noticed Andrew had no visa. An hour or two went by as an officer sorted through voluminous folders and made numerous phone calls. Finally, his secretary cut and pasted a document on the computer headed in Portuguese "Notification of Infraction." To my surprise, he and the secretary then signaled for Gary and I to get in his car, parked just outside the office, and we left at high speed for the boatyard. When we arrived at Brian's office, he translated: Andrew had to be officially told he must leave, and he had to sign the impressive document the secretary had brought along. But where was he? Andrew was supposed to be on the boat, as he was a non-person. While Brian stalled the officials, Gary and I searched frantically for Andrew, even co-opting Brian's car and one of his workers as the driver. We finally discovered Andrew loung-ing on the beach about two miles away. Fortunately, the police were still in Brian's office when we got back. Andrew was told he had three days to leave Brazil, and he signed the notification; Brazilian honor was satisfied.

Three days was fine by me, as we were running very late if we were to spend much time in the Antarctic summer season. It was also too hot in Jacare—it hit the 90s by lunch. So, we changed to the heavy weather sails, refueled by jerry jug, restocked the fresh food, and pre-pared to leave on a direct shot to Port Stanley, 3,000 miles away.

It was curious shopping in the large "Hiper" market at João Pessoa. The P.A. system pumped out Christmas music, and the clerks wore cute little Santa hats, but the temperature was sweltering. However, it was refreshingly inexpensive in Brazil, especially after Europe. I bought a few bottles of local rum at about $2.50 per liter.

The policeman came down to the boatyard just to make sure we were really leaving, and we got our passports stamped and departed on December 17th. Just before we left, I picked up a parcel from Bren-da at the post office, and in it were a couple of Christmas presents and back copies of the *Guardian Weeklies*. (Sadly, "Manchester" had been dropped from the name some years earlier.)

The South Atlantic Ocean

The winds were generally light for the trip south, apart from the inevitable squalls. We were just about on the Tropic of Capricorn for Christmas Day. The boat was decorated with the traditional tree and we had turkey (canned) with all the trimmings for dinner. In the afternoon we watched *Christmas Story*, one of the videos Brenda had sent to Jacare.

Just after Christmas I was horrified to learn of the tsunami in the Far East on the BBC short-wave broadcasts. On the 1995-1997 circum-navigation, I had cruised through that region, including Thailand, Sri Lanka, and the Maldives.

This tree, along with the canned turkey and cranber-ries, served to brighten up many Christmases celebrat-ed aboard.

At Phuket, I couldn't imagine the effects of the tidal wave, as the bay is so shallow for up to a mile from shore. Many yachts must have been swept onto the land and the crews killed. It was sobering news.

For the next week, we had mostly calm weather in the South Atlantic, and early in the New Year we cut back on engine usage as the fuel supply on board was down to about 20 gallons. We needed to save this for our arrival in the vicinity of the Falkland Islands. This was the first time in many years that I have had to curtail engine use at sea because of fuel shortage.

Every evening the Southern Cross rose higher and higher on the port bow. Near 40° S we spotted our first albatrosses, but the wind remained light—no Roaring Forties where we were. In fact, the weather got milder and milder for a while. We had warm, sunny days with cloudless skies, and a sea as calm as a millpond. But the wind had disappeared. Between lunchtime on January 6th and lunch on January 7th, we sailed only 36 nm.

The boat rolled lazily in the swell and the sails slatted—it was very frustrating. Stanley still lay 700 miles away. To make matters worse, we encountered the current that streamed round Cape Horn and headed into the Atlantic, where it was called the Falklands Current. This was running between 1 and 2 knots on the nose. By the 10th we were experiencing more typical weather for the Forties, with winds up to 30 knots.

The next night we reefed the mainsail in a wind that gusted up to 35 knots. When we retired into the cabin to enjoy a well-earned cup of tea, the boat was suddenly rolled by an immense wave and I was catapulted against one of the vertical steel posts by the companionway steps. I was left winded, and when I tried to get up, a familiar pain shot through my side—I had obviously cracked a rib. This made watch-keeping a little tough on Andrew and Gary. Until we got to the Falkland Islands, anytime I needed to adjust the sails, or even open the main hatch on my watch, I had to call on them.

We had another slow day between the 12th and 13th when we made good only 35 miles towards Stanley, noon to noon, but this was because we were fighting very strong head winds and we sailed over a 100 miles in tacks. Fortunately, the wind then backed and decreased to 20-25 knots and we were able to lay a course directly to our destination. We tied up at the floating dock in Stanley at about 2:30 pm on the 14th. After a shower at the Seaman's Center, I hitched a ride to the local hospital and checked into the casualty department for an examination. An x-ray did not show a significant crack, but the doctor said that this was fairly usual until calcification started in a few days after the break.

The Falkland Islands and South America

The injury made any muscular activity and even sleeping very painful. I had planned for Port Stanley to be the penultimate stop before a dash to the Antarctic Peninsula, the goal of the whole crazy trip since leaving the Baltic. I put together a revised schedule for the next month, bearing in mind that we had to be in Montevideo, Uruguay, in mid-February to meet the next crew, who would be with me as far as New York. I allowed a week for the 900-nm passage to Port Lockroy, six days for the leg back to Port Williams, and two weeks from there to Uruguay. There would be almost no time in each port. Bearing in mind the vagaries of the Southern Ocean, it was extremely optimistic.

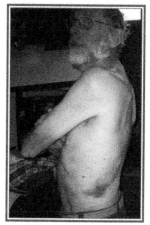

Eric shows his cracked rib, South Atlantic, 2004

When I discussed it with Andrew and Gary I detected, shall we say, reservations? They pointed out that I was not a fully-functioning crew member, that they had no experience of the Southern Ocean or of sailing in ice, and that without me being 100 percent effective they were somewhat apprehensive about the plan. I brooded about their concerns for a day as we lay at the massive floating dock a mile or so east of Stanley. I decided they were probably right, and more to the point, if one of them suffered an injury we would be down to one able-bodied crew, and the Antarctic is not a place to be so short-handed.

So I made the decision to skip the Antarctic in 2005. I was very frustrated. I had made a massive investment in time and labor the previous winter to get the boat ready and had spent months sailing as far as Port Stanley. Later, two reports of sailing in Antarctica in 2005 had confirmed ice conditions were bad. The Bransfield Strait, for example, was choked with ice from Deception Island to Port Lockroy. This was a passage we sailed in 1999, encountering only a few icebergs and no pack ice. So prudence was a bitter, but wise choice.

To fill time before we were due in Montevideo, we decided to spend a couple of weeks in the Falkland Islands. I had never cruised the dozens of islands that make up this archipelago. We spent a pleasant week

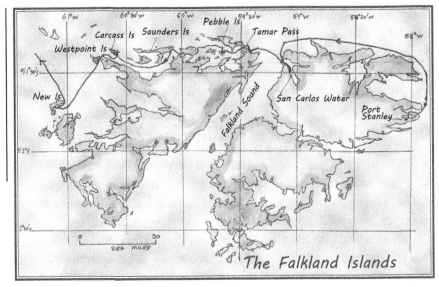

The Falkland Islands

in Stanley, a little longer than we planned, as we were trapped in port by a strong northerly gale. We were tied up only a few yards from Seamen's Mission, which provided many comforts and services. Stanley itself was a 30-minute walk along the shore, usually done in the rain. We were "adopted" by a native "kelper," Patrick, who gave us lots of local advice and a package of over a dozen books when we left. He and his friend Paul in turn appreciated our stock of rum.

We had a fascinating visit by three deck-hands off a Danish freighter that tied up near to us. The ship plied regularly between the Falklands and England. Besides the three, the entire crew consisted of two officers and a cook. I was amazed to learn that only the officers stood watches on the bridge, four hours on and four hours off. During the watch, the duty officer took care of the engines, communications, and paper work. The last thing they did was look out of the window. This confirmed my long-held suspicion that the odd ship we meet at sea was certainly not looking out for us; the watch was probably down below changing the oil in the engine!

I visited the Governor, whom I had met on our last trip to South Georgia Island in 2003. He said the old whaling station at Grytviken had mostly been demolished because of the asbestos contamination. Of course, we spent convivial times at the watering holes, such as The Globe and The Victory. Before leaving for our cruise, I had to phone the owners of the islands we planned to visit; all the islands are privately owned and it was necessary to get permission to land, but we were warmly welcomed. Outside of Stanley, the outlying islands are known locally as "camp." I was also lucky to meet my friends, Jen and Pete Clements, who were very familiar with the area—just by chance the cruise ship on which they served as guides, *Explorer II*, was tied up to the dock for a few hours. Jen and Pete lived in Brookhaven just a mile from my house. Pete was born in the Falklands and made very helpful suggestions for our local itinerary.

After a one-day passage along the north coast, during which we endured southwest winds up to 40 knots, with hail, we anchored in San Carlos Water. The next day we entered a labyrinth of small islands and rocks via the Tamar Pass. Although we had tide tables for Stanley, we did not know the time difference to get a favorable current and we were wrong by hours—the current was ebbing strongly against us. With Gary at the wheel and Andrew on look-out at the bow, I tried to navigate the zig-zag course past several shoals. Things just didn't seem to be going right. I kept popping up the companionway for a look and glancing at the radar, and finally the GPS read-out solved the mystery.

As we penetrated the pass, the current overwhelmed the roaring diesel and we were going backwards over the bottom. The pass teemed with life, birds of all descriptions fluttered and swooped overhead, and dolphins and penguins bobbed alongside. Eventually, we got through to more open water and after a couple of hours, we anchored for the night. We inflated the dinghy, but when I tried to fire up the outboard engine it refused to start. It was about two miles from our anchorage to the Pebble Island settlement, so we decided to skip a visit there. Instead, after supper, we watched Laurel and Hardy as the wind howled on deck, and kept a close eye on nearby landmarks to make sure the anchor was not dragging. Before we left Stanley, we had attached the 65 lb. fisherman's anchor to the chain as a precaution against the kelp that litters the bottom in many bays and harbors of the Falklands.

Darkness came late and only lasted a few hours. In the morning, we traversed an intricate channel to Saunders Island called Woolly Gut, sailing by such eye-catching names as Nipple Point, Golding Channel, Anxious Passage, and Dirty Ditch Passage. When we dropped anchor at the settlement we used the 37-year-old Seagull engine to power the inflatable. Normally, I only used this engine to propel the rigid dinghy, as the 8 hp Nissan was too heavy for that small boat. But the Nissan had suffered terminal ignition failure and would not run again until I arranged for a new module to be brought by the incoming crew.

We were greeted at the farmhouse by Biffo, the owner's sister, and her father-in-law. She told us they farmed 7,500 sheep and 200 head of cattle, and ran a small guesthouse for about a dozen visitors, mostly birders and photographers. Later we met the owner himself, David, at one of the farm buildings. I was very interested to inspect a wind generator installed a couple of years before, following a government subsidy for this purpose to all the camp farmers. This had reduced his diesel fuel consumption by 75 percent. Biffo suggested we move our anchorage to a bay a few miles away which was populated by penguins and was only a short walk to an albatross breeding colony. This we did and while we were on the beach, Biffo showed up with a couple of sturdy, baffled-looking sheep which she had man-handled into the back of her Land Rover. We walked to the cliffs to inspect the birds, but one disappointment was that my video camera malfunctioned, and the only shots I could get were with the digital still camera. The next day, we made our way to Carcass Island, and en route I called my daughter, Brenda, on the Iridium satellite phone so that an ignition module for the Nissan engine could be added to all the other spare parts the new crew was bringing. We anchored off the farmhouse and started to chug ashore in the inflatable. Immediately, we were surrounded by cavorting dolphins that seemed delighted to have a new playmate. They were quite gaudily striped, black and white, and later we found out they were a sub-species called Commerson's Dolphin.

On Carcass Island, the owners Lorraine and Rob farm a few hundred sheep to keep the grass cut, but they mainly run a guesthouse for visiting tourists and scientists. Throughout the islands these visitors, residents, and even freight are moved by the Falkland Islands Government Airline that rarely operates above a few hundred feet, and lands on the grass near the settlements. After tea and cake, we explored the shoreline, inhabited by burrowing Magellanic penguins, until driving rain drove us back to the boat.

It was just five miles to Westpoint Island and we had our anchor down well before darkness. (I nearly wrote "before the sun set," but we rarely saw the sun.) I first sailed to Westpoint Island in 1992; it had its share of unique kelper names such as Death Cove, Cape Terrible, Mount Misery, Cat Cove, and Grave Cove. Westpoint was owned by Lily and Roddy Napier, and we shared a friendship with Dennis Puleston, Jen's father, who lived near me in Brookhaven and was a frequent visitor to the Falklands. No doubt inspired by Dennis, Roddy was a leading player in the development of conservation plans for the Falklands.

We dinghied ashore in the morning and said hello to Lily and Roddy. Chatting over a cup of tea, we discussed all that had happened since my last visit, and then Lily drove us to the west side of the island in the ubiquitous Land Rover. Hundreds of birds, mainly albatrosses, nested together in the tussock grass; it was an amazing sight. Rockhopper penguins made their way down the cliff face to fish in the turbulent sea breaking on the beach. However, it was my impression that their numbers were considerably down since my last visit. We walked back to the farm and made our goodbyes. We had a great run with a brisk wind to New Island but the land was shrouded in fog when we arrived. We groped our way in by radar, dropped the anchor and decided to wait until morning before running ashore. The land and settlement buildings were intermittently visible in the drizzle, as wraiths of fog came and went. We shut the hatch, fired up the heater and watched a W.C. Fields movie after supper.

New Island was divided into two halves with different owners; their houses were only a few hundred yards apart. The first house we visited was owned by the author of a wonderful guide to the wildlife of the area, but unfortunately, he had flown off to Stanley. Much to Andrew's delight, his daughter Georgina was in residence. He had met her previously during our sojourn in Stanley. We bought a copy of her father's book, *Wildlife of the Falkland Islands*, by J. J. Strange.

Next we visited Kim and Tony, an American and a Brit who met working on cruise ships and fell in love with the Falklands and each other. They bought the house on New Island and lived a happy but isolated life. They had one young son, aged about three, I would guess. It turns out Tony was also a friend of Dennis Puleston, my neighbor from back home. He gave us tips on the local wildlife colonies and Gary and I made a long trek over a headland to try to find some seals. On the way, we passed the beached wreck of a WWII Canadian minesweeper called *Protector*.

This was to be our last little adventure in the Falklands, so we put away the dinghy, hauled up the anchor, and by mid-afternoon New

Cruise to Ireland, the Baltic, England, Portugal, Brazil and the Falklands, 2004-2005

Island faded from view on the stern as we sailed away to Uruguay. The latitude of the Falklands is in the 50s south, and as we sailed north into the Roaring Forties, I confidently expected mostly strong, westerly winds, such as we experienced in 2003 when we sailed from South Georgia to Santos. It was not to be. Instead, we had calms, north or northeasterly winds on the nose, and choppy seas that precluded running the engine. These conditions worsened as we got into the 120-mile wide estuary of the River Plate. Here, the water shoaled to about 30 feet and the chop kicked up by the long fetch reminded me of Buzzards Bay at its worst. It took us two days to sail across the estuary to the approach channel for Montevideo. On the way we passed within a couple of miles of the sunken hulk of the WWII German battleship *Graf Spee*. The ship was scuttled by the captain in neutral waters after a brush with British cruisers. Several books describe this fascinating story and it was also a movie.

I called the harbor control on the VHF radio as we approached, and in faltering English we were told it was a commercial harbor only and yachts were not accommodated. This was a problem. We had a minor repair to make to the running rigging before we could sail to the next port, Punta del Este, which I knew had a yacht marina. I asked permission to anchor off the beach fringing the wide Montevideo Bay while we affected repairs before an overnight sail to Punta. For some reason this seemed to trigger their suspicions and we were told quite peremptorily to return to the approach channel and enter the harbor. Our position was monitored by the harbor radar and we were issued several course changes before we were met by a launch that guided us to a quay full of Uruguayan navy ships, one of which swung out of the way to allow us to tie up, and then came back alongside, hemming us in. I was quite apprehensive; had we inadvertently violated some local law? In these security-conscious times you never know! A naval seaman escorted me with the ship's papers to the headquarters building. Here, the boat was cleared into Uruguay with little fuss and our passports examined. I was told we were free to enter the city. What was going on? Due to their general lack of English and my lack of Spanish, I never found out. It was late afternoon when we walked into the old city. Near the dock area it was pretty much run-down, with crumbling buildings and cracked, uneven sidewalks. After a mile or so, we found the more modern center, and even more importantly, we found an ATM which disgorged local currency, so we treated ourselves to a beer and then a pizza. We had arrived in civilization. What we did not know at the time was that Andrew lost his credit card after using the machine, and replacing it took much of his time later when he was in Uruguay.

Unfortunately, there were no bathroom facilities or showers at the quay we were tied to, and so smelling slightly high we walked back into town the next morning after a traditional pancake breakfast aboard the boat. I passed an internet outlet and checked my e-mail, which had built up to an enormous list since we left Port Stanley. Then I looked for a barber, as my beard had not been trimmed since I started to grow it after leaving Lisbon. I had tried in Stanley, but the only barber on the island was on vacation in England. Eventually, I chanced upon the most up-market hair dressing salon I have ever visited. I asked for a beard and hair trim. This required the attention of a male barber and three quite curvaceous young ladies who wound up by shampooing my hair as I sat in a special chair that tilted to immerse my head in a bowl at the rear. Total price: $20. I think at home that session would have cost $100. After a light lunch, I found the section of town where the automotive shops clustered and bought a new car radio for the main cabin, the third to be installed on the trip. These units do not tolerate well the salt and humidity of an ocean-going sailboat.

I had arranged to leave for Punta del Este at 4:30 pm and to my surprise, the crew of the outboard vessel showed up on time, and we left promptly for a very pleasant night sail to the next port. As our heading was easterly for this short, 60-mile leg, we were able reach when a light wind came after midnight. We tied up at Punta bow-to with help from another yachtie, who attached our stern to a mooring buoy. Quite a few sea lions make the harbor their home, and it is spectacular to see these 500-pound beasts propel themselves onto a jetty four feet above the water and settle down for a nice sunbath. My next crew was due to arrive in a week, so this gave us time to carry out a few minor repairs, bend on the genoa jib, change the anchor, get the laundry done, and explore the town.

Punta is a modern, clean town on a peninsula, with a beach on one side and the harbor on the other. It is a popular vacation resort for Argentineans from the south side of the River Plate. Many owned apartments in the town. In the evening, it did not come alive until after nine, and in fact, many restaurants did not even open until that hour.

At midnight, the main street was thronged by crowds of gaily-clad, mostly young people. All the shops were open until one or two in the morning. There were some oddities in the Uruguayan way of life to an American eye. For example, restaurants charge about a dollar for using their cutlery with a meal. There were no postal collection boxes; you must go to a post office.

Gary returned to South Africa after a few days. When I rented a car to pick up the incoming crew at the airport, I discovered driving habits were also a little different. Signs were few and far between, and often they were painted right on the road—you must look down, not up! I got lost driving to the airport, as the single sign indicating the turn-off read "Carrasco," not "Montevideo Airport," as one would expect, and I missed it. It was a bit like labeling JFK Airport "Queens Airport." I arrived just as Ruth and Sasha were pushing their heavily-loaded luggage carts into the lobby. Both these ladies had spotted my crew call on the website and signed up for the remainder of the cruise. Ruth was a friend I first met at vintage car rallies; she owned a red 3-liter Bentley that was very sporty. She had crewed on ocean passages some years before. I had not met Sasha previously, but she owned a 32-foot sailboat, had a CG Captain's license and wanted to get some ocean time.

Once they had settled in and seen a little of Punta, we drove the rental car to Montevideo for an afternoon. In the center of town, there were many street buskers and traders selling antiques and souvenirs from scores of small stalls. As usual, I was pushed for time, so three days after the new crew signed on, we left for Santos, Brazil. Andrew waved goodbye from the dock; he intended to fly to New York in a couple of days. It was about 850 sea miles to Santos from Punta del Este. I decided to leave the storm mainsail bent on the boom, as this would minimize the chances of having to reef it. But the down-side was a lack of drive in light winds. Naturally, we encountered just such conditions most of the time. Although we had some wind from the south at the beginning, the weather soon settled into pattern that would persist for much of our sail off the Brazilian coast—light north or northeast winds or calms. We rarely saw the wind speed exceed 15 knots except in the odd squall.

On the way north, with the boat completely becalmed, we were twice able to slip over the side for a swim. We made our landfall just as the sun was setting, and an atypical south wind wafted us into Santos

Bay past a dozen anchored freighters waiting their turn to go upriver to the docks. As we entered the river mouth, it began to rain heavily—not ideal conditions for the ladies to drop the mainsail for the first time. I turned the boat into wind just below the old Portuguese fort that many centuries ago had been attacked by Francis Drake. Ruth and Sasha rigged the unfamiliar lazy jacks, dropped the boom into the gallows and secured the mainsail with gaskets. All things considered, it went well.

Chugging the last mile up the river to the turn-off for the yacht club, I was momentarily disoriented by a huge blue and orange building on the east bank, which was not there two years ago. It was the new ferry and bus terminal, which had replaced the ramshackle building that I was used to. We tied up at the familiar Santos Yacht Club with some help from the fellows on the dock. We had logged 1,352 miles from Punta and taken 10 days. Unfortunately, the combination of head winds and choppy seas would persist for nearly another 2,500 miles as we clawed our way north along the east coast of South America. In addition, the southern branch of the equatorial current bucked us to the tune of 15 to 25 miles a day. The next morning, we organized the laundry, had a shower, and took a taxi into the old town to complete the dreary ritual of checking in. The Brazilian bureaucracy was always slow, but this time our visas were in order, and eventually, after visiting three separate offices, we had all our documents stamped, something I would have to repeat when we left. Back at the Yacht Club, I met Dancini, a friend from my last visit to Santos. Now, though, he was the captain of an impressive motor yacht that belonged to a TV personality.

In the evening, we took a bus into Guaruja to check our e-mail at the local Dunkin' Donuts (truly, that was where the terminals were) and had dinner. Unfortunately, it rained steadily for much of our stay in Santos, which dampened the sightseeing for the ladies. In the morning we restocked at the local supermarket, and this they enjoyed, getting to know unfamiliar brands. After lugging all the stuff back to the boat and cramming it into lockers, Ruth and Sasha went back to Guaruja for the shopping.

The next morning, I repeated the clearance procedure for a departure the next day, and in the afternoon we all went to a ritzy section of Santos on the beach called Gonzaga. Our evening meal was at the Yacht Club, so we dressed up a little and Ruth and Sasha enjoyed sushi. We refueled and spent the evening tied to the gas dock so that we could make an early start. In windless conditions we powered for a day and a half to the scenic cruising area centered in Ilha Grande. We anchored in the pretty port of Abraão for the night. We had dinner ashore and discovered our waiter had lived in Danbury, Connecticut, quite close to Ruth's home. The next day we moved down the coast for another night at anchor. The crew went swimming on the beach and we had dinner at a small bar. Several dogs waited patiently and expectantly in the shadows for their share. The next morning when we went back for a final swim, they recognized their benefactors and followed us to the beach.

Our first navigational problem was to round Cabo Frio (Spanish for "cold"), so named because of the upwelling of Antarctic water in the region. The sailing conditions were particularly frustrating—light head winds, a choppy sea surface, and an adverse current. At one point, we tacked south for several hours and then tacked backed, and made good only about ten miles towards the Cape for all that time. Under power, it was very hot in the engine room and George, the autopilot, began to wilt under the heat. Eventually, we rounded the Cape and slowly beat our way north towards Cabedelo, our last chance to re-stock before the long leg to the Caribbean .

One morning we sailed into a small fishing port called Guarapari and pushed our way in between the local boats to the fuel dock. Sasha and I filled the tanks, while Ruth rushed off to the market to get fresh fruit and veggies. We were soon off again. The sailing conditions were not unpleasant—mostly light wind or none at all, with a calm sea.

Eric carrying out repairs at the masthead

Two days later the jib began to luff badly and I discovered the halyard had either broken or detached from the upper swivel. This meant a trip to the masthead for me to rig the spare halyard. If things went wrong, God forbid, what would the relatively inexperienced crew do? We discussed this possibility before I climbed into the bosun's chair and Ruth and Sasha winched me to the top of the mast. Head for the nearest sizable port, I suggested, which happened to be Salvador. We programmed the waypoint for this port into the GPS and then up I went. George steered the boat slowly down-wind to minimize pitching, but we rolled badly. An hour later I was back on deck, safe and sound, a little stiff from holding onto the mast like grim death, but the halyard was attached, and we didn't have to go to Salvador!

We continued our slow beat north, and Saint Patrick's Day came and went. We had a double slug for happy hour and Irish Stew with real pratties for supper. Often when under sail, we watched a movie after happy hour. Ruth had brought three Marx Brothers comedies on DVD and we greatly enjoyed these vintage classics.

Two days from Cabedelo, the wind backed a little and we were able to lay a direct course, but it remained light. We anchored in the Paraiba River at the small village of Jacare, in sight of Brian's familiar boat yard.

To the Caribbean and Home

We spent only two days at Jacare but we got a lot done. The major job was to replace the engine exhaust hose, which was leaking fumes and sea water. The owner of the marina, Brian, managed to find me a piece of hose that was a little too thick and a little too large, but in this remote part of Brazil you work with what you've got. It was very sweaty work installing it; the temperature in the engine room was close to 100° F and every few minutes I had to stop to drink copious drafts of water. I rarely drink water, as I remember the remark made by W.C. Fields when he inadvertently tried some—"I don't know what it is but it won't sell!"

The two ladies retired to the Orca Pousada, a Brazilian B&B, so at least they were spared the salty language emanating from the engine room. When the engine was running again, we restocked at the Hiper-market and refueled by jerry jug, transferring 90 gallons of diesel by dinghy into our thirsty tanks. After a delicious home-made dinner at the pousada, which cost all of $4, we left in the late evening, sailing down the Paraiba River.

On the open sea there was no wind, and as we powered towards the equator the electric autopilot, George, began to show signs of heat prostration. It was located only a couple of feet above the engine and was so hot I could not touch the case. I cannibalized a blower and hose from the cabin heater and rigged a cooling breeze for the unit. After a day, we encountered the doldrums—grey skies, plenty of rain squalls, and fitful winds. Five days out from Brazil, we crossed the equator and Ruth and Sasha joined the many pollywog crews who have made their first crossing aboard *Fiona*. Naturally, Father Neptune showed up and we killed a bottle of champagne that Sasha had brought along.

199

A day or so north of the equator, we picked up the northeast trade winds. We made good time compared to our beat along the South American coast in 1995. Our best day was 151 miles, made good towards St. Martin. But the winds were not as favorable as those we encountered on the same leg on the 2002-2003 cruise, when we averaged nearly 170 miles a day during the last week on the way to Barbados. Another reason was that we bucked a countercurrent that at times ran as high as 2 knots. Although the Pilot Charts showed a smooth flow of ocean current from the equator, which eventually turns into the Gulf Stream, in practice the flow was obviously very turbulent, with many whirls and eddies.

The nice weather gave Ruth and Sasha a chance to practice celestial navigation, but I did not have the *Nautical Almanac* for 2005. Then I remembered that Cathy had installed a program in the laptop when we were cruising in the Baltic. Sure enough, this had all the data we needed for about the next 50 years. The ladies were quite good at using this program, and our position lines coincided with the GPS to within three miles. Before we got to St. Martin, the wind veered so that we sailed past Barbuda and Antigua on a run. We arrived at Marigot before lunch after a 16-day passage. After refueling, we dropped anchor in the bay just north of Kay's condo.

St. Martin was getting over-developed, which resulted in terrible traffic problems, but I could still get the finest croissants and coffee for breakfast that I ever tasted. Once again, our visit was brief. We replenished the propane, bought some rum and had dinner a couple times with Kay and some guests who were staying with her. We left after two days for Bermuda as the sun was setting.

We sailed with the trade winds until about 24° N, but after that we experienced indifferent winds, sometimes on the nose. One afternoon, two large whales surfaced just behind the boat. I think they were Minke. The whales came just in time for my birthday (I turned 39 again). I baked a cake and the ladies sang the traditional song, though I have never liked birthdays. We had made the passage in just over a week.

My daughter Brenda and old friend Lew were waiting to greet us in Bermuda. Brenda decided to stay at small B&B in St. George's. Lew, who had edited many of my cruising videos, moved onto the boat.

Sasha decided to leave the cruise in Bermuda and I went into a flurry of e-mail activity to find a replacement. I also put up a notice at the Royal Bermuda Yacht Club, and that produced several enquiries from young people who were signing off a large Canadian ex-fishing boat called *Farley Mowat*. Perhaps the ship should be called Fairly Militant, as it was run by conservationists who did such things as harass sealers.

One reason for pushing to get to Bermuda was that the spring meeting of the Cruising Club of America (CCA) was coincidentally being held there at the same time. The opening reception was in the afternoon of the day we arrived. We all enjoyed this party and the next evening, Brenda and I attended a ritzy dinner celebrating the centennial of the founding of the Bermuda Race. When Brenda left, we sailed to the west end for a couple of days to anchor in Mangrove Bay and Ely's Harbour.

I had sailed to Bermuda many times since my first visit in 1968, and there have been great changes in that period. For example, black Bermudians were virtually invisible in the 1960s, but by 2005, they ran the government. But there were signs of stress in the society of this beautiful island. A symptom was that Trimingham's, a flagship department store chain, was closing down after 160 years in business. The reason given to me by a Bermudian friend was that the offshore banking and insurance sector of the economy paid such high salaries that the cost of living had sky-rocketed. The other major sector, tourism, could not match these salaries and remain competitive with other vacation destinations. As there were many more unskilled and semi-skilled jobs in servicing the tourism sector than there were in the offshore sector, that was the problem.

Lew flew home after a week and Mahius joined us from the *Farley Mowat*. Ruth, Mahius and I set sail on the last leg of the cruise to Long Island after refueling with duty-free diesel. A large high pressure zone had settled over Bermuda when we left, and this provided nice sailing with northeast winds in the 15-knot range for a couple of days. Then we ran into the inevitable front that always seems to lurk between the island and the mainland. But the winds remained fairly light and we crossed the Gulf Stream in cloudy weather with moderate seas. It certainly felt colder after our sojourn in the Tropics. Again, we sailed into high pressure, which killed the wind and so we powered for the last day and a half across a sea that was so calm we could see stars reflected in it at night. Soon we were picking up New York radio stations, and a small land bird found a temporary home on the boat.

We got stuck in the Patchogue River, just as we were almost at our home dock, but my friend Bob on *Fireplace* pulled us through the mud. Perhaps one day they will dredge it. Gale warnings were broadcast for the day after we arrived, so we had timed it just right. The leg home from Bermuda was 680 miles, making a total of 3,789 miles for the leg from Brazil to Long Island. It had not been one of my most enjoyable cruises, but I think my crews had a good time, except perhaps for Sean and poor, mixed-up Celeste. I had 15 different crew members during the cruise and therein was one of the key problems—only four had sailed with me before, and the rest had literally to learn the ropes as they cruised, a period that can be trying for me.

I was also very disappointed we did not achieve the ultimate goal of sailing once again to Antarctica. This was largely my fault, as the strategic planning of the trip was poor. With hindsight, it was obvious I should have planned to fly home from Lisbon, not London. We would have had better weather in the Channel and the Bay of Biscay and would probably not have lost as much time as we did in port. I should have planned to arrive at Port Stanley much earlier to leave a bigger margin for contingencies, such as breaking a bone or two. You live and learn.

The cruise was also plagued by mild or non-existent winds. Although we experienced heavy weather in the North Sea, the Bay of Biscay, and the South Atlantic near the Falklands, the rest of the trip was very benign. For example, we never reefed the mainsail all the way north from Port Stanley to Long Island, a distance of about 8,000 nm. I see from the log that about 14 percent of all the time accrued on the diesel engine since the boat was launched in 1983 was added on this single trip. Days on end under power were not much fun.

There were a few highlights, of course. The Baltic, London at St. Katharine's Dock, cruising the Falkland Islands, and our visit to Uruguay were all very enjoyable. Perhaps that was because they were new for me. To be fun, cruises must reach fresh places. We watched many movies on DVD using the laptop computer, and I read a good deal. Outstanding books were *Into Thin Air* by Jon Krakauer, *The Selfish Gene* by Richard Dawkins, and *Ice with Everything* by H. W. Tilman.

Fiction I enjoyed included *A Soldier of the Great War* by Mark Helprin, *Birdsong* by Sebastian Faulks, and *Bright Day* by J.B. Priestley.

When I got home, I proposed to the Cruising Club of America that they should sponsor a new ocean race for sailboats with no fossil fuel on board. All energy would be supplied by the motion of the boat or sunlight. Of course, this was based on my own experience with the shaft generator on *Fiona*. Although I have every admiration for single-handed racers such as Ellen MacArthur, who had, in fact, sailed past the Falklands just before we arrived on her record-breaking circumnavigation, I feel it is somewhat ironic that they depend on a throbbing diesel to provide power for everything on board except propulsion.

Fiona Log, 2004 - 2005

PORTS	LEFT / ARR'D	COMMENT	NAUTICAL MILES
Patchogue-Provincetown	6/12 to 6/17	Stopped Block Is and Newport	214
P'town-St Johns, Nfld	6/18 to 6/27	Stopped Lunenburg	1,027
St Johns-Kinsale, Ireland	7/1 to 7/16	Atlantic Crossing	1,805
Kinsale-Bantry Bay	7/19 to 7/23	ICC/CCA cruise	131
Bantry Bay to Inverness, UK	7/25 to 8/1	via Caledonian Canal	657
Inverness to Thuro Is, Denmark	8/3 to 8/10	North Sea, Linfjorden Canal	731
Thuro to Kiel Canal, Germany	8/11 to 9/10	Cruised Baltic to Sweden	952
Kiel Canal to London, UK	9/11 to 9/17	North Sea. Flew to NY	661
London to Falmouth	10/13 to 10/18	English Channel	403
Falmouth to Lisbon, Portugal	10/25 to 11/2	Bay of Biscay	941
Lisbon to Tenerife, Canary Is	11/15 to 11/21	Tied up Santa Cruz	728
Tenerife to Cape Verde Is	11/22 to 11/30	Anchored Mindelo	976

PORTS	LEFT / ARR'D	COMMENT	NAUTICAL MILES
Cape V' Is to Cabedelo, Brazil	12/1 to 12/13	Atlantic Crossing	1,438
Cabedelo to Stanley, Falkland Is	12/15 to 1/14	South Atlantic	3,186
Stanley to New Is	1/22 to 1/28	Cruised Falkland Is	258
New Is to Montevideo, Uruguay	1/29 to 2/8	Passage to S. America	1,049
M'V to Punta del Este	2/9 to 2/10	Shifted Port	41
P del E to Santos, Brazil	2/20 to 3/2	Head-winds, contrary current	1,088
Santos to Ihla Grande	3/5 to 3/8	Cruised Ihla Grande	164
Ihla Grande to Cabedelo	3/9 to 3/22	Head-winds, contrary current	1,444
Cabedelo to St. Martin	3/25 to 4/11	Crossed equator at 39° 27' W	2,274
St. Martin to Bermuda	4/13 to 4/21	CCA Spring Meet	835
Bermuda to Patchogue	4/30 to 5/06	Crossing the Gulf Stream	680
Total	**6/2004 to 5/2005**		**21,683**

7

Cruise to Antarctica Again
2006-2007

In the late summer and early fall of 2005, I spent six weeks cruising Maine and cogitating about the coming year. After the disappointment of the 2004-2005 cruise there was really no question of where to head for in 2006—Antarctica.

I also decided to have the diesel engine rebuilt during the winter. Lube oil consumption was up; oil pressure was down. Weeks Yard lifted the engine from the hull using the travel-lift. When the mechanic, Richie, at Long Island Diesel removed the balance unit from the bottom of the engine the cause of the problems was obvious; a bushing had seized on the oil pump shaft and was machining the casing away. Numerous parts were replaced during the rebuild, and the old Perkins was ready to put in another 12,000 hours of service.

Fiona *anchored at Butter Island, Maine*

In planning the trip, I was not going to mess around, I decided to head directly for the South Atlantic, but allow some time for poking into a few Brazilian ports. To add some novelty to the cruise, I planned to return along the west coast of South America and pop back in the Atlantic via the Panama Canal. This would be an east-to-west rounding of the Horn, although I hoped to sail far south of that lonely cape.

205

The crew consisted of Mickey, who had signed up for the whole trip, and Dan, on board just for the Atlantic crossing. An old friend of my son, Peg, bummed a ride as far as Block Island. Mickey had just retired; he worked for many years as an electrician for the New York City subway system and sailed his own boat with the South Bay Cruising Club (SBCC).

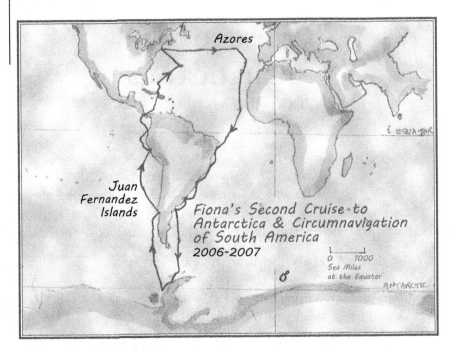

The Azores to Brazil

We shoved off in mid-June and negotiated the Patchogue River without going aground, although as usual, Bob on *Fireplace* escorted us for a few miles as insurance against that eventuality. There was no wind when we powered through Fire Island Inlet and it was a dull ride a couple of miles south of the coast as we chugged east past all the familiar lights at Moriches, Shinnecock, Amagansett, and on to the powerful light at Montauk Point. Here we picked up an early morning breeze and had a great sail across Block Island Sound to the Great Salt Pond.

Activities ashore included our traditional walk to Southeast Light, and then Peg caught the afternoon ferry back to Long Island. The next morning, we refueled and left for Flores in the Azores. Our trip across the Atlantic was dominated by areas of high pressure. At first there was a high to our south and we enjoyed good sailing with the clockwise winds on the starboard quarter. Then the high moved north and we sailed into the center. This gave us days of fairly light winds interspersed with squalls. The crossing from Block Island of a little more than 2,000 nm took 15 days. It was a mild introduction to ocean sailing for Mickey and Dan, as the highest wind we encountered was a brief 40 knots in a squall, but mostly the wind was in the 15-knot range. On the way over, we were able to try for the first time receiving e-mail using the Iridium satellite phone.

Flores was as beautiful as ever and the locals just as nice as ever. We anchored north of the new jetty at Lajes, and took a spectacular taxi ride to the main town, Santa Cruz, where we had a vast lunch at a restaurant overlooking the harbor, if you could call it that. In fact, I marveled again at how on earth we got *Fiona* into such a tight space during our 1986 cruise to the Azores. It was tiny, with fearsome rocks guarding the entrance, lying opposite the dock.

An overnight passage in windless conditions brought us to the huge marina at Horta on Faial Island. Hundreds of yachts from many countries make Horta a stopover for almost any Atlantic cruise. As usual, I freshened up *Fiona*'s sign on the jetty and updated it to include cruises made since we were last in Horta in 2002. Dan left the boat a day after we arrived and Louise joined the crew a couple of days later. Louise had crewed sporadically since 1986, taking time off from her work as a scientist at Brookhaven National Laboratory. Shortly after that, Mickey's wife, son, and mother-in-law flew in and checked into the hotel behind the marina. We all took a taxi tour of the island; a highlight was the view of the caldera (crater) of the huge volcano in the middle of the island. It was also interesting to visit the site and museum of earthquakes and volcanic eruptions that rocked the west end of the island for several months in 1957-58. The lighthouse was destroyed and the gaunt ruins now stand in the center of a field of ash. The Azores lie on the junction of three tectonic plates and all the islands were formed by volcanic activity.

We had a fascinating visit to the youngest island, Pico, whose 7,700-foot volcano dominated the view to the east from Faial. The short ferry ride across the channel separating the two islands took a half-hour to the port of Madalena. Just a few minutes from Madalena was a newly-opened visitor center at a lava tube. These tubes were formed when rivers of lava cooled and solidified on the outside, but liquid lava continued to flow on the inside. If the lava flow decreased, the level dropped and when the whole thing cooled off, a tube was left. The one on Pico was over three miles long, and in places the ceiling was nearly 50 feet high. A short section was open to the public, which we traversed with a guide. Underfoot it was very rough and stout shoes were needed. The guide showed us evidence that over the centuries, the tube carried lava from several eruptions.

On Pico we also visited a whaling museum. Whaling was a major industry until it was banned about 25 years earlier. I was glad this barbaric practice had stopped, but it was interesting to see a movie made in the 1970s; the islanders hunted from open boats like the New Eng-

landers a century earlier. When Mickey's family left, we made the crossing to São Jorge with a nice southwest wind, anchoring in the small harbor for a couple of days in the lee of a high, steep cliff. We discovered that vast numbers of shearwaters nested in the cliff; in the evenings and mornings the racket they made was unbelievable. It sounded like a thousand tinny loudspeakers playing steel band music. One afternoon we climbed a volcanic hill overlooking the town of Velas, and at the top we met a charming Swedish couple that we invited to the boat for happy hour.

View of Pico from the marina at Horta

We sailed the next morning to the island of Graciosa and anchored in the lee of a new jetty at Praia. Only a few miles from Praia lies a fantastic volcanic crater I remembered vividly from my visit in 1986. In the center of the crater a tunnel sloped down to an underground lake in a cavern called Furna do Enxofre—sulfur furnace. To get to the cavern, we descended down a spiral staircase inside a tower built a hundred years ago. At the bottom, the smell of sulfur was overpowering and gas bubbled up from mud holes in the rocks. It was all very reminiscent of "Lord of the Rings."

The next day we sailed to our last island in the Azores, Terceira. This was the third island of the group to be discovered in the 15th century after Santa Maria and São Miguel. Clearly, the early navigators were not very imaginative that day; Terceira means "third" in Portuguese. We tied up at a new marina in Angra do Heroísmo, so named because of heroic fighting there in a civil war. It was damaged in an earthquake in 1980 and had been attractively rebuilt. Here was our chance to do some laundry in the new facilities and stock up for the trip to Madeira, 600 miles to the southeast. We had supper on our first night at an up-market restaurant strongly recommended by the marina manager. Unfortunately, Mickey's fish could apparently have been fresher and he was laid low the next day by tummy trouble.

While he suffered, Louise and I climbed a steep hill overlooking the harbor and at the top, to our surprise, we found a cluster of old anti-aircraft guns installed by the British in WWII to protect an airfield built by the RAF. As the nearest mainland, Portugal, was over 700 miles away and was neutral in the war, I was puzzled about where they expected the enemy to come from. Later, I realized the attacker would probably be the Vichy French in Algeria or Morocco. I remembered when we visited Gibraltar that the French had bombed the place many times in WWII.

When we left, Mickey was still under the weather but gamely stood his watches, even though he was not able to eat for a couple of days. The first day and a half saw us chugging along under power in windless, rainy weather. Then in the middle of the second night, a steady wind developed from the northeast and we enjoyed a great sail to Madeira. On the last day we slowed the boat in order to arrive at the capital, Funchal, in daylight. The inner harbor was little changed from when Bill Steenberg and I visited in 2000, except there were more local pleasure boats, leaving even less room for visiting yachts. We tied up three abreast and went for a shower. Louise reported that the ladies room was infested with cockroaches. (Ah! The pleasures of the cruising life.) In the afternoon we all took a ride on the telefericos (cable car) over the rooftops of Funchal to a cloudy summit overlooking the town. The highlight was watching nervous tourists being propelled downhill in wicker sleds guided by two grinning natives in white suits with straw hats. We took the cable car back. The next day we booked a fascinating tour of the island in a minivan. Once clear of the Funchal conurbation, the interior was wildly beautiful—the high mountains and steep valleys told the story of the island's turbulent birth in volcanic eruptions a million years ago.

After a day of boat repairs, shopping and, for one member of the crew, a visit to the beauty parlor, we left for La Palma Island in the Canaries. Once clear of the wind shadow off the south coast, we enjoyed strong northerly winds that drove *Fiona* to her destination in less than two days. When we tied up at the yacht club in Santa Cruz de La Palma, we had entered Spanish territory. However, as we were already in the European Union there was no bureaucratic hassle to deal with. The town is built on the edge of a huge, ancient crater, and the buildings in the center date from the 16th century, with doors and windows framed in massive stone blocks. The second floor of these buildings usually carried an elaborately carved balcony. Once again, we signed up for a tour of the island. The northern part was very agricultural; La Palma supplies a large percentage of the bananas consumed in the EU. As part of the tour we visited a plantation. These were located near sea level and bananas were a popular crop with farmers because the fruit was produced continuously, independent of the season. We also visited a rain forest at an altitude of over 2,000 feet. The guide explained that a million years ago, the whole of Europe was covered with the same sort of forests, known as Mediterranean type, but after the last ice-age they only survived in the Atlantic islands.

Another interesting fact is that when the Spanish arrived in the 15th century, the Canaries had an indigenous population of white, blonde-haired natives (Guanches) who had been there for about 1,500 years. Mummified bodies of tribal leaders have been discovered in caves with funeral offerings of weapons and food. It was speculated that they were related to the present day Berber tribes of North Africa. Sporadic contact was maintained with Europe and they were known to the Romans. When the Spanish decided to conquer the Canaries in the early 15th century, it took nearly a hundred years; the Guanches resisted fiercely and many men were killed. Finally, they were enslaved and assimilated. The Canaries were so named because of the indigenous dogs also discovered when the Spanish arrived—the name is derived from Latin, and has nothing to do with small yellow birds.

From La Palma we sailed to La Gomera Island. We had intended to push on to Tenerife but the marinas there were either full or not functioning very well, so we stayed on La Gomera for eight days while waiting for the new crew to join the boat. We went to Tenerife by ferry and took the bus to Santa Cruz, and found that the amount of construction under way was staggering, testimony to the deep pockets of the EU. In Santa Cruz itself, the beautiful waterfront plaza had been demolished because they were constructing a light rail system. We visited the Military Museum where they celebrated the defeat of Admiral Nelson when he attacked Tenerife in 1797. At the Museum of Humanity and Natural History, we were able to view many Guanche relics, including a few mummies.

Back on La Gomera, we took a public bus across the island to a town on the west coast and returned on a ferry to the terminal near the marina. The roads were precipitous, with many scary hairpin turns over sheer cliffs. Despite that, one day we rented a car and visited an ancient rain forest in the center of the island, which was a National Park and a World Heritage site. There was virtually no flat land, and for hundreds of years the inhabitants farmed by building stone terraces in the sides of the steep hills. There were literally thousands of them, many still in use, but a fair number were abandoned as banana farming near the coast became common. The amount of labor to build the terraces over the centuries is unimaginable, but throughout the Canaries and Madeira I was sure the effort was comparable to building the Pyramids.

Finally, our new crew, Marco, showed up. He was from Serbia and a keen racing sailor. We departed for the Cape Verde Islands the next day. On the day we left, Louise signed off and caught a plane to Madrid for a connection to a New York flight. A few hours after we sailed, on Marco's first watch, he spotted a boat on the horizon which turned out to be loaded with illegal immigrants from Africa. We passed within half a mile and called the Spanish coast guard on the radio. The boat was less than ten miles from the La Gomera shore and they were in no danger of starving. When we looked at the blow-up of a digital picture that Mickey had taken, we counted more than fifty heads. These immigrants were a real problem for the Spanish authorities; the newspapers reported more than a thousand arrived in the Canaries every week, sometimes as many as five hundred in one day.

After a couple of days, we began to find a few flying fish on deck in the mornings, and early on the third day we crossed the Tropic of Cancer. *Fiona* rolled sedately before the northeast trade winds which usually blew between 10 and 15 knots and sometimes failed altogether for a few hours. After four days the wind picked up and we sailed wing-and-wing with the jib on a whisker pole to port, and two reefs in the mainsail. About midnight, on my watch, a seam on the mainsail split wide open. We dropped the sail and continued on under jib alone. The next morning, we took the sail off the boom and bent on the storm mainsail. That same morning, we found we had been inundated with flying fish that crashed onto the deck during the night. Mickey estimated that he threw fifty over the side.

We arrived at Mindelo as the sun set on the sixth day after leaving La Gomera. It was blowing up to 30 knots in the harbor as we attempted to anchor. We dragged, so we raised the anchor and reset it with more chain, and by then the sun had set with tropical abruptness. We toasted ourselves with rum in the darkened cockpit and I threw together a quick meal of spaghetti Bolognese. We waited until morning before venturing ashore. We did not intend to stay long at Mindelo. Mickey's Brazilian visa had to be activated by entering the country not more than 90 days from when it was obtained; that gave us until September 10th to check in at Cabedelo. On the shore we encountered the "beach boys," always a problem at Mindelo. For a fee they guard your dinghy—the threat they were guarding against was, of course, themselves, if you didn't pay up. Having got that out of the way, we checked with the immigration officer and the port captain. We arranged to be refueled in the afternoon and checked our e-mail. Returning to the boat, we found it had dragged again in the wind that still howled over the mountain. Our vigilant minder had tied a rope to another boat, and when I paid him for his attention to *Fiona*'s safety, he showed up later blind drunk.

The next morning, we restocked the fresh food and left by lunchtime. The strong winds were probably associated with an easterly wave, the precursor of hurricanes, and later I heard from a ham radio operator that tropical storm "Debbie" had formed 300 miles west of the Cape Verde islands. The trip across the doldrums to Fernando de Noronha turned out to be more complicated than previous passages, because we were much earlier than usual and ran into the southwest monsoon that developed over West Africa until the end of September. Instead of glassy calms, we experienced choppy seas, headwinds, and squalls. At one stage, it seemed like we were going to beat to our destination, tack after tack, which would have taken weeks. But a ham radio operator I was in touch with advised that the winds swung southerly below four degrees north, so we made a long tack to the southeast and found she was right. From there, we sailed on port tack to Fernando.

We had to make a slight detour to avoid St. Peter and Paul Rocks, a lonely archipelago that suddenly rises from the seabed to trap unwary sailors hundreds of miles from land. On a later cruise, I aimed to visit the forbidding rocks. (See Chapter 10)

An hour after sunrise, we crossed the line at 30° 01'W on September 3rd. Naturally, Father Neptune made his appearance for happy hour that day. Fernando de Noronha was obviously booming. It was promoted heavily in Brazil as an "eco-tourist" resort, with numerous pousadas (B&Bs). Bars and restaurants had sprung up since my last visit. The harbor was choc-a-block with small boats providing scuba diving and marine sight-seeing. Unfortunately, some government bureaucrat must had figured yachties were getting all this good stuff cheap because the harbor fees, which had previously been non-existent, had been pushed up to $20/person/day. We arrived on September 5th and left on the 6th, but we were dunned for two days—an expensive stop-over.

Marco managed to see the spinning dolphins by getting up at 4 am, and also to swim with a bale, or group, of turtles. Mickey and I toured the village using the old cobbled roads through the jungle, built by convict labor centuries ago when Fernando de Noronha was a penal colony. My old friend Elda, whose bar overlooked the harbor, was still there, but now she was a proud mother.

The iconic pinnacle at Fernando de Noronha

When we left, the wind slowly swung on the nose and we spent the last two days of the trip tacking to windward, something cruising sailors always try to avoid. With the coast in sight, we tried motor sailing, but the constant motion stirred up the debris in the fuel tanks and the engine kept stopping. Finally, a day and a half behind our expected time, we had the entrance channel to Cabedelo in sight. It threaded a serpentine path through sandbars, and just when we needed it most, the engine died. While Mickey and Marco tacked through the channel, I slaved below in the hot engine room cleaning filters. It was close to sunset on the 9th—Mickey's visa would expire the next day! Fortunately, the old diesel fired up again once it got a steady diet of clean fuel, and we anchored at Jacare just as the sun set. The band was still playing Ravel's "Bolero"; all was right with the world.

Marco and Mickey had both decided to leave the boat once we reached Cabedelo, Mickey because of a medical condition that needed attention in New York. But he hoped the rejoin the boat in Uruguay. We had the usual hassle with the bureaucracy, but our papers were in order, although Mickey just scraped in on the last day of the 90-day grace period, which had been allowed after the issuance of his visa. Marco had also decided to leave. I think he was a little disappointed that we had not pushed the boat harder in the style he was used to as a racer.

Brian Stevens, the British owner of the boat yard in Cabedelo, was very helpful in getting my repairs attended to, especially the rip in the mainsail. One night in the small hours, we drove to the airport at João Pessoa to meet the new crew, Mike, who flew in via São Paulo from Moscow where he worked for an internet company. Mike's brother Chris had crewed for me from Puerto Rico to the Bahamas during the 2000-2001 cruise. Mike's computer skills were soon put to work trying to fix a problem that had developed with the e-mail feature of the Iridium satellite phone. In the end, we decided the problem was the hardware, not the software. As a replacement I signed up for e-mail that used the shortwave transmitter via a program called "Sailmail." This was slower, but served for the rest of the cruise.

Brian found a 19-year old Brazilian lad, Andre, who wanted a ride to Salvador, so I signed him up. Andre spoke passable English, but had no sailing experience. I thought he would be an intellectual when he was older; his constant reading companions were Stendhal and the chess corner in old copies of *Guardian Weeklies*.

Shortly after Mike arrived, I took him to João Pessoa for a quick tour. An election was pending and the streets were packed with people, many wearing the colors of their party and waving flags. As we walked along one of the main streets, a couple of cars came right by us, and in one was the President of Brazil, Lula, beaming at the crowd. There seemed to be virtually no security.

I repeated the bureaucratic process in reverse for our clearance to Salvador. I had to visit offices in Cabedelo and João Pessoa because one closed after lunchtime, and I travelled on the rattletrap train that connected the towns—fare: 50 cents U.S. As soon as the repaired sail was delivered, we were off.

The Brazilian Coast to Uruguay

At sea we found a brisk southerly wind, but an afternoon on starboard tack to the east put us far enough offshore that we could sail on port tack to Brazil's ancient capital of Salvador. The leg took four days. Salvador is a stunning city, built on an escarpment a couple of hundred feet above the sea. The marina was located directly opposite an elevator that whisked you up in a few seconds, all for 2 cents U.S. On leaving the elevator, there were a series of old squares, each with a vast church. Salvador was the slaving center of Brazil, and in fact slavery was abolished only late in the 19th century. The squares were thronged with people, mostly black. Some of the women, for the benefit of the tourists, were dressed in costumes of the pre-abolition days, hooped skirts, and colorful bandanas.

Public marina and elevator (on left) at Salvador, Brazil

One evening we chanced upon a weekly bash in a square where bands entertained a crowd with lively music until exhausted, when another group took over. One band in particular was outstanding, all women. The rhythm was carried by two drummers who flung their arms so wildly that I was amazed they managed to get the sticks back in time to catch the beat. However, walking back to the elevator, I noticed many people, and especially small children, huddled in the archways of the ancient churches for the night. The northern part of Brazil was very poor, but smiles and laughter abounded, and there was always the sound of music in the warm air.

Ladies dressed in slave-era dresses, Salvador, Brazil

At night the narrow streets off the squares were alive with small shops and restaurants. On our last night, Mike and I decided to eat Italian. We sat outside at a table precariously balanced on the uneven cobblestones. Just as we finished the appetizer, which was excellent, the heavens opened, but there was no room inside. The waiter put our plates and drinks on a cabinet holding crockery, and we stood there feeling slightly stupid but no one offered to seat us. Finally, we reluctantly cancelled our order for pasta and trudged off in the rain. When the rain stopped we poked into a few shops. At a small gallery run by a pleasant lady artist, I bought one of her colorful depictions of Salvador.

Our next port was Ilheus, where we anchored off the yacht club, which was really a restaurant, and wandered into town. Once again, we encountered an election day in process. Andre went to a polling center to file an excuse for not voting, as every Brazilian has to vote, or file an excuse. Failure to vote could result in a fine or other penalties. We had hoped to take a tour to a nearby rain forest, but almost everything was closed due to the election. We inspected the particularly fine cathedral and found a nice place to eat.

The next day we sailed for the Albrolhos Reef, which lies about 20 to 60 miles offshore, and anchored near a couple of small islands. The navy had a station on one which controlled access, as the whole area was a national park. It was overcast and windy. We inflated the dinghy and anchored it near a reef, donned mask and snorkel—but I was not very impressed. Certainly there were some colorful fish, but I had seen better. Our requests over the radio to the navy for permission to go ashore were unanswered.

We sailed in the late afternoon for Vitória, arriving three days later early in the morning. Despite directions from someone at the yacht club, translated by Andre, we went aground and had to wait an hour for the tide to float us off. We picked up a mooring and got to the shore using the dinghy. In the city I noticed an art exhibition featuring local talent, so I wandered in, suspecting it would be very modern and boring. But in fact, the featured artist was a woman born in Brazil in the 19th century called Claudel. She trained as a sculptor, and went to Paris and became Rodin's mistress. I was impressed by her work and for comparison, there was a piece by Rodin himself. To my eye, she seemed just as good. I was sorry I could not read the copious notes in Portuguese about Claudel and her work.

For dinner, we went to a steak and hamburger joint that passed itself off as American. I must say, in general, I did not enjoy the food in Brazil, as they use far too much salt in the cooking. While Mike and Andre tucked into steak, I ordered a chiliburger. But when it came, it looked rather odd, and on investigation turned out to be eggplant and fish. I grumbled to the manager, who spoke some English. "But that is what they eat in Chile," he explained: a Chile-burger.

Our next leg took us round Cabo Frio, past the bright lights of Rio de Janeiro and on to Ilha Grande. We anchored at Abraão, a village I was getting to know well through my travels. The next day we spent the morning at the beach on the seaward side of Das Palmas Bay and sailed to Saco do Ceu (Sky Cove) in the afternoon. We got a free mooring at a fairly upmarket hotel on the shore called the "Green Coconut." We ate at the hotel and explored the area a little in the morning. The Ilha Grande area was undergoing rapid development, but at a settlement near the hotel we found two dug-out canoes, relics of an old way of life, fast disappearing.

The next day we squeezed in a quick lunchtime stop for some snorkeling at a reef and then sailed to the old town of Paraty. This was a National Heritage site because the old center has been preserved and no cars were allowed in the narrow streets. The buildings were low and rather dull; it was simply where the poor people lived a century ago. An odd feature was that the streets flooded at spring high tides, which is one way to keep them clean, I guess. Our next stop was the yacht club at Santos, which I first visited in 1992. It had changed very little since. It was the club of the super-rich who lived in São Paulo about 60 miles away. The club was immaculate, very up market, but as soon as we stepped outside the single-guarded gate, we were in grungy Guarujá, very down market. The super-rich usually visited their yachts by helicopter, thus avoiding the mean streets outside the club. Mike took a bus to Rio for a few days, and Andre went home to São Paulo, but he promised to return for the rest of the trip to Uruguay—at that point, we were about half-way down the east coast of Brazil.

To my surprise, Andre showed up for the next leg to the south, to the city of Florianopolis. This took about two days. We anchored 10 miles north of the city, as it was traversed by a bridge about 6 feet lower than our mast. The local yacht club had an annex at the anchorage, which was very convenient. We took a bus to the city, which was quite complicated. The local bus dropped us off at a transfer terminal and we then got on an express bus in to the city. All Brazilian cities had comprehensive bus networks which were well-used. The city itself was not remarkable. For some reason, Andre decided to leave us at this point, and he took a bus back to São Paulo. Although not legally required to do so, I forked over the money for the ticket, as Andre was in his own country. He seemed like a nice lad—when he had come back to the boat at Santos, he had brought me a present from his mother, a CD of classical music.

Mike and I sailed on for Rio Grande, our last port in Brazil, but for the first time since we left Jacare, we ran into heavy weather. The wind piped up to gale force for about 12 hours and as it was on the nose, we just furled the jib and lay hove-to under a double-reefed mainsail. This was a sign we were working our way south, as the weather was often dominated by fronts coming from Argentina. After Mike got the e-mail working, using the SSB radio to get a weather forecast service called GRIB, by and large it worked well. The wind arrows were generated by a computer but it did not get the gale quite right. But no harm came to us or the boat, and after things died down, we were soon under way for Rio Grande, which lay up a ten-mile-long channel. Our cruising guide suggested tying up at the local yacht club, but as we approached, the reading on the depth finder dropped and dropped until we were nearly aground. I reversed before we touched bottom, and just before we reached the club we passed a dock with a Swedish yacht tied up. The captain waved us over and we found we were guests of the Oceanographic Museum. We could not have been more fortunate, as the Director, Lauro Barcellos, had studied in the U.S. and was delighted to welcome an American boat.

We walked into town for the usual bureaucratic clearances, but these were postponed until Monday as we had arrived on a Saturday. On Sunday, Lauro laid on a delightful lunch for Mike and me and the crew of an Argentinean boat, which had managed to get into the yacht club. The Swedish captain, Len, had a Danish friend whose son picked us up on Monday to get our clearances.

Rio Grande was quite the worst place I had experienced for bureaucratic regulations, and that's saying something in Brazil. On Saturday, I had been told at the Port Captain's office that a health and sanitary clearance was essential. What did this mean? My yellow fever vaccination certificate was out-of-date and Mike didn't even have one. Perhaps they wanted to inspect the holding tank. My fears turned out to be groundless, as the certificate was intended for large ships and covered illness on board such as plague, when the ship had last been de-ratted, and how we handled ballast water. After a half-hour of filling out forms, mostly with the notation "N/A," we had our clearance. But the Port Captain closed at 11:30 am; we were too late, and we wanted to leave on Tuesday, before they opened again. As it turned out, Len's friend's mother worked at the Port Captain's office, and she was head of the maritime school. Soon we had our exit permission, and the only price we had to pay was that Len and I had to spend a few minutes answering questions from her students about sailing the oceans in a yacht. One question I fielded was: How much did it cost? It must have seemed an impossible dream to the poor Brazilian sailors; their average wage was a few hundred U.S. dollars a month.

We sailed for La Paloma in Uruguay, a small fishing village I first visited in 1992 on the way back from my first voyage to the Pacific. It was also a middle-class seaside resort, but the season had barely begun. The fish factory was still in business, and down in the dock area the smell was pretty overpowering. We got our entry clearance at the Port Captain's office, and it was very simple compared to Brazil. We checked our e-mail and then pushed on the next day for Punta del Este. We had a really fantastic sail with a 20-knot wind just forward of the beam, and tied up in the marina which I had left in the summer of 2005 on the way north with Ruth and Sasha as crew. I planned to spend only a couple of days at Punta and then move on to Piriapolis, about 25 miles to the west. This port was a hangout for cruisers and seemed a better spot to leave the boat while I flew to New York. To look the place over, I took a bus from Punta. Piriapolis turned out to be a pleasant seaside resort with a small marina. At the dock, I ran into Dave and Marcie on *Nine of Cups*, fellow members of the Seven Seas Cruising Association. They were very helpful and confirmed it was a good place to leave the boat.

After another day at Punta, Mike and I planned to sail early in the morning. Mike intended to take a bus to the Buenos Aires ferry across the River Plate, and ultimately return to Moscow. Alas for the plans of mice and men—by 4 am Mike and I were on the dock adding extra fenders and moorings, and as dawn broke, I discovered the harbormaster had shut the port. The dreaded Pampero—a burst of cold polar air—was about to fall on us. I told Mike to take the bus anyway and then, with the help of some marina workers, I moved *Fiona* to a safer spot. The wind howled for two days, and I began to worry that I might not be able to move the boat and make my flight. But the on the third day, I was able to make a single-handed passage to Piriapolis. I alerted Dave and Marcie by radio and they rounded up a gang of cruisers to help me tie up. I had two days to get organized and pack all the boat gear I was taking home for repair, before I caught a bus to the Montevideo airport.

The flight via Buenos Aires went as advertised and I staggered out of JFK with my luggage about 7 am the next day. Mickey and Barbara were there to meet me. After breakfast at the Blue Point Diner, they dropped me off at home. It was then that I discovered that my laptop computer had disappeared from the large canvas duffel bag I had packed it in. It seemed pretty obvious it was stolen at Montevideo airport, as the security x-ray was the only way the thieves would know where to look. Replacing it and loading the programs I needed took a fair amount of time during my stay at Brookhaven.

I returned in two weeks, and one of the new crew, Ware, synchronized his flight so that he caught the same plane from Buenos Aires. We were met at the Montevideo airport by an obliging Uruguayan sailor, Alberto, who had noticed my plans to visit Uruguay and contacted me by e-mail. But Ware's luggage did not appear on the carousel, and when he did eventually get it, several expensive items had been pilfered. In the next two days, the rest of the crew for the Antarctic leg joined the boat, Paul and Joey. Paul was an experienced sailor from Vermont, and Joey was a sailmaker and rigger who had been working in Maryland. Ware had experience only on power boats, but it seemed like I had a good crew on board for this venture to the Antarctic.

When we left for a return to Punta del Este, we had 20 to 25 knots of wind on the beam and made the trip in three hours. Alberto met us at Punta and took me shopping at quite a ritzy supermarket on the outskirts of Punta called "The English Store." The next day, Alberto took us to his house for a BBQ, as he owned a cattle ranch in the interior. The meat was exceptional. One more day and then we got rid of our Uruguayan pesos and left early in the morning for Argentina. I was sorry to leave, as the people of Uruguay were very friendly, apart from the light-fingered blighters at the airport.

Argentina

The two-day trip to Mar del Plata, Argentina, was a mild introduction to sailing *Fiona* for the new crew. We arrived at yacht basin early in the morning and found ourselves a slip, though it was very crowded. After breakfast, I faced the usual chore of clearing in with the bureaucracy, which took all morning. At the immigration office, the passports were stamped and the usual entry forms completed but when I told them our next port was Puerto Stanley in the Falklands, I was gently corrected; we were going to the "Malvinas," as the Argentineans call the Falklands. I did not need to return to immigration when we left, as the Malvinas belonged to Argentina, they claimed.

Back at the marina, I arranged to get fuel delivered and we explored the port area. Some redevelopment was underway and we had a nice dinner at a small complex of new restaurants and shops. The next day, we bent on the storm sails in preparation for the Antarctic leg and got a few maintenance jobs out of the way. The crew took a taxi to the jazzier part of town lying north of the port, and I entertained an interesting American couple, Mary and Scott, who lived on a Nordhavn power boat, *Egret*, and who had crossed the Atlantic a couple of times and cruised the Med.

The next day, our fuel arrived by truck. There was no gauge, and I am sure I paid for a lot more fuel than was actually delivered, but at least all our tanks were full. There was no need to linger, so we stocked at the supermarket and left the next day. The Argentineans had been very hospitable and the yacht club let us stay for nothing. The trip to Port Stanley took seven and a half days. At first, we had a nice westerly breeze, but after a few hours, it died and we were left wallowing in the seaway. For the next couple of days, we ran under power or sailed in erratic light winds. But then the wind came up rapidly, and within a few hours we had the sails reefed and a wind up to gale force. The wind veered and continued to increase; soon we were running under just the double-reefed storm mainsail. The wind rose to 50 knots, with gusts to 55 knots. But *Fiona* was used to winds like that—we had sailed for days under similar conditions in the Southern Ocean in the 2002-2003 circumnavigation.

After a week out, we had the Falklands in sight and we entered the harbor at Port Stanley very early in the morning. I decided to anchor and tie up when it was light. When we got on shore, we heard that the storm we had experienced was much worse at Stanley—winds of 70 to 90 knots had been reported. The weather below about 50° S is dominated by low pressure systems which track east every few days, and before leaving we monitored them carefully to pick the best time to go. We moored at the huge floating dock about a mile and a half east of Stanley. It was very convenient to the Seaman's Center, which provided meals, showers, toilets, games, and laundry—all the things a sailor needs in port, except booze. It was run by a Christian organization called the Seafarer's Trust out of the U.K.

Stanley was quite familiar to me from our cruise in the Falklands in 2005. We made the trip into town many times, mostly using the scenic path along the shore, and mostly in the rain and 30-knot winds. We worked through our list of maintenance jobs in the mornings and explored the area in the afternoons and evenings. Paul and Ware flew to Sea Lion Island for a night and Joey went camping. Before he left town, he got a map of the minefields left by the Argentineans after the 1982 war from the British Army bomb disposal unit, which was still stationed at Port Stanley. We refueled and restocked, and I found lots of British epicurean delights, such as mushy peas.

On Christmas Day, the main cabin sprouted the old tree and Santa left a few tidbits under it. The crew paid for a traditional dinner at one of the best restaurants in town, the Brasserie. The customs officer who checked us in, Mick, invited us to his house for drinks, and we met his Chilean wife, Celia, and family. To my surprise, the Seaman's Center was open and we recuperated from an excess of food and drink by watching stultifying British soaps on TV. The day after Christmas is called Boxing Day, and it is a holiday in Britain. In the Falklands, there was a traditional Race Meeting, and scores of local horses competed at the straight track just west of Stanley. There was a very festive air, as people munched hotdogs and hamburgers and scoffed drinks, while watching the tug-of-wars and sack races in-between the horse racing.

Antarctica

The inhabitants of Port Stanley were exhausted after the excesses of Christmas and Boxing Day, and nearly all the shops were closed until New Year, but we managed to buy some fresh fruits and veggies. The baker was closed all week, but the West Store had some frozen bread, so I bought 10 loaves and cranked down the temperature of the freezer. We prepared for the expected rough crossing across the Drake Passage by double-lashing the rigid dinghy on the foredeck and mounting metal covers on the main cabin windows, called "deadlights."

We left on December 28th with what looked like a favorable wind forecast. But, alas, by the 30th we were hove-to with a head wind of 35 knots, gusting to 50 knots. By the evening we were able to sail again, but by the next day we were becalmed! This was a part of the world where the weather changed quickly. Our destination was King George Island in the South Shetland group. On New Year's Day, I made a tra-

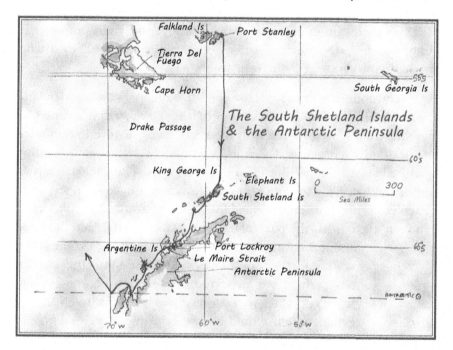

ditional canned turkey dinner, originally intended for Christmas but, of course, we had eaten out in Port Stanley. The weather was a mixed bag as we approached the island chain, and each morning I talked to a radio ham in the Falklands, Bob, who provided forecasts for yachts in the Cape Horn region.

As we approached King George at night, the weather was atrocious. We also had to battle an unfavorable current running over 3 knots, with the wind on the nose. We started the engine, but we scarcely gained ground. Sleet accumulated in big piles on the deck and on the rigging. Joey made a small snowman in the cockpit—he was from South Carolina and said he had never seen snow before.

We anchored in a bay on Nelson Island, just south of King George, which I had chosen by inspecting the chart for a sheltered haven. As it got lighter, we saw we were surrounded by large chunks of ice breaking away from a glacier at the head of the bay. I contacted a Russian base on King George by radio, and they gave directions to a better anchorage nearer their station, which we moved to as soon as was practical. A lone scientist on the shore of Nelson Island waved and called us on the radio, but it was too deep to anchor near him. As we approached the anchorage at King George, we found a charter yacht was also there. Although cruising boats are relatively rare, a few charter boats bring adventurous tourists, often bird watchers. They usually originate the cruise at Ushuaia in Argentina.

Several countries operated bases on the island. As we walked over to the few buildings forming the center of "town," we passed several Chinese from a research station near the anchorage. The terrain reminded me of South Georgia, as it was not completely devoid of vegetation like the true Antarctica, but most of it was moss. The Chileans ran an airport with service to Punta Arenas. How things have changed since Shackleton made his epic voyage 90 years ago from Elephant Island, not far to the east! At the control tower, we talked to the meteorologist about the forecast and tried to find out the extent of the sea ice further south. We were invited into the Russian base, where we inspected the research equipment and had a cup of tea in the lounge. We were able to check our e-mail, which would be the last time in several weeks. All in all, I thought the Russians were very comfortable there. Our host, Sasha, then walked us over to a Russian Orthodox Church, which had been prefabricated and then erected near the top of a hill overlooking the site. It was small but the Orthodox Russian ornamentation was very impressive in the otherwise barren surroundings.

Orthodox Russian Church on King George Island, Antarctica

The next day, we left for Greenwich Island. I had a note on the chart that there was a penguin rookery near a good anchorage. I was determined to sail there to conserve fuel, despite a head wind. We beat down the Bransfield Strait all night, but of course it was fairly light in the long Antarctic twilight. The radar died and there were scattered icebergs about. On Paul's watch he spotted a huge shelf 'berg, the first he had ever seen of that kind. It was so big he thought we were approaching land; we tacked around it.

By morning, we approached the anchorage, a small bay formed by a finger of volcanic ash called Yankee Harbour. The guys took the dinghy ashore to look for penguins while I fiddled with the radar without success. I also had no luck getting the cabin heater to work. Why do these devices die just when you need them the most?

During the night, a flotilla of small growlers, lumps of floating ice, drifted in to share our anchorage. Our next stop was Deception Island. Many years ago, it was a whaling station which was built on the shore inside an old volcanic crater. The volcano was still active, and several times the base had to be evacuated due to eruptions. Thermal springs dribble hot water into the sea at low tide. I first visited here on the 1998-1999 cruise. Since then, the British tidied the place up, and much of the old equipment was gone, including the fuselage of a deHaviland Beaver plane, which had been abandoned by the British Antarctic Survey. But there still plenty to see, including several de-

Eric at the wheel cruising off Greenwich Island, Antarctica

caying huts and the aircraft hangar, which was still in good shape. When we were there before, the hangar was full of snow, but now it had all gone. In fact, my impression was that there was much less snow and ice than there was in 1999.

We spent a morning exploring and digging holes in the ash, and then watching them fill with water that was too hot to touch. The wind was fair, and so after lunch we left for a day-long sail to Port Lockroy. It was cold, and heavy sleet fell, gathering in the fold of the reefed mainsail. When we started the engine, and hauled in the boom as the wind died in the lee of Brabant Island, I noticed that the sleet had frozen into a solid bar inside the fold of the sail. We wouldn't be able to shake the reef out until it got warmer.

After Brabant, the wind howled again in the Gerlache Strait and we dropped anchor at Port Lockroy in the evening, with the sun shining brightly. During the 1998-199 cruise, this had been our first stop, and there were quite a few changes. To start with, we anchored in a bay behind Goudier Island, which had been frozen solid on our first visit. There were three other yachts at anchor, all charter boats operating out of Ushiai in Argentina. A large cruise ship was anchored nearby, and while we were there, a half-dozen ships stopped, loaded with tourists. Port Lockroy had been discovered. The post office had been expanded into a gift shop and the resident staff increased from two to three.

Anchored at Port Lockroy, Antarctica

A whale skeleton on the shore, Port Lockroy, Antarctica

In the morning we introduced ourselves to the staff, a male manager and two lady assistants. One of them, Jo, was leaving the next day on one of the cruise ships. We were told the revenue from the shop paid all the operating expenses of the base, and provided a surplus to help the British Antarctic Heritage Trust. In the afternoon, we explored the extensive Gentoo penguin rookery on a nearby shore, and took pictures of huge whale skeletons left there probably a century ago by the whalers. After supper, we went back to the base to say goodbye to Jo, and as a precaution against the cold, we took along a bottle of Mount Gay rum. Quite a party developed.

In the morning, we dinghied over to the charter sailboat we had first encountered at Port Stanley, *Pelagic Australis*. It was operated by a well-known captain, Skip Novak, who also happened to be a member of the Cruising Club of America. Using this slender excuse, I got us invited on board. There was a well-heeled party of ten British charterers having breakfast in the main cabin, so we stayed in the pilot house. The boat was interesting, as it was specially constructed in South Africa of aluminum for Antarctic chartering.

In the afternoon, we watched a movie on board *Fiona* and transferred our extra fuel from jerry jugs into the main tank. After deflating the dinghy, we left in the morning for a quick race to the Antarctic Circle, the ultimate goal of this part of the cruise. Our route took us through the Lemaire Strait, which had been impassable due to ice in 1999. This year, it was cluttered in places by growlers and brash ice, but we had no difficulty finding a way through. It was spectacular sailing; the strait is five miles long and less than a half-mile wide. Immense black cliffs, split by great glaciers and walls of snow, towered up thousands of feet. Looking up almost vertically as we sailed through, one couldn't help wondering what would happen if the snow banks, high above our heads, decided to detach themselves at that moment and fall into the sea.

The wind was failing so I decided to anchor for the night. The chart showed a group ahead called the Argentine Islands. A British base was shown on one island, Galindez, but I suspected it was closed. However, it had a nice-looking anchorage and we headed for it. Soon, some buildings and radio antennas came in sight and a flag was flying; it was blue and yellow—Ukraine. When we dropped the hook in front of the largest hut, a Zodiac dinghy roared out to greet us and later returned with a scientist, Andriy, who spoke English. He persuaded us to move to a very secluded bay behind the station, but it was so confined we had to tie the stern to a rock to avoid drifting onto the shore.

Sailing through the Le Maire Strait, Antarctica

Later, the Zodiac returned to take us to the base. It was formerly British, but had been taken over by the Ukrainians about four years before. It was used for atmospheric radio research. The Polar Regions are especially suitable for this, as signals generated by lightning strokes in the northern hemisphere are conducted by the earth's magnetic field to the south, where they can be detected as very low frequency waves, called "whistlers." As it happened, it was the station chief's birthday. We helped ourselves to a splendid assortment of buffet food and frequently toasted someone or something with vodka in the Russian style—down in one gulp. Speakers played loud ethnic music and we were made to join in the dancing, everyone in a circle jumping up and down, arms linked. Unfortunately, there were no women stationed on the base. The chef brought in an impressive three-tier birthday cake with three candles, which the chief extinguished with one puff. A small room off the bar served as the library, and I was amused to find shelves full of old British periodicals such as *Punch*. Many were nearly 30 years old and, of course, very few of the current residents could read them.

It was after midnight before we got back to the boat. In the morning, Andriy and two other scientists came to visit us. They were particularly interested in our e-mail capability, which used SSB radio and the service I had signed up for when we were in Brazil to get the GRIB weather charts. As Andriy was leaving, I asked if they could spare some diesel fuel, and he departed with our empty jerry jugs. Just after lunch, the Zodiac returned with 60 liters of fuel, and they would accept no payment. The Ukrainians had been very hospitable to us, and the brief break at their base was our last encounter with "civilization" for several weeks. Our course south took us down the Grandidier Channel. On our left were massive headlands of black rock and ice towering thousands of feet. As the sun inched infinitesimally towards the horizon, the pale horizontal rays dramatically illuminated the gaunt cliffs, whose tops by then were enveloped in cloud. *Fiona* plowed on, almost as though she was sailing into a vast stage setting of Wagnerian grandeur. When Ware was on watch at about midnight, the density of the floating ice around the boat suddenly increased and he called me on deck. There seemed to be no way through. We were at 65° 35' S, only 60 miles from the Antarctic Circle. A glance at the chart showed we could reach more open water west of the Biscoe Islands by backtracking about 20 miles.

The wind had died away, and I was reluctant to use precious fuel, but we were so close to our goal that we put the wheel over and headed northwest with the engine. When we were able to head south again the wind slowly returned and strengthened. We crossed the Antarctic Circle at 66° 33.5' S and 68° 59' W at about 5 am local time the next day in gale force winds. It was bitterly cold, with sleet falling. Working on deck was not very pleasant, but we got the boat gybed over and heading northwest.

Heading North to the Panama Canal

The wind increased and backed. We tied the second reef in the storm mainsail and ran, as the seas built up, with a wind that gusted up to 55 knots. Later in the day, the wind began to subside, and we slowly set more sail. But we made a tedious trip across the Drake Passage as a large high pressure system settled in. It took us a week to reach 55° S, but at least it was getting a little warmer. We were usually close-hauled in light or moderate winds that blew between northeast and northwest for most of the cruise up the coast.

We talked to Bob on ham radio every morning, and he passed on the latest weather forecast. It was a slow, tedious sail until we got north of 48° S, when the wind veered to the west. A week before we got to Chile, the sky cleared, and hanging over the stern of the boat in the southern sky was the most brilliant comet I had ever seen. The tiny head glowed diamond white and a vast, bushy green tail illuminated a large segment of the sky. I asked Bob on our next radio contact what it was called, but he didn't know. In fact, he had not even seen it where he was in Port Stanley.

A couple of days later, we took the metal covers (deadlights) off the main cabin windows, which greatly lightened our space below. Abeam of the large island of Chiloe, which I first visited in 1998, the wind died entirely and I decided to make for Ancud, a small town just inside the Canal Chacao, as we did not have enough fuel to get to Puerto Montt if the calm persisted. During the night the engine stopped half a dozen times, as dirt in the bottom of the nearly empty tank was stirred up by the swell. I think the fuel we got in Mar del Plata had been particularly dirty. Each time it stopped, I had to clean the filters and purge air out of the fuel lines. Eventually, the feed line from the tank became so clogged we couldn't clear it. As a last resort, I drilled a hole in the top of the tank and pushed in a piece of hose from which the engine could suck fuel. To complicate matters, a fuel return line sprang a leak, and about seven gallons of our precious fuel went into the pan under the engine before I noticed. We pumped it out via a filter and put it back in the tank. It was a busy time and I stank of diesel fuel.

I was heartily pleased when we chugged into Ancud just after lunch, and tied up to a fishing boat on the jetty. Fortunately, there was a nearby gas station where we filled our jerry jugs. Then I had to clear in at the Port Captain's office. As Ancud was our first Chilean stop, the paperwork took some time. When I got back to the boat, the crew were enjoying a party on the foredeck of the fishing boat, swigging Chilean wine and eating raw shellfish. Several fishermen came to inspect the boat, as we were the first American yacht to stop there in years. Unfortunately, one of them took the opportunity to swipe Paul's cell phone. Later, we had a celebratory dinner at a very pleasant restaurant overlooking the bay, but appearances belied the food. It was the worst celebratory dinner I had ever eaten—my chicken was practically raw and still frozen on the inside. Ah, well, you can't win 'em all, and we were home and dry. We had made it to the Antarctic Circle and rounded Cape Horn westabout. It was a voyage definitely worth celebrating, even with raw chicken.

It was about 60 miles to Puerto Montt from Ancud, and the first part of the passage was through a fairly narrow waterway called the Chacao Canal, which was notorious for the fierce current. As the moon was full, I expected it would be especially strong, and we timed our departure to take maximum advantage of the east-setting current. There was no wind, so we chugged along under power at about 5 knots, but when the current grabbed the boat, I noticed the GPS showing our speed over the bottom as 11.4 knots—a boost from the current of 6.4 knots.

We arrived at the marina about 7 pm. I was fairly familiar with the local set-up, as we had stayed at the same marina in 1998, when we were on our way south to the Antarctic. The next day, we tackled the maintenance problems that had accumulated during the Antarctic leg, the most serious being the fracture of a stainless bracket holding the starboard side of the bow platform. I crawled into the chain locker to hold the nuts, while Paul unfastened the bolts on the outside, and we removed the bracket. I gave it to the marina manager, Rodrigo, who arranged to have it welded. We also needed a new cockpit seat cushion to replace one that had been washed overboard in the storm that hit us when we left Stanley. Down came the Yankee jib, as we intended to use the large Genoa for the rest of the trip north.

Puerto Montt was founded by Germans in the nineteenth century. Very little architectural evidence of that remained, but one nice relic was the German Club. Here one could eat from immaculately set tables, be served by punctilious waiters, and enjoy good food. One evening, we all went to a restaurant that a guidebook claimed served the best beef steak in Chile. It was full, so we ate next door, where the food turned out to be mediocre.

Soon the crew began to change. Paul left for Santiago, and Mickey showed up with his wife Barbara. Mickey and I made a new feed pipe to put in the hole I had drilled into the fuel tank. One afternoon, while we still had a rental car, Barbara, Mickey and I did the food shopping to restock the boat to get us as far as Ecuador, nearly 3,000 miles away. When Barbara left, Mickey moved back on board and, eventually, Joe took a bus to Santiago, 600 miles to the north.

The days soon passed and then it was time for Ware, Mickey, and me to start the long haul up the Pacific to the Panama Canal. Five days after leaving the Chacao Canal, we arrived at Robinson Crusoe Island in the Juan Fernandez archipelago, the very island on which Alexander Selkirk was marooned in the early 18th century, and which was the inspiration for the novel of the same name, written by Daniel Defoe. We had to slow down in order to arrive with the first glimmer of daylight because our radar was still defunct, and we anchored just clear of a couple of dozen small fishing boats in Cumberland Bay. The only sign of civilization was a small village. Otherwise the verdant, steep mountains looked just as they must have to Mr. Selkirk. There were a few unpaved roads in the village but they did not seem to go far. When an airstrip was built, the only flat land they could find was on a peninsula on the other side of the island; potential passengers must make an eight-hour trek by foot or a two-hour boat ride. There were a few small restaurants, a couple of shops selling mostly canned or dry food, and a large Catholic church. A supply boat came from the mainland 300 miles away about once a month.

The place reminded me of the first visit Edith and I made to the smaller Caribbean islands in the early '60s—muddy tracks, chickens everywhere, and the cockcrow of roosters. After a pleasant lunch, fish of course, Ware and I hiked up to a pass between vertiginous peaks. A lookout at the top permits a view of both sides of the island. Ware climbed down to the other side, but I had had enough exercise; it was a steep climb of nearly 2,000 feet straight up from sea level. After another fish dinner I slept like a log.

The next day I took care of the mandatory postcards and got our clearance to leave for Ecuador from the Chilean Navy. Mickey and I looked for a memorial to a famous sea battle that took place here in WWI; the German battleship *Dresden* was trapped by the British and sunk in Cumberland Bay. The only evidence left was a number of gun turrets that rather incongruously lined the muddy main street.

We had a very pleasant fish lunch at the yacht club overlooking the bay, and then weighed anchor after spending the last of our Chilean pesos on canned fruit in one of the small shops. On the night of February 20th, we crossed the Tropic of Capricorn. It was surprising, I thought, that one could cruise from the Antarctic Circle to the tropics in less than four weeks of sailing. We had steady, but gentle southeast winds for almost the entire trip to Ecuador. We used the engine only sparingly for the 2,000 nm leg to La Libertad, which took 16 days.

A curious incident occurred when we were sailing north, about 200 miles off the coast of Peru. At happy hour, Ware asked me about pirates, and I started to say I had never met any, and then I glanced out of the port window, and said, "Except for those guys hanging off the port side!" To my amazement, a small skiff with two fellows in ski masks had met my gaze. We all rushed into the cockpit, not knowing what to expect. They turned out to be fishermen, operating off a mother ship we met an hour or two later. The poor chaps were hungry and thirsty, so we gave them a sandwich and a couple of cold beers. The masks were simply to keep the equatorial sun off their skin. When we passed the mother ship, another skiff stopped by and we gave them a beer, too. I felt sorry for these poor fishermen, floating about in a small boat 200 miles offshore, with just a rusty-looking outboard. It could have been very dangerous if they were caught in a squall.

In the Gulf of Guayaquil, the wind died completely and we finished the leg under power. The Puerto Lucia Yacht Club at La Libertad where we tied up was very luxurious. It incorporated a hotel, pool, and pleasant restaurant, and the architecture was very modern and striking. We stayed for three days, which was spent refueling, replenishing the propane, checking e-mail and, of course, clearing in and out. The Ecuadorian bureaucracy was like most in South America, slow and cumbersome.

Ware met some young friends and spent a day at a resort up the coast surfing. There was a group of live-aboard yachties at the club, mostly Canadian and American. They were taking advantage of the very low labor rates to get major boat work done—labor cost about $5 per day. We enjoyed our stay. Taxis were also very inexpensive and the Ecuadorian currency was the U.S. dollar, which made things simple. But we were running a few days behind schedule, and the winds in the Gulf of Panama were notoriously fickle, so we left to make a shot directly to the Canal.

The trip to Panama was frustrating. For the first five days, we managed to sail for only 10 hours, and otherwise we powered over an oily sea. As we approached Punta Mala, we were very low on fuel, so naturally, we then ran into headwinds and strong countercurrents. We had to beat up to the Gulf of Panama, making good only 50 miles a day, but sailing over 120. We anchored for the night with the great bridge carrying the Pan American Highway over the Panama Canal in sight. It was exactly two months since we had left the Antarctic Circle.

The next day, we began the tedious process of renting a mooring, clearing in, and starting the paperwork to get through the canal. It was very hot, with the temperature touching 90°F by midday. Still, at the same time my home base, Long Island, was enduring another very cold spell, so things could have been worse.

The Canal, Bahamas, Bermuda, and Home

The transit was my fourth passage of the Panama Canal, but my first from south to north. The canal had become wholly-owned by Panama since my previous passage, and obviously they were trying to maximize income. For example, a new charge since I last transited was a deposit to cover the extra cost of launches and pilot, should the passage take two days. In the past, I made the trip in one or two days, depending on what time the pilot showed up. As we made the transit in less than twelve hours from start to finish, it still took several letters when I got home to extract a refund. Yachts must carry a crew of at least four for the transit, in addition to the captain and pilot. These men handle the lines to the chamber sides from each "corner" of the boat. We got two British backpackers to help, via the notice board at the Balboa Yacht Club bar. The yacht club, by the way, was finally being rebuilt after it burned down in 1998.

We transited eight days after we arrived in Panama, and I got my outward clearance directly for the Bahamas, without stopping at Colón on the Caribbean side. The town had a terrible reputation for violence, and I was mugged there myself on my second visit to Panama during the 1995-1997 circumnavigation. Actually, we cheated slightly and sailed to the San Blas Islands after we dropped off the Brits in Colón, with advice to take a bus immediately back to Balboa.

The San Blas are home to Kuna Indians who make the most wonderful, colorful embroidery called "molas," which I have mentioned earlier. We anchored in the dark, but shortly after sunrise a small skiff pulled alongside with two Indians. One of them, Venencio, was the master artist, and he had scores of his molas packed in water-tight containers, and he spread them out in the cockpit. We all bought samples, and after prolonged haggling, Venencio departed considerably richer.

Selling embroidered cloth molas, San Blas Islands

After one more night in the archipelago we sailed for the Windward Passage between Haiti and Cuba and the gateway out of the Caribbean. The Windward Passage is well-named, as it lies to the northeast of Panama, and the wind blows from the same direction. Rather than face that trip, the captains of the old Spanish galleons usually sailed much further to clear the Caribbean by heading for the Yucatan Channel between the west end of Cuba and Mexico. Not only was the wind on the nose, we found that we were set to the west by a current that ran up to two knots. The direct distance to the Passage was about 700 nm, and it took us ten days and sailing about 1,100 nm to do it.

We were heartily tired of beating to windward when we finally raised the east end of Cuba. At that point, the wind died and we powered into the Atlantic. Just before midnight, Mickey, who was on watch, was startled by the antics of a ship that illuminated us with a powerful searchlight. It turned out to be a U.S. Coast Guard cutter. They called on the radio and said they intended to board. Before long, a sturdy rubber boat drew alongside; we were all told to stay in the cockpit as four heavily-armed sailors climbed aboard. After a search to make sure the boat was safe and seaworthy, they inspected the safety gear, engine room and our documents. They were very polite, and in the end, all they could cite me for was a lack of a written waste management plan. It sounded very bureaucratic to me and I wasn't aware we should have one. I have been inspected several times over the years by the U.S. Coast Guard, and apparently it is always necessary for them to find something to justify a citation for an infraction. When the Coast Guard left, we headed for Matthew Town on Great Inagua Island, where I hoped to pick up some fuel. No dice. When we got there, everything was closed because it was Good Friday. (You tend to lose track of the days when sailing.)

I was pushing to get to George Town in the Exumas by the following Sunday to meet Lew, the editor of my cruising videos, who planned to spend a week on the boat and then leave from Marsh Harbour in the Abacos. This meant we would have to sail most of the way, but after leaving the Windward Passage the wind was fickle. Suffice to say we dropped our anchor in George Town just about the same time as Lew's plane landed, and we tapped into the last few gallons to power to the anchorage inside the reef. We couldn't get any fuel there until Tuesday because of the Easter weekend, but it gave us the chance to repair the masthead light, which had literally been shaken off by the swaying and rolling during our beat to the Passage. Lew had brought along a spare.

I planned two stops in the Exumas, one at Big Farmer's Cay and Norman Cay, and then an overnight sail to Marsh Harbour. At Big Farmer Cay, we anchored half a mile from the settlement. After happy hour, we rode over in the dinghy and tied up to the dock, not knowing what to expect in the village. A very bright young lad of about nine years of age met us when we climbed ashore. "Is there a restaurant?" we asked. "Sure," he said, and he led us to a simple building with two tables outside. I think it belonged to his aunt. She made us a delicious meal of fresh fish, rice and corn for a very reasonable price.

The morning dawned cloudy and windy, but as we left the sky grew blacker and we were racked by squalls on the way to Norman Cay. I had been there several times before, beginning in 1969 when Edith, Colin, and I returned from the Caribbean on *Iona*. On this trip, Mickey collapsed in his bunk, and when he refused lunch, I realized there was something wrong. The weather cleared up and the wind died, so I started the engine, as I wanted to make Norman before dark. I became increasingly concerned about Mickey, who had become incoherent and virtually comatose. Eventually, I called Bahamas Air Sea Rescue for medical advice; they suggested an air ambulance meet the boat at Norman Cay. I also spoke to the manager of the restaurant/hotel facility there and discovered the dock was in poor shape but usable. I told him we would need help to get Mickey ashore; perhaps he could round up a few strong yachties.

235

The sun was low when we got to the pass through the reef. I spoke to the pilot of the plane, which was already waiting on the runway. He told me that if the patient was comatose, he would have to be accompanied to Nassau by someone off the boat. Lew volunteered to go, packed his bags, and put some clothes for Mickey in a backpack. The pilot also said he would have to leave before sunset, which wasn't far off. It was a struggle to get the boat to the dock—we touched bottom a couple of times and protruding timbers damaged the bow pulpit, but four husky yachties man-handled Mickey onto the dock and on to a waiting pick-up. The pilot kept calling on the VHF to say he was leaving, but I urged him to wait. It was a two-minute ride to the airstrip, and the plane was still there with one engine turning over. We loaded Mickey through the door, Lew climbed in, the other engine spun into life and they were gone. I thanked everyone for their help and offered to stand a round at the bar, but it was closed, as the facility was being refurbished.

Ware and I returned to the boat, cast off and anchored in the bay, and then we had a well-deserved, delayed happy hour cocktail. Later I talked to Lew, who was still at the hospital, on the Iridium satellite phone. Mickey had been in great pain from a blocked prostate, but he had foolishly tried to alleviate the pain with generous nips from a bottle of rum. The next day, Ware and I left for Marsh Harbour, where my daughter, Brenda, planned to join us for a couple of days to celebrate my birthday—39 again. Brenda showed up on schedule. She had booked at a small hotel just across the street from the marina. We took the ferry to Hope Town for lunch; I had sailed there in the past, but judging by the number of yachts in the harbor, it had become very popular and anchoring was no longer permitted, only permanent moorings. We had a pleasant lunch at a restaurant on the water, starting off with a local specialty, conch fritters. Hope Town was very scenic with delightful twisting lanes shaded by colorful tropical trees. The houses were mostly small, immaculately maintained, and the pastel-colored paint reminded me of Bermuda. The red-and-white striped lighthouse must be the most photographed in the world.

Hope Town, Bahamas

The next day, we took care of food restocking for the next leg to Bermuda and then we walked to a marina on the north side of the harbor from which Edith and I, with the kids, had rented a charter boat more than 30 years before. Naturally, nothing looked familiar. Brenda cooked a birthday dinner for us in the kitchen, which was part of her suite at the hotel. The next day, I took Brenda to the airport early in the morning and returned to the marina hoping to leave. However, a bad nor'easter was ravaging New England and I discovered Ware had become very concerned that we would run into the same weather near Bermuda. I could not convince him that the low would be well into the Atlantic long before we got to Bermuda, but he had already packed his gear and decided to quit that morning. I was a little put out that Ware had trusted me to take him to the Antarctic Circle, but did not trust me to sail safely from the Bahamas to Bermuda. I left anyway for a single-handed passage.

I already had crew lined up to meet the boat in Bermuda for the final leg to Long Island. He was a doctor, and had rearranged his busy practice to get a week clear, which is why I could not delay. En route I was able to contact a friend from the local yacht club, Mike, who had sailed with me previously, to take Ware's place. This brought the crew strength back up to three for the Gulf Stream crossing, which sometimes could be rough.

To Bermuda

The trip to Bermuda started well with brisk northwest winds that backed to west, so I was able to run for a while with jib poled out to starboard. After a couple of days, it got noticeably cooler and I started to wear a sweater. I made the halfway mark in a little over three days, but then the wind swung onto the nose. A large high had settled over Bermuda and I was in the southeast quadrant with subsequent northeast winds. As always on a dead beat, it was frustrating sailing; the last 150 nm took me three days, and that includes the last 12 hours under power, when the wind eventually diminished. On arrival in Bermuda, I contacted my old friend, Bernie Oatley, who had been greeting arriving yachts for as long as I could remember. He arranged a slip at a marina so that I could get the bow pulpit repaired—it had been damaged in the Bahamas in the confusion when Mickey was landed. A very competent young man, Stuart, convinced me it would be as cheap to make a new pulpit as repair the old. I went to his shop in an old building on the waterfront in St. George's and discovered the work he did with stainless steel was excellent. But could he do it in a couple of days? In a word, yes! He cut the old pulpit from the bowsprit to use that as a pattern, and two days later had a new one made.

The next day the new crew, Gary and Mike, arrived for the last leg to Long Island. They helped to get the pulpit positioned when Stuart brought it down to the boat. After a couple of hours of welding, the job was done. We also found a cracked bracket which supported the bow platform, and Stuart welded that also, and when we bolted it back on, we were ready to sail. The forecast looked good, apart from the first evening, when light headwinds were predicted. From then on it looked like two days of reaching. We left in mid-afternoon after clearing customs and buying some last-minute groceries. We did, indeed, find a light headwind, but by sunset we were under power. The wind picked up in the night from the west and we made good progress on a close reach. The wind died in the vicinity of the Gulf Stream and we completed the last day and a half to the Fire Island Inlet under power over a calm sea.

We entered the Inlet five and a half days after leaving Bermuda and anchored for the night just east of the Robert Moses Bridge to await a favorable tide at the Patchogue River. When we awoke the weather was foul, with a northeast wind gusting up to 30 knots. We slogged down Great South Bay and managed to avoid all the shallow spots. Bob Lyons was waiting in the river aboard *Fireplace* with friends to assist if we got stuck in the mud, as happened when we returned from the Falklands in 2005. But we made it okay and tied up at Weeks Yacht Yard just after lunch on May 6th, 2007, 11 months after leaving, with 19,830 nm logged.

This was a successful cruise. We achieved the goal of crossing the Antarctic Circle. But it was a somewhat hollow triumph. The crossing was just a set of numbers on the GPS screen, the view on deck was the same old sea in fog and sleet, but the seed was sewn for a longer cruise to the deep south. Many highpoints remained in my memory—the Ukrainian and Russian bases, Salvador, and Juan Fernandez Island. I enjoyed Port Stanley over the holiday season. The kindness of Alberto in Uruguay went a long way towards erasing my annoyance at the theft of my laptop at Montevideo. I was very concerned about Mickey's collapse in the Exumas, but I was impressed with the competent way the Bahamas Air Sea Rescue went into action and got him to hospital.

8

A Summer Cruise to Greenland

2008

T his cruise was an experiment to see how enjoyable a four-month voyage would be. My plan was a reconnaissance of the west coast of Greenland, possibly leading to a trip to the Northwest Passage at a later time. I did not want to traverse the Canadian coast twice, going north and returning, so I decided to sail to Greenland via the Azores, which I had always enjoyed visiting. On the way back, I planned a fairly leisurely sail to Newfoundland, Nova Scotia and Maine. Wayne, a retired National Park ranger, Jim a small boat sailor from Florida, and Louise, a friend who had sailed with me previously on many occasions, signed up for the leg to the Azores.

Sisimuit

Azores

The Davis Strait
& Greenland
2008

0   1000
Sea Miles
at the Equator

The Atlantic Crossing

Our cruise started on time—no last minute crises, apart from Louise, who misplaced her passport on a trip the previous week and just managed to get it back in the nick of time. We were all on board for high water and, although we were accompanied by Bob on *Fireplace* to give us the usual assist in the Patchogue River, we had never less than two feet under the keel as we powered into the Bay. Clearly, the dredging the previous winter had really made a difference. As we sailed along the south coast of Fire Island, we experienced some of the worst weather of the trip, when frontal squalls came though about 9:30 pm when we were south of Shinnecock Inlet. The wind gusted up to 30 knots and veered violently. There was a lot of confusion and some sail flogging, but we got through without damage, although later in the passage across the Atlantic a tear developed in the jib; it may have had its origin in those wild moments.

At Block Island we picked up a mooring and made our traditional walk to the southeast lighthouse. In town, I ran into my old sailing buddy, Dr. Charles Starke, who had crewed for me with his wife, Mary, aboard *Iona* back in the early '70s. After happy hour in the cockpit and dinner at The Oar, we left early in the morning for Flores, in the Azores. The first day, we had light winds and headed a little south to clear Georges Bank. The winds became erratic and we powered, or sailed if we could. A few days out, we noticed the tear in the genoa jib and when we got a chance, we bent on the Yankee. The GRIB wind forecast, which we received daily via Sailmail, showed a huge high pressure system settling over the Atlantic from New England to the Azores. We edged up to 42° 30' N to find some wind, although our destination, Flores, lay about 39° N. Sometimes the wind picked up to a little under 30 knots, and we reefed the mainsail, but mostly we had light sailing.

Two new pieces of equipment installed in the past winter worked well. A new autopilot, George II, replaced the old Benmar, George I, which was given honorable retirement after 24 years of service. A device called AIS (Automatic Identification System) displayed the position, course, and speed of nearby large ships, which improved our feeling of security when we spotted massive freighters on the horizon, as it made it easier to avoid them.

Louise and Wayne were enthusiastic birders and chattered about the birds near the boat as much as the birds chattered about them. A couple of times we watched a movie during an extended happy hour and almost before we knew it, two weeks had slipped by and we had Flores in sight. The trip from Block Island was a shade over 2,000 nm and took 15 days.

The Azores

With masterly timing, Wayne's wife, Paula, was visiting Flores when we arrived; she caught up with us again when we pulled into the huge marina at Horta after an overnight sail. Wayne's place was taken by Teresa, a veteran crew who was making her fifth trip aboard the boat, although she only signed up as far as Terceira. We had our first supper together at a rather unique restaurant, which served one's order of meat or fish raw. After contemplating it with some alarm, I was relieved when the waitress brought each diner a nearly red-hot brick in a special holder, with condiments arranged on it, so that you could grill the meal to your own idea of perfection.

The next day we took care of many routine matters such as laundry, getting the jib repaired, and updating *Fiona*'s sign on the famous pictorial seawall. One evening, Louise and I attended a traveling circus featuring a couple of moth-eaten lions, two incomprehensible clowns, and a shapely young lady swinging from a trapeze. It was great fun, reminiscent of an era that seems to have passed in the States.

Our next stop was the island of São Jorge. Since we had been there two years prior to this, they had built a marina. It was not a very large marina, and had no facilities, as those were due the following year. But with the marina, came a charge and, worse, bureaucracy, which was absent on the previous visit. The highlight of our stay was accidentally catching a display of peasant dancers in the front of the church on the main plaza as we wandered back to the boat after dinner. About 16 men and women in traditional costumes, some bare-footed, performed an intricate square dance to a four-piece string band. They were very good. The next day, an eight-hour sail took us to Graciosa, where they were also building a new marina, which also wasn't finished. Nevertheless, the bureaucracy was in place and I had to sign in at the police station. The next day we took a cab to the famous Sulfur Cavern, a sloping volcanic crater. We descended into it via an impressive stone tower with spiral steps. Bubbling springs and a warm smell of sulfur awaited us at the bottom. Afterwards, we walked back into the village and took a taxi to the main town of Santa Cruz for a late lunch. We found a quaint museum with early apparatus for crushing grapes. The taxi driver, on the way back, told us that he had lived many years in Boston; New England had been a destination for Azorean immigrants for centuries.

Our sail to Terceira the next day was a lovely reach. We tied up at the familiar marina at Angra, and the next day, I left bright and early for a bus ride to Praia to meet the incoming crew at the airport. Anita was a former naval lawyer who had crewed in Bermuda Races. Bill was a small boat sailor from Hawaii who had been injured in a car accident several years earlier. He was very keen to complete an ocean passage to demonstrate that the injury had no lasting effects, and I was ready to give him a chance. Anita and Bill arrived on schedule and we taxied back to Angra, while Jim and Teresa moved to a hotel for a couple of days before their departure for home.

The next day, Louise organized a taxi tour of the island. The highlights included a lava tube called Christmas Cave—an immense cavern, certainly the biggest I had ever been in, and the unique swimming beach at Biscoitos. The "beach" consisted of a large plain of huge jumbled pieces of lava at the water's edge; areas between the boulders had been leveled off with concrete to provide numerous smooth sunbathing platforms. We sailed the boat to Praia on the east coast, our final stop in the Azores before leaving for Greenland. Praia was by no means as attractive as Angra, but there were well-stocked supermarkets and we got all our supplies for the next leg. When I reviewed some video tape, I discovered to my dismay that the video recorder had been malfunctioning for the entire trip, but thanks to the presence of the large American air base near Praia I was able to replace it with a unit that used the U.S. format, which Anita picked up at the PX. Locally-sold cameras used the European system, which would have certainly made editing more difficult in the fall.

Louise left on a direct flight to Boston, but our departure was delayed by the arrival of another lady—Hurricane Bertha. Bertha had been hovering near Bermuda for several days, but the track forecasts intersected exactly with our rhumb line course to the Davis Strait. Although Bertha was eventually downgraded to a tropical storm, she still packed winds of 50 knots and I wasn't keen to risk an encounter with a crew that had not yet got used to the boat. We waited three days before I could be certain that we would not make the acquaintance of Bertha.

The Complicated Route to Greenland

A high pressure zone lay to the north of Terceira, and after we left, we powered for about a day on our way to the Davis Strait. After that, we got light winds with sunny skies. Anita and Bill learned how to take a noon sight with the sextant. Eventually, the weather deteriorated and we furled the jib in winds of 25 knots, gusting to 30 knots.

The next day, Anita came down with terrible abdominal pains and other symptoms. It was clearly not just seasickness. She could not urinate, shades of Mickey's problems the year before in the Bahamas. We exchanged e-mails with her physician, who provided some sound advice and suggested we use a catheter. I carried a good stock of them but I felt too embarrassed to insert it, and so Anita managed to do it herself. Obviously we had to get her medical attention, and so I altered course for St. John's, Newfoundland, which lay just under a thousand miles to the west.

I was then alerted by an e-mail from Charles (the same buddy we met at Block Island) that another tropical storm, Cristobal, was heading in our general direction. Fortunately, Cristobal just seemed to evaporate after a few days, but we ran into a huge stationary high pressure cell that was located south of Newfoundland, and this gave us several days of beating to weather, something no gentleman should ever have to do. The seas were moderately rough and *Fiona* slogged to windward, often under staysail and main for several days. We typically sailed 120 nm in 24 hours to make good only 60 miles towards the destination. It was difficult for all of us, but especially Anita, who took to her bunk, nursing a hot compress to alleviate her pain.

Thirteen days after leaving Terceira, we pulled into St. John's, a port I was very familiar with. It lies only 1,200 nm from Terceira but we sailed 1,631 nm. Anita left right away to arrange transportation home, although fortunately, she was feeling somewhat better. Later, she sent me an e-mail to say she needed a minor surgical procedure. I contacted some old friends in the area to find replacement crew.

Bill and I greatly enjoyed St. John's, which was in the middle of a music festival. Crowds thronged the downtown streets, so great was the influx of tourists that I was unable to rent a car, which I really needed to get some parts, fill the propane tank, and transport other supplies. A part I had to find was a new fuel filter, as the old one had developed a crack which allowed air to get into the fuel supply—bad news for a diesel engine. I took a bus to a possible source, but they didn't have one. However, when I explained I was on a sailboat and car-less, the salesman commandeered a company pick-up and drove me all over the industrial parks on the outskirts of St. John's until we found one. People were very nice there, which was one reason I liked higher latitude cruising.

There were a couple of new museums since I was last in the town. The Rooms, which sounded like a run-down boarding house, was, in fact, a very imaginative ethnic museum and art gallery. The Geo Centre was located on the road up to Signal Hill. The main emphasis was a local geology; the museum building had been chiseled out of the rock and one wall was open to display the strata. They also had an exhibit about the sinking of the *Titanic*, which happened not far away, off Cape Race on the southeast coast of Newfoundland.

The weather since our arrival was damp and cold, and on the morning of the annual regatta, the radio announced that it had been postponed for a day due to high winds and driving rain, which would have cramped business at the numerous concession stands. At the same time, they mentioned the temperature was 13°C (about 58°F), which, combined with the humidity, led to a dreary day. Eventually, the Regatta was held after a two-day weather delay, the first time it had been delayed that much in its 190-year history. I wandered off to Quidi Vidi Lake to view the festivities. Scores of stands offered food and drink, cotton candy, ice cream, and games. A brass band tootled away, and on the lake the racing skiffs flashed towards the finish-line to the encouraging shouts of their supporters. The whole of St. John's was there, and all the downtown shops closed for the day. Not many cities will close for a day at the whim of a race committee.

During our first week, we had no luck finding a new crew, and Bill and I decided we would leave for a shorter cruise to Labrador. Then the local newspaper ran an article about the boat and in no time I was inundated by potential crew. Anita was replaced by Bianca, a young

American who had sailed to Newfoundland as crew on a charter yacht and then fell out with the skipper. Bill also took the chance to step down without leaving me in a hole. He had been frank in telling me that he had been partially disabled by an auto accident several years earlier; he had not expected that working on the foredeck in a seaway would be quite that difficult. His berth was taken by Ray, a native Newfoundlander, who was a professional seaman with a sailboat of his own.

Just before we left, a charming young lady appeared with a TV camera for an interview. Apparently, the show was broadcast across Newfoundland, and when we popped into a bar in St. Anthony, I was recognized as that notorious sailor who had been in the news.

Our trip to St. Anthony, on the northern tip of the Newfoundland Peninsula, went well. After powering to clear the coast of Avalon, we picked up a great beam wind and reached most of the way, though it was in rain and fog. We tied up with the fishing boats, arranged to top off the tanks before sallying forth into the Davis Strait, and set about arranging a trip to the Norse site at L'Anse aux Meadows. A very obliging fellow, Charley, offered to lend us his pick-up the next morning for the 30-mile ride. Such is the informality in these northern settlements that we never even discovered his last name. The site was much the same as my visit in 1994: actors dressed in period clothes sitting in the replica Norse sod huts, describing the tough life led by these settlers. The site interested me as a sailor; there was no lee for west to north winds. I assume they dragged their ships up the sloping shore. We drove back to St. Anthony and left in mid-afternoon.

The trip to Godthaab, or Nuuk as it is now called, in Greenland was very routine. The small town is the capital and lies at 64° N. We did not see wind over 25 knots and frequently had to resort to powering. We were often shrouded by thick fog and glimpses of the sun were rare. The sea water temperature stayed in the low 50s (Fahrenheit), and we never saw any ice. This was completely at variance with my preconceived notions of the passage—I thought we might well have to hove-to at night to avoid icebergs, as we did on previous trips to the Antarctic. Instead, we ploughed on, 24/7, keeping a close eye on the radar.

The leg from St. Anthony took seven days. We tied up next to a raft of six boats in the crowded inner harbor. But we had to move several times, as inside boats came and went. The town center was a 20-minute walk from the dock. There were numerous restaurants and bars, and the bars often featured Danish pool, which was played with three balls and five skittles in the center of the table. The rules were complicated, but Bianca and I shot a few racks. It was quite a fun game. The place was fairly civilized with a good hotel, banks, and a couple of super-markets. But food and most things were very expensive. Surprisingly, many young women from Thailand were working in the shops and hotels. At the harbor, the Seaman's Hostel provided showers, laundry, and a pleasant cafeteria. We refueled at the fuel dock on a spit east of the approach lead-in light. Diesel was inexpensive by northern stand-ards, $3.33 a gallon. Ray helped to refuel, and to his eternal chagrin, accidentally put a few liters of fuel in a water tank because he opened the wrong deck plate. But we purged the tank over the next couple of weeks, first with sea water, and then fresh and no permanent harm was done.

The National Museum and Tourist Gift shop on the site of old God-thaab had interesting Inuit artifacts, especially two women and a child who died in the 15th century. The freezing temperatures and dry air had mummified them. Their clothes were made from animal skins and stitched with sinew, and were amazing examples of craftsmanship. The women were tattooed. The remains in the museum were part of a larger group found in the same grave in 1972 consisting of six women and two children.

To the Arctic Circle and Labrador

We sailed up the Godthaabsfjord hoping to find Old Norse sites. We had a little map bought at the Greenland National Museum to help us. Our first stop was the island of Qornoq, where we discovered a small community of weekend cottages, but no ruins. A few people we talked to professed ignorance, but they were Inuits; perhaps the old hostilities persisted to this day. The next day, we set off for Anavik, where, according to the guide there were a few standing walls. The fjord became choked with growlers, 'bergey bits, and even a couple of icebergs coming from the glacier at the head of the fjord. The wind picked up to nearly 30 knots, on the nose, and as we approached the coastal area of the site, it became clear that there was no lee for a wind of that strength and anchoring would be impossible. I reluctantly turned around, and we whisked back to Qornoq at over 7 knots. Dodging the ice became a problem as the sun sank and glare blinded us. But we dropped the hook at the old spot and enjoyed a fine supper with celebratory champagne, followed by a movie. Such was our sybaritic life in the frozen wastes.

We left for Sisimiut, formerly Holsteinborg, the next morning. The anchor was badly fouled by seaweed that looked like maiden's hair, a weed that used to be common in Great South Bay. Ray and Bianca finally got the ground tackle clear and we scooted down the fjord back to Nuuk. We quickly refueled, as it looked like we had a window devoid of the persistent northerly winds. But the wind was light, on the nose, and died completely after the first night. It took a day and a half to raise Sisimiut. Just about 20 miles before we got there, we crossed the Arctic Circle at 51° 02'W. The small harbor was crowded with fishing boats. We refueled and found a vacant piece of dock wall to tie to, but later, other boats rafted to us.

The town was small. With a population of about 5,000, it is Greenland's second-largest settlement. A resident told us we were only the second yacht he ever remembered visiting the place, although I doubted that. Most locals seemed to live by fishing or hunting. I saw some Inuits unloading a skiff loaded with skins and pieces of carcass. There was a small museum and some restored old buildings, but the medieval Viking settlements did not extend this far north. Dog sleds and huskies were used north of Sisimiut in winter, and I was able to photograph a few huskies waiting for the return of the snow. We had a shower and a pleasant meal at the Seaman's Hostel on our last evening. Then we disentangled ourselves from the fishing boats rafted to us, and set off for Labrador in the early morning after a two-day stopover. The trip south down the Davis Strait to Nain in Labrador took six days. We experienced a mix of calms, head winds, and, occasionally, nice beam reaches. One morning, the wind piped up and a block strap on the staysail outhaul broke. Ray and I struggled on the foredeck to shackle on a replacement. Then we furled the jib and eventually reefed the mainsail as the wind increased to 30 knots. On two nights, the clouds cleared and we witnessed the ever-changing kaleidoscope of the Northern Lights. I had thought we might finally see some icebergs drifting south with the Labrador Current, but we saw nary a one.

On the whole it was an uneventful leg until we reached the coast near Hen and Chickens Reef. We arrived in the early morning on a south-southwest course. The wind was forecast to be 20 to 25 knots from the west. From the reef, the course to Nain was generally west along a twisting passage strewn with rocks and small islands. It was dead to windward, so we tried motor sailing with the engine assisting the sail, but the angle of heel caused the engine to overheat. The wind increased to 30 knots, and our speed dropped to virtually zero. It was about 30 more miles to Nain. I looked at the rocks and islets that already encumbered our route and decided we weren't going to make Nain that year.

Huskies wait for winter at Sisimuit, Greenland

We spun the boat around and headed for the open sea with strong wind on our back. The wind increased to 40 knots, the spume flew off the rising waves, and *Fiona* became very difficult to steer. We had to reef the mainsail. Somehow, we managed to do this in the shrieking wind and got the boat settled into a broad reach to the southeast. We were going to Battle Harbour, 350 miles down the coast on the Belle Island Strait. Actually, we headed for Mary's Harbour, which was about eight miles on the mainland from the island of Battle Harbour. Here, we tied up to the semi-deserted government wharf late in the afternoon and walked into the village for a meal. Ray was horrified to find that in the depths of Labrador he was unable to get fish for dinner. I asked a fisherman on the dock what they fished for, and he said they caught shrimp, but that "wasn't really fishing." The officer at the Royal Canadian Mounted Police station on the road into town was happy to stamp our passports to show we had officially arrived in Canada again.

At lunchtime, we left for Battle Harbour, but just as we approached the rather tricky inlet on which it was located, our chart blew out of the cockpit! We got it back in a soggy state, but it was still good enough to read. Battle Harbour was an important trading center for salt cod for centuries, and about 14 years prior to this, a bunch of enthusiasts began restoration of the old warehouse buildings. I remembered visiting during the '94 cruise, and I was skeptical then that anyone would come to see them—Battle Harbour is a small island with no runway.

But I was wrong; there was a small guest house and a ferry service from Mary's Harbour. Even small cruise ships stopped by.

We had a pleasant supper with the guests, and afterwards the manager, Mike, show some slides and videos of a pod of Orcas he had spotted nearby the day before. They were incredible—at least eight animals together, frolicking and coming right alongside his skiff. He actually touched their shiny skins several times. The next day the weather forecasted for our trip down the Newfoundland coast looked bad, but we had a one-day window to work to the south. We left early and, despite directions from Mike, I managed to touch bottom, that is, hit a rock, on the tickle south of the settlement. "Tickle" was a Newfie word for a passage so narrow it tickles the side of the boat. For a few hours we had good sailing, but the wind picked up as we headed for the coast of Newfoundland.

In order to get in before nightfall, I chose a small bay about five miles north of St. Anthony called St. Lunaire. Our offshore chart was useless for detailed navigation in the bay, but we slowly made our way inside, avoiding rocks and small islets. We got the anchor down in sight of a small village just before sunset. Although the water was only 12 feet deep, we let out 120 feet of chain as we were expecting a blow. It came! About 6

The crew at Battle Harbour, Labrador: Bianca, Eric, and Ray

am the next morning, I was awakened by the boat bumping on some rocks on the shore in a wind of 25 knots. Ray and Bianca struggled to get the anchor up as I maneuvered with engine to find water deep enough to keep the boat floating. A couple of fishermen stopped by in the melee and offered to guide us to better shelter once the anchor was up. We moved a couple of miles, following their skiff in driving rain and a headwind gusting up to 30 knots.

When we came to re-anchor we discovered why we had dragged—entangled with our own anchor was a large, rusty grapnel we had picked up. I couldn't believe we would drag with a ten-to-one scope under normal circumstances. The west wind that followed the gale whisked us to St. John's in less than two days of glorious sailing.

Nova Scotia and Maine

We stayed four days in St. John's to change crew and wait out Hurricane Ike, which produced a strong wind from the south as it passed over Labrador. Meg and Bryan replaced Bianca and Ray. Meg was a former certified merchant marine officer, while Bryan was young man with no sailboat experience but who was looking for a little adventure before starting the college term. Meg was moving back to Georgia and arranged for Bianca to leave with her pickup truck a few weeks after we departed. The idea was to rendezvous on Long Island when *Fiona* got there.

A view of St. John's, Newfoundland, Canada

We stopped at Ferryland on the way south. It was the site of an early English settlement funded by Lord Baltimore in the 17th century, called Avalon. Extensive excavations had revealed many foundations, the cobbled main street and the seawall. At the museum, they had over a million artifacts dug up so far, with over 60 percent of the site still to be explored. The settlement thrived for several decades, but then the Dutch burned it to the ground. They did not kill the inhabitants; they were simply eliminating competition for the Grand Banks fisheries. The site disappeared back to the earth and was never built on again, which is why the archeologists found it so rewarding.

Bryan contacted his uncle and aunt who lived nearby, and they gave us a huge box of snow crab legs, which we ate on the dock after all the visitors had left. We also had 17th century bread to eat that the lady in the reproduction colonial kitchen had given us. All was washed down with Mount Gay rum, a very colonial era supper.

Our next port was Louisburg on Cape Breton Island. The main attraction was the reconstructed French fortress. In the early 18th century, it was the main French base on the Atlantic seaboard, and it was a thorn in the side of the British. It was captured, returned to the French under treaty and captured again in 1758. This last time, it was demolished by colonial troops from Boston, who were fed up with being attacked by the French. In the 1960s, the coal mining industry in Cape Breton collapsed and the government came up with the imaginative idea of retraining the miners and using them to rebuild a section of the old town and fort. Copies of old plans were forthcoming from Paris, and archeologists dug up numerous artifacts that were used as patterns. Now you can spend a very interesting day there, with actors dressed in period clothes pretending it was 1744, at the height of French power. They served meals from the period, fired muskets and cannons, and played old music. All great fun. In the evening, I attended a musical at the local playhouse, where young musicians and singers performed Nova Scotia ballads, mostly about the demise of the way of the life they loved, that is, the end of the cod fisheries.

From Louisburg, we sailed directly to Lunenburg in Nova Scotia, arriving well after dark, so I decided to anchor in Puffeycup Bay and wait for daylight before finding a place to tie up. When that was settled, I heard from a Canadian sailor on a nearby yacht that a tropical storm was expected to hit Nova Scotia by the weekend. It was Thursday. A quick check of the marine weather forecast showed that we had a one-day window to get to Maine. Otherwise, we would probably be trapped in Lunenburg until it blew over. I was reluctant to leave after such a short time; I had first sailed there with *Iona* in 1967 and I had quite a fondness for the old place.

After Meg and Bryan enjoyed an early supper of lobster on the dock, we left before sunset. We had to power to Cape Sable, but then picked up a good breeze and sailed through the night across the Gulf of Maine. We arrived at the entrance to Frenchman's Bay with rising winds in thick fog. Fortunately, the old radar was working well and we groped our way into Bar Harbor where we picked up a mooring. For the first time on this cruise, we pumped up the inflatable (we had used the rigid dinghy up to that point) and chugged over to the dock master's office, where we checked in with customs; we were back in the U.S. of A., thank goodness. When we returned to the dock after quite a fancy supper, we were drenched with rain preceding the arrival of Tropical Storm Kyle the next day. Despite frightening forecasts from the Coast Guard of gusts to 65 knots and 30-foot seas, nothing materialized and we spent a quiet night. The storm had veered towards Nova Scotia; I think we got out just in time.

Maine

Bryan returned to Canada on the ferry to join his father for an annual moose hunt. Meg and I sailed over to Stonington and anchored for the night. In the morning, we found we were gently bumping on the bottom, so we left quite early and anchored at Butter Island. The owners, the old line Cabot family, encouraged visitors to use the shoreline and had put a nice granite bench on top of a hill with a wonderful view of Penobscot Bay. From Butter, we chugged over to Belfast where we spent two nights tied up at the city dock. We ran into a cruising

Granite bench on top of hill at Butter Island, with view of Penobscot Bay

English couple, Robin and Jackie, and enjoyed a happy hour on board with them and the two dock masters, Kathy and Malcolm. Meg decided to walk in to town for supper, but I stayed on the boat. When she got back, I enquired about her meal but she said she hadn't had one, and instead had stopped by a police station and reported Bianca had stolen her pickup. I was astounded, but it was the beginning of increasingly erratic behavior on Meg's part.

The wind was light when we left Belfast, and I made the mistake of towing the dinghy. Later in the morning, the wind picked up to 25 knots and, inevitably, the dinghy capsized. We were making little progress despite setting the mainsail. Camden was abeam, so we altered course and anchored in the bay to the east of the inner harbor. Here we righted the dinghy, drained and dried the outboard motor, and replaced a section of the towing bridle which had broken. It was fortunate indeed that we had diverted into Camden; if the other half of the bridle had broken we would have lost the dinghy, and trying to recover a capsized dinghy with a broken towline would have been very difficult in the seas that were running by then.

After a couple of hours, we set off again for Rockland, this time with the dinghy on deck. Unfortunately, this delay meant we arrived in Rockland quite late. We just had enough time for supper ashore before retiring to the boat. We left early for the leg to Port Clyde. I had always relished the old-fashioned grocery store there which never seemed to change much. After lunch we walked over to Marshall Point lighthouse. The next day, Meg took the ferry for a day on Monhegan Island. When she returned, we had just enough time to power to an anchor-

age five miles away, before darkness made the navigation too dangerous in the rocky waters of Muscongus Bay.

Our next mooring was at Boothbay, and from there we sailed over
to Orr's Island. The route past many small islands and rocky outcroppings required a careful lookout. Twice while I briefly left the cockpit
with *Fiona* under control of George, the autopilot, Meg turned it off
without saying anything and I returned to the cockpit to find the boat
heading for the rocks. Her actions were becoming very erratic and
her attitude was quite bellicose. Then she mentioned she had been
pensioned off from the merchant marine because of a head injury she
had received aboard a ship.

We anchored at the Orr's Island Yacht Club to
visit a friend I had first met in the Azores when
I was on the circumnavigation via the Capes. We
had a very pleasant dinner with several of my
host's friends, only to be brought back to reality
by watching the debate between Obama and Mc-
Cain on TV. We had been isolated from the political hoopla in the U.S. on the boat.

After a lunch-time stop at Jewel Island, we
picked up a mooring at Portland. Meg had trained
at a maritime school there many years before, so
she had lots of friends to contact. I browsed the

Marshall Point Lighthouse, Port Clyde, Maine

many used book stores and spent a morning at the wonderful art museum; the special exhibit was French and American Impressionists, a
period I loved.

Chuck joined the boat for the last leg to New York. He had been
browsing the boat website and caught my crew call. He had known me
briefly years before when he worked at the laboratory as a contractor.
We left early for the leg to Isles of Shoals, which lies a few miles east
of Portsmouth, New Hampshire. The wind deserted us and so we powered all the way, but we arrived in time for Meg and Chuck to explore
the island, which houses a religious retreat belonging to the Unitarian
Church. By this time, relations between Meg and I were frosty and we
mutually agreed her early departure would be a good idea. The next
day we powered to Rockport, Massachusetts, where Meg had friends

and she disembarked there. To my surprise, she stopped by the dock before we left the next day and thanked me for a wonderful cruise.

Fortunately, the wind came back and we had a great sail to Provincetown. On the way, we saw quite a few whales, and some were breaching. Next we transited the Cape Cod Canal and tied up at Marion, at the head of Sippican Bay. Chuck's son Mark met us on the dock, bringing with him a huge supper.

Our next stop was Newport, Rhode Island, followed by a good sail to Block Island. Our intention had been to sail the following night down the Long Island coast, but when we awoke there was a strong wind from the north and we left immediately. Unfortunately, the wind conked out by the afternoon, and so we powered and entered Fire Island Inlet about 10:30 pm. We negotiated the tricky shallows east of the Robert Moses Bridge and anchored for the night. By morning, the wind was blowing strongly from the northeast as we chugged up Great South Bay. As usual, Bob aboard *Fireplace* was waiting to greet us off Blue Point to offer a tow up the river if needed. But the previous year's dredging gave us a foot clearance, even though we were coming in a little before high tide. We arrived at Weeks Yacht Yard at noon, and several old crew and friends were waiting.

Although the cruise had lasted only four months, I had had 11 different crew, and only Louise and Teresa were repeaters. I had been very surprised by Greenland; along the coast as far north as we sailed, about 67° N, it was quite green. So Eric the Red got a bum rap when he was accused of "spin" by naming the country "Green." I thought we might meet considerable floating ice in the Davis Strait, but we saw none; even the west side in the Labrador Current was clear. I was pleasantly surprised to find a lot of Thai nationals working in Nuuk, and the women were very pretty.

There had been considerably fewer sailboats cruising Maine and New England than on previous cruises I have made at the same time of year. We logged 8,058 nm and added 468 hours on the rebuilt engine. Based on this trip, the Northwest Passage cruise looked feasible, at least as far as Greenland.

Around North America via the Northwest Passage
2009-2010

9

This was going to be a tricky cruise. No one can predict if the ice will open up, but if it does, the boat would have to be located about 75°N to take advantage and push west as quickly as possible. If the passage showed signs of closing before completing the transit, I would have to back-track to the North Atlantic before being frozen in for the winter. In that case, an alternative cruise had to be planned. Preparations for the trip began months before our departure in mid-June, 2009. I greatly appreciated the reports and videos made by Roger Swanson and Gaynelle Templin of their attempts on the passage aboard *Cloud Nine*, which were ultimately successful in 2007. Scores of charts had to be ordered from catalogs and collated into convenient packages for each leg. This onerous task was greatly helped by my old shipmate, Louise. Advice on getting ice and weather data via satellite was offered by Bob Forman, a fellow member of the South Bay Cruising Club (SBCC), based on his extensive use of these services in the Bermuda Race.

The colonization of South America by Spain in the 16th century spurred immense efforts by other European countries to find a way to sail to China from the Atlantic round the north of the American continent. In the early 17th century, the English explorer Henry Hudson discovered the bay later named after him, and set in motion the lucrative trade in furs. Names on charts often reflect discoveries made by the early explorers, and remain as an epitaph for many. Attempts to find a northwest passage to the Pacific were made starting from both the

Atlantic and Pacific ends. As described in this chapter, *Fiona* sailed in the waters where, on one of the most famous expeditions to attempt the passage, every man-jack aboard two English ships died, about 240 years after Hudson. It was another 50 years before a Norwegian sailor, Admundsen, finally sailed from the Atlantic to the Pacific via the North-west Passage. A few years later he became famous as the leader of the first expedition to reach the South Pole. I think the ice conditions and the weather were a good deal more benign for our passage than those experienced by earlier voyagers to the High Arctic.

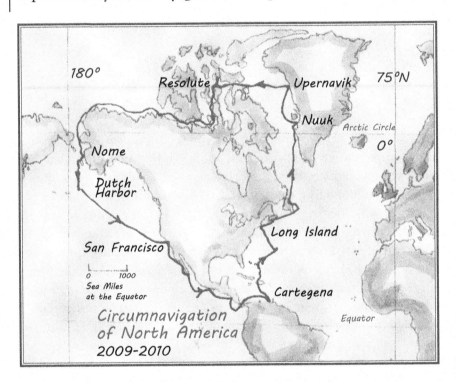

Crew had to be contacted and arrangements made for each leg. Ed, also a fellow member of the SBCC, took the drastic step of resigning from his job in the city to sign up for the complete trip. Joey, a veteran of the 2007 Antarctic Cruise, signed up for as far as San Francisco. Russ, a Delta Airlines pilot, organized a few weeks off work so he could join us at Nuuk, Greenland, just for the actual passage in northern Canada.

Many orders for bulk food supplies had to be placed. Special equipment was needed. For example: a spare propeller, a ten-foot-long pole and spike to fend off ice floes, and a shotgun, should we be unlucky enough to meet a hungry polar bear. Ten five-gallon jerry jugs of diesel were fastened to the lower life-lines. Besides all these tasks were the normal launch activities: painting the bottom, launching and stepping the mast, all performed by Weeks Yard. I started the engine, filled the water tanks, and checked out all the various systems. I organized the ritualistic Bon Voyage Party. Somehow the whole ball of wax came together, and we left on schedule at noon on June 15th, 2009.

Long Island to Greenland

Our cruise up the coast to Block Island and on to the Cape Cod Canal was fairly routine. As we popped out of the canal, a steady south wind was forecast for a couple of days and I decided to bypass my usual stopover at Provincetown and head straight for Nova Scotia. We enjoyed a good passage across the Gulf of Maine, but bad weather awaited near Cape Sable, at the south end of Nova Scotia. In went the reefs as we fought our way up the coast to Lunenburg. In the fog and rain, we tacked to avoid a trawler which then promptly reversed course and, in the confusion, the jib sheets got tangled, and the sail flogged and then tore. We set the staysail and motor-sailed the last ten miles to port in gale force winds.

Jennifer and Kathy at North Sails soon had the jib back in shape and after three days we left for St. John's, Newfoundland. It was a windless day with thick fog. Despite all the modern appurtenances, such as radar and GPS, we got a shock as a rocky shore and breakers loomed out of the fog on the bow and a swift turn was needed to avoid an early end to the cruise. Once clear of Lunenburg Bay, the fog lifted, we set sail, and five days later we had the imposing headlands on either side of the Narrows in sight. St. John's was very familiar from previous visits and my sojourn there in 2008. Soon a friendly face appeared, Jim Winter, who was able to find a machine shop to repair a stainless steel elbow from the engine exhaust system. St. John's is a pleasant place with many coffee shops, bars, and old book stores, and George Street was a magnet for Joey at night. But we had to keep moving; the window for good ice much further north was opening and we had to be there. I replaced much of the food we had used, as food prices would escalate in Greenland and the Arctic.

We left after a week, but our visit wasn't over. Twenty miles out, the steering chain which connects the wheel to the quadrant broke. The emergency tiller was quickly rigged and we tied up again at St. John's just after midnight. Repairs were made in daylight and by happy hour we were on our way again. It was only in Mexico, months later, that we were able to pinpoint the cause of the steering failures.

Ice charts obtained from the Canadian Coast Guard indicated we might find icebergs coming south with the Labrador Current; we shaped a course to cross this region as quickly as possible and then headed due north to Nuuk. We encountered no icebergs at the start of the nine-day leg, but sailed by plenty as we approached Nuuk. The harbor scene was just the same as in 2008—chaos! Numerous small boats

Fiona *moored alongside this barge in Nuuk, Greenland*

Joey *gets a friendly kiss from a Thai girl, Nuuk, Greenland*

and medium-sized ships were rafted together on the west side of the inner pool. We tied up alongside a French cruising boat, *Fleur Austral,* we would run into again further north. We checked with the police for immigration clearance but they weren't very interested in us. We moved to the fuel station, our last chance to get cheap diesel. When we returned, *Fleur Austral* had gone.

We tied up next to an old steel barge, about six boats out from the dock. This turned out to be my undoing—to get to *Fiona,* I had to walk around a narrow catwalk surrounding an empty hold, and there were no rails. The catwalk was only about nine inches wide and littered with wire rope, rusty shackles, and other marine bits and pieces. Returning to the boat, I missed my footing and tumbled heavily into the hold, landing on a steel rib. As soon as I tried to get up, I realized I had cracked one of my own ribs, which are not made of steel. I have broken enough of them over the years to know the symptoms. For the next few weeks, I suffered considerable pain using my arms and when trying to find a comfortable sleeping position. Sneezing was agony.

Russ had stayed in touch by e-mail, and arrived on schedule via Iceland. However, an unfortunate development was that Ed decided to quit the cruise at this stage. He had suffered from sea-sickness and I think that colored his view of the possibly arduous sailing still lying ahead. After we left Nuuk, we experienced mostly windless conditions and as we motored up the coast, I decided to put into Sisimiut to top off the tanks. This port was the furthest north that we reached in 2008, and just before arriving we crossed the Arctic Circle, the traditional marker of the start of the Northwest Passage. On the way to Upernarvik, our last stop in Greenland, we cranked up the Iridium satellite telephone to download charts of ice conditions at the north end of Baffin Island. Every year, ice accumulates in this region, often blocking the entrance to Lancaster Sound, which is the start of the tortuous route through the archipelago of Arctic islands. Thus, it was important to know the precise edge of the pack ice to avoid sailing too far north. As it was, we had to sail to very nearly 75° N before turning west.

There were plenty of icebergs about, but they were fairly widely scattered, and avoiding them mainly involved a careful look-out. As it turned out, there were plenty of ice charts available, but some were not complete, and it proved expensive in terms of download minutes to get the information we wanted and needed. Russ had a brilliant idea: have his sister, Debbie, scan the ice charts on the internet, which was essentially free, and send us ice limit coordinates and the best charts to use via Sailmail, which is the low bandwidth bread-and-butter e-mail server for the boat. Russ also had a SPOT transceiver, which enables GPS coordinates to be relayed to a web site along with a reassuring message that everything is okay, or not. Rich, the *Fiona* webmaster, was able to establish a link to the SPOT display from FNN on the boat web site, so that anyone logging on could follow our progress. This proved to be very popular with friends interested in following our cruise.

Upernarvik is an old whaling port, though now it is a small, mostly Inuit, village clinging to the sides of the hills. We dodged numerous icebergs on the way to the dock. I arranged for a fuel delivery by truck. There were dogs everywhere, as they were used to pull sleds in winter, but there were also plenty of snowmobiles lying outside the simple dwellings. In summer, the universal form of transport is the all-terrain vehicle, or ATV.

Approaching Upernavik, Greenland, 2009. Traditional igloos have long ago been replaced by prefabricated houses.

We found a small museum with an old kayak and hunting implements from the Stone Age Inuit culture. I was continuously impressed during our sojourn in the High Arctic by the astonishing way the Inuits had managed to survive in one of the most hostile environments in the world. Several books we carried on board described their way of life before it was swept away in a generation in the 20th century. Now, the salient feature of all the Inuit villages we visited was a tank farm, replenished every summer with oil and gasoline, without which they would not survive winter. In Upernarvik, we met an elderly French couple living in a tent on the shore. They had flown in from France with a canoe and their camping gear and were planning to cruise along the Greenland coast, camping at night. Suddenly *Fiona* seemed the height of luxury.

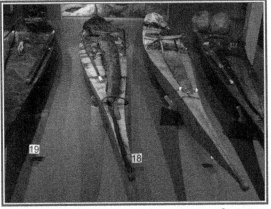

Old Inuit kayaks in a museum at Upernavik, Greenland

The Trip to Resolute

From Upernarvik our route took us through Lancaster Sound, with the ice-bound coast of Baffin Island on our left, and the dramatic cliffs of Devon Island on our right. Our destination was Resolute Bay near 75° N, where we would wait for the ice to open up in Peel Sound and the Franklin Strait, if, indeed, it was going to open up at all in 2009. Before reaching Resolute we anchored for a night

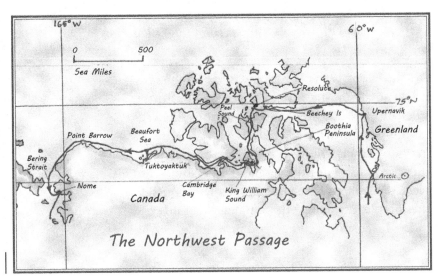

at Beechey Island. This desolate spot was where the famous Franklin expedition wintered over in 1845-1846. Two ships of the most modern design, equipped with early steam engines, had left England in the spring of 1845 with orders to force a way through the Northwest Passage from the Atlantic to the Pacific. Much of the route had already been explored, especially the Beaufort Sea, the coast of the Arctic Sea of northern Canada, and the region around Lancaster Sound. It was felt only a few hundred unknown miles separated these two areas, and Sir John Franklin, with the ice-strengthened *Erebus* and *Terror* would have no difficulty completing the passage, to the greater glory of British Empire, and the Royal Navy.

The immediate focus of interest was three graves on the shore. These belonged to two sailors and a marine from Franklin's ships who died during that first winter. They had been buried in permafrost, thus the bodies were well preserved. In 1984, Canadian scientists received permission to exhume the bodies and conduct autopsies, providing the graves and bodies were returned to their original state. There was great interest in how these men died, as the expedition disappeared from human ken after their stay at Beechey Island, and only a few scattered remains were found many years later, leaving no written record. The story of the exhumation and autopsy is told in a fascinating book by O. Beattie and J. Geiger, *Frozen in Time*. They found the bodies to be in almost perfect condition, and spooky photos show the poor mariners as they looked when they died. They died of TB and respiratory problems, but analysis of their hair showed excessive lead accumulation. Samples taken along the length of the hair showed how the lead built up with time. The scientists theorize that lead from the new method used to preserve food on the ships, namely canned meat and vegetables, got into their systems from the solder. It seems likely that a year or two later the whole expedition was suffering from serious lead poisoning and this

Eric, toting a shotgun stands at the graves on Beechey Island

Remains of old Arctic expeditions and cairns on Beechey Island

could have been a major factor in the failure of the venture. Along the beach were remains from later expeditions and a few cairns contained the ashes of prominent Canadian Arctic pioneers.

The ice charts showed a band of drifting ice blocking the entrance to Resolute Bay, but it was only two- to three-tenths density and we figured we could work through it. We eventually anchored at the head of the bay near the small Inuit village of only about 250 souls. *Fleur Austral* was already anchored there. We checked in with local Royal Canadian Mounted Police post, as this was our first official stop in Canada. Then it was a few yards to the local hotel called the South Camp Inn, operated by an entrepreneur called Azzie, who was originally from Pakistan and was married to a local Inuit lady. The hotel was more like a youth hostel, but Azzie offered us a free lunch, showers, and free e-mail. We couldn't have found a finer friend.

The hotel serviced passengers arriving at the airstrip, often government officials or workers at the mining companies further north. Also it was nice and warm, and so we often found ourselves in the lounge watching mindless TV. Azzie arranged for a fuel delivery by truck, so we had to bring the boat into the shallow water at the beach and carry the hose out on the dinghy. I stopped by the French boat to let them know about these arrangements, which were laid on for the next day. All went well and the captain invited us on board for happy hour. His name was Phillipe Poupon; he was a celebrated French racer in the 1970s and '80s, winning the Global Vendee a couple of times, which is a very tough single-handed circumnavigation. His charming wife, Geraldine, was a film actress who appeared with such stars as Gene Hackman. They were attempting the Northwest Passage with their four children, ranging in age from about one to 14 years, and an old friend with little sailing experience. The boat was quite new, designed by Phillipe and built of aluminum, about 68 feet long. We were all awed by both the family and their boat.

A day after refueling at about 4 o'clock in the morning, it was broad daylight of course, and we were awakened by a shout from shore. Ice floes were moving into the bay at an astonishing rate.

Aground at Resolute, Nunavut, Canada, 2009

Fleur Austral was just clearing out through the last remaining clear lead right against the eastern shore of the bay. It was shallow there, but with centerboard up, the French boat had a very small draft. We raised the anchor and motored into the clear pools between the floes, but these got smaller and smaller until finally, we were forced right against the shore, and unfortunately, it was high tide. By the afternoon *Fiona* was hard aground with her port bilge resting on the sea bottom. However, with her long straight keel and generous beam *Fiona*, can take that sort of treatment without damage if the sea is calm, unlike many more modern boats with skeg keels. The keel-to-hull attachment can be subjected to high forces if the weight of the boat is taken in the keel, leading to stress failures. Skeg keels exert far more stress on this critical joint than straight keels.

A German boat, *Perithia*, which had anchored the day before, was in the same predicament, although they managed to stay afloat. We floated off at the next high tide and pushed our way through the floes to deeper water. The same afternoon, we were hailed by a young fellow, Dave, who was standing on the shore. We invited him aboard for happy hour. He was a visiting workman from New Brunswick who had been hired for maintenance work on the government-supplied houses. Unfortunately, he had had a contretemps with the local board and had been summarily fired, and so wanted out as soon as possible. He was volunteering to come aboard as crew. I was delighted, as ever since Ed left us in Nuuk, I had been hoping we would have four on board for the transit of the Passage. In the finest tradition of the old British naval press-gangs, he was immediately signed onto the crew list, although he had no sailing experience. How many young men have had their first sailing lessons in the Northwest Passage?

We had some excitement when a polar bear swam by, climbed onto a floe, and sunned itself for a few hours. The next day, we went ashore to investigate the wreck of a WWII Lancaster, which had crashed in 1950 on the approach to the runway. The local con-

Polar bear on a floe, Resolute, Canadian Artic

Exploring the wreck of a Lancaster bomber, Resolute, Canada

servation officer, a young woman, spotted us on the road and made us return to the boat to get our old shotgun—the bear had allegedly chased someone on a bike in the village the evening before.

One afternoon we climbed Signal Hill, a 600-foot eminence overlooking the village. Each evening we talked on shortwave to Peter Semotiuk, a resident of Cambridge Bay who ran a radio net for cruising boats. He kept us up to date on ice conditions, though we also had our own ice charts downloaded via the Iridium satellite radio, and of course we had Debbie's e-mail messages. Finally, after ten days of waiting, it appeared the ice was clearing in Peel Sound and Franklin Strait, and a narrow lead existed on the east side.

Peter Semotiuk with Eric in the cabin, Cambridge Bay

The Heart of the Northwest Passage

Early on the morning we planned to leave Resolute, ice floes again started to invade the bay, so we simply upped anchor and threaded our way out. Once clear of the bay, only a few growlers and 'bergey bits dotted the sea. There was a light head wind as we powered past Griffith Island and into Peel Sound. We had started in the heart of the Northwest Passage, and this was likely to be the most difficult section. For over a day, we powered south with only a light wind. In fact, we experienced only light winds during most of the time we were in the middle portion of the passage. In 2005, my friends Roger and Gaynelle aboard *Cloud Nine*, had to turn back in this region after they were freed from the ice by a Canadian icebreaker.

Late on the second day after leaving Resolute Bay, we entered the ice field that lay north of the Tasmania Islands, an archipelago lying off the east coast of the Boothia Peninsula. There were several channels shown on the chart which led south. I elected to use the most easterly, marked the Shortland Canal, and despite fairly thick ice, we were able to negotiate a way through in a few hours using a spotter perched in the ratlines. I should mention that the compass and autopilot were both not functioning properly due to the proximity of the North Magnetic Pole, which was located north of Resolute. We got directional info from the GPS; the helmsman had a battery-operated unit in the cockpit.

The weather turned nasty, with sleet and fog. Fortunately, with engine running we had some heat in the cabin. By noon, south of the Tasmanias, the ice really thickened, and in the fog we could see very few leads of clear water, and these usually tapered out with little progress. The radar was deceptive, as it only picked up the larger floes, and apparent leads turned out to be choked with smaller floes as we got closer. We pushed on for nearly 12 hours before we had to admit we were stuck, and so we tied ourselves to an iceberg just before midnight, although the light from a watery sun illuminated the fog and the gloomy scene around us.

Later, I was awakened by a crash and the sudden tilting of my bunk. We all rushed on deck; a 'berg had collided with our own icy haven. It had rotated and the underwater mass had lifted *Fiona*'s bow clear of the surface. With the stern still in deep water I started the engine, put the transmission in reverse and we slid back into the sea as though we were on a slipway. We found another floe to attach ourselves to on the lee side using the dinghy anchor—one piece of equipment I

Fiona *anchored to an ice floe, Peel Sound, Nunavut*

had forgotten to bring was a four-pronged grapnel, which would have served much better as an "anchor" to attach *Fiona* to the 'bergs.

The fog started to lift and soon the shore of the Boothia Peninsula was visible less than half a mile to the east. It looked rocky and very bleak. A check of our position on the GPS showed that we were moving north with the ice-field. We were still in a clear pool of water, but it was shrinking, and by lunchtime clear water had virtually disappeared. We were surrounded by ice, some of which was obviously "old" ice with thick pieces tilted up on edge.

After lunch, I checked our progress north in the field. We were heading back towards the Tasmanias at about 7 nm a day. The chart showed a promontory and bay on the coast just before the islands. I was concerned the ice might push us into them. I decided to call the Canadian Coast Guard to advise them of our position and see if there was an ice breaker in the vicinity. I told them we were not in immediate danger and they advised getting the inflatable ready so that we could reach the shore of the Boothia Peninsula if *Fiona* was crushed and sank. They also recommended putting survival gear and important personal possessions in handy bags. They said a breaker could be there in one or two days if needed.

As we blew up the dinghy on the foredeck, we could hear the "song" of Beluga whales coming through the hull. They must have been under the boat, which was in about 170 feet of water. Their tune sounded like someone playing a saw with a violin bow. All afternoon, we fended off floes with the 10-foot pole and spike I had brought along just for this purpose. In the evening, we watched a movie on DVD.

Fiona *trapped in ice, Franklin Strait, Nunavut*

The next day was much the same, with ice now forming virtually 100 percent coverage. Every six hours, I checked in with the coast guard as they had requested, but they said an ice-breaker would not be heading our way, as we were not in immediate danger. By then, we had moved 14 miles north and the cape and Tasmania Islands were clearly visible. As we maneuvered to avoid being crushed, using the engine and the poles, I was very concerned about the vulnerability of the rudder, the top of which stuck out of the water by an inch or two at the stern and clearly would not survive an impact from a rampaging heavy floe.

By the third day, a northeast wind developed and almost unperceptively, the clear areas between the floes began to widen. From the spreader, a clear lead extending to the south about a mile away was visible. We began to push floes out the way and generally make our way in that direction. It looked like we were going to break out after all.

After a couple of hours, we made it to the lead, which by then, of course, had changed its character and developed tributaries. We worked our way generally south and edged away from the coast. The value of having four on board was apparent; we split into two watches of two men, one spotting from the ratlines and one hand-steering. I called the coast guard to let them know we were on our way again. When we found a clear patch a few hundred yards in extent, we anchored to a floe in the evening,

The nights were now getting noticeably darker. Within a few hours the patch usually shrank, and we had to re-anchor by sailing up to another substantial floe and tossing our dinghy anchor onto it until it wedged firmly on a protuberance. We were now headed for the James Ross Channel, east of King William Island. Perhaps this is the time for a little history of Arctic exploration.

In the middle of the 19th century, most Arctic experts, including apparently Sir John Franklin, believed that King William Island was a peninsula attached to the Boothia Peninsula. Thus, to proceed south, King William had to be passed to the west with land on the port hand. Unfortunately, the M'Clure Channel lying to the west of King William brought down a continuous stream of heavy old ice floes from the north and was very rarely passable. The Franklin expedition in 1846 was trapped in ice west of King William, probably for two winters, and ultimately the ships were crushed and sank. Some members made it to shore and trekked south, and their remains were discovered many years later. No one survived to tell the tale. By 1847-1848, there was concern in London about the fate of the expedition and mostly at the urging of Sir John's wife Jane, several rescue attempts were organized, all without success. Later Dr. John Rae, an employee of the Hudson's Bay Company, met Inuits possessing relics of the expedition and oral stories of the white men who perished. In extremis some of the survivors had resorted to cannibalism. His findings caused a sensation, but his mention of cannibalism earned lifelong opprobrium, as it was contrary to the heroic image of Sir John fostered by his wife, and, strangely, Charles Dickens.

Tribute to Roald Amundsen, Gjoa Haven, Nunavut

It was Dr. Rae, exploring the Boothia Peninsula on foot, not by sea, who made the discovery that King William was an island, and that the channel separating it from Boothia was apparently navigable when the ice melted in summer. King William forms a barrier that prevents the ice from the M'Clure Channel from blocking the passage most summers. This crucial knowledge was exploited by the Norwegian Roald Amundsen when he made the first transit of the Northwest Passage. Amundsen sailed his 58-foot sailboat, which had a small engine, through the passage in three years starting in 1903, wintering twice in a small bay on the southeast side of King William Island he called Gjoa Haven, named after his boat *Gjoa*. His arrival attracted nomadic Inuits to Gjoa Haven because westerners were a source of invaluable (to them) wood and iron. Amundsen was probably one of the last Europeans to experience firsthand the Stone Age culture of the Inuits before it disappeared in the 20th century. His account of their way of life in that demanding environment makes for interesting reading, as he lived very closely with them.

Our down-loaded ice charts and e-mails indicated that the only way south was close to the shore of the Boothia Peninsula. We began to slowly work our way east and south, again with two men on watch, one in the rigging, spotting the best route through the ice. A hazard we learned to avoid while zigzagging between the floes was that many had underwater projections protruding well beyond the surface contour. We called them "horns," presumably caused by wave action eroding the edges of the floe faster than the underwater part was melting. The ice reports were right; close to the coast was a fairly clear channel with patches of heavier ice concentration.

We sailed past the point on Boothia where Dr. Rae had observed the strait separating King William Island and, six days after leaving Resolute, we anchored in the bay at Gjoa Haven. We had been luckier than Amundsen, who went hard aground in this part of the Passage and lost some of his keel, although we did have a near miss with a rocky islet. We had the benefit of GPS and modern charts, but what was going on? I suddenly noticed a small note on the margin of the chart: "Horizontal datum not determined." In other words, the chart was not quite as modern as I thought, and dated from the days when longitude was harder to measure accurately and a world-wide reference datum for latitude and longitude had not yet been established.

We inflated the dinghy and motored to the pebbly shore. The fresh water creek, which attracted Amundsen in choosing the site, flowed down a steep gully, but now it was littered with debris. There was a hotel, a market, and the Royal Canadian Mounted Police station. Residents zipped about on ATVs, and snowmobiles lay around, waiting for winter. The nondescript houses looked exactly like those at Resolute, somewhat depressing. I arranged for a fuel delivery by truck, and the manageress of the market walked with me to a small section of bulk-headed dock to show me where the truck would come. The water was shallow and encumbered by a couple of abandoned kids' bikes.

Gjoa Haven is now a permanent settlement of about a thousand souls. The Gjoa Haven Hamlet office building had a small exhibit devoted to Amundsen. At one point during our visit, an elderly man introduced himself as Amundsen's grandson. Later investigations using DNA disproved the old man's claim. However, it was quite possible as the Inuit culture regarded wives as chattel and they were often lent to visitors. For warmth, the whole family usually slept together naked between animal skins—good heat transfer engineering, perhaps, but .... While Amundsen's detailed account of his nearly two-year stay at Gjoa makes no mention of any liaisons, other Arctic explorers clearly did. Peary and his navigator Matthew Henson both fathered children with Inuit women in Greenland while wintering over prior to their dash to the North Pole.

We went back to the boat to await the fuel truck and tied to the dock, but a few feet out. Unfortunately, the water was shallower ahead of the bow and we were soon aground forward as we waited all afternoon for the truck. When it came,

Inuit locals come down to the dock at Gjoa Haven, Nunavut, Canada.

we filled the tanks and finally got back into deep water about 11 pm by using the dinghy to pull the bow round at high tide. Just as we re-anchored, the lights of a boat were spotted heading into the bay. We knew from radio chatter with Peter that this was *Ocean Watch*, a 68-foot sailboat which had left Seattle in May, 2009, and was making a west-to-east transit of the Northwest Passage. We called on VHF and arranged to meet for brunch the next day at the snack bar in the hotel. The captain, Mark Schrader, was, like me, a member of the Cruising Club of America, so it was fitting that our two cruises should cross paths at Gjoa Haven. When we all gathered for a late breakfast, Mark explained he was trying to circumnavigate both North and South America in a year. He had also aroused some media interest in his cruise, as he carried two scientists among the crew who were studying global warming in these northern climes.

We left in the afternoon, as we had a fair wind to carry us to the south end of King William Island. We rounded the point and hung a right up to the Simpson Strait, the boisterous wind was then dead on the nose, and I did not fancy tacking up the rock-strewn water. A cozy-looking bay lay on the right, on the shore of King William, and we headed for that. When we had a lee, we dropped the anchor in 20 feet and settled down for the night. Nursing a rum and apple juice, I stared at the bleak shore a quarter of a mile to windward. I pondered about the desperate crews of Franklin's ships trying to make it overland back to the Canadian mainland. We were probably very close to a path they would have chosen—some relics, skeletons and a whaleboat were found near the estuary of the Back's River, which lay to our south on the other side of the Simpson Strait. The site was later called "Starvation Cove." I raised a toast to their ghosts and went below into the warm cabin.

Meeting the cruise ship, Hanseatic, in the Northwest Passage

It took another day for the wind to drop, and then we negotiated the tricky Simpson Strait under power. Halfway through, we passed the cruise liner *Hanseatic* which was heading east. The passengers lined the rail and waved enthusiastically. *Fiona* must have looked very small to them, and they probably wondered what those crazy New Yorkers were doing so far north.

The next section of our route, Requisite Channel, also looked rather difficult, with numerous shoals and small rocks, so I decided to leave that for the morrow and anchor in M'Clintock Bay. This turned out to be quite interesting. A Dew Line radar was visible on the horizon, and when we dinghied ashore we found an airstrip along the beach. There were some large fuel tanks and a hut, all obviously abandoned. On the shore was the wreck of a wooden fishing boat called the *Sea Otter*. Joey managed to climb aboard, and reported everything of value had been stripped from the hulk. I wonder what dramatic circumstances led to her demise.

Wrecked boat on the shore of Simpson Strait, Nunavut, Canada. It is mandatory to carry a gun as protection against wandering polar bears.

In the morning it was cold, 22°F, and a heavy frost lay on deck. We left bright and early and navigated very carefully through the Requisite

Channel, which fortunately was almost free of ice. We tied up at Cambridge Bay two days after leaving M'Clintock; it was August 25th. In the early planning of the trip, I had chosen August 22nd as the drop-dead date for a decision on whether we were going to make it through or turn back to the Atlantic before the Passage closed due to winter ice. According to Peter, we had seen the worst ice, and the route along the Arctic coast of the Canadian mainland and in the Beaufort Sea would be largely free of ice if we hurried.

Even though we were running a little late, I decided to push on to Alaska, which was still a long way off. Russ decided Cambridge Bay was as far west as he had time for, and wisely decided to fly out and rejoin the workaday world.

Cambridge Bay to the Aleutian Islands

Anchored near the dock at Cambridge Bay was an American power boat, *Bagan*, which was also making an east-to-west passage. Sprague, the owner, and a cameraman visited us later for some footage for his passage video. Ashore, I was able to arrange for a fuel delivery to top off the tanks and to have fresh water delivered, the first we had taken aboard since Nuuk. Both were expensive, but I was surprised at the cost of water—35 cents per gallon, despite the numerous lakes which abounded north of the village. I asked the truck driver why this was and discovered the water was stored in a heated building so it was available all winter. Such were the complexities of living so far north.

Cambridge Bay was a notch above the villages we had visited previously—it had a couple of supermarkets, one of which featured a Pizza Hut in the foyer. Western civilization was creeping in. We were able to get showers at the Visitor Centre and Keith Peterson came down to the dock for a drink at happy hour. A local politician, whom we had first met at Resolute, he gave us some souvenir items from his election campaign. Keith is a member of the Nunavut Legislature, an entity that split off from the Northern Territories by the Canadians some years ago, the idea being to give the Inuit some measure of autonomy.

When we left, we aimed for our last port in Canada, Tuktoyaktuk, on the western side of the MacKenzie River Delta and about 600 nm away. We encountered only scattered ice. Many of the geographical features had names reflecting the intense interest in the region during the 18th and 19th centuries: Lady Franklin, Bathurst, Dease and Union, and Dolphin. The Northern Lights laid on a show for us. It was nearly midnight when we arrived at Tuktoyaktuk to discover *Bagan* tied to the dock. We rafted alongside. They were heading next for Barrow, in Alaska, to pick up some spare parts that had been shipped there. We left a few hours after them but our destination was Nome, on the other side of the Bering Strait. We had a tedious sail along the north coast of Alaska in the Beaufort Sea. Occasionally, we could see the edge of the pack ice on the starboard horizon, but we had no serious problems with ice. It was 500 nm to Point Barrow, the most northern extremity of Alaska, and then we turned south in the Chukchi Sea.

A book I carried on board described a scientific expedition launched in 1913. In October of that year, the ship *Karluk*, captained by Bob Bartlett, was trapped in thick ice five miles from Point Barrow, exactly where we were. It certainly seems that the climate had warmed since then; there was no sign of ice.

Two days later, in heavy seas roiling up from astern, the roller chain of the steering system broke. This was the second time the chain had broken. It took another failure later in Mexico before we put our finger on the cause. We hove-to for a while to rig the emergency tiller, and then resumed our course to Nome, hand-steering during two-hour watches. It was strenuous, cold duty for the two-and-a-half days it took us to raise Nome, ten days and over 1,100 nm out of Tuktoyaktuk.

We crossed the Arctic Circle, thus completing the Northwest Passage transit. From crossing the circle heading north, to crossing heading south, took 49 days, including 34 sailing days, and we logged 3,440 nm. Peter sent me an e-mail to say he believed 11 private boats had made the passage the same year. The day before our arrival, we surfed through the Bering Strait with Russia just a few miles on our starboard. We were surprisingly far west—not far from the International Date Line, further west even than Hawaii.

We arrived at Nome just before midnight and tied up to the rather forbidding ten-foot high dock wall; *Bagan* was tied up just around the corner. In the morning we were cleared back into the U.S. by a very pleasant border control officer. I was disappointed to discover Nome charged a stiff nightly fee for dockage; I had got used to the free dockage in Canada.

I replaced the broken steering chain and in the afternoon, we topped off the tanks from a fuel truck. The next day I wandered around Nome, which is quite a small place, made famous by the Gold Rush in the late 1880s. Some entrepreneurs still operated dredges just off the shoreline, prospecting for gold. All the rip-roaring bars, bordellos, honky-tonks, and hotels had been swept away by the tide of time, but a small section of Front Street has been re-created to evoke that time, although it reminded me of Disney World. There is no direct road connection with the rest of Alaska.

Dave came to me in the afternoon and told me he was going to leave the boat in Nome and move to a hotel. I was disappointed because it was nearly 3,000 nm to San Francisco, where I intended to make our landfall on the mainland after leaving Dutch Harbor in the Aleutians. Both the Bering Sea to Dutch Harbor and the Gulf of Alaska have a bad reputation for heavy weather and winter was approaching; I wanted to leave as soon as possible with at least three on board to give easy watch-keeping hours.

Joey, Dave, and a crew member from *Bagan* went on quite a pub-crawl that night, and about 2 am I was awakened by a cry from Dave. Joey and his friend from *Bagan* had fallen into the harbor returning to the power boat. Dave had managed to get them to the ladders on the dock wall and needed help getting Joey onto *Fiona*. He probably saved their lives, as hypothermia sets in quickly up there. We stripped Joey, wrapped him in blankets, made him hot tea and got him into his bunk. In the morning, Joey was very contrite but also very depressed that Dave was leaving us. He did not relish the thought of double-handing to Dutch Harbor, lying about 650 nm to the south across the Bering Sea.

I was planning to leave by lunchtime, as it looked like a great weather window had opened with northerly winds forecast for four days. The three of us sat down over the breakfast table at a local café and the emotional upshot was that Joey decided to join Dave. We went back to the boat, Joey packed his gear, and my former crew pushed *Fiona*'s bow clear of the dock as I started a single-handed leg to Dutch Harbor where I felt sure I could enlist new crew.

I was exceptionally lucky with the weather. The wind remained on the stern at moderate strength, and I sailed or motor-sailed without much difficulty. I remembered that Roger and Gaynelle on *Cloud Nine* had encountered a 60-knot storm on this leg of their 2007 passage and sought shelter at Nunavik Island. When Nunavik came up on the port side, the weather was fine and I pushed on. I was receiving GRIB wind forecasts via Sailmail, and Debbie was still sending a daily weather updates. Only as I neared Dutch Harbor did the forecast began to look ominous, with gale force winds. Fortunately, however, they were from the northwest, not on the nose.

I arrived in the vicinity of Dutch Harbor near midnight; I had picked out a spot on the chart to anchor that provided a good lee from the gale. My greatest difficulty was getting the 65 lb. fisherman's anchor deployed, as the crew had secured it inside the pulpit and I had to lift it, plus chain, over the rail. Once I got the anchor down, I slept like baby. I had made the leg in four and a half days from Nome—respectable even for a fully-crewed boat. In the morning, I called the harbormaster on VHF for directions into the secluded inner boat harbor, and tied up next to a Swedish motor-sailer which had just completed the Northeast Passage from Sweden via the Russian and Siberian coast to Alaska. The Swedish captain, Nicholas, had a rented van and very kindly drove me to the harbor master's office, and later to a gas station to refill the jerry jugs. Dutch Harbor is one of the busiest fishing ports in the U.S., with many boats coming and going. Some had been featured in the TV series "Deadliest Catch." I posted notices at chandleries, bars, and the recreation center for new crew, and also posted a crew call on the website. I walked over to the small village of Unalaska for a shower at the recreation center, and toured the Russian Orthodox Church, with its characteristic onion-shaped towers, a reminder that this whole region was once part of Russia.

WWII era radio equipment, Dutch Harbor, Alaska

Standing on the bridge over the river I saw dozens of salmon spawning in the gravel, which they disturbed by furiously wriggling their bodies. Then they died, and the seagulls were having a feast. I went with Nicholas for a drive up Ballyhoo Mountain to see the remains of extensive WWII gun batteries. This area was now tribal land and we had to buy a day permit for $5. In 1942, the Japanese invaded Attu further west in the Aleutians, and there was fear they would work down the chain. Dutch

Harbor was converted into a submarine base and bombed by planes from Japanese carriers. There was a museum devoted to the wartime period, and some of the old military radios there were familiar—I had bought them as surplus when I was a teen-ager. Unfortunately, in the paranoia that swept the country at that time, the native population was deported and spent the war in deplorable conditions.

There was a very pleasant hotel where I had lunch a couple of times; the free wi-fi in the lobby was perfect for dealing with my e-mail. Eventually, Harry, a former coast guard sailor from Oregon, and Ben, a fisherman from Homer, Alaska, signed up for the leg to San Francisco. Before we left, Nicholas and I paid a call on one of the ship's pilots who guided vessels into Dutch Harbor. We wanted advice on transiting the pass into the North Pacific Ocean, as the passes can have fierce currents and rough seas if the wind opposes the current. He was very helpful and gave us both a booklet of local tidal information.

Across the Gulf of Alaska to San Francisco

We left in a gap between the passing low pressure cells, and transited the Unalga Pass on the ebb, as the pilot advised, without problems. Once into the North Pacific, the next low caught up with us and we experienced gale force winds that put the lee rail under. Unfortunately, the crew had not had time to find their sea-legs, so it was a rough introduction to the boat. Harry was badly seasick, complicated by his affliction of sleep apnea. He had to sleep with a special mask strapped over his face, connected to a 120-volt outlet. Because of that, I had to keep the inverter running most of the leg.

A couple of days out, the staysail halyard snapped. The break was next to the swaged shackle, so repair was just a question of reeving the line back through the block on the mast and swaging another thimble. Fortunately, Ben was an experienced rock climber and he shinnied up the ratlines and mast steps to reeve the halyard with the wind still howling. We had the new swage fitting on, and the sail drawing again within two hours. I was fortunate this failure did not occur while I was single-handing from Nome.

A few days later there was a mysterious engine stoppage, which I eventually traced to copious amounts of water in the fuel. The only explanation seemed to be leakage through the deck plate into the tank when the deck was awash during the gale. In the end, I removed about five gallons of water from the tank and then discovered it was nearly empty because the gauge was over-reading by about 30 gallons. About this time, we sailed into a large, stationary high pressure system that gave us light head winds for a couple of days—always frustrating sailing.

By this time, Harry had pretty well recovered from his sea-sickness, but his personality had undergone a complete change. He was extremely rude to me, but I bit my lip and did not provoke a quarrel. We pressed on towards the Golden Gate Bridge and passed the half-way mark eight days out from Dutch Harbor. A few days later, a low pressure cell crossed our track with strong gale force winds for a day, so we reefed down and survived without problems. As we wallowed in the aftermath of the storm, with high seas and light winds, the faithful Perkins engine overheated. I dealt with all the usual suspects such as raw water intake filter and a replacement pump impeller, but sea water was simply not getting pumped around the engine. It was baffling, but as an expedient solution, I rigged an electric pump which might allow the engine to run for about 30 minutes as we approached the dock.

I gloomily contemplated an expensive repair in port and, as I read through the shop manual, a throwaway remark in the book mentioned loss of pump performance due to a worn cover plate and suggested simply reversing it. It seemed too simple a solution, but half an hour later, Ben and I working in the cramped, rolling engine room, had the plate off and put it back with the outside face on the inside. It worked like a charm and the engine ran cooler than it had for months.

The next challenge was to plan our arrival in San Francisco. I contacted Bill Steenberg, a veteran of two *Fiona* Atlantic crossings, from Cape Town and Portugal. (Chapters 3 and 8) He lived nearby and was able to arrange a slip in Emeryville, near Oakland. I intended to fly home for a couple of weeks before resuming the cruise to Panama, and the return leg to Long Island. The pilot chart recommended entering San Francisco Bay with the flood tide. By estimating our arrival date, when we still had about 500 miles to go, I was able to look up the tide table and discover the tide turned about 5 am. This was perfect— we would be entering the Golden Gate as the sun rose, and would cross the bay to Emeryville by mid-morning. We might even see the Golden Gate Bridge if it wasn't foggy.

The problem was the wind; it had swung around to the southeast, on the nose as usual, and dropped. We did not have enough fuel to power all the way there and the seas were too high anyway. We emptied the last of the jerry jugs into the tank and sailed whenever we could. The wind for the last day was forecast to be very light and the seas had calmed down. We powered very slowly to conserve fuel, and eventually we picked up a fair wind for a few hours. A thick fog descended on us and we cautiously made our way across the busy sea lanes leading to San Francisco. At one time on a 12-to-2 am watch I had to sail a holding pattern to ensure we arrived off the Golden Gate Bridge with a favorable tide. Unfortunately, a thick fog enveloped the famous bridge as we approached, but it lifted a little and we could see portions of the span. The fog signal on the south side hooted ominously as we slipped into the bay.

As we approached the jetty, Bill and his family waved a welcome. Later we had champagne and hors d'oeuvres in the clubhouse. Harry had his bags packed and bummed a ride to the airport with Bill's daughter within minutes of us tying up. Once *Fiona* was safely tied up in the marina, I flew home to Long Island.

Bill Steenberg greeting Eric on arrival in San Francisco

The first phase of the cruise was over. Since leaving Long Island on June 15th we logged 8,873 nm in 124 days. We spent 45 days in various ports, yielding an average of 112 miles per sailing day, including those in which we were trapped in ice.

Southern California and the Mexican Coast

After nearly three weeks at home, I returned to California in mid-November. Probably the most noteworthy thing I accomplished at home was, at the urging of one of my old crew, to put together a PowerPoint slide show of my transit of the Northwest Passage. I gave the talk for the benefit of the Carmen's River Maritime Center to a sell-out crowd at the local church hall. Bill met me at the San Francisco Airport and was his usual hospitable self, insisting that I stay with him, and running me down to the marina every day. I was able to squeeze in a presentation of my slide show at a local yacht club and meet many of his sailing friends. In return, I was given charts and advice on sailing southern California and Mexico.

Two young men signed up for the initial stages of the trip south, Quentin and Bart, having seen the call for crew on my web site. Quentin and his girlfriend Emilyn carried out a complete inventory of the food left on board while I was away. Later in Mexico, Emilyn swapped places with Bart. Quentin and Bart had had some sailing experience and turned out to be enjoyable companions. We made a short haul to Monterey and left the boat there for a few days to celebrate Thanksgiving. Bart and Quentin spent some time at their respective homes and Bill took me to his charming weekend house at La Selvas. I feasted at his traditional family gathering and reluctantly made my farewells.

The lads rejoined the boat and we chugged past the breakwater, which was crowded with honking sea lions. We headed for Santa Cruz Island, with the wind on the starboard stern quarter blowing about 25 knots. We had a sleigh ride to the island and anchored at the ominously named Prisoner's Harbor a day and a half out of Monterey. After inflating the dinghy, we headed for the shore and took a short walk, but there was really nothing to see. The island is a park and, apart from a worker that passed us in his pickup, we saw no one.

On returning to the beach, we found the surf had picked up, but I foolishly decided to launch the dinghy, which capsized, dumping us in the sea. As we were wet anyway, we pushed it beyond the breaking waves and climbed aboard. Fortunately, the outboard engine started and we returned to *Fiona* to dry out. Both my still and video cameras had been ruined and, although Quentin tinkered with his camera for a few days, he never got it to work. It turned out to have been a rather expensive excursion.

Our next stop was Avalon on Catalina Island. This is a very popular spot for Californian boaters from the San Diego region and the harbor had over 400 moorings, but there were not many boats there so late in the season and we enjoyed the town without standing in long lines. A landmark is the old Casino; never a gambling center, it was built in Art Deco style as a dance hall. Several movies were shot on the island at the height of the Hollywood era, and the Casino had an interesting museum showing snaps of '30s and '40s film stars, such as Clark Gable and Humphrey Bogart, at Avalon with their yachts. Nowadays, the Casino is mostly used to screen movies; we went to see *Christmas Carol*, mainly so we could inspect the wonderful Art Deco interior. One movie shot on the island before the war was a western, for which the producers imported a herd of buffalo. After the film was finished the animals were released into the wild, and now the herd is quite a tourist attraction.

I knew that Jack Carstarphen's wife Ruth and son Orne lived at Avalon. Jack was the captain of *Maverick* when we chartered aboard in the 1960's. When we sailed our own boat down there, *Iona*, in the late '60s they had separated but Ruth was pregnant with a son, Orne. I kept in casual touch with Ruth via Christmas cards and I knew she had moved to Avalon where Orne grew up. Ruth had died a few years ago, but to my delight Orne was listed in the local phone book. I gave him a call and discovered he was deputy harbor master. Obviously, salt water must run in his veins. He was very pleased I called and we got together on the boat. The next day he gave us a tour of the island. This was a rare treat because much of the island is a land trust administered by the Wrigley (chewing gum) family, who have owned it for decades. As a resident, Orne had all the permits to drive into the restricted parts and we even saw the fabulous buffalo herd.

At San Diego, we were given a complimentary berth at Cabrillo Island Marina, thanks to Bill's friend Craig, who I'd met at the slide show. A new edition of the popular California boating magazine *Latitude 38* appeared with an article about my Northwest Passage, and the ladies in the office posted a copy on the notice board with the caption "Famous Sailor Visits Our Marina." I was a little embarrassed, but such is fame! Quentin and I both bought new still cameras and I met up with an old sailing friend, BettyLou, who took me to a vast supermarket to re-provision for the leg to Mexico. BettyLou was married to Arnie when he built *Sea Swan* in Patchogue, near me on Long Island. One night it was very windy, and the crew furled a runaway jib on a nearby boat. The owner was so grateful, he got them $50 credit at the marina café. I also contacted one of my old flying buddies from those dim and distant RAF days. He was still flying his own plane and aroused my envy by telling me he had gotten a ride in a MIG 21.

It was just an overnight sail to cross the border into Mexico. We tied up at a marina in Ensenada and completed the paperwork to enter the country. If you do it after 2:30 pm the fees double! Obviously, the Mexican bureaucrats do not like working late. Viagra is sold everywhere with suggestive posters to attract the border tourists. The town was quite pleasant, with numerous restaurants, though meals and food at the markets were only slightly below New York prices. But Ensenada is too close to the U.S. border to be very inexpensive except at the taco stands. It was still fairly chilly in the mornings—40s F, an incentive to work our way south as quickly as possible. It took us two days to sail to Bahia de Tortugas, a small, more typical Mexican town than Ensenada. Although the bay is named for turtles, I had never seen so many pelicans in my life. They flocked on the jetty and every unoccupied boat. We sampled the local eateries and moved on.

Pelican crew, Bahia de Tortugas, Mexico

During the night the steering chain broke, the third time this had happened on this cruise. The weather was mild, so obviously something was going on. We hand-steered with the tiller to Bahia Asuncion and anchored off the village to repair the chain. We discovered that all the breakages of this trip were due to a pin in the lower sprocket assembly working loose and fouling the chain. We replaced chain and pin and secured the pin with stainless safety wire. A major overhaul of the steering system was obviously needed when I got home.

We left the same afternoon, bound for Magdalena Bay. Keeping busy, we took care of minor maintenance and I showed the lads how to use a sextant. We plotted a running fix using sun position lines; the GPS seemed reasonably accurate (GPS is the gold standard for fixes). We anchored in Santa Maria Cove. It was getting much warmer with the mid-day temperature climbing to nearly 80°F. Bart and Quentin overhauled the jib sheet winches and had a swim. A boat we had seen earlier showed up, *Fire Water*. We talked to the elderly captain, Richard, and his wife Doris, who had lived aboard 35 years making yearly round trips between Mexico and Hawaii. For the first time since leaving Long Island, I donned short pants. We were now nearing the southern tip of Baja California. On the way to a marina at San Jose del Cabo, we passed two large whales and a baby.

Bart signed off at the marina and we were joined by Quentin's girl-friend, Emilyn, who planned to sail to Panama. The marina manager, Jim, had written an informative and humorous guide to sailing the coast called *Baja Bash II*. He gave us a complimentary copy. The town was rather dusty, but boasted several inexpensive restaurants and internet cafes. We left to cross the southern end of the Sea of Cortez, bound for La Cruz, and it turned out to be a pleasant sail, in contrast to the mostly windless passages along Baja. We enjoyed La Cruz, a small, modest town with no overwhelming development.

Our next stop was Zihautanejo, where we stayed a few extra days because all the offices were shut for the New Year holiday. This was our last port in Mexico and we needed a zarpe (official clearance to leave for a foreign port) from the Port Captain, so that we had the necessary documents to enter Costa Rica. Edith and I had visited Zihautanejo about 22 years before, by air. We had stayed at a small hotel on the beach, but such had been the scale of development that I couldn't recognize much from my previous trip.

After leaving Zihautanejo, we experienced flat calm for a couple of days and motored. We were heading for Costa Rica, about a thousand miles away. The seas began to rise, although we still had no wind; we were nearing the infamous Gulf of Tehauntepec, where very strong winds, sometimes up to hurricane strength, can be generated. The boat rolled ferociously, but eventually we had enough wind to sail. This stabilized the boat, but the wind increased to about 30 knots and we tied two reefs in the mainsail, doused the genoa jib and set the staysail. We made good progress across the gulf, but before we furled the jib, a small tear developed. We exchanged the genoa for the Yankee jib in a lull, but the wind soon came back. We sailed with the reefed mainsail, staysail, and Yankee jib for the remaining 500 nm to Puntarenas in Costa Rica, which took ten days against heavy head winds.

When Emilyn was on watch one night, she spotted the freighter *Efficiency* approaching on a collision course at 20 knots on our bow. The first warning came on our Automatic Identification System (AIS) receiver, our relatively new aid which plotted the position of nearby ships using relayed GPS coordinates. She called on channel 16, but the reply was in poor English. Despite repeated warnings to change course to port, they finally said they could see our green light and then turned starboard across our bow. They passed only 100 yards on our port side, which was very scary in the dark with tumultuous seas running.

Costa Rica, Panama and the Canal

South of the Gulf we passed Guatemala, El Salvador and Nicaragua without seeing the coast line. We had winds on the nose up to gale force, with seas running 10 to 12 feet and strong currents. Sometimes we sailed with a triple-reefed mainsail and the staysail. The weather was atrocious—by far the worst I had experienced since being in Alaskan waters. In one 24-hour period, I found on checking the GPS that our distance to the destination had increased by about 30 miles.

As we approached Costa Rica, another hazard loomed, an area of hundreds of square miles littered with "Sea Mounts." These are stupendous pinnacles rising from the sea-floor 6,000 feet below to within a few feet of the surface. They ranged in diameter from a few miles to 20 miles, and more than two dozen were scattered in the area. They had not been surveyed for decades, and clearly it would not be prudent to sail across one in such heavy weather. We had to tack and zig-zag between these obstructions; it was uncomfortable and stressful sailing.

Eventually, we arrived in Costa Rica and anchored for the night in the lee of a small island before heading for the port of Puntarenas. We had no idea where the Port Captain was located, so we anchored in the narrow estuary by the fish market and wandered ashore in the dinghy. Fortunately, Emilyn was fluent in Spanish and soon got directions. We shouldered our way through the packed and noisy streets, stopping at an ATM to get some local pesos.

After a long wait in the Port Captain's office we were told an agent was essential. This was arranged and Jorge met us at the dinghy. He asked us to move the boat to the proximity of the Port Captain; we chugged a few hundred yards up the river and re-anchored. The reason for an agent soon became apparent; after a couple of hours, Jorge had assembled four officials on the dock opposite the boat to start our entry paperwork—Customs, Health, Immigration, and Police. When all that was done, Jorge piloted the boat up the river to the yacht club, about three miles out of town. The route was encumbered by sandbars and wrecks. We tied up to a float, and communication to the shore was accomplished by the ubiquitous "Pangas"—small narrow skiffs with outboard engines and propellers at the end of long shafts.

The club facilities were excellent and we were able to enjoy a shower, drinks and a meal. We contacted Andy, an expat who lived in Costa Rica. He planned to sail to Panama with us and make a video of the Canal transit. The next day, he and his wife showed up and we drove in their van to a town about 12 miles away to complete our entry into the country. We had to obtain a temporary import license for the boat. We found a sailmaker to repair the jib, and I visited a barber, who shaved off my beard and gave me a haircut that would have passed muster in the marines. After some shopping for food and beer we contacted Jorge to get us the necessary papers to clear out for Panama.

We had calm weather for a leg under power to the western boundary of Panama, and we anchored at several verdant islands for swimming and snorkeling. These islands were almost deserted; some were part of a national park and were wonderful tropical cruising. To get to the canal we still had one more hurdle to pass—Cabo Mala (Bad Cape, in Spanish). Many capes throughout the world produce their own weather and Bad Cape was no exception. We encountered fairly stiff winds almost on the nose. It took us two days to batter through to the lovely, tranquil Las Perlas Islands. This was Andy's first exposure to roughish weather at sea, and he was clearly not impressed.

We cruised to a few anchorages in the island group and then sailed for the canal entrance. In the distance, we could see the skyscrapers of modern Panama City on the starboard, and ahead, the numerous freighters at anchor waiting their turn for the transit. We refueled at a marina, which was too crowded with a "Round the World" rally to find a slip for us. I had run into such rallies in the past; the Trade Winds Rally encountered during *Fiona*'s first circumnavigation comes to mind. (Chapter 2) They are like an infestation of locusts, often exhausting fuel and provisions in small ports and crowding out anchorages.

We had to anchor for a couple of nights, and so we dinghied ashore to clear into Panama and start the paperwork for the canal passage. Andy checked into a fancy hotel to indulge himself in luxury and to await the start of our transit. This was my fifth transit of the Panama Canal aboard *Fiona*. In the past I handled the paperwork myself, but this time, after we had cleared into Panama, I hired an agent who scheduled our transit and dealt with the Canal Authority. We eventually managed to get a mooring at the Balboa Yacht Club and spent two days watching the endless stream of ships passing just a hundred yards to the north as they entered or left the canal.

The Canal Authority requires a small boat to be manned by a captain and four crew in order to make the transit, and they provide an advisor. To make up our crew strength, we were joined by another Bill, who flew down from New Hampshire, and who planned to stay aboard as far as New York. He was an experienced small boat sailor. On the appointed day, we were joined by the advisor, Robin, at 7 am and we powered up to the Mira Flores locks. Fortunately, we were able to tie up to a tug boat also making the transit, which is much simpler then tying the boat in mid-lock with two lines to both the bow and stern. All went well to the Gaillard Cut and the Gatun Lake. At the other end of the lake, Robin told us that delays had occurred with freighters ahead of us and we would have to anchor for the night.

Then something happened and we were offered the chance to make the last Caribbean-bound transit of the day, but we would have to be tied to the lock wall. We jumped at the chance, but as it turned out, it was not such a good idea. There are three locks to get vessels down to sea level. We entered the first lock behind a tug that was shepherding a disabled ship. I soon discovered the disadvantage of being tied to the dock wall—turbulence from the tug ahead, which was constantly maneuvering, caused us to bang against the wall, and the mast spreaders came dangerously close to colliding with it. In the second lock, a loss of communication between Robin and the dockside line-handlers allowed us to drift away from the wall, and twice I had to make a scary 360-degree, three-point turn in the turbulent water inside the lock, between the stern of the tug and its charge and the lock gate.

When we were finally tied up, spectators in the public viewing stand applauded. After dropping down to sea level in the third lock, we headed for Colon to disembark our advisor. In my previous trips, I stayed at the Colon Yacht Club, but in a dispute with the people who ran the container dock, who wanted to expand, the club had been bull-dozed out of existence literally overnight. It was still light, and I decided to head over to a new yacht club near the start of the north breakwater. Fortunately, we were able to tie up and Andy, who was desperate to get home, hitched a ride to the Colon bus station. After a couple of days, Emilyn and Quentin also signed off. They proposed to explore the natural wonders of Panama and Costa Rica on foot before heading home to California. Bill and I were joined by Louise, a veteran of many *Fiona* cruises, who flew in for a month aboard.

The San Blas Islands and Colombia

We left for the short leg to Portobello. This was a major port in the glory days of the Spanish Main; much of the loot extracted from the New World passed through it for trans-shipment to Spain. None of its former importance remained; it is a small, scruffy village without even a bank. The remains of forts built to protect the town line the shore and we wandered among the stone ruins. The forts had been knocked about a bit in the 16th and 17th centuries, mostly by the English. Children now played football in the flat spaces between the walls. We moved down the coast, stopping at a scenic bay and then anchoring in the San Blas Islands.

Louise and Bill pose with a Kuna Indian lady and her molas, San Blas Islands, Panama.

I had visited these islands on several occasions, starting with a cruise to French Polynesia in 1990, the circumnavigation in 1995-1997, and the trip to Antarctica in 1998-1999. They are inhabited by an indigenous Indian tribe called Kuna. For centuries, the occupiers of the mainland, first the Spanish and then the Panamanians, had tried to eliminate them. But they are fiercely independent and now have a degree of autonomy, which has allowed them to prevent any wide scale development in their country. They still move around in dug-out canoes, some with outboards, but many paddled or sailed with a lug rig. The women dress with a characteristic tight skirt and bodice decorated with molas, multi-colored cloth embroidery. The molas are also sold to tourists. There are several small villages scattered through the islands, with the bamboo huts densely crowded together, and though their lifestyle seems primitive, most of them carry cell phones! We snorkeled on a wrecked freighter and enjoyed a few meals ashore in primitive Kuna restaurants. Louise indulged in langouste, a clawless local lobster.

It was time to move on to Colombia, a 200-mile leg across a great bay, usually against the northeast trade winds. By watching the weather forecasts carefully, we were able to make the crossing mostly under sail, close-hauled on port tack with a wind from the north. We arrived in the late afternoon, and were heading up the inlet channel, when we had a scare when the engine overheated. We nursed the boat to an anchorage and when the engine cooled down, we discovered a hose clamp had broken and the cooling fresh water had drained away.

In the morning, we tied up at the yacht club in Cartagena. It was quite primitive, as the whole place was undergoing an extensive re-build. However, the dock master was very helpful and we enjoyed our stay. It was very hot and humid, and afternoon temperatures of 95°F were common, so we sweltered. Cartagena was another important port for the colonial Spanish. The town was built on several islands inside a bay, and each had its defending forts, which were mostly in good repair. The downtown central area inside the old walls was very attractive; we spent some time visiting the historic buildings and the stunning art museum. Fortunately, most of our everyday needs were met by a modern air-conditioned supermarket located close to the club, which featured a pleasant cafeteria, toilets, and an internet snack bar, as well as a well-stocked food section.

Louise flew home from here and her place was taken by Bert, a New Yorker originally from Germany. Bert kept a boat at Weeks Yard, *Fiona*'s home port, and we had exchanged yarns when we were both there working on our boats.

While in Colombia, I began to get disturbing e-mails about the con-dition of the Fire Island Inlet, which had shoaled due to heavy weather in winter. This was my point of entry to the Great South Bay, a last ob-stacle before pulling into my home port. I assumed that the problem would be sorted out somehow, but it raised the possibility of being stalled only 20 miles from home after circumnavigating the whole of the North American continent.

The Bahamas

We left for the Bahamas with a head wind and we had to beat our way clear of the coast, but after a day the wind veered and we were able to sail for the Windward Passage close-hauled. Gaining this favo-rable slant was one reason why we had sailed to Colombia; in 2007, returning from Antarctica, I sailed directly for the Passage from the San

Blas Islands and endured a long slog upwind. The wind died and then backed to northerly as we sailed past Cuba, but we made it to Matthew Town on Great Inagua Island in five and a half days after leaving Cartagena, five days shorter than the leg in 2007.

It was considerably colder in the southern Bahamas. We anchored a quarter mile off the beach—it was an open roadstead and we rolled badly. We inflated the dinghy and chugged over to the beach. The settlement was quite small, and only had the basic necessities: a store, bar, police station, school, and not much else. The economy depended entirely on the Morton salt company, which operated large ponds in the interior to make salt by the evaporation of sea water. As we left, we could see huge piles of salt glistening in the sun. It looked more like the Arctic than the tropics.

The northerly winds persisted and we powered to a more protected anchorage on Long Cay. It was very remote, and apart from a couple of yachts, we saw no one for a few days. The water was like crystal; we could see the bottom clearly 20 feet down. On the shore were thousands, if not millions, of conch shells displaying the characteristic slot were the shell had been cut to release the animal inside for food. Unfortunately, the shore was also littered by plastic debris of every description—bottles, flip flops, buckets, and packaging.

We indulged in a leisurely cruise through the Bahamas, stopping most nights—gunk holing, as sailors call it. We moved to Clarence Town on Long Island, and then to Rum Cay where we were disappointed to find the first bar we stopped at had no rum. The second had rum, but if we wanted a meal it had to be ordered hours before. Fortunately, the old lady running the place was able to produce some delicious conch fritters for us.

Eventually, we fetched up at George Town in the Exumas chain. This is the favorite spot for many snowbirds who bring their boats here year after year in winter. It is especially popular with Canadian boaters. We were able to re-provision, take a shower, do the laundry, and check our e-mail. For Bert, the e-mail proved urgent—business problems called him back to New York.

Bill and I sailed north, usually spending one night at each anchorage. At Farmer's Cay, we went aground near low tide. An obliging yachtie helped set a kedge and we got off as the tide came in. It was a warning that *Fiona*'s six-foot draft was tight for cruising in much of the Bahamas.

We had a wonderful sail across the Exumas Bank with a 15-knot beam wind and absolutely calm water provided by the islands to windward. A cold front pinned us down for three nights at Staniel Cay, an island Edith and I had visited in 1969 aboard *Iona*. Once again, I was unable to recognize much of the place, due to extensive development in the intervening years.

We sailed to a beautiful national park, unscarred by development, called Wardrick Wells. On shore we explored the remains of a settlement started by Empire Loyalists, who moved to the island after the American "Rebellion," as the British termed that historic event. It was abandoned after a few years. Scrubby bushes hid the moldering piles of coral bricks used to build the small houses. Reading a display about the history of the Bahamas, I was surprised to discover the islands had been covered by thick forests of exotic hardwoods, such as lignum vitae (a trade wood, also called guayacan; it is the national tree of the Bahamas and the Jamaican national flower). The trees were logged by early European explorers and the soil washed away, leaving the islands in the semi-arid state they are today.

Our final stop in the Exumas was Norman Cay. This was the scene of the dramatic evacuation of a sick crew member by air ambulance during the 2006-2007 cruise. (Chapter 7) My plan was to leave early in the morning for a 30-mile leg to Eleuthera, but the combination of choppy water and low sun on the bow got us into serious trouble. The entrance through the outer coral is tricky and narrow, so Bill went ahead in the dinghy sounding a route, but it was difficult to "'read'" the depth. Although the depth finder (located near the stern) showed several feet under the keel, *Fiona*'s bow struck heavily and the flooding current pushed the boat sideways onto rocks. Poor *Fiona* bounced in the shallow water. I sent Bill back to the anchorage to see if he could get a cruiser to come and help, but by using all the power available from the trusty Perkins engine, I was eventually able to get the bow pointing seaward again as the tide rose, and then power into deep water. Bill rejoined the boat a few hundred yards offshore and we winched the dinghy back on board. Later I was able to inspect the damage by diving with a mask; it looked like more work for Weeks

Yard when we got back.

We stopped at several small ports on Eleuthera. Perhaps the most interesting thing we visited was a "Blue Hole" a half-mile inland from the village of Rock Sound. These geological features are not unusual in the Bahamas, and this one was nearly circular, with a diameter of about 400 feet. They are very deep and the water level rises and falls with the tide, showing that there is an underground connection with the sea. The indigenous Indians had regarded them as very sacred places.

We left from Hatchet Bay for a fine 24-hour sail to the Abacos Islands. En route, we had to take evasive action in the middle of the night to avoid a small freighter, even though we were under sail and had right of way. But as they say, "Might is right." By daylight, we were off Great Abaco Island; we carefully navigated through a cut in the reef into the Sea of Abaco, and anchored a quarter-mile off New Plymouth. This charming village was established by Empire Loyalists and some of the families still living there can trace their roots back to these early pioneers. Bill and I visited an old house belonging to one of these families, the Lowes, which is now a museum.

Our next stop was Treasure Cay, which used to be a nice marina; I had anchored there several times in previous cruises. But now, so many condos had been built that the marina was rather overwhelmed and the matey bar I remember was deserted. Although the bar on the magnificent beach was functioning, for some strange reason it closed at 5 pm.

The next day we were off to Man-o-War Cay. We left at high tide, which meant we arrived near low tide, and so we bumped slightly entering the small, shallow harbor. This was getting to be a feature of Bahamas cruising with six feet hanging under the boat. Man-o-War is an old village, and for a couple of centuries the residents specialized in boat building. We were able to look in a couple of the sheds where work was in progress, though now the boats are made of fiberglass. We had lunch and dinner at the local restaurant, Dock and Dine. The island was dry, we discovered; no Heineken with our meals. Transportation on the narrow roads was by golf cart.

It was only an hour's sail to Marsh Harbour, our final port in the Bahamas, here we checked into a marina, expecting to be in port only a couple of days, but strong northeast winds kept us pinned there a few days longer. We were joined by Wayne, who flew in for some scuba diving before he signed on. Wayne was a veteran of the 2008 cruise (Chapter 8), across the Atlantic to the Azores leg.

Bermuda and Home

When the strong northeast winds finally let up, we left for Bermuda, although initially we were pushed a little north of the rhumb line. Then the wind petered out before switching to the southeast, so we enjoyed a pleasant sail with no heavy weather to deal with and arrived in Bermuda six days out, just before midnight. After clearing customs, we tied up at the dock wall on Ordnance Island, very close to where I secured on my first visit to Bermuda in 1968. There were plenty of signs that the economic downturn had hit Bermuda. The cruise ship terminal on Ordnance Island was now a yacht center, featuring easy chairs, wi-fi, and a clean toilet. It is ironic that in 1968 the same site was occupied by the dinghy club, subsequently moved to make way for the cruise ship terminal.

There were quite a few shops for rent in St. George's and the pub on the north side of the square was closed. Bill's wife, Kathy, was already in Bermuda when we arrived, and Bill, who was feeling unwell, left the cruise to join her before flying back to New Hampshire. My old friend Lew flew in for a few days' vacation on the boat; he is the editor of the famous *Fiona* cruising videos. We discussed plans for the next in the series; *Fiona* Challenges the Northwest Passage. I had hoped to sail to the west side of Bermuda for a couple of days and anchor on the reef, but very strong westerly winds prevailed, with gusts to 45 knots, and so we stayed securely tied up to Ordnance Island. Before the wind piped up, Lew and I changed the mainsail for the storm main; I was expecting bad weather for the last leg to Long Island, and thought that changing to heavy weather sails would be a good preventative.

I always enjoy Bermuda, and the rides in the pink and blue buses along the narrow roads with breathtaking views of the azure sea are a real pleasure. Wayne managed to squeeze in nine diving sessions, and then he, too, was joined by his wife for a few days and they moved to a nearby hotel. There remained the problem of replacing Bill, but my friends in the South Bay Cruising Club came through, and we were joined by Allan, who flew in the day before we left for the last leg of the North American circumnavigation.

We enjoyed good weather for the five-and-a-half-day cruise to Long Island. Allan was greatly impressed by a pod of fin whales which gamboled around the boat. A problem which developed the first day out was that the engine was overheating. I traced this to the fresh water circulation system. After changing a few components without any success, I finally converted the cooling system temporarily to direct sea water cooling, and this fix got us home. I knew we would need reliable power to transit Fire Island Inlet. The parlous state of the Inlet, caused by winter storms, had been the subject of numerous e-mails since I had arrived in Colombia. At first the news was very depressing, but more careful surveys made as the spring weather improved indicated I should be able to make it at the peak of high tide. Bob Forman, who brought his own boat through the Inlet a few days before *Fiona*'s passage, e-mailed detailed instructions on the zig-zag course in the channel to avoid shoal spots.

As we neared the coast I was faced with a dilemma; I had originally intended to enter on the high tide about 4 pm on Saturday, but the forecast showed gale force winds developing. I decided to enter on the earlier tide about 3 am and risk a night passage. The weather was still calm and we transited without difficulty, and the minimum depth we experienced was a little over two feet under the keel. A thick fog developed as we passed under the Robert Moses Bridge, and in the tricky channel through Great South Bay, we missed a turn and bumped onto a sand bar but easily powered off. Bob Lyons met us off Sayville with his beautiful Matthews power boat, *Fireplace*, carrying Wayne's better half and some friends. We tied up at Weeks Yard about 7:20 am on May 8th, on schedule.

The last few hours had been a dramatic finale to *Fiona*'s circumnavigation of North America. It had been an exciting 47-week cruise— *Fiona* logged 16,333 nm, although towards the end the log tended to under-read; the true distance was probably nearer 17,000 miles. For the statistically minded, I received 228 GRIB weather forecasts, entered 337 GPS waypoints, and exhausted 16 different crew members during the course of the cruise.

An Inexplicable Attraction: My Fifty Years of Ocean Sailing

10 | A Cruise to Some Small Atlantic Islands
2011-2012

This cruise was a ten-month, 12,500-mile odyssey along the rim of the Atlantic. *Fiona* sailed to Canada, Iceland, the Faroes, Scotland, Ireland, Portugal, the Canary Islands, the Cape Verde Islands, Brazil, French Guiana, and home via the Caribbean and Bermuda. The boat experienced heavy weather on the way to Iceland and off the Irish coast, and there was a fairly high crew turnover—19 signed on during the cruise.

On the way, expeditions were made to several islands which are hard to get to except by boat: Sable Island, Heimaey, St. Peter and Paul Rocks, and Devil's Island. We enjoyed a beautiful aquatic display by dolphins off Portugal. On Sable Island we met the legendary herd of wild horses. Horses also featured in a visit to a fair in rural Ireland. At the same location I visited the South Pole Inn, famously built by Tom Crean, a survivor of the Shackleton Antarctic expedition, so that he could always quaff a beer at the South Pole!

To Canada and Iceland

Fiona left Long Island in mid-July, 2011, with a crew of three besides myself. Sue was a teacher determined to make a significant offshore passage, and Wayne was a veteran of the 2008 Atlantic crossing and the 2010 leg from the Bahamas to Long Island. Ryan, a young man with seven years' experience in the Navy, intended to complete the ten-month cruise.

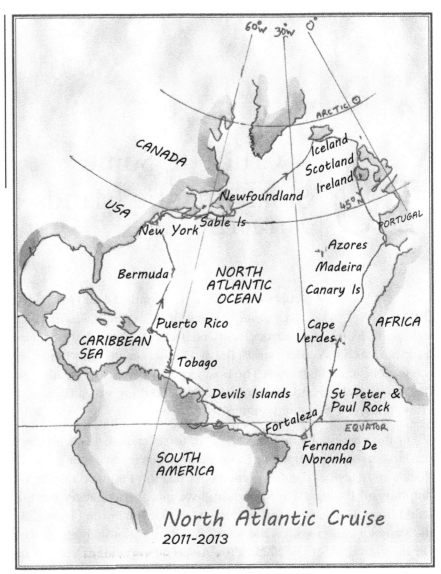

North Atlantic Cruise
2011-2013

We had no problems with shoaling in Fire Island Inlet and mostly powered in very calm conditions to Block Island. We took our usual walk to the southeast lighthouse and had supper at The Oar, which was crowded with yachties. We enjoyed a pleasant sail along Block Island Sound to Megansett Bay and rose at 5 am to catch the flood tide in the Cape Cod Canal. After refueling at the service station next to the power plant, we left the canal and sailed to Provincetown, where we spent two nights.

Wayne renewed his acquaintance with National Park rangers and went on nature walks. Our timing to leave Buzzard's Bay had been perfect; it got very windy in the anchorage we had just left, as we hung on a sheltered mooring at Provincetown. The big event in town was "Bear Week"— corpulent gay men, mostly with beards and combat boots, lumbered around the town. When the wind died down, a big high settled over the rhumb line to Nova Scotia. Later the wind perked up, and we crossed the Gulf of Maine under sail. Apart from one 12-hour spell using the engine, the weather was very mild compared to many of my trips across the same piece of water.

We arrived at Lunenburg about 6:30 am in the morning and discovered the Yachtshop marina was no more; the name had been changed to the "Boat Locker." Several floating pontoons had appeared since our last visit in 2009, as part of a waterfront revitalization. Lunenburg was our first Canadian port, so we had to clear customs. I had obtained a Canpass certificate before leaving, which saved a lot of paperwork on arrival. The Victorian architecture is a great feature of Lunenburg, especially the Academy on Kaulbach Street. We left after a day, as a weather window opened up for a leg to Sable Island, for which we also had prior permission to visit.

The Academy, Lunenburg, Nova Scotia

Sable Island is a sand spit lying on the very edge of the continental shelf, about 100 miles off Nova Scotia. It is about 20 miles long and less than a mile wide. In past centuries it was a graveyard of shipwrecks. We arrived off the north beach at 1 am and contacted Sable Island by radio, and when we were about ten miles out, we arranged to meet a guide on the beach about 9 am. We anchored in 15 feet and found a reasonable lee from the west-southwest wind. In the morning, we dinghied ashore and met Zoe, a very experienced botanist who gave us a wonderful three-mile walking tour around the west end of the island. To my disappointment, she said the wild horses, which are an exotic feature of Sable, did not escape from a wrecked ship, but were taken there in

Eric with wild horses on Sable Island

the 18th century as a commercial venture to take advantage of the free grazing, and to harvest the foals. I had always believed the shipwreck legend, which seems much more thrilling. There are now about 500 of the original horses' descendants roaming the island. The Canadian government took over the island in 1801 and proceeded to protect the horses and establish a life-saving service, as the island continued to attract ships to their doom. We followed the narrow pathways made by the horses through the grass, and wild flowers of every color littered our way, which Zoe identified. The horses we met were fairly tame and we could approach quite close to them. Several mares had new foals.

Seals gather off the beach to see the rare visitors to Sable Island

A highlight for me was to come across a rusty, abandoned Bren gun carrier of WWII vintage. Also, on the south beach, we found hundreds of grey seals enjoying the surf and sunning themselves on the sand. Our tour concluded with a visit to the scientific laboratories and instruments led by the station commander, Gerry Forbes. He told us *Fiona*'s crew was the first to make it ashore in 2011. There is an extensive program under the aegis of Environment Canada to study everything from airborne pollutants to continental lightning strokes. Twice a day, they launch balloons to collect upper atmosphere data. About eight people live permanently in a neat settlement. They are resupplied mostly by air—the planes land on a huge sand flat which is actually the remains of an old lake.

Gerry took us for a look around in his van with four-wheel drive and balloon tires. On the way, we drove down a narrow lane in the tussock grass that was inhabited by thousands of terns, who made their concern obvious by wheeling and diving at the van with shrill cries. Gerry called it "The Valley of Death." We also saw the island's only tree—after 50 years it was only about four feet tall. Zoe explained it was the scouring action of the sand that inhibited growth, not the wind. After all, in Patagonia, I saw many trees that simply grew parallel to the ground in very windy places. (Chapter 3)

Back at the base, we met three sailors off a small boat who were on their way to France. We agreed to meet again at St. John's, Newfoundland. Bad weather was forecast to be on the way and we raised anchor in mid-afternoon. We were all profoundly impressed by Sable Island and the pleasant, courteous staff who took time off their own work to make us welcome. Shortly after we left, the weather deteriorated, with 30-knot winds, fortunately from astern. We were obviously very lucky that we had gotten a weather window to visit Sable Island. With reefed main and jib, *Fiona* forged downwind at speeds of up to 9 knots. But the blow lived up to the old sailor's aphorism—quick to come, quick to go. By the morning, the winds decreased to 10 knots or less, leaving us wallowing in the heavy seas with no wind to stabilize the sails. A low to our north had quickly intensified and then scooted rapidly to the east. We started the trusty Perkins. Three days out from Sable Island the familiar coast of southern Newfoundland at Cape Race appeared on the port bow and we enjoyed a sail north to the Narrows. We checked in with the St. John's harbor radio and tied up at Queen's Wharf by lunch time.

The weather was very pleasant for a couple of days but then turned into typical St. John's clammy, damp days. Nevertheless, the crew enjoyed the great social life and managed to visit the wonderful museums. We climbed Signal Hill and walked to Quidi Vidi village. I looked up my old friend Jim Winter who drove me all over the city to find obscure spare parts. We refueled and changed to heavy weather sails.

After leaving St. John's on August 1st, we shaped a course somewhat south of the direct rhumb line to Iceland. The intention was to cross the Labrador Current as quickly as possible and to give a greater offing to Cape Farewell on the southern tip of Greenland. This area is notorious for heavy weather. The Arctic to our north was lying under a huge high pressure cell and we did not see a wind over 20 knots for a week after leaving. In fact, the winds were in the 10- to 15-knot range with sunny skies. The down side was that the wind was east to northeast, for the most part, on the nose. We made slow but steady progress, mostly under sail across calm seas.

The horizon on the port shimmered under the Northern Lights. After about a week the wind picked up to 20 to 25 knots, with higher gusts, and we ploughed to windward under staysail and reefed mainsail. Due to a combination of lows to our south and highs to our north, the wind blew persistently from the northeast and we beat slowly towards Iceland, not the pleasantest kind of sailing.

Wayne and Ryan were both laid low by seasickness, but Sue remained cheerful and even stood a few watches for Ryan. On August 9th we sailed 133 nm, noon to noon, only to make good 54 nm towards our destination. The same day we got a scare when copious amounts of water began sloshing about in the bilge and occasionally washing onto the cabin sole; the hose on the sink drain had come adrift and water spurted into the boat as *Fiona* slammed into the waves. Fortunately, the through-hull valve worked perfectly, and furious pumping by hand and using the electric pump brought the situation under control.

When we were about 600 nm from Reykjavik the weather worsened, and for a week we had to deal with strong winds with a large sea running. We hove-to for a day and a half under double-reefed main, with gale force winds gusting to 50 knots. When conditions improved a little, we set a reefed mainsail and staysail and commenced again the dreary beat towards Iceland. When Wayne and I were working in the cockpit, a big wave burst aboard and caused to us hang on for dear life. The life rings were washed away and even the bracket holding one was broken. The MOB (Man Overboard) flasher disappeared forever. Tack after tack, we worked our tedious way to the northeast, and on the 17th, Iceland was in sight. We tied up at Reykjavik before dawn on the 18th. We had logged 1,914 nm to make good 1,400 nm from St. John's, Newfoundland, to Iceland, a reflection of the long slog to windward.

The impressive glass building called "Harpa" at Reykjavik, Iceland

Unfortunately, Ryan quit the cruise at Reykjavik. He had originally signed up for the complete Atlantic circuit and his departure left me struggling for crew at each major port. Sue and Wayne had all along planned to leave when we reached Iceland. Their places were taken by Marc, a retired dentist, and Arlene, a retired accountant. Both had considerable sailing experience.

We tied up at the Reykjavik Sailing Club, a new facility since my visit in 2000. It was located next to a spectacular glass building called Harpa. Besides the waterfront there had been considerable development in the town itself. We were only ten minutes from the town center, which boasted numerous restaurants, shops, and internet cafes. My friend Eli, whom I first met during the cruise to the Arctic in 2000, had married Hildur in the interim. We had dinner at their beautiful house with their three children and their parents. The Icelanders enjoy a very high standard of living, but it comes at a price—food, fuel, and other necessities are very expensive by American standards. Eli was very generous with his time and he took a day to give us a wonderful tour of some of the natural wonders of Iceland. Naturally, the crew all had a swim at the famous Blue Lagoon, a geothermal spa located in a lava field, one of the most-visited spots in Iceland.

We refueled before leaving, though the pump was a temperamental automatic thing that kicked out my credit card after we got our tanks half-filled. From Reykjavik, we made a 24-hour sail to Heimaey in the Vestmann Islands. On the way we sailed past Surtsey, an island created several miles offshore by a volcanic eruption in 1963. But Surtsey was disappearing fast; about half the island has been eroded away by the action of wind and tide. Just over 4,000 people lived on Heimaey, where the major occupation was fishing, and therefore the harbor was very busy. In 1973, a new volcano inundated the town and everyone was evacuated.

The "Blue Lagoon" heated by thermal springs, Iceland

Volunteers managed to contain the lava flow by cooling it with sea-water, using massive diesel-powered pumps, so that most of the houses and the harbor entrance were saved. We completed refueling and left after two nights for the leg to the Faroe Islands.

The Faroe Islands, Scotland and Ireland

We had a wonderful downwind sail to the Faroes and arrived off the islands after two days. Unfortunately, the current was against us as we struggled to Torshavn. The tidal currents are strong in these islands and cruisers are warned always to plan inter-island trips in conjunction with current tables. Off the island of Hestur, we came to a complete standstill. The trusty Perkins engine was roaring away, but we made no forward progress as the currents spun the boat in whirlpools. Close to the rocky shore, we found a counter-current. but it didn't last long and it took us a long time to battle past the cape at the southeast corner of the island. Eventually, we sailed out of the grip of the worst of the currents and pulled up to the dock for visiting yachts at Torshavn in the late afternoon.

A customs official cleared us in and we were free to wander round the town, which had a distinctly Scandinavian look. We asked the skipper of a local schooner moored just ahead of us about eateries and he promptly gave us soup and crab's claws, which he had prepared for a charter party who had cancelled out. There were plenty of coffee shops and restaurants, and even a few take-out places, such as pizza and fish and chips, but prices were up there. Coffee and a small cookie-sized pastry at the coffee shop near the dock ran about $10. There is an extensive bus and ferry network connecting the Faroe Islands, some of which are joined by undersea tunnels, with more planned. We visited several sites on Streymoy Island by road that had interesting relics going back to Viking times. At Kirkjuboes, there was an old church and 13th century cathedral undergoing restoration. The 900-year old log cabin farmhouse had been occupied by the same family for 18 generations, and their graves proliferated in the cemetery. One day, a very pleasant tour guide we met arranged for us to bum a ride to the ferry to Sandoy island, where we enjoyed a brisk walk, though there was not a lot to see except the old church with its sod-covered roof. The Nordic museum, located a couple of miles northeast of Torshavn, was well worth a visit, however. A highlight was a visit to Torshavn by the travelling "Baldoni" circus. The show took place in the town sports center. There were no animals, just acrobats, magicians, and clowns.

House with a sod roof, Faroe Islands, family graves in foreground

Scotland

On leaving the Faroes, we had hoped to make our first stop in the U.K. at St. Kilda Island, which lies about 35 miles west of the Hebrides. It was occupied for centuries by very hardy shepherds and fishermen, but was eventually abandoned. Very calm weather is needed for a visit; and, as it was blowing 25 to 30 knots during our trip south, we gave up on the idea and headed for the North Minch in the Hebrides. The southwest wind forced us to tack around various headlands as we aimed for an anchorage at Rum Island. We arrived about 3 am, but the anchor chain was firmly wedged in the chain locker and would not budge. Instead of dropping the hook, we tied up to the massive concrete ferry dock for a couple of hours until the falling tide forced us to cast off. Apart from its name, the main attraction at Rum is an elaborate Edwardian mansion built without regard to cost by a Lancashire industrialist who had made a fortune manufacturing cotton spinning machines.

We headed for Tobermory on the Isle of Mull, a quaint village I had visited before. It had been enhanced by a large number of pontoons for visiting yachts. The next day we endured a wet and windy sail down the Sound of Mull, with the wind was on the nose, to Oban on the Scottish mainland. The marina was on a small island, Kerrera, about a mile west of the town. An hourly ferry connected it to downtown Oban. During the weekend, we had a visit from an old sailing friend, Pauline Chapman, who had been following *Fiona*'s website and was touring in the area. My cousin Philip Forsyth, his daughter Sheena, and her partner also managed to get across on the ferry for a few hours—a visit made short when the weather deteriorated as the remnants of hurricane Katia approached; they faced a three-hour car ride to the east coast.

Highland cattle on Kerrera Island, Scotland

The next day, Marc and Arlene decided that Oban was far enough for them, and signed off. As Katia howled in the rigging, I removed the engine exhaust hose and manifold. The hose was clearly very tired (I had installed it in Brazil in 2007), and a stud broke on the manifold, which had to be replaced. The marina manager arranged for a machinist to remove the broken stud on the mainland. This turned a three-hour job into a two-day job.

Low tide at Oban, Scotland

Unfortunately, after a couple of days at Oban, I discovered a sore on my forehead. On my next visit to the town on the hourly ferry, I asked the pharmacist at Boots chemist shop for some ointment, but she was adamant that I should see a doctor. She told me where the medical center was, and a pleasant receptionist arranged an appointment in about four hours, even though I was not a resident of the U.K. The doctor diagnosed shingles and gave me a prescription for week's supply of pills. I had it filled at the nearby pharmacy, and when I asked the price, I was told firmly, "Och, prrrescrriptions are frree in Scotland." I also began what was becoming a familiar routine of filling the crew berths. Sometimes I ate in the restaurant of the marina, which was quite unique, at least for that climate—it was in a tent. I got the boat ready for the next leg, which included refueling at US$7 per gallon for diesel.

The days passed by, mostly wet and windy, and my old friend Barbara Fitzgibbon, whom I first met in Thailand sailing round the world, found a volunteer to sail to Portugal. The new crew, Conor, flew to Glasgow from Cork and caught a train to Oban. He came across to the marina on the ferry and we left early the next day with a fairly grungy weather forecast, but Conor only had a limited time available to make the trip.

Ireland

The trip to Dingle in southwest Ireland took a week, but we logged only 591 nm. That's because we had winds persistently on the nose, sometimes up to gale force, and we hove-to on three occasions, once for a day and a half. Setting the second reef in preparation for heaving-to, the storm mainsail tore along the leach, though fortunately it was below the reefing cringle. When the weather eased up, we removed the sail and bent on the regular mainsail, but within a few hours, we had that sail reefed down as we hove-to again. We also suffered a scary repeat of the incident off Iceland that nearly sunk the boat—the hose to the galley sink came adrift. Fortunately, I caught it in time before the water in the bilge reached a dangerous level. The weather moderated for the last day, and we powered into Dingle Bay with a mild wind. I was very sorry that Conor had endured such bad weather for his first offshore passage, but he kept a stiff upper lip.

The crew at the Dingle Marina—Sean, Peter, and the Harbor Master, Brian—were very helpful in taking care of our needs. We refueled from a truck at US$4.80 per gallon, a steal compared to Scotland, and a young woman, Monza, repaired our sail with an old sewing machine she normally used to stitch skins for the traditional Irish currachs. In the evenings, we enjoyed the matchless Irish music available in almost countless pubs. A cruising American, Kevin on *Exodus*, put me in touch with a fellow Westsail 42 owner, Drake, who readily agreed to take Conor's berth for the leg to Lisbon. A local sailor, Eanna, who was completing his yacht master certificate, was also happy to gain ocean time by signing up for the leg to Lisbon. Frank and Barbara Fitzgibbon found time to drive over and gave Conor a lift back to Kinsale. The afternoon we planned to leave was complicated by the refusal of the engine to start, due to an ominously silent starter motor. We substituted the spare starter and that one also refused to function. We rushed the original starter to the only auto service shop in Dingle and, to my relief, a competent mechanic stripped it down and got it working inside of an hour.

Portugal

We left at 6:30 pm on Friday afternoon, only a few hours after our planned departure, and were soon enjoying a great sail, close-hauled on starboard tack as we headed for Portugal. The wind held for over three days before dying, as we moved into the center of a high pressure cell. We completed the leg to Viana do Castelo under power in a little under five days, a distance of 713 nm. Drake turned out to be a very enthusiastic videographer, and he made extensive video records of *Fiona*'s deck and interior to assist in an upgrade he was planning of his Westsail 42. It was a real pleasure after the rain and chills of Scotland and Ireland to enjoy happy hour in the cockpit dressed in a t-shirt. The change in climate achieved by sailing a few hundred miles south was astonishing.

I had first sailed to Viana do Castelo after the cruise to the Arctic in 2000. The waterfront had changed dramatically as Portugal spent the Euros gained by joining the Common Market. The small marina, for example, where we stayed during my first visit, was blocked by a new swing bridge that formed part of a scenic riverside walk. I elected to tie up on the river bank to a small pontoon. Fortunately, the old part of town was little changed and I was able to enjoy coffee and pastry at the quaint pastelerias on the medieval square that Bill Steenberg and myself had patronized eleven years earlier. I introduced the crew to the unique "elevador," a cable railway going up the hill to the massive Basilica overlooking the town. The weather was perfect for strolling the quaint streets in shirtsleeves. On our last night, we had supper at a restaurant in an old building with massive stone arches and a fireplace about ten feet wide.

We left the next day for a port 130 miles down the coast called Nazaré. The GRIB forecast predicted completely calm conditions and that is what we found. We were a little short of fuel by this stage, and so we motored at a sedate 5 knots over a flat sea. We soon attracted a large school of dolphins which gamboled round the boat for hours, much to Drake's delight. He shot gigabytes of video from the bow platform. While we were still sailing, he edited the footage into a charming four-minute video with captions and music, and posted it on Facebook when we got to port.

When we pulled into Nazaré, we tied up at a prominent BP sign, but it turned out that the station was disused. When I attempted to start the engine to move, the starter refused to budge. We removed it (again) and began some serious maintenance. A couple of mechanics sent over by the dock master, Captain Hadley, whom I had called on VHF to explain our tardiness in departing the dock, quickly took over and had the starter stripped, cleaned and functioning again in about an hour. We refueled at a pontoon, paying the outrageous price of US$7.30 a gallon, and then tied up at the marina.

The next day, we explored the town and took the cable railway, of which the Portuguese seem very fond, to the top of the precipitous peninsular jutting out into the Atlantic north of the town. In a supermarket, I discovered one of my favorite Portuguese delights—white port—a bottle of which lubricated happy hour that evening. We left for Cascais (pronounced, inexplicably, as "Kas Keyesh"), where I intended to leave the boat while I returned for a couple of weeks to New York. We sailed overnight to Cascais with a fine northeast breeze and tied up before the marina was even open. The marina had grown enormously since I spent a night there in 2000. A vast complex of shops and restaurants had been built, along with many more boat slips.

After we were tied up, we walked into town and caught a train to Lisbon. Eanna was returning to Ireland the next day, and I wanted him to see a little of Portugal's capital. After he departed, Drake and I stayed for a few more days. One day, we took a bus to Sintra, where there is a palace of the former royal family. On October 25th, I flew to

Long Island for my usual mid-cruise sojourn in Brookhaven, carrying numerous parts that needed repair. I returned to Portugal with a few days to spare before a new crew showed up, and spent time installing the parts I had brought back with me. Unfortunately, only one of my crew that I had connected with through e-mail actually showed up— Markus, a German professional musician.

We enjoyed a very easy sail to Porto Santo in the Madeira archipelago with light winds from astern, which died after three days, and so we powered the last 115 miles. I had never been to Porto Santo before. The big attraction is the white sand beach, which is popular with people from Madeira, where the beaches are black. Christopher Columbus had a house there. The cruisers at the marina staged an impromptu musical evening on a German cruising boat; Markus played some bongo drums they had on board, and was very good.

We sailed on, as the following day was a public holiday and I did not want to arrive at Funchal and find everything shut. The harbor was crowded, as usual, but mostly with local boats, which seemed to be more numerous every time I visited Funchal. I took a tour of the spectacular mountain landscape and Markus hiked along the central ridge, in clammy cloud all the way. I took the teleferico to the top of the hill in Funchal, but the season was getting late; no tourists were taking a chance on the mad toboggan ride from the top of El Monte on the wicker sleds. This was a little curious, as there were several cruise ships visiting the island, sometimes two at a time. And they were huge—5,000 passengers, although the customs man said they usually carried only 3,500.

If Portugal was facing a financial crisis, as the papers said it was, it was not obvious in Madeira. The streets were crowded with new cars, the women were elegantly dressed, and even in the villages there were no overt signs of poverty. The Great Depression it was not. In the harbor was a Dutch brigantine, *Tres Hombres*, originally built in Germany in WWII, which the skipper assured me made money carrying freight between the islands of the Caribbean and Europe. However, he made most of the crew pay $1,500/month each for the experience. This was similar to the old ways on the square riggers. Apprentices paid to go to sea, as time on square riggers was necessary to achieve a mate's "ticket."

We had a great beam wind for the leg to La Gomera in the Canaries, and in fact we had to slow down by striking the jib so that we arrived in daylight after a two-day sail. Markus, who had suffered from mal de mer through most of the trip, even under calm conditions, flew home the day after we arrived. Thus, I again faced the problem of finding crew for the leg to the Caribbean. The marina had an extensive notice board and several people advertised for crew positions, and so within the week I was able to recruit Marco, a young German cabinet maker on a walk-about, and Jorden, an even younger Israeli woman. Marco had completed a three-year apprenticeship, and it is a German tradition for the newly-qualified man to leave the area where he had trained, so as not to compete with the former master. Hence, the term "journeyman." Neither had much sailing experience but they spoke adequate English.

The town of San Sebastian is a pleasant place, not overly crowded, and with lunch-time temperatures in the 70s. I thoroughly enjoyed my quiet hiatus as I waited for the crew. On a Saturday night, there was a concert in the main square with a sprinkling of Christmas music. Marko signed on the day before we left and we had a final shore-side pizza with an English cruising couple. Jorden, the young Israeli woman, arrived very early on the ferry from La Palma, and after getting a few last minute grocery items, we pushed off.

Cape Verde Islands

We refueled and headed for Mindelo in the Cape Verde Islands. Apart from a few hours when the wind was upset by the proximity of the islands, we had great trade wind sailing to the Cape Verdes. Unfortunately, the refurbished shaft generator I had installed at Cascais died, due to a failure of the pulley for the driving belt. It was made of an aluminum alloy and had simply machined itself away. This meant we were a little short of 12-volt power, but Victor the Vane performed well as the autopilot, which eased the load on the battery.

We dawdled as we approached Mindelo, so as to arrive with sun-up. Good thing we did; since my last visit, a huge marina had materialized. A couple of lads in a dinghy helped us secure to mooring ball and we tied up stern-to, Med style, to a floating pontoon. The place had improved since my last visit. Jorden had not been too happy with thought of the long haul to Brazil and the Caribbean awaiting us, and had decided Christmas at Mindelo sounded better. Marko ran into a French backpacker, Damian, who had sailed as crew to Mindelo on another boat, and so Damian signed on the day we left, Christmas Eve.

Crossing the Atlantic, St. Peter and Paul Rocks, and Brazil

Poor Damian was terribly seasick as we headed down the choppy St. Vincent Channel on our way to St. Peter and Paul Rocks. As soon as we got out of the wind shadow of the island, we picked up good trade winds that blew for days. On Christmas Day, we rigged the traditional tree in the cabin. On our first day out from Mindelo, we reeled off 162 nm in 24 hours with the reefed storm mainsail. Apart from one four-hour hiatus, the winds continued strong until the 30th.

On New Year's day, the wind became erratic, with numerous squalls. We had entered the doldrums at about three and a half degrees north. We ran the engine periodically to keep up some progress, and on New Year's Day, we sighted St. Peter and Paul Rocks, which lie about 55 miles north of the equator and 500 nm from the Brazilian coast. As we approached, the weather deteriorated. To our surprise, as we neared the rock we found a fishing boat at anchor, called *Natamar*. As they pitched and rolled at the end of a long anchor rode, we called them on VHF. The occupants were scientists. There was a heavy swell running, a stiff wind with rain, and obviously, there was no chance of a dinghy ride to the rock. Saints Peter and Paul actually comprises about four rocks in a

St. Peter and Paul Rocks, near the Brazilian coast

cluster, and on the largest we could see a small hut with a parabolic antenna. To the south, there was a navigational warning beacon on a short pole. We circled around for a while and then set a course for Fernando de Noronha. I was very disappointed that I could not actually set foot on the rock, but I got close!

We had good winds and a favorable current to whisk us to Fernando in less than three days. We anchored to seaward of the crowded harbor at 3 am local time. A cruise ship, *Ocean Dream*, was still blasting out loud music at that hour. In the morning, we pumped up the inflatable and launched it over the side. It was the first time it had been used since we visited Sable Island in Canada. The Japanese outboard refused to start and we substituted the old Seagull engine I had first used during *Iona*'s 1968-1969 Caribbean cruise. We chugged our asthmatic way to the jetty, pouring out copious smoke and oil.

As we had no Brazilian currency, we walked up the hill under a blazing tropical sun to the old village I remembered well from previous visits, Vila de Remedios. When Fernando de Noronha was a prison island, this is where released inmates lived; they were not repatriated to the mainland. After vainly trying my card at the bank, we discovered the only place to use an international card was at the airport. We took a taxi, which turned out to be rather expensive, and returned to the village for lunch. On the way back to the port, we stopped for a few groceries, and then at the port I checked in with the Port Captain. The authorities had come up with a new way to tax yachties—an anchoring fee, which for *Fiona* amounted to $89 per night. This is in addition to the head tax imposed on all crew members (except for the first day) of $22 per night. Soon the small office was filled with Federal Police, Maritime Police, and goodness knows what other officials, all filling out forms. I said we would stay one day, and was informed in no uncertain terms that the next day began at 8 am, so we must be gone before that.

I discovered Elda no longer owned the bar nearby which had been our watering hole on other visits. Also, the large wind generator, which had disappeared, had been hit by lightning and pulled down. We chugged back to the boat, dismantled the dinghy and I felt a lot better after a couple of *Fiona* cocktails. The depredations of the taxi, lunch, and the voracious port captain had depleted all the cash I had gotten from the ATM, except for about $30. Clearly, the cost of living on the island had skyrocketed since my last visit, and I wondered if this was a consequence of introducing cruise ships. The half-hourly bus service from the dock to the village, about a mile and a half, which used to cost about a buck, had escalated to $7 one way.

To Devil's Island

We enjoyed a really pleasant downwind sail to Fortaleza under a tropical moon that got bigger every night. We arrived about midnight, and the small marina looked rather complicated to enter in the dark, so we anchored just outside until dawn. It was a good thing we did. Shortly after sunrise, a sailboat emerged and the captain asked us if we intended to enter. When I said we that did plan to do so, he warned us not to proceed past a large catamaran which had lines stretching right across the harbor due to the heavy surge. Interestingly, the boat was a Westsail 42, very similar to *Fiona* except it was yawl-rigged. It had formerly belonged to Walter Cronkite, and was now called *Mailee*. We dropped our hook just to the seaward of the cat and backed up to the massive steel pontoons which formed the marina. We secured the boat about four feet from the pontoons because we were warned again by the crew on the cat about the surge to be expected, and rigged a gang-plank using a fender board.

The marina had no facilities except use of the showers and toilets at the nearby swimming pool, part of the hotel complex. But marina guests could use all the hotel services, and there was a handy fast food bar and an internet café. The dock master, Amando, arranged for us to get diesel from a local entrepreneur who had a pick-up with a 200-gallon tank in the back. We drove to the local gas station, put 100 gallons in the tank and drove back to the marina, where the driver tossed a line on to the dock, and we hauled his hose across to *Fiona*. The cost was about US$4 per gallon, plus US$80 for the use of the truck.

Fortaleza is the largest city on the north coast of Brazil, but there was little architecture of note and much of the place had a run-down air. About a ten-minute walk from the marina was the huge municipal market, which was architecturally interesting; inside were four floors connected by spiraling walkways hanging in space. But the place was separated from the marina by a very busy highway, where trucks, motorbikes and cars screamed by at full throttle. When I was crossing a side street to enter the market one day, on a pedestrian crosswalk, a maniacal driver saw his chance and I escaped only by propelling myself violently forward by pushing off the fender on the driver's side.

We handled maintenance chores in the mornings; I went over the side with scuba gear to replace the zincs on the prop shaft, but the water was too murky for me to see more than a few inches. And so I postponed the job until I was in clear water in the Caribbean. I spent a lot of time fiddling with the shaft generator, which hadn't worked right since the Cape Verdes, despite the new pulley installed there, but I was unsuccessful. Marco and I rebuilt parts of the Aries wind vane, which gets a lot of wear and tear on a trip like this. Damian took our laundry to some machines a taxi-ride away.

Damian had decided to sign off the trip at this point, and we went with him to the bus station. He was heading for Recife, several hundred miles away. It was interesting to see the numerous destinations and inspect a large map of the routes. Brazil is a HUGE country, only slightly smaller than the U.S. in area. Marco and I left after five days for French Guiana.

Marco and I double-handed to Kourou in French Guiana, a leg of over 1,000 nm, but it took us a little over six days, due to the 45 nm per-day boost we got from the Equatorial Current. The sea is very shallow along this part of the South American coast; even thirty miles from shore, the depth varies between 30 and 50 feet. Following the channel to the Kourou River entrance, we often had only two or three feet under the keel, although it was nearly high tide.

Once in the river, we spotted a small stone jetty and what looked like a boatyard, so I decided to anchor there. After the tide turn, the ebb ran very fast and we dragged, so we re-anchored with more chain. As it turned out, we should have anchored further up the river, which would have put us nearer to the town of Kourou. This illustrates my unfamiliarity with electronic chart plotters, which I was using for the first time. Basically, I found it like navigating on a postage stamp—better yet, a beer-mat. Either you can zoom in and see great detail over a small area, or zoom out and see a wide area without detail. The display on my plotter was only four inches square.

Once settled, we launched the rigid dinghy and puttered to the jetty using the old Seagull engine. It was about a half-hour walk into town, where we bought a few groceries and took a taxi back. We were only five degrees above the equator. You may remember the line about mad dogs and Englishmen and the mid-day sun, and there we were, the two of us, out in the midday sun (although Marco is German).

The next day we were fortunate enough to bum a ride to the port area to clear in at Customs. The port is divided into two parts: the commercial port, where we eventually located the Customs, and the space launch dock, which is protected by three rows of barbed and razor wire, as well as an electrified fence. Kourou is where the European Space Agency launches rockets. After a pleasant but expensive lunch at a restaurant near the dock, we walked back to town, mailed a few cards and attempted unsuccessfully to log onto the internet at a bar with a gorgeous barmaid and lousy wi-fi. After more grocery shopping, we taxied back to the dinghy and boarded the boat just in time for happy hour.

In the morning, we weighed anchor and sailed for Devil's Island, seven miles offshore, in rain and squally winds. Several small boats carrying tourists passed us in the channel. They were all catamarans, with both sail and power capabilities. In the 18th century, the French were impressed with the British development of Botany Bay using transported criminals. They decided it would work for French Guiana. Devil's Island was only one of numerous convict settlements. In a bit of pre-Orwellian double-speak they were named Iles du Salut (Salvation Islands, in English). The group consists of three islands: Royale, St. Joseph, and Devil. Royale is the largest and was the main prison and administrative center. St. Joseph was used for hard cases. Some cells there were built with no roofs, just iron bars, so that the prisoners could be monitored continuously. Other cells, for solitary confinement, allowed no light to enter. All these remains have returned to the jungle, and although we dinghied over to St. Joseph Island, the interior was inaccessible and we were confined to a shoreline footpath. It is now forbidden to land on Devil's Island.

The cemetery at Royale Island, French Guiana

We spent two days at Iles du Salut, mostly visiting Royale Island. Most of the buildings were originally made by the convicts using stone quarried on the island, so they are substantial. One building had been converted into a hotel. Each day we concluded our tour at the bar. There was a very interesting museum which depicted the hard life of the convicts in graphic detail. The punishment for infractions was often death, and the prison had a guillotine set up in an inside court yard. The yard and the cells for condemned men next door were still open to visitors. We inspected a cemetery on Royale Island for warders and their families, as convicts were buried at sea.

The most famous prisoner was Captain Dreyfuss, a French army officer, falsely accused of treason in an anti-Semitic plot. A special cell was built for him on Devil's Island, where he spent several years in solitary. Warders were forbidden to speak to him. If a strange ship was sighted near the island, the warder held a pistol to his head until the ship disappeared. Finally, a campaign to exonerate him, led by Emile Zola, was successful, but Dreyfuss returned to France broken by his experience. Guiana was taken over by the Vichy government in WWII and was blockaded by the U.S., causing half the prisoners to starve to death or die from lack of medicine. The prison was shut down after the war.

The Caribbean

We left early in the morning and headed for Barbados in the West Indies. It took us a day to sail out of the shallow water that extended for miles from the coast, and we were driven by strong northeast winds. But then the wind died and in the sail slatting that followed, the mainsail developed a couple of tears. We took it down and bent on the spare. That night the wind came back with such force that we had to reef the sail we had just installed. This burst carried us through the next day and we dropped anchor in Carlisle Bay, Bridgetown, just about midnight. It was very windy in the bay, and in fact for most of our stay.

The Bridgetown Signal Station instructed us to tie up in the main cruise ship harbor, something I try to avoid, as it is designed for very large ships, not yachts. The last time I was there the rail cap was damaged, but this time we managed to slip in behind the huge sailing schooner, *Spirit of the Wind*, without trouble. The terminal building was packed with the passengers of three cruise ships, but eventually I got the clearance papers signed by officials in several offices and we returned to the anchorage in Carlisle Bay.

The next step was to inflate the dinghy. When we launched it, Marco suddenly yelled, "Eric, the dinghy!" I glanced aft—the dinghy was free of *Fiona*, and rapidly heading for the horizon under the 20-knot breeze. Marco dived in and swam to the dink, but he could not start the outboard, and it was impossible to row and make headway against the wind. I started the engine on *Fiona*, raised the anchor and started in pursuit of Marco and dinghy, which was now far to the west. Some tourists on jet skis tried to help, but without a painter, there was nothing to tow with. Eventually, we sorted it out and re-anchored the boat. It turned out that the strap on the dinghy holding the eye for the painter had broken.

We headed for a look at Bridgetown by taking the dinghy up the Careenage, under the bridge and tying up at a new dinghy dock. We spent a few days doing boat maintenance in the mornings and dinghying to shore for meals and shopping. I donned the scuba gear again and went over the side to change the zincs on the prop shaft. We rigged a line from one side of the boat to the other, so that I could pull myself down to the prop. I had one scary moment when the tank got wedged between the line and the hull, and I could not get back to the surface. Fortunately, by banging on the hull I alerted Marco that something was wrong, and he eased the tension on the line.

The Boatyard, despite its name, was a bar/restaurant with a pier and dinghy dock on the beach, about half-mile south of the entrance to the Careenage. The dock was in disrepair, and care was needed on tying up to ensure the dink did not get caught under the rotting vertical planks. Entrance was by means of a wristband costing US$10, which was redeemed as drinks and food were consumed. There were several inexpensive Asian and Indian restaurants about a 15-minute walk south along Bay Road, just past the yacht club.

I made my usual pilgrimage to visit my great-grandmother's grave in the military cemetery, number 58. Susannah Forsyth was still there, but the structure was showing the effects of 132 years of weathering. We also visited the Mount Gay Rum Distillery, but the tour was disappointing; all the old oak barrels which used to age rum in huge warehouses had been moved, and the plant near Bridgetown just bottled rum. The tour was basically a video promoting Mount Gay rum and a free sample. The old firm, founded 1703, was taken over by Remy-Martin in 1989, and I suspect was greatly expanded, probably at the expense of the quality of the rum, although Mount Gay is still what we drink on the boat every happy hour.

It took a little less than 24 hours to sail to Charlotteville on Tobago. We anchored in 40 feet at Pirates Bay, on the north side of Man of War Bay. It was a Saturday when we arrived, which meant I was hit with a fee of US$45 for overtime for the Immigration and Customs officials. Charlotteville was like going back in time to when Edith and I cruised the Caribbean in the 1960s—a simple village with roosters crowing and hens running around followed by their chicks. There was an ATM next to the customs office, but I was never able to actually extract money from it. Prices were relatively low, and there were a couple of small markets and a restaurant. A shop on the waterfront provided internet and laundry at very reasonable prices. The Trinidad Tobago government now required all yachts to clear in and out of each port; we cleared Immigration and Customs for Scarborough and planned to sail there the next day.

Instead, we anchored at Store Bay, just on the southwest corner of the island. This was more popular than Scarborough, which has very little room north of the jetty and is constrained by the busy ferry terminal. There were quite a number of small shops and restaurants clustered around Pigeon Point Road. Bagos Beach Bar and the adjacent store, Store Bay Marine Services, provided for immediate needs—book swap, laundry, and internet. Some protection from the surf when landing the dinghy was provided by the artificial reef of the Coco Reef Hotel. We landed on the beach as far south as possible.

We cleared Immigration and Customs in Scarborough—both were located in or near the ferry terminal building. Transportation was provided by the public taxis, which were not marked. One just stood at the bus stop at the corner of Pigeon Point Road and waved a hand, just like one does for the "publicos" in the Dominican Republic. The trip cost one dollar.

At this point, Marco decided to become a backpacker again and took the ferry to Port of Spain. I spent a few days anchored in Store Bay until the new crew arrived, Louise and Bob. Louise was a veteran of many *Fiona* cruises, but this was to be Bob's introduction to living and cruising on a sailboat. Louise was a keen bird watcher, so we arranged a tour of the rain forest on the north of the island. This was conducted by Harris, who was very knowledgeable, and Louise collected several new sightings. We were all issued rubber boots, as the trails were very muddy.

After clearing out, we sailed the next night to Grenada with a lovely beam reach, the wind touching 25 knots. We dropped anchor in crowded Prickly Bay, where the marina provided inexpensive showers and meals. Getting the local currency, the EC dollar, was a minor problem, as it took an expensive taxi ride to an ATM a couple of miles away.

The next day we rounded Point Saline and tied up at Port St. Louise Marina. This was a new facility which was making every effort to attract cruisers. We rented a car to explore the hinterland, but that turned out to be rather a bust; nothing was sign-posted, so we didn't find a single scenic waterfall. No doubt the taxi drivers' union tried to make sure local knowledge was needed! However, we did find Lake Grand Etang, a crater lake, where we examined the nature center.

Arriving in the coastal town of Grenville in time for lunch, the only place we found open was a Kentucky Fried Chicken. We drove back to another nature center on a mangrove swamp, but the birding was poor and we treated ourselves to a drink at a nearby hotel.

From St. George's harbor, we sailed to Carriacou and cleared out of Grenada for Union Island in St. Vincent at the south end of the Grenadines. When we cruised these waters many years ago, some of the islands had boats under construction on the beach. Tourism and fiberglass seemed to have killed that, but before we left Carriacou, we had a couple of suppers at an old shipyard on the south side of the bay, which had metamorphosed into a restaurant called the Slipway. Indeed, the rusty rails and winding winch could still be seen. Near the bar were two large belt-driven saws that must have dated to the 19th century. And plastic sheets on the original platens provided a convenient stop to rest your rum punch. The food was excellent, too.

We cleared into St. Vincent at the small airport and then enjoyed sundowner rum punches at a unique bar on the small island in the harbor accessible only by dinghy. High winds kept us pinned in the harbor for another day, and we were entertained by the incredibly skilled kite surfers, who used the high wind to zip to and fro along the reef, occasionally launching themselves into the air.

Our next stop was Salt Whistle Bay, Mayreau Island. Considerable development has occurred since Edith and I had the anchorage to ourselves in the late '60s. A paved road now ran from Salt Whistle to Saline Bay. A large Club Med cruise ship disgorged hundreds of tourists for a few hours of beach fun. But Anna Maria Alexander (1837 to 1950) is still sleeping peacefully in the little cemetery near the top of the hill. We stopped at Canouan Island, but heavy surf and discouraging signs on the jetties prevented us from landing the dinghy. We moved on to the much more attractive Admiralty Bay at Bequia overnight and anchored before picking up a mooring. Port Elizabeth is a quaint village which hasn't changed too much over the years. We walked over the hill to one of my favorite spots, Friendship Bay, but discovered the beachside hotel had closed. Perhaps it was another victim of the economic downturn.

The next day we took the ferry to Kingstown on St. Vincent's main island. The ferry was old and decrepit. It had apparently begun life in Scandinavia; it rattled and shuddered its way for an hour to cross the passage. The streets were alive with colorful vendors shouting their wares. It was very much the West Indies of my earlier visits. We found a peaceful restaurant on the top floor of the Cobblestone Inn for morning coffee and returned later for lunch. A little shopping and a walk through the busy fish market completed our tour and we returned at 4 pm on the same rattletrap ferry. Dinner at a small beachside bar rounded out the day.

The next day we set out for St. Lucia, and to break up the trip we anchored at Chateau Belair Bay, near the north end of St. Vincent. It was a rolly night, shared with two other sailboats that had adopted the same tactic of breaking up the trip by anchoring overnight. Early the next day, we started for the passage crossing. The northern cape of St. Vincent is notorious for high wind and seas, and in 2004 *Fiona* was badly damaged when we made the same trip. A wind gust broke the bobstay, which in turn caused the roller-furler to break, and the bow platform to shear the attachment lugs, which bent the tubing forming the platform (Chapter 5). This time, we did not set sail until we were clear of the cape, although it was a slow, rough ride under engine. The lumpy ride stirred up dirt and sediment in the fuel tanks and the engine stopped, but fortunately after that, we cleared land.

As we sailed along the coast of St. Lucia, I spent an uncomfortable hour or two in the engine room changing fuel filters. We anchored in Rodney Bay as the sun set. Early the next day, we tied up at the Rodney Bay Marina, a well-organized operation, which was relatively inexpensive. We met some folks from the CCA we had first run into at Bequia (*Eight Bells*) and also a fellow retiree from Brookhaven National Laboratory, Mike and June on *Idunno*. A water taxi took us over to Pigeon Island, now connected to the mainland by a causeway. When *Iona* first cruised this way in 1969, it was still an island. During the Napoleonic wars, the British Navy built a large fort on Pigeon Island, much of which still remains. We got our laundry done by "Suds," who delivered it to the boat the same day. I also got a local worker to touch up the oil on the teak, for the relatively reasonable labor charge of US$15 per hour.

We took a full day's taxi ride the next day to the volcanic south end of the island, to Soufriere, from the French for "smelling of sulfur." On the way, we stopped at a few spots so that the locals could pester us with items for sale. I am sure the taxi driver was in cahoots with them. However, one stop was fairly unique; for a couple of dollars, Louise got to pose with a boa constrictor wrapped round her shoulders. We were told snakes had been introduced to the island to discourage slaves from running away.

After supper at one of the marina restaurants, it was early to bed; we were up just after sunrise for the sail to Martinique. We anchored just after lunch at Anse Mitan in 25 feet and took the ferry, which runs hourly to Fort de France. Here I cleared in, and instead of the usual customs and immigration officials, I was eventually directed to a small snack bar near a gas station in the commercial port. On an old cable reel sat a laptop computer. After filling out a complicated spreadsheet, mostly in French, I hit "Enter," and thus, literally entered the boat into Martinique. The old-time officers with their kepis had been replaced by a push-button!

Louise wrapped up in a boa constrictor, St. Lucia, Caribbean

The next morning, we motored across the bay and anchored just a hundred yards east of the old fort. The morning was spent exploring the old town, where we photographed the famous statue of Empress Josephine, who hailed from these parts. Her head was still missing; it had disappeared even before Edith and I first visited the island in the early '60s. We had lunch at one of the stalls in a small square. In the afternoon, we toured the ethnological museum which had a good exhibition of Carib and Arawak Indian artifacts. Supper was in the restaurant of a high-class hotel where we brought down the tone of the place in our grungy sailing clothes, compared to the well-dressed resident diners.

We left early the next day to push 20 miles up the coast to St. Pierre, the former capital which was wiped out in 1902 by a volcanic eruption of Mount Peleé. When we anchored *Iona* there in 1969, there were just ruins with virtually nobody living there. Now it is a thriving village with a bustling market and traffic jams. The Museum Volcanique has some interesting photos of before and after, along with a lot of battered and melted remnants. In 1902 an election was pending, and the governor somehow felt that to acknowledge the possibility of an eruption was a reflection on his regime, despite many signs Mount Peleé was going to blow. He used troops to prevent people fleeing and he was killed along with about 30,000 others when the volcano blew its top at 8:40 am on the 8th of May, 1902. Only one person survived—a prisoner in the deepest cell of the jail. It can still be seen, next to the remains of the elaborate former theatre.

After supper ashore, we dinghied back to the boat in the crowded anchorage and left the next day for the long haul to Dominica. Prince Rupert Bay was just an overnight stop that was rather rolly, and so early in the morning at first light, we raised the anchor and sailed with a good wind to Iles des Saintes. We arrived at lunch time, and finally got the anchor down in 50 feet, after dragging a couple of times, and dinghied ashore. Our plan was to visit the fort perched on a hill overlooking the harbor. These small islands were the scene of an important naval battle between the French and the British in the 18th century. The British victory under Admiral Rodney assured their dominance in the West Indies during the rest of the Napoleonic Wars. As we trudged up the hill under the burning sun, we ran into a bunch of French tourists who told us the fort was closed, and we thankfully walked back to a bar on the dock to sink a beer and watch passengers boarding the ferry to Guadeloupe.

When we returned to the boat for happy hour, a small launch came alongside. We were told that anchoring was no longer permitted and we had to pick up a mooring, which cost US$15 per night. This was to become a pattern as we worked our way north; permanent moorings protected reefs from damage caused by anchoring and, of course, the local authorities don't mind the extra income. The next day we sailed past the long coast of Guadeloupe, sometimes with an assist from the engine as we fell into the lee caused by the high mountains, and headed for Montserrat. In 1995, the southern part of the island was inundated with ash and boulders from another volcanic eruption of Soufriere. The capital town, Plymouth, had to be abandoned. We had

a great view of the destruction as we sailed a couple of miles off the coast. The tops of buildings poked out of the ash and lava and black smoke still rolled down the hillside. We anchored for the night at Little Bay, a rather gloomy place with high cliffs surrounding the anchorage, and we rolled badly as swell came in from the north.

We were glad to leave at first light. From Montserrat we sailed to Nevis, part of the twin island country of Nevis-St. Kitts. At first we anchored at Charlestown, but, as was becoming common, we had to move to a mooring after clearing in at customs and immigration. In the morning, we contacted a British expat who had e-mailed me with an invitation to visit him while at Nevis. He was a retired surgeon called Desmond Fosberg, who had spent most of his career at St. Kitts. We moved down the coast to pick up a mooring opposite his charming cottage on Tamarind Bay. We met Desmond and his wife, Catherine, and over lunch heard many interesting stories of his life as a surgeon in the West Indies. Desmond swam out to the boat for happy hour and we had dinner at a lovely beachside restaurant called Gallipot, run by his step-daughter.

From Nevis we sailed to St. Martin on the French side. The first order of business was to contact Kay Pope, our old friend from *Iona*'s cruise in the '60s. We had a pleasant lunch at her beautiful apartment overlooking Marigot Bay. After a shopping spree in tax-free Philipsburg, we sailed overnight across the Anegada Passage to Virgin Gorda. The area was inundated with bare boat charters, captained by idiots with no apparent knowledge of the rules of the road. Soon after we cleared in, we escaped to tranquil Anegada Island. Louise went on a hunt for the pink flamingos. The original flock became extinct many years ago, and the taxi driver confessed his grandfather had shot one of the last ones. New birds were introduced from Bermuda about 20 years ago.

We stopped for a night at Jost Van Dyke, where we ran into two other CCA boats (*Phoenix* and *Delawana*) and organized an impromptu CCA rendezvous. The island has many memories for me of the time Edith and I spent a year cruising in the Caribbean when we were both young, but not so foolish. From Jost, it was a few hours downwind to Culebrita, where we anchored for the night and also tried a little snorkeling on the reef.

Puerto Rico

The next day we officially entered the U.S. at Culebra Island, a small part of Puerto Rico. We soon moved on to the huge Marina del Rey on the main island. Bob left almost immediately to visit friends on the west side of the island. The next day, I rented a car and Louise and I toured the impressive El Yunque, the "rainmaker," which is part of the Caribbean National Forest. Walking along a mile-long footpath to a waterfall, we were drenched by a downpour, but what can you expect in a rain forest?

Waterfall in the El Yunque National Rain Forest

Louise flew home at this point and I picked up the new crew, George and Peg, at San Juan airport. Both were local sailors from Long Island, and Peg had made short trips with me before. On the way back to the marina we discovered the highway had been flooded and police were diverting traffic. Our rental car maps were useless to find the minor roads back to the marina, but George and Peg fished out their iPhones and soon brought up Google Earth and navigated us back to the boat. Obviously, I had a 21st century crew!

Bermuda and Home

We left with a stiff easterly wind blowing into the marina entrance, and after 20 minutes the chop stirred up the sediment in the fuel tank and the engine stopped. A rocky islet lay 200 yards on our lee; Peg and George got a quick introduction to sail setting. We sailed without difficulty through the pass in the reef and on to Bermuda, 840 nm away. For several days we had a beam wind and enjoyed great sailing. Peg was a naturalist and found the ocean a marine desert—no dolphins, no whales, just a few flying fish. About half way, the Trades petered out, but we kept sailing. The light on Gibbs Hill hove into view and we tied up in Bermuda after a week's sailing. Friends and family planned to visit and I spent a couple of weeks at Captain Smokes Marina in St. George's. After Peg and George returned home, Lew flew in for a week. He is the editor of the *Fiona* sailing videos. Wandering the quaint streets, he encountered again the St. George's' town cat, Flea. In 2010 when *Fiona* was tied up at Ordnance Island, Lew awoke with a shock

Flea, the St. George's town cat, Bermuda

when Flea jumped on his chest in the middle of the night. Apparently Flea is a well-known night-time prowler.

A few days later my son Colin, granddaughter Gabriella, my daughter Brenda, and her friend Gina, all arrived at the airport. The reason was a celebration for my 80th birthday. Before the party we managed a quick sail up Ferry Reach, and had lunch anchored at Whalebone Bay, followed by a return to St. George's via the Town Cut. We all gathered at the Carriage House for a quiet dinner, and I received several presents and read choice pieces from a collection of witty sayings about growing old, given to me by a Bermudian friend.

With that out of the way, my new crew for the last leg to Long Island flew in. Bob Forman was an old friend from the South Bay Cruising Club who intended to sail the Newport to Bermuda Race in June, and he wanted a preview of the Gulf Stream., especially the accuracy of the current predictions. John was an experienced sailor who once rowed across the Atlantic. It was pleasure to have such an expert crew aboard. There was little wind as we left and we powered for a few hours

Family gathering for Eric's 80th birthday in Bermuda, 2012. Standing, L to R: Daughter Brenda, son Colin, and grand-daughter, Gabriella.

until Bermuda sank over the stern. And then some wind developed. As we entered the vicinity of the Gulf Stream, we motor-sailed in a light wind, but the engine overheated. The cause was apparently the very warm sea water, which peaked at 85.8°F. Once clear of the Stream, the engine ran normally (but see Chapter 11).

There was almost no wind north of the Stream and we powered to Fire Island Inlet, entering at midnight. Bob had surveyed the Inlet the week before and we had no difficulty with shoaling, which had been such a problem when we entered after the 2009-2010 cruise. The wind picked up as we threaded our way down Great South Bay with light rain and fog. Alerted by e-mail, Wayne was waiting to take our lines as we approached Weeks Yard about 4 am. We had logged 12,515 nm since we left in July, 2011. The cruise had been enjoyable on the whole, but it had been plagued by the constant need to find crew; 19 altogether. And I literally had to teach most of them the ropes. I began to think about the next year's trip. Antarctica beckoned, but I would have to find crew who were prepared to stick with me for the duration.

11 A Frustrated Attempt to Circumnavigate Antarctica
2013-2014

When the 2011-2012 cruise was finished, I contemplated what to do next. I was not getting any younger and neither was *Fiona*, so the next cruise had to be a cruise of stature, possibly my last major trip. I had always enjoyed sailing in Antarctica, the only drawback being that it took months to get there and back. I had attempted to sail to Antarctica three times in the past—two had been successful. The wind near the coast had usually been east or southeasterly, something one would expect from the low pressure systems that circulate the world between the Antarctic continent and Cape Horn. Would it be possible to circumnavigate Antarctica heading west, the wind from astern or on the port beam? I began to check wind forecasts on the internet for the areas I had in mind; I assumed the average winds would be much the same for a year later.

There were many other potential problems—how far north was the fast ice (the ice connected to land); how to provision for about 10 to 12 weeks where there would be no supplies or help; how to get crew for an extended, arduous cruise.

Nevertheless, I decided to give it a shot, and we left as planned on July 5th, 2013.

Eastwards Across the Atlantic

One crew member, Wade, signed on the day after our Bon Voyage party, but the other member, Joey, a veteran of previous trips aboard

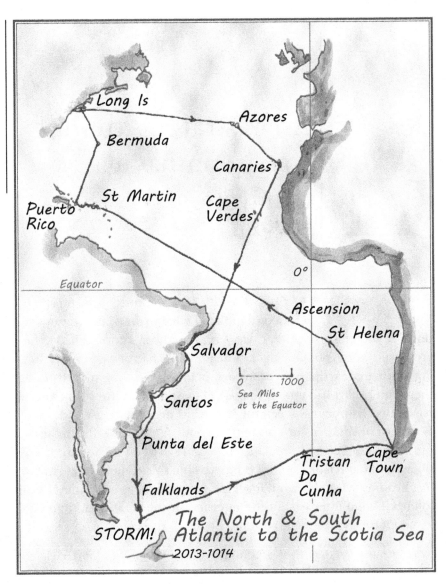

Long Is

Azores

Bermuda

Canaries

St Martin

Cape
Verdes

Puerto
Rico

0°

Equator

Ascension

St Helena

Salvador

0   1000
Sea Miles
at the Equator

Santos

Punta del Este

Cape
Town

Tristan
Da
Cunha

Falklands

The North & South
STORM! Atlantic to the Scotia Sea
2013-1014

Fiona (Chapters 3 and 9), failed to appear on time despite numerous
e-mails and telephone calls, and we reluctantly left for the Azores without him. His place was taken by Pat, just for the run to Block Island.

Transiting Fire Island Inlet, we bumped on the bottom for a short
distance, but without damage. We had a glorious sail along the coast of
Long Island, thanks to a high pressure system lying to the south, which
provided a wind of 10 to 12 knots on the starboard quarter. When we
arrived in Great Salt Pond, we found an interloper had attached him-

self to one of the CCA moorings, but he soon relinquished it to us. The anchorage was chockablock with boats enjoying the Independence Day weekend. After lunch at Ballards, we made the traditional walk to the southeast lighthouse, enjoyed our last ice cream in New Shoreham, and walked backed to New Harbor, where Pat caught the Viking ferry back to Long Island. I had hoped Wade and I would be able to have supper at The Oar, which is very much a "yachtie" bar, but it was so crowded, we made do with a scratch supper on the boat and retired early. It had been a long day.

The next day, we took care of some small maintenance tasks and left just after 8 am. The same high pressure dominated and we had wonderful sailing as we headed for Flores, in the Azores. Wade turned out to be a gentle giant. At 6 feet, 3 inches, he also had immense strength. When we set the whisker pole for the first time, I asked him to pull the foreguy as tight as he could, and then noticed the pole had developed a significant bend! I modified the request to "as tight as I could get it" and the pole straightened as he eased the line off the cleat. The weather continued hot, with a gentle wind from between southwest and west.

For about a week, each day was much the same—reaching or running with winds in the 12-knot range. We averaged about 130 nm per day. Most of the time, Victor the Vane was in control of the helm; when the wind fluctuated for a spell, George the autopilot steered the boat. Wade and I read a lot and took care of maintenance chores. We divided the daytime period, 8 am to 8 pm, into two six-hour shifts. At night, 8 pm to 8 am, we served three four-hour shifts.

As we sailed near the center of the high, the wind died and, for a day and a half, we chugged along under power. When the wind came back, it was southerly. This was rather a surprise, as I expected north or northwest winds on the east side of the high. However, a low was developing to the east and this upset the wind pattern. A couple of squalls gave us wild sailing, followed by little wind as they moved off. A passing freighter gave us a call on channel 16. The captain, who had an Indian accent, was astonished to meet a sailboat so far from land and wanted details of our departure, destination, and time at sea!

The wind continued to be mild, but a low-pressure area produced rain and squalls. When the wind died completely, we started the engine. It was hard to have to endure the noise and heat after the tranquility of the great sailing we had enjoyed in the earlier part of the trip. I was devouring a book a day and Wade was very interested in learning something about celestial navigation. We broke out the old sextant, a veteran of all of *Fiona*'s cruises, and checked the GPS with a noon sight. About 600 nm from Flores, the wind was frustratingly erratic for half a day; we shifted the whisker pole from one side to the other three times before lunch. Then, the wind settled down to blow strongly from the northwest. *Fiona* picked up her skirt and just flew on a broad reach. It was a wonderful change after listening to the engine for over a day. Victor the Vane coped admirably; Wade logged 29 nm on his 8 pm to midnight watch, an average of over 7 knots. Then, the wind conked out very quickly and for half a day we tried to squeeze what progress we could from a 5- to 8-knot breezes.

We also had engine problems, overheating, and signs of water in the lube oil. Also, the engine start battery gave up the ghost, but no problem, we had plenty of other batteries on board. We dealt with each situation as best we could, including changing the oil and filter. For the night watches, we ran the engine slowly. We then had a good night of sailing, followed by a day of fickle winds and finally a complete calm. Whales, dolphins, the occasional sea turtle, and even a few flying fish enlivened the watches. And then a high developed to our south and favorable winds propelled us to Flores, which was good, as I was becoming concerned about our fuel usage.

We made our landfall as light was fading, and entered the harbor at Lajes about midnight, local time. It had been five years since my last visit. Since then, the industrious Portuguese, no doubt with EU money, had constructed a small marina in the northwest corner of the bay. Fortunately, a "yachtie" answered my call on Channel 16 and let us know there was room for us. We slowly negotiated the unfamiliar passage between flashing red and green lights, and our friend on the radio was waiting to take our lines. In the morning, we officially checked in and were free to explore beautiful Flores. We had logged 1,864 nm from Block Island, and the passage had taken 15 days, which was pretty typical.

We walked up the hill to the village above the harbor to get some euros. The ATM at the bank behind the church rather reluctantly, I thought, disgorged some notes and we treated ourselves to a beer and some lunch. Actually, only I had the beer, as Wade is a teetotaler, and he settled for a Coke. After picking up a few groceries at the market, we returned to the marina. We got to talk to a few of the crews, who were an international lot—Canadian, British, French and German. Here we met Kieron for the first time; later he joined the boat in Puerto Rico on the leg home.

Later, many of us retired to the Beira-Mar Pizzeria, located a short distance up the hill. I remembered it with some affection from my last visit. In the morning, Wade and I hired a taxi, driven by Mr. Fonseca, and toured the gorgeous island. Mr. Fonseca had lived in Canada for 15 years and spoke English very well. He gave us a lot of local history, including the sad fact that, although Flores was charming, it was a tough place for locals to live in. Our driver told us that most people had a job with the government or got by on unemployment relief.

Wade was very impressed by the place as we drove along the winding roads, edged with miles of stone walls, which were covered in great profusion by hydrangea flowers. Like all the Azorean islands, Flores was made in recent geological times by violent volcanic upheavals, which produced a landscape of dramatic valleys and mountains. We had a "very local" lunch at a small café in the capital, Santa Cruz, and Wade declared it to be the best fish he had ever tasted. Afterwards, we walked to the dock, where I nearly lost *Fiona* during my first visit in 1986. For happy hour, we entertained the crew from a British yacht, the one that had responded to our radio call the night before, and later, had supper at the pizzeria with the gang from a Canadian boat, which was tied up next to us. The next day, we left soon after sunrise for the leg to Horta on Faial Island.

Horta was an old friend. I first sailed there in 1986 and this was *Fiona*'s fifth visit. Wade took the ferry to Pico one day with some fellows off the Canadian yacht we had met at Flores. They climbed the great volcano and the clouds cleared way for a wonderful view from the 7,500-foot summit. I also introduced Wade to Peter's Café Sport, a de rigueur stop for any yachtsman, although sadly, it was tourist-ified from the old days. Duncan and Hilda at Mid-Atlantic Yacht Services provided a number of essential spares. We took care of numerous maintenance jobs. I spent some time at the masthead rewiring the anemometer and stringing cord between the mast steps and the outer shrouds. The idea was to prevent the mainsail halyard from wrapping round a step when it was flopping about. I repainted the *Fiona* sign on the seawall; it was quite faded from my last touch-up in 2008. I also had a warm shower, my first since leaving home. We tried to recruit a third crew member for the leg to the Canaries and on to Brazil, but without success. All-in-all, we had a very pleasant four days.

When we left, we powered to the south coast of Pico and then picked a wonderful breeze as we got out of the wind shadow of the island. The wind blew initially from the southwest, and then veered with squalls and rain. We reefed—the first time since leaving Long Island—and the wind settled into the northeast with clear skies. It blew reliably for hundreds of miles. Victor the Vane dealt with the steering and we didn't use the engine again until we got to the breakwater at San Sebastian, La Gomera, a leg of 951 nm. Unfortunately, the notorious acceleration zone between La Gomera and Tenerife lived up to its name and we had a tough few hours until we finally staggered into the lee of the harbor at San Sebastian. This is because the northeast winds are funneled into the narrow channel by "El Tiede," the 12,200-foot volcano on Tenerife.

A Solo Trip Westwards Across the Atlantic

When Wade checked his e-mail after we arrived, he discovered his son had developed a serious medical condition; he decided to fly home and left on the ferry to Tenerife after a few days to catch a flight to the U.S. That left me with no crew—exactly what happened on my last visit, in 2011. A cruising couple we had gotten to know at the marina was interested in sailing to South America, and so ultimately, Nicole and Chris signed up to cruise as far as Uruguay. They had been living on their sloop, *Mew Gull*, for many years, and the last five years had berthed at La Gomera. Unfortunately, when the time came to actually untie the lines and shove off, they changed their minds and unloaded the gear they had previously stored on *Fiona*.

This left me with a dilemma—if I stayed any longer, I would probably be late getting to Uruguay and may even miss the Antarctic summer window. So I sailed anyway, single-handed, bound for the Cape Verde Islands. The weather was fairly benign, but after a few days, the wind failed and I started the engine. The overheating problem which first emerged on the transatlantic leg was still there, despite serious attempts to solve the problem in Horta. I had about a half-dozen promising replies to my crew call for the Antarctic leg and every night I spent as much as an hour on the computer dealing with questions via Sailmail.

The wind piped up the morning I arrived at the Cape Verde Islands, with gusts over 40 knots. But as I rounded the cape into Porto Grande, I got a good lee and I was able to furl the sails without too much hassle. I arrived just six days after leaving La Gomera, but the marina was almost deserted; the busy season for Caribbean-bound yachts had not yet started. Finally, a marina crew appeared and made me tie-up to a pontoon bow first, which created a problem getting off and on the boat. Later, the captain and crew off a charter boat helped me turn *Fiona* around so that I could clamber on and off at the stern.

Water was still scarce here; yachties bought an electronic card which permitted entry through the security gates, but also docked the allowance you were initially given (100 liters) when you used the toilet or shower.

The Aries wind steerer needed TLC; a spring-loaded pin had rusted in place and I had to find a machinist to make a stainless-steel copy. I got a lead on a machine shop, but how on the earth the taxi driver found it I'll never know. It was in the middle a run-down industrial area, but they made me a perfect copy for less than the taxi fare! I also discovered a broken spring in the hub of the Aries; the machinist put me onto a wonderful store called Zepherino. They seemed to sell everything and it was always crowded; I was able to get a spring about a foot long, from which I cut a piece about an inch long, which was a perfect replacement for the broken bit.

While I had access to the internet, I tried to sort out the applicants for the crew positions on the Antarctic leg. Ultimately, a couple dropped out and I made an offer to one without getting a reply before I left. For the leg to Brazil, I posted a "crew wanted" sign on the marina notice board, but without any bites. I reluctantly resigned myself to single-handed passage to Brazil. The Bulgarian crew from a next-door boat helped me to take off the working mainsail and bend on the storm main. This reduced my average speed a bit but meant I wouldn't need to reef for the usual winds I expected to meet on the leg to Brazil. I stocked up with plenty of beer and apple juice. I was mildly cheated when I checked-out by being charged for an extra night, based on the way they calculated arrival and departure times. I refueled at only $3.00 per gallon for diesel, which more than compensated for being short-changed for dockage, and left before 10 am local time for the roughly 1,800 nm leg to my intended destination, Jacare, on the Paraiba River in Brazil.

Naturally, the wind was very calm for the first few days, because I had mounted the storm sails. I managed some sailing in light winds, getting the boat up to 4 knots, but when the speed dropped to 2.5 knots, I ran the sturdy Perkins diesel. The light winds continued for five days; I judiciously used the engine, when possible, in combination with the sails, yet progress was slow. It was also very hot: temperature in the main cabin was in the 90s by lunchtime. It was even hotter in the aft cabin, and I temporarily moved onto the port berth, in the main cabin, when I slept. One squall packed a wind that gusted to 37 knots with driving, cold rain. That was when bending on the storm mainsail paid off.

A week after leaving the Cape Verdes, I was not quite half way to Cabedelo, the entry port for Jacare, and about half the fuel on board had been used. Then, the wind finally came back, but it was from the southwest, blowing straight from Cabedelo! I began to tack, about 12 hours on each tack, but it is hard to make progress that way. The navigation was complicated by the Equatorial Counter Current, setting strongly to the east, and by numerous squalls.

On the crew front, I confirmed two applicants for the Antarctic leg: Clay and Simon. I debated with myself about a third, as "insurance" against one dropping-out, and also to make watch-keeping easier. The down side was food and water storage. For the leg from Jacare, a former crew member had indicated interest, but as the days went by, he remained silent, despite numerous e-mails. I decided that without a definite commitment within a few days I, would sail directly to Salvador, where I had arranged to sign on a Long Island couple, John and Helena Almberg.

After a night of severe squalls, the, weather improved, but the wind was still on the nose—tack after tack, maybe making a good 50 nm a day. *Fiona* crossed the equator at 32" 22' W. The putative crew eventually decided not to meet me in Jacare and I switched course a few degrees, to head directly to Salvador. Unfortunately, the wind was not too favorable, and I was pushed to the right. I passed Fernando de Noronha, 45 miles to the west, so there was a problem rounding Cabo Branco if the wind persisted without veering. An American living in Budapest, David, agreed to crew from Santos.

One morning, I discovered the propeller was not turning, producing horrible thoughts of failure of the Borg Warner transmission, yet surprisingly, I found all four bolts holding the coupling had become unscrewed. It was a tricky job getting it put back together with the boat sailing; the propeller kept turning despite free sheets, which reduced the boat speed to nearly zero.

The weather did not improve, and there were frequent squalls. I made one short tack to the east and one long tack to the southwest each day. At times, the wind speed picked up to 25 knots, with gusts to 30 knots. I spent a lot of time furling or reefing the jib. For me, it was quite demanding physical work. I was about 250 nm from Salvador, and *Fiona* was running down the coast, when the wind moderated and veered, permitting a wonderful reach. There were plenty of steamers also skirting the coast; at one point I had three registering on the Automatic Identification System (AIS). I handled e-mails twice a day, when shortwave conditions were good for Sailmail. Minor maintenance continued, the most serious being that the mounting bolts for the Aries worked loose. Hanging over the stern to tighten them was difficult, and I used George the autopilot for the last 300 miles.

South to Uruguay

When I arrived at Salvador, I discovered the marina I had stayed at before was not functioning, but I was able to get a slip nearby. Just to complicate life, the depth-finder display quit. I walked to a shopping area, but the banks were all closed so I could not use my card at an ATM. Fortunately, however, I had a few dollars that I was able to change into reals at a "cambio." To start the clearance process, I found the Policia Federales Office in the dock area, but they told me to come back the next day. After three quiet weeks alone on the boat, I found the traffic and noise very disturbing.

I took a taxi back to the marina and poured a stiff rum, or two. Naturally, when I went back to the Policia Federales they were closed—it was a Saturday. John and Helena arrived at the marina, lugging tons of stuff, most important of which was a new water pump for the engine, which my son Colin had located. John is a wooden boat enthusiast, and owns a Tom Gilmer design, *Blue Moon*. He also runs his own computer consulting business. Helena grew up in Brazil, but has lived in the States since she married John; she is a former concert pianist. So I had a very talented crew. John and I tackled some of the maintenance chores that had accumulated, which were more easily fixed by two people.

When we left the following Tuesday, the boat was in fairly good shape. The new water pump was a tremendous improvement. Helena was extremely helpful in dealing with the bureaucracy, including two more visits to the Policia Federales Office to clear in and out. After refueling, we left the marina on Tuesday morning for a 24-hour sail to Ilheus, a small town 120 miles down the coast.

The depth finder problem, which had first surfaced when I arrived at Salvador, came back, but John and I were able to partially fix it with some parts from my collection of electronic bits. However, it was obvious that a new unit would have to be found before I departed for Antarctica.

We anchored off the yacht club at Ilheus and went ashore via a tender with a wheezing diesel, run by the club. When we returned, the young men operating the tender told us that *Fiona* had dragged her anchor and they had tried to tow her, but the strain had been too much for their old engine, which had given up the ghost. The wind and seas in the exposed bay had indeed strengthened. We got a ride to the boat, started the engine and re-anchored. Instead of a planned dinner ashore, John cooked some beans and ham. Early the next morning, we left with a fairly stiff breeze, which was on the nose as we cleared the nasty-looking reef on our starboard. Not unexpectedly, the choppy seas stirred-up sediment in the fuel tank, which blocked a filter and the engine quietly died with the reef only 200 yards on our lee. We hurriedly set sail; Helena and John were getting a taste of the little adventures that make sailboat cruising so interesting.

We planned to sail overnight to the famous Abrolhos Reef, which is a huge complex of coral and small islands that pokes out 60 miles from the coast into the South Atlantic. Indifferent winds caused us to be a little late and it was after nightfall on the following day when we arrived at Santa Barbara Island, which carried the lighthouse that warned shipping of the reef. Fortunately, there was a gorgeous full moon. Using radar, GPS and a chart-plotter, we were able to safely negotiate the reef and anchor in the lee of the island about 11 pm, local time. Santa Barbara is the base for the National Park Service, which controls part of the reef. A charming young ranger stopped by in his dinghy in the morning to tell us about the anchorage, and to arrange a tour of a nearby island. Later, he picked us up for a ride to Siriba Island; halfway there, the engine spluttered and died, but the wind pushed us towards the island anyway. On shore, a young woman, Rachel, acted as a guide. The island is a bird sanctuary, which supports a large population of breeding pairs. Only three kinds of birds live there: brown boobies, white boobies, and tropic birds. They were astonishingly tame; we could walk within a couple of feet of the raucous creatures. Rachel told us the reef was a hazard to sailors from the time Portugal discovered Brazil, and the name "Abrolhos" comes from the exhortation to coastal mariners in Portuguese to "open your eyes."

The weather forecast spoke of impeding high winds, so we left in the afternoon for the 200-mile leg to Vitória, in an attempt to get there before they did. The high winds came in the evening, with gusts to 30 knots. Yet the wind was behind us, so we set up the whisker pole and sailed wing and wing. We made great time and arrived off the busy commercial harbor of Vitória about an hour after sunset. A dozen large freighters lay anchored at the entrance; we dodged between them and headed for the inner harbor. We sailed very carefully across a reef, which extends for a mile, using the chart-plotter to find the pass. Once inside, we anchored for the night. I knew from previous visits that the water around the yacht club was rather shallow and finding our way in the dark was too risky. (See Chapter 5.)

In the morning, we contacted the club on VHF and they found us a pier to moor to. It was not very comfortable, and we had to use the dinghy to get ashore. John had lost his glasses overboard during a gybe, so the first order of business was to find an optician who could make another pair. After several tries, we hit pay dirt, and John had a new pair within a day. In the evening, we walked to an area near the yacht club called "The Bermuda Triangle." Compared to Salvador, Vitória was very affluent and the triangle consisted of restaurants and small businesses that seemed quite upmarket.

The next day, the weather deteriorated, due to an offshore low, and our departure for points south had to be postponed. It did not look like we would get favorable winds for several days. Helena and John took the opportunity to visit some interior beauty spots for a couple of days. The wind at the yacht club switched from easterly to westerly, which was not good. Originally, we were blown away from the dock, but now *Fiona* was pressed by the wind on the stern and we were hanging on just one mooring buoy. The wind increased to 30 knots, and *Fiona*'s bow bucked wildly—only two feet from the concrete pier. I looked anxiously at the line holding the stern cleat to the mooring; it was only 3/8-inch diameter, but at least it was new. If it let go or the mooring anchor dragged, the expedition to the Antarctic would have been over in minutes. After a fairly bad night the wind subsided, and I was able to breathe easier.

We lost a couple of days because of the bad weather at Vitória, but finally left with the wind on the nose. We clawed offshore and set course for Cabo Frio. It took two days to get there. It was a significant rounding, as Cabo Frio divides the passage along the South American coast into the north and south parts. We anchored at Abraão on Ilha

Crew member Helena with the trusty old Seagull engine, Abraão

Grande about an hour after sunset. I persuaded the old Seagull engine to propel us to the shore, where we enjoyed a very pleasant meal. Unfortunately, John had to row back; the fuel shut-off valve leaked and the tank was dry. However, in the morning it performed flawlessly after some maintenance. After breakfast we weighed anchor and set off for Santos, in calm conditions. A few hours later, the wind built up, on the nose of course, and by nightfall we were tacking under sail, with 20 knots of wind in coastal waters full of anchored freighters and numerous small fishing boats, carrying bewildering lights. We sailed far enough offshore to lay a good course for St. Sebastian Island, close-hauled, and made it to Santos Bay just before dark. It was foggy and rainy, but we pulled into the sanctuary of the Santos Yacht Club without incident.

We tied up to the fuel dock and tried to refuel, but after about 25 gallons the pump ran out of fuel. At that point, we got permission to stay on the dock for the night and retired to the luxurious club bar/ restaurant for supper, which, fortunately, was still open. What a contrast! The next day, we waited for fuel to be restored. Helena and John caught a taxi, and the new crew member, David, appeared. David had signed up via the web site. He was employed by an American company in Europe and between jobs had a couple of months to spare. He was a good seaman, as well as being computer savvy.

In visits past, I have had a good deal of trouble dealing with the bureaucracy in Santos, a major port. This time it took us nearly a full day, but David and I managed to get clearance to depart from the Federal Police, customs, and the Port Captain all in one day—an accomplishment which needed a small fortune in taxi fare, yet it was well worth it. We spent our last full day clearing up some minor maintenance and exploring the upmarket part of Santos, called Gonzaga. I bought an oil painting from a booth at a beach-side craft fair, something that has become a bit of a tradition. I had bought a painting at the same place in 2005.

We left before lunch the next day, having spent all our remaining reals on lube oil and groceries. The day was bright and sunny, but the wind was light and on the nose. We powered down the coast, heading for Punta del Este in Uruguay, the jumping-off point for the Antarctic leg. The wind slowly picked up, and after three days we were running wing and wing in near gale-force conditions. David got a taste of deep water sailing when we had to gybe and shift the whisker pole over. The run continued for a couple of days before the wind faded.

David was interested in learning something about celestial navigation and I again got out the old sextant and showed David how to take a noon sight, the traditional navigation method of the square-riggers for centuries. The wind petered out and we powered south to an area for which the forecast showed a southeast wind. Sure enough, when we were nearly 200 nm from Punta del Este, a light wind appeared and we sailed close reaching across a calm sea. This wind wafted us to Punta, which disappeared in a thick coastal fog as we approached. With radar, GPS and a chart-plotter, such conditions are no problem, and we tied up at the ANCAP fuel station without difficulty. However, it was Sunday and the place was shut tight. I did manage to contact an immigration official and get us stamped in, however. We spent the night at the fuel dock and arranged for a slip when the marina office opened in the morning.

South to the Falkland Islands

I was able to reacquaint myself with Punta del Este, which I had last visited in 2006 (see Chapter 7). Prices had really gone up, as inflation is a problem in both Uruguay and Brazil. One day, David and I took a bus to Piriapolis, a small town about 20 miles along the coast of the River Plate from Punta. On my previous visit, I had left the boat there while I flew to New York. I was very disappointed to discover the marina I had stayed at had obviously gone downhill. Boats were crammed together along the inside of the breakwater, and some had clearly been abandoned. I decided to leave the boat at Punta this time when I flew home. David agreed to stay on board and keep an eye on things. There were no other cruising boats in the marina, except for a couple of Argentine boats that stopped for a few hours to re-water. Life was fairly quiet, enlivened only by the local fishing boats that tied up each morning to sell their catch. The seagulls screamed and fought over the scraps as the fishermen cleaned the fish; huge sea lions broke the surface to gobble up the larger pieces. Before I left for the U.S. by air, we labored each morning for several days, to empty and inventory the many lockers used to store food on *Fiona*. Based on restocking for four men, for 12 weeks, we prepared shopping lists and took a taxi to the largest supermarket, Tiende Inglesio. On the way, we usually treated ourselves to coffee and pastelerias; the coffee was served in tiny cups and was very strong.

A week quickly passed and almost before I knew it, I was on a plane to New York. I had a long list of things to bring back, and within a day of my return from Long Island, we were joined by Bob and Simon, who completed the crew roster for the Antarctic leg. Bob was an American, about 60 years old. Simon was a Canadian in his twenties and had considerable sailing experience. I asked David to be responsible for satellite communications and computer data handling. Simon was appointed Sailing Master. And Bob was to be ship's doctor and photographer. We put last minute provisions on board; most of what we would need had already been loaded the week before I left for New York. We experienced mostly calm weather as we headed south across the wide estuary of the River Plate. For two days, we motored in fog, then a light wind materialized and we sailed for a half a day before the wind picked up and veered to the southeast. Within a day, the wind had picked up to 30 knots and the crew got a chance to reef the mainsail for the first time.

The wind continued to increase to gale force, with gusts to 45 knots. Talk about changeable weather! A heavy wave struck *Fiona*'s bow with a violent crash—it displaced the rigid dinghy on the fore-deck and broke the mounting chocks. The guys went forward in driving spray to secure more lashings. After about a day, the wind rapidly dropped, and after a short spell under power, a westerly wind developed in the range of 10 to 20 knots, which kept us moving until we made landfall on the north coast of East Falkland Island. We tied up at the massive floating dock installed after the Argentinian War of 1982, called FIPASS. The leg from Punta del Este had taken 10 days and we logged about 1,300 nm.

The Antarctic Crew: Eric, David, Bob, and Simon

Port Stanley is fairly bleak, but the people are very friendly. There is a Seaman's Center near FIPASS, which has all the necessary facilities and a snack bar. It had been six years since I had last been there. Every day I walked the three miles round trip along the shore footpath into Port Stanley, often in rain and a brisk wind. The path is frequently inhabited by magnificent birds. In town, there are three cozy pubs and several restaurants. Cruise ships visit in "season," which was just beginning. One day I stopped by to see some old friends I had made on previous visits, Lily and Roddy Napier. Now they live in Stanley, but I first visited them on their Westpoint Island farm when we rounded Cape Horn in 1992.

Our time was mostly spent in preparation for the trip to Antarctica. We replaced the CQR anchor with a 65-pound fisherman type, and we bolted aluminum plates called "deadlights" over the main cabin's windows. David crafted a wooden cover for the aft cabin hatch from surplus pallets that were scattered on the dock. I finally got the Espar diesel heater to function. Simon and Bob repaired the broken chocks for the rigid dinghy. David used the wi-fi at the Center to scan internet data on Antarctic ice. It did not look good—there was pack ice as far north as 64 degrees south. Records from earlier Antarctic voyagers have reported ice-free conditions as far as 70 degrees south. This did not bode well for our attempt to circumnavigate Antarctica westabout.

There was some social activity, and we invited Roger and Flo off *Australis* over for happy hour drinks. One evening, the captain of a Belgian cruising boat invited the crews of the boats at FIPASS over for a potluck supper on board *Buena*. A few locals stopped by, and the cabin was packed. We loaded fresh fruit and veggies, bought some frozen and double-baked bread and some British delicacies such as mushy peas, Marmite, and Bassetts Liquorice All-Sorts. We were ready!

Storm Damage on the Way to Antarctica

The forecast for the day we left was 30 knots from the west, which was okay, as this would give us a beam reach. Our destination was King George Island in the South Shetland group, which lay almost due south of the Falklands. We left with the storm mainsail bent on—this is smaller than the working mainsail and has two reefs, the second being very deep, leaving almost a trysail when set. In Port William Sound, before we encountered the offshore wind, we tied in the first reef. Thirty-knot winds may seem like a lot, but in my experience of the region, such winds are not uncommon and it is almost impossible to make a transit of the Drake Passage and Scotia Sea without meeting winds like that at some stage.

Offshore, the wind was blowing hard, with gusts to 50 knots, so we furled the jib and sailed with the reefed main and staysail. My sailmaker, Mark, had me told the staysail was "bulletproof." We tied the second and last remaining reef in the mainsail—it was well-timed; I had watched with amazement and some trepidation as the anemometer climbed over 60 knots—the needle was vibrating madly on the end-peg. That night, we ploughed south with shortened rig in rising seas. As the gloomy scene lightened with sunrise, the wind dropped into the 30-knot range—I figured the early turbulence might have been due to East Falkland Island lying to windward, and as we headed into more open water, the wind would settle down.

The boat was taking a battering from huge waves, but we shook out the second reef with *Fiona*'s foredeck gang wearing harnesses as they worked at the mast. The sea conditions were very rough. I had just retired to my bunk in the aft cabin for a post-lunch nap, when

Simon shouted that the forward bilge pump wasn't working and the head was flooding. I worked my way forward, grabbing the uprights in the heaving cabin; there was a lot more water than just a stuck pump would account for. As we watched, the water level rose rapidly; we were clearly sinking by the bow. By the time we had assembled a couple of pumps, the water was over the cabin sole—we got a "bucket brigade" going and I went into the water in the forward head to find the leak.

A copious stream of water was running down the inside of the hull on the port side, from somewhere behind a locker. The only thing up there, out of sight, was the gooseneck for the head. I shut the main through-hull valve for the toilet and the stream greatly slowed down. When we got the water level down to a manageable level, I peered behind the panel in front of the gooseneck, and found that the hose from the through-hull valve was detached from the plastic "U"—almost certainly caused by excessive pressure as the huge waves slammed into the bow. Water had been pouring into the boat through an inch-and-a-half hose opening to the sea. I figure we were minutes away from sinking, or at least shipping enough water to cause a capsize.

The problem in reassembling the gooseneck was that the white sanitary hose used in marine toilets hardens like steel when it is cold. To get the thing back together, David and I had to put the ends of the hose in boiling water to soften the plastic so it would slide over the barbs on the through-hull valve and the "U" fitting. Working in the pitching bow with sea water and the contents of the discharge hose sloshing about was tough, and for the first time in more than 30 years, I was seasick.

Later, we found the forward bilge pump was completely clogged by debris, which always happens when the water rises to new levels. The interior of the boat was saturated. Besides the water splashing about from what was left in the bilge, the pounding seas found every crack in the caulking and forced water in. On the starboard side of the main cabin, the pressure of the waves thudding on the sides forced the rubber gasket out from between the movable port and its frame—water gushed onto Simon's bunk every time a wave hit. All the other bunks were soaked, as well. As evening fell on the second day we re-tied the second reef in the mainsail in a wind that gusted to 45 knots.

The wind slowly veered to the southwest and *Fiona* began to sail east of the rhumb line as she slogged to the south. After a few hours, we gybed onto port tack and headed west. This produced an entire new set of leaks as the waves slammed against the port side. The navigation table was flooded and my laptop computer went the way of all flesh. The inverter in the engine room failed, along with many other victims of the flood. Two five-gallon jerry jugs filled with diesel disappeared from the aft deck. In due course, I decided we had sailed far enough to the west and asked Simon, who was on watch at the time, to gybe onto starboard tack. When Simon grabbed the wheel, which had been locked to the wind vane, he found it spun freely—the steering chain was broken!

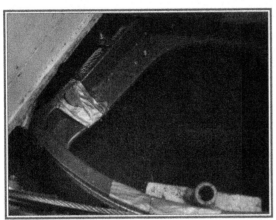

The problematic quadrant box

It is testimony to *Fiona*'s sailing ability that, for some time, she had been holding a good course in tremendous seas and strong winds without any rudder control. A quick look under the pedestal revealed the failure: the master link fastening the chain, which passes over the wheel sprocket to the wire rope leading to the quadrant, had snapped under the tension needed to swing the rudder in the heavy seas. Fitting a new master link took only a few moments, and I noted in passing that there was only one other master link left in the spares kit. The problem was that the wire rope leading to the quadrant had come off the sheaves, and the grooves in the quadrant, which was swinging violently as the rudder oscillated in the heavy seas. Getting the wire back was not going to be easy—the quadrant, which is a heavy bronze casting, fitted neatly in the quadrant box, with little room to spare. With Bob helping, I lashed the quadrant to the end-stop with rope, and slipped my fingers between the quadrant and the sides of the box to get the wire back in the grooves. If the quadrant slipped its moorings to the stop, I was going to be short a few digits. Bob guided the rope into sheaves under the aft cabin sole at the same time.

Eventually we got everything in place and tightened up. As we went on deck to try the wheel, Simon gasped and pointed ahead—looming out of the gloom and spray were the rocky cliffs of lonely Beauchene Island only a couple of miles ahead. This was the most southerly outpost of the Falkland archipelago. We had got the steering fixed just in time to gybe over and head southeast again. The wind was 40 to 50 knots with occasional gusts that touched 60 knots.

A few minutes later I was below when I heard violent sail flogging and Bob poked his head through the companionway hatch to say the staysail boom had broken! I rushed on deck to view a scene of devastation on the foredeck—shreds of Dacron lashed by the wind flew from the forestay and a port shroud. Bob and Simon struggled to get the staysail halyard down, as the sail had split in half. When we got things a little more under control, it was possible to figure out what had happened: the swivel on the staysail outhaul block had sheared, and the adjacent cleat had been wrenched out of the staysail boom. With this mess attached to the staysail clew, the sail had rapidly flogged itself to destruction. Although the boom had fallen to the deck, it was not actually broken.

I now faced a difficult situation: although I carried spares for the jib and mainsail, I did not have a second staysail. Without the staysail, *Fiona*'s ability to sail to windward, particularly with winds over 25 to 30 knots when the jib was furled, was seriously compromised. Most of the other failures already mentioned could be dealt with, and Antarctica was still within reach. Yet, the loss of the staysail forced a reappraisal of the cruise objectives. I knew there was nowhere nearby that could provide another sail. Probably Santos in Brazil was the best bet, but if we sailed to Santos there would be no time to head south again in the 2013-2014 season, so Antarctica was out.

I was bitterly disappointed. The cruise had been in preparation for nearly a year, and of course, David, Simon and Bob had signed up specifically to visit the Antarctic continent. Standing in the heaving cockpit with the spray flying in the howling wind, my heart was heavy. It looked like this was as close as we were going to get to Antarctica on this cruise. I told the crew that I thought we had done our best, that we had been very unlucky to run into weather like this, and that we had to consider how to get ourselves home in one piece. I felt our best strategy was to head to Cape Town; all the facilities were there that we required. It was a long way, but it was downwind! Accordingly, at 53 degrees south and 59 degrees west, we turned the boat around and headed northeast.

Sometimes, turning around when the destination is so close is the hardest decision one can make. The trip to Cape Town would be no picnic—it was about 3,500 nm away, mostly sailed in the Furious Fifties and Roaring Forties. As it turned out, the decision was the smartest thing I could have done. We later discovered the main water tank had shifted in the melee and cracked, and half of our fresh water had leaked out.

East to Cape Town

During the next couple of days, we rolled downwind, cleaned up the boat and tried to dry out our clothing and bedding. David rescued the hard drive from my flooded computer and pronounced that the data could be retrieved. He managed to transfer the program used for Sailmail to his own laptop, so we again had limited e-mail capability, a major feat in the soggy, bouncing boat. One of the first e-mail messages I received was that the Antarctic pack ice was the furthest north it had been for 34 years, confirming that even if we had made it to the Peninsula, my original plan of an Antarctic circumnavigation would not have been feasible.

The wind was variable and at times fell to 10 knots, but mostly the log mentions relative winds of 20 knots with swells rolling past the stern. I decided we would visit Tristan da Cunha Island, as it was almost on the direct path to Cape Town. I had sailed there once before, 12 years earlier, and I felt the crew would enjoy the chance to visit this isolated community. It was a leg of about 2,000 nm.

Four days later, after enjoying typical Fifties sailing, that is, frequent swells washing into the cockpit, the nemesis I had been dreading occurred—the steering failed again. Fortunately, the wind was in the 15-knot range and we hove-to under the reefed mainsail. On inspection, I again found that wire rope was dangling from the quadrant and at first, I just assumed the wire had stretched and dropped out of the grooves. In order to keep the quadrant from shifting, we rigged the emergency tiller to the rudder post extension, and Simon sat on deck holding the tiller over. Although the wind was not strong, there was a heavy sea running and he had to work hard to hold the rudder in position.

As Bob and I toiled in the aft cabin, the boat rolled quite violently. Suddenly, there was a bang like a gunshot and the quadrant crashed to the other side, though fortunately our fingers were not in the way at the time. Simon was still holding the tiller in the original position, but the substantial cast iron universal joint between the rudder post and the extension had fractured, and this was entirely due to the force of a wave hitting the rudder. As we had done on the previous failure, Bob and I tied the quadrant down with rope and finished re-positioning the wire rope. When this was done, it was obvious that the problem was not the wire stretching; something was broken.

By this time, we were all exhausted. The motion of the boat was fatiguing, and night had fallen, so we let *Fiona* lie hove-to while we ate a simple supper and caught some sleep. I lay in my bunk with dark thoughts. Without the emergency tiller, there was no way of steering the boat if we could not fix the original system. We were hundreds of miles from the nearest land—South Georgia Island, which was hardly a haven. I had no idea how we would steer if we could not fix the failure. In the morning, at first light, I discovered that the chain had broken inside the steering wheel pedestal. To get at it, the compass and engine controls had to be removed. We all gathered in the cockpit and carefully stored each part as I removed them, so that they

The fractured cast iron universal joint

would not get lost in the pitching, rolling boat. We fished out the chain from the sprocket attached to the wheel and I removed the broken link, using a grinder on the universally versatile Dremel tool. I inserted the last master link in the spares kit to join the chain together.

This was the last major failure, although I felt the Sword of Damocles was hanging over us each time I saw the wheel working hard. Running down the Forties, we had the usual minor problems: chafe of the Aries lines, and whisker pole topping lift breaking, and yet basically, the boat held together, and as we worked to the east-northeast, the weather moderated and it got perceptively warmer. Three weeks after leaving Port Stanley, the misty outline of Tristan da Cunha hove into view—we had sailed about 2,500 nm, including the exciting attempt to get to the Antarctic.

Tristan was occupied by the British in 1815 to prevent any attempt by the French to rescue Napoleon from St. Helena, 1,000 miles to the north. When Napoleon died in 1821, a small group, under Corporal Glass, received permission to stay there. There is a settlement on the north coast called Edinburgh, where a few hundred souls scratch out a living by fishing.

When we arrived, the wind was quite light and we anchored with some difficulty, caused by thick beds of kelp a few hundred yards off the shore. Being an open roadstead with no lee, it was rolly. The person on the marine radio told us we could not land, as the place was shut down for a public holiday. We inflated the dinghy, persuaded the reluctant outboard to start and waited. We kept an anchor watch all night, and at first light, tried to get permission to land, but it was too late. The wind had picked up and surf at the jetty was too high. Simon, David, and Bob dinghied over to the jetty, while I stood by on *Fiona*. It was too dangerous to leave the boat alone, as the anchor was slowly dragging. The harbor master assessed the conditions at the jetty and waved them away. So they returned to the boat, we put the inflatable away and upped anchor in a rising wind. Simon, on the bow, had to pull masses of kelp off the chain as it came up. We were all disappointed not to have made a landing, but that's the cruising life. We bore away for Cape Town—1,500 miles to the east.

The weather north of 40 degrees south was pleasant and we enjoyed wonderful sailing with favorable winds. Six days after leaving Tristan it was Christmas. Out came our traditional tree and, to no one's surprise, Santa Claus managed to leave us a few small presents. We opened a bottle of wine someone had given us, but the motion on the boat had not agreed with it—it tasted terrible. Fortunately, we still had plenty of rum. Shortly after, we found the bread was going moldy and I baked a loaf, using the old Swedish oven. The crew loved it. I was going to bake a cake, but discovered all the eggs had gone funny.

Yet Cape Town was not far away and, early on the morning of January 2nd, 2014, the distinctive outline of Table Mountain and the Twelve Apostles to the south welcomed us to South Africa. We tied up at the Royal Cape Yacht Club at lunchtime. We had sailed 4,090 nm from Port Stanley in 36 days.

South Africa

Simon knew a charming young lady in Cape Town and she ran us to the Immigration Office so that we could get our passports stamped, and after a quick visit to customs, we were officially in South Africa.

The first order of business was to get the major repairs under way, but it is a tradition in Cape Town to take a couple of weeks' vacation after Christmas. It was the start of summer, and so organizing repairs to the sails and steering system was slow to start. But there was plenty to do on the boat and for a while, we monopolized the washing machines in the club laundry, not to mention the showers.

Eventually, the staysail was deemed beyond repair and I ordered a new one. We dissembled the steering system, and I was a little horrified to notice the side plates of two links in the steering chain were cracked. These were potential failures that would have been very difficult to repair, given the fact that I had no master links left. A helpful rigger promised to make new steering cables and to find replacement chain. While still at sea, I had e-mailed my son, Colin, who put together a package of spare parts, including an order at a store in Cape Town for a new laptop. He also FedExed a universal joint, which he modified before shipping, so that the length dimension matched the original. It was made for the inch-and-a-quarter-diameter shaft of the rudder post extension. I figured I had little hope of finding one in South Africa, which uses the metric system.

Each morning we worked on the boat, and in the afternoon we sampled the delights of Cape Town, which is a modern, clean city. We usually ate at the yacht club, which in my opinion is one of the finest in the world. We were there in time for the start of the biannual Cape to Rio Race. After the frenzied pre-race parties, the participants headed out into terrible weather, and one skipper was killed when the mast collapsed. Many boats returned, beaten and bedraggled.

One day we took the train, which rattles and squeals its slow way from Cape Town to Simon's Town on False Bay. It is a naval base, Dutch in centuries past, British during WWII, and now South African. We toured an obsolete submarine and looked at the penguin colony which makes a home on the shore. Poor Bob was scammed when he used an ATM machine—slick operators stole his PIN number and within minutes, cleaned out his account using an ATM in a village several miles away.

In Cape Town, a trip to the top of Table Mountain is de rigueur, but can be chancy; the cable car is often closed due to high winds, and if it is calm, the top of the mountain can be covered in thick cloud, known locally as a "Table Cloth." Nevertheless, David and I found the right combination one afternoon and ascended in the cable car to the top. The view from the over 3,000-foot summit is, of course, wonderful. Several walks of varying lengths are laid out on the rocky terrain, and there is a charming restaurant and gift shop.

David and I were sobered by the District Six Museum, a Bohemian area in the 1920s and 1930s where many biracial couples and Jewish immigrants lived. It was ethnically cleansed and bulldozed, and now the museum is the only reminder of that long-bygone way of life.

Slowly the crew dispersed. Simon flew to Canada. A few days later, Bob and David flew to their homes in the U.S. and Hungary, respectively. One day after the crew had left, I made another trip to Simon's Town, and in a gallery there I saw a picture of a Can-Can dancer done in pastel that I really liked. And after a couple of weeks of negotiation via e-mail, it was mine. I had to take it frame and all, as it was drawn on board and could not be rolled up. The Can-Can lady travelled back to Long Island in the aft cabin starboard bunk.

I made several interesting excursions while in Cape Town, due to a curious coincidence; visiting at the same time as myself was an 85-year-old sailor named Karl Burton, who was making a solo circumnavigation. He was tied up at the marina at the Victoria and Alfred complex. In the course of tracking down the whereabouts of an old South African crew, Pattie, on the internet, his wife back in California discovered he wasn't the only octogenarian sailor visiting Cape Town. So, once Pattie and Karl were re-united, they included me in their social plans.

Sunday at lunchtime, Pattie, her friend Lynn, and Karl picked me up at the Yacht Club with her 21-year-old Land Rover. We drove through the scenic country east of Cape Town to Stellenbosch, an entrancing town with lots of Old Dutch architecture. At the old arsenal, in the shade of some trees on a small square, we spotted about a dozen antique cars—we had happened on an informal Sunday gathering of old car buffs. There was 1941 Cadillac, a Hudson Terraplane, and a Rolls Royce, among others. Naturally, we stopped to shoot the breeze, and I discovered we had a common acquaintance, a South African Bentley driver I had met years before. Small world!

Later, we visited a winery for some wine tasting and wound up at a very up-market restaurant for a Thai lunch. We were joined by some of Pattie's friends—Ian, his son Russel, and Russel's girlfriend. Ian is a dentist from Scotland who has made a second home near Cape Town, where he stays for about three months every year during the northern winter. I think Ian was getting a little bored, because he was fascinated to meet Karl and me, and he insisted on arranging for all of us to see an outdoor production of *Richard III*, which was playing in the area.

Before the crew left, we had a farewell supper at an Indian restaurant near Long Street. I set about recruiting crew for the leg to St. Martin, and Jon Lihou, another Canadian, signed up via my website. Amy had posted a "crew available" card on the club notice board, so we arranged an interview on the boat. She came with her father. All seemed to go well, but the next day she e-mailed me to say she had a berth on another boat. Fortunately, another potential crew also posted a card on the club board, a young Frenchman called Mathieu. He had little sailing experience, but he seemed very intelligent and spoke English well. The problem with recruiting South Africans, which I tried to do, was that they needed a visa to visit St. Martin, a lengthy bureaucratic process involving the French consulate in Cape Town.

Later in the week, Pattie contacted me to say Ian had been able to get tickets for *Richard III* and prior to the show, she planned an afternoon of sight-seeing. Sure enough, at the appointed time the old Land Rover chugged up to the club entrance, with Pattie and Karl aboard. First we drove to an unusual café in a warehouse in the dock area called "Panama Jacks." After lunch, Pattie showed us some of the interesting spots in Cape Town, finishing up near the terminus of the cable car with Table Mountain looming over us. Then we drove along a spectacular winding road along the west coast to Hout Bay. The road clung to the side of almost vertical cliffs in places, and I could only admire the engineers and crew that built it. We stopped by Ian's lovely ranch for supper and cocktails before driving to the outdoor theatre. The stage used a few simple props and a natural grove of trees. It was very well done—Mr. Shakespeare would have enjoyed it.

Mathieu signed on, and a few days later Jon flew in from Vancouver via Hong Kong. Naturally, he needed a few days to decompress, so I took him on a tour of the downtown flea markets and souvenir stalls and suggested a train ride to Simon's Town. After nearly five weeks at Cape Town it was time to go. Pattie and Karl came to the yacht club to say au revoir and help untie lines. We left with gentle winds for St. Helena, and ultimately, the Caribbean.

Northwest to Long Island and Home

The 1,800-nautical-mile leg to St. Helena took two weeks. We saw no winds over 15 knots, and mostly had winds under 10 knots. We picked up a mooring in James Bay and within an hour, a lighter was alongside replenishing our fuel. Jamestown did not seem very different from my last visit in 1999, but changes were in the works; as we approached on the last night we could see intense lighting on the southeast corner. This was the 24/7 construction site of an airfield by a South African company. Once there is air service, the character of a place will change. But at that point, Jamestown reminded me of a small English village of the 1950s.

Mathieu and Jon repaired to the best hotel in town, the Consulate, for a few days of elegant luxury, while I stayed on the boat. In the evening, there was a long toot on the horn from the venerable Royal Mail Ship *Saint Helena* as she gathered way for a run to Ascension Island, and then on to Cape Town. This ship has been the island's only connection with the outside world, something that will end when the runway is completed.

*Consulate Hotel, Jamestown, St. Helena.
Note colonial soldier on the balcony.*

The next day ashore I did a little laundry and had a shower in a substantial stone building that looked like it predated Napoleon's exile on St. Helena. I had hoped to visit the Napoleon residence, but I waited until Sunday when the whole place just seemed to shut down. No taxis, in fact, and so I was lucky to get a lunch. Even the hotel was shut down. Monday morning, the troops came back to the boat and, after a little food shopping, we left for Ascension Island. It had been a pleasant hiatus.

The leg to Ascension was also plagued by very light winds, and the trip took a week to cover just over 700 nm. We also burned up about 60 gallons of diesel, some of which I was able to replace in port by paying a local entrepreneur to run four five-gallon jerry jugs over to the gas station. When we arrived,

Jon and Mathieu decided to hole up the Obsidian Hotel. I wandered over the next day to check my e-mail and Jon told me he was quitting and flying out from the island. Somehow I wasn't surprised, as he obviously had not been enjoying the sailing experience and was very tense, which led to unexpected flashes of temper. I stayed aboard *Fiona*, and this had its complications. The outboard engine was not behaving properly and the dinghy dock at Georgetown was positively dangerous in any kind of swell.

On the second day, we took a tour of the island in a Land Rover provided by the Conservation Centre. Ascension is of fairly recent volcanic origin and is mostly covered with brown cinders. Just like Tristan da Cunha, it was occupied by the Royal Navy in 1815 to forestall any attempt by the French to rescue Napoleon from St. Helena. It must have been a dreadful posting, but somehow the marines built sturdy stone buildings still standing today. The item of real interest in the tour was to ascend Green Mountain (2,817 feet) via a tortuous switchback road. Near the summit, which was often covered with cloud, was a small tropical rain forest. Apparently, when Darwin visited the island aboard the *Beagle* he suggested the moisture at the mountain summit could support vegetation and this in turn would cause more rain. The idea was followed up and now there is this miniature paradise on an otherwise arid, cindery island. The beaches are one of the world's largest nesting areas for Green Turtles. Hundreds come ashore every night to lay their eggs, as they have been doing for millions of years. During WWII, the U.S. built a runway which is still in use.

The next day, after clearing with customs and immigration, Mathieu and I spent our last St. Helena pound notes at the grocery store, boarded *Fiona*, stored the inflatable dinghy, and sailed for St. Martin, 3,700 nm away. The wind varied from good to light and, on the average, we made good about 100 nm a day until we got north of the doldrums. Some evenings we whiled away a couple of hours by watching a video. Mathieu belonged to another generation and had never heard of cinema greats like Marilyn Monroe and Humphrey Bogart. I tried to correct that lack of knowledge by showing old movies like *Some Like It Hot* and *Casablanca*. For several nights in a row, a handful of birds hitched a ride by perching on the aft rail and the radar. Mathieu looked them up in our bird book and pronounced then to be petrels.

When we got to the doldrums we encountered the usual squally weather and fickle winds, so we powered for about a day and a half using our carefully-husbanded reserve of fuel. We crossed the equator at 28° 31'W, and the next day Father Neptune duly appeared to induct Mathieu as a "Son of Neptune." North of the doldrums, the trade winds picked up and occasionally we were forced to reef the mainsail. This was more to keep the boat balanced and make life easier for Victor the Vane, which steered virtually all the time. We also encountered the North Equatorial Current and reeled off some good daily mileages, the best being 170 nm, noon to noon.

We sailed through the Sargasso Sea, and as we made good our westing, we kept putting the ship's time back by an hour at a time. It was very hot by lunch time, and the heat also brought a plague of fruit flies who had matured in the drink locker where leaky beer cans provided their nourishment. Every morning a crop of flying fish lay hardening on deck. I worked the shortwave radio every day to get weather forecasts and to recruit a new crew for the Caribbean leg. Eventually, Helena and John, veterans of the earlier cruise along the Brazilian coast, signed up to sail from St. Martin to Puerto Rico.

Mathieu and Eric toast the completion of the 6,000 nm leg from Cape Town to St. Martin in the Caribbean

We arrived at the south coast of St. Martin on the first of April and with very light winds ghosted to the Fort Louise Marina at Marigot. The leg from Ascension had taken 27 days. Within a couple of days, Mathieu flew to Nicaragua to join his brother on a Central American vacation.

My friend Eric Freedman, captain of *Kimberlite*, happened to be in St. Martin. We linked up and he drove me, with the torn mainsail, to a sailmaker on the Dutch side. Then, with his striking Colombian companion Betty we enjoyed a leisurely lunch. The boat next to *Fiona* at the marina, *Selkie*, was captained by a fellow member of the Cruising Club of America, Paul, who had been an investment banker with an interest in energy. We retired on several evenings to the friendly bar across the street to sort out the energy problems of the world.

When Helena and John showed up, we spent a day in Philipsburg, and then left for an overnight sail across the Anegada Passage and then cleared into the British Virgin Islands at Virgin Gorda. We could not get the fancy Japanese outboard engine to run, and so we powered the inflatable dinghy once again with the venerable Seagull engine. The trip to Anegada Island was a gentle beam reach of about three hours, and then we anchored to windward of a mooring field of bareboat charterers—there must have been about fifty of them. It was a measure of how popular that kind of cruising has become, and how popular Anegada is, which was rarely visited when Edith and I lived in the islands, due to the danger of crossing the reef. A buoyed channel and GPS had fixed that problem.

Our next anchorage was Jost Van Dyke, with a stop on the way over at Sandy Cay for a swim. Before dinner I stopped to talk to a shopkeeper who turned out to be a Chinnery, an old family name on Jost Van Dyke. When Edith and I first visited the Virgins in the early '60s, we spent a week on an old Brixham trawler called *Maverick*, anchored at Jost Van Dyke for New Year's Eve, when we were entertained by Lionel Chinnery on his guitar. I learned Lionel had been dead for many years, but I was able to talk to his sister. This brought back wonderful memories of cruising with Edith and Colin on *Iona* in those waters.

We cleared out of the Virgins at Jost Van Dyke and entered the U.S. at Culebra. We had a great downwind run to the huge Marina del Rey, where Helena and John left to meet John's mother for a short family vacation at San Juan. I had a day to myself before I rented a car and drove to the San Juan airport to meet the incoming crew, Kieron and Denis. I had met Kieron earlier in the cruise at Flores; he was crewing on a Canadian boat. We used the rental car for a tour of the wonderful El Yunque National Forest and left early the next day for the leg to Bermuda.

Normally, I would have expected the Trades to carry us north, at least to latitude 24°, but they did not develop. Instead, we sailed in light intermittent airs, and powered when the wind died. The day before we arrived in Bermuda, we picked up a good northwest wind and sailed for a day before the wind veered to northerly, which put it on the nose. We powered the last 20 miles with the lights of the island visible on the port bow, especially the powerful beam of the Gibbs Hill lighthouse. We entered the Town Cut about 2 am after contacting Bermuda Radio. Customs officers were waiting to inspect our documents and enter us into Bermuda.

My old friend, Bernie, who had been greeting boats to Bermuda for as long as I can remember, met us on the dock shortly after sunrise and arranged a slip at Captain Smokes Marina. Tying up there was tricky with a good breeze on the beam. Denis and Kieron had never been to Bermuda before, so the novelty of the pink and blue buses, pastel colored houses, and lush greenery was a delight for them. My old friend Gillian stopped by for happy hour, and she brought a good supply of "Dark and Stormy" cans and some egg rolls. In the morning, she had some business to conduct in Hamilton and gave us a ride into the city. I got some spare parts and then showed the guys some of my favorite spots—the Art Gallery, the Royal Bermuda Yacht Club, and the Princess Hotel. We had a pub lunch at the Hog Penny Inn.

In the morning we did some boat maintenance in preparation for the leg to Long Island, followed by sight-seeing in St. George's. We had a final dinner at the White Horse. In the morning we cleared out with customs and immigration and checked the long-range weather forecast. To my surprise, the official would not give me a copy of the print-out, claiming they were saving money by cutting back on paper. Talk about penny-wise and pound foolish! But the forecast looked good for the first day but then head winds would be a problem. We decided to leave anyway.

Kieron displays his glued-on finger

The forecast turned out to be exactly right—a wonderful sail the first day after we cleared Kitchen Shoal, and then four days of head winds. We made some progress under sail but used far too much engine. One evening as we tacked, the boat gave an unexpected lurch, and Kieron caught his hand between the barrel of the winch and the jib sheet. The top one inch of his right hand middle finger was just about amputated and was hanging by a shred of skin. There was blood everywhere. After packing the wound with paper towel and Neosporin I called a sailing friend, Charles Starke, who had sailed on *Iona* when he was a medical student. Charles advised me to use an antibiotic, which we had in the medical kit. He also suggested gluing the severed part of the finger back on with Krazy Glue, which fortunately I had on board. We were 300 miles from Fire Island Inlet. We found a plastic tube that would keep the parts together and dressed the wound two or three time a day. Fortunately, the weather improved and we made good time to Fire Island Inlet under sail.

Eric, the owner of *Kimberlite*, had e-mailed me the time of high tide at the Inlet and we arrived just a few minutes after high. The sea was calm but thick fog had descended. Fire Island Inlet is constantly shifting and the Coast Guard is hard pressed to keep the buoys in place which mark the deep channel. Mike, a friend from the South Bay Cruising Club, sent me the latest information on the buoys and we picked them up on radar without difficulty.

We then made the 20-mile leg to Patchogue inside Great South Bay without going aground, and when we arrived at Weeks Yacht Yard, Peg, a veteran of the 2011-2012 cruise, was waiting to greet us and take the lines. I dropped Denis off at the Port Jefferson ferry and a day later Kieron flew home. He later e-mailed to say the doctors thought his finger would be saved intact.

Last Thoughts

It had been a strange cruise. I had not achieved the primary goal, which was probably over-ambitious, but I made great new friends in South Africa. It was my fourth attempt to sail to Antarctica—I do not include my two trips to South Georgia, which is sub-Antarctica—only two of which had been successful. I guess this gives some idea of the statistics for a small boat to traverse the Scotia Sea.

The weather after we left the Falklands was atrocious, and bore little resemblance to the forecast. It wasn't the worst weather I have ever been in, but it was close. I felt particularly chagrined that I had exposed the crew to this rough treatment by Mother Nature, when nothing in their previous sailing had prepared them for it. But they bore up wonderfully, and David, Bob, and Simon were great crew. I was very apologetic that we had not made it to the Antarctic Peninsula, which is what they had signed up to see.

As for me, it is almost impossible to express the disappointment I felt when I made the prudent decision to turn away from Antarctica.

Dealing with the details of the trip had been a constant companion during planning for most of the past year. When we swung *Fiona's* heading to the northeast on that stormy night, I knew I was not going to make my goal, and I wasn't getting any younger either. Looking at it philosophically, cruising is all about the experience, and *Fiona* will be as good as new after a few repairs, and there were still cruises to be made.

12 | Long Distance Ocean Cruising— *The Nuts and Bolts*

Although I had been sailing for many years prior to retirement, I accumulated the bulk of my sea miles during the cruises outlined in the previous chapters. In this chapter, however, I want to offer some practical words of advice. If you have no intention of ever setting foot on a sailboat you can skip what follows.

My style of cruising evolved, although it was based on my own special circumstances, and sailing with many different crews, who usually signed on for only a few weeks or months. Only two crew members completed a cruise with me from start to finish. Walter sailed round the world, 1995 to 1997, and Mike sailed to Antarctica, 1998 to 1999. David and Bob, who made a circumnavigation with me in 2002 and 2003, almost made a complete trip, but they left the boat at Barbados, which was a planned departure for them.

One necessity forced by this mode of sailing was that I had to come up with a schedule before the trip began and stick to it, so that crew joining me later in the cruise, who might well have taken time off work, could count on me showing up at some intermediate port more or less when I said I would. It probably led to more use of engine than was desirable. Typically, about 10 to 15 percent of a cruise mileage was under power.

Many long-distance cruisers are couples, and usually their schedule is fairly elastic, so they often spend long periods in the same place between ocean legs. This isn't for me; I discovered during the first circumnavigation that dealing with shore-side problems didn't appeal to me. Perhaps that was what I was trying to escape from. Although I was usually glad to make port after a long leg, after a few days or a week I was just as glad to shove off.

As you might deduce from some of my comments about bureaucracy in foreign countries, I have a low tolerance for that kind of nonsense. Unfortunately, the tensions arising from the 9/11 attacks have only made this aspect of cruising worse. I have my own way of dealing with it—when I am stuck in some hot, dusty office filling out numerous forms, watched by a puffed-up official, I tell myself that in a few days or possibly a week or two I shall back on the open sea, free, and he will still be stuck in the same office, probably for years. That usually works and I wind up feeling sorry for the fellow, who is only try to make a living in a boring, useless job. Of course, there are also the ones who enjoy their moment of power, exemplified by the postal clerks around the world that gossip to each other while the queue stretches through the door. Thus, my cruises started to reflect more time at sea and less time in port.

In my second circumnavigation, the boat spent 184 days at sea and 72 days in port, and that included a month while I flew home. Of course, once I sailed through the Caribbean and later to Maine, the ratio changed considerably. I guess I had got my long-distance fix for that year. However, there are exemptions to this addiction; on seven occasions between 1995 and 2014, I spent about six weeks in the fall cruising Maine. On these trips I would often take a month to cover the 100 miles or so as the crow flies from Bar Harbor to Portland. The coast is so indented by deep, wonderfully scenic bays, that you could spend a lifetime cruising Maine and not experience all of it.

Watch Keeping

My preference is to sail with a crew of two, plus myself. With three of us that means, on average, each person spends eight hours on watch per day. I break the 24 hours into two periods: 8 am to 8 pm, ship's time, and 8 pm to 8 am. The daylight watches are three hours long and the night watches are two hours long. By day, a person has six hours free after a watch, and at night, four hours free before going on watch again. This system has the advantage that the watches "dog."

That means you serve a different watch on consecutive days, with the pattern repeating every three days, so that no one is stuck with a permanent graveyard shift of midnight to 2 am—you are "dogging" a watch.

If I am sailing with just one other crew member, the two of us divide the night watches into three four-hour shifts and two six-hour daylight shifts. This system also dogs the watches, with the pattern repeating every two days. I should mention that ship's time can be set to anything that is convenient. Navigation, of course, uses Universal or Greenwich Mean Time, but I like to set ship's time so that it gets dark about 8 pm. As the boat crosses lines of longitude, ship's time has to be reset every fifteen degrees or so.

On the boat, I do the cooking, and the crew washes up. Setting ship's time for nightfall at 8 pm gives them some daylight to get the galley cleaned up and all the pots and pans put away before the night watches begin. In port, I usually set ship's time to local time. Occasionally, I sail with four on board, and in that case we do two-hour watches, with one-hour dog watches from 4 to 5 pm and 5 to 6 pm, and this fits in with happy hour.

Of course, the routine is often disturbed by events that require several people on deck, tying in a reef for example. When the activity is over, the person whose watch it would have been takes over, if the time for a watch change has slipped by. Whenever anyone comes off watch, they make a brief annotation in the logbook, showing time, log reading, compass course, and barometric pressure. They can also add anything else of interest, such as sea conditions or wind speed and direction and changes in sail plan. Nowadays, with AIS we often log the names of ships that we pass. Once a day at noon, I usually write down in the log the ship's GPS position, course, and distance to a waypoint.

Only rarely do I ask the crew to spend the whole watch in the cockpit. Most times it is sufficient to glance around on deck every ten or fifteen minutes to make sure there is not a 20,000-ton freighter bearing down on the boat. If it is foggy, the watch performs a radar scan every half hour or so, but under sail I do not have enough power to keep the radar on continuously. With the engine running, that is not a problem. Otherwise, the watch consists of making sure we are on course, or as close as we can get if headed by the wind, and that the sails are trimmed. Under sail, the wind vane may require adjustment.

Once the crew gets used to the boat I expect them to trim and reef the jib by themselves, as this does not require them to leave the cockpit. If conditions justify reefing the mainsail or shaking out a reef, they wake me if I am asleep. I stress that no one leaves the cockpit unless someone else is watching them; this usually means that small jobs on the foredeck can be done only during watch changes.

Navigation and Maintenance

Safe navigation is the skipper's responsibility. To do this you need charts, and for a long voyage the charts can be a problem. When I built the boat, I incorporated two charts lockers in the forward head, about 3 feet long by 20 inches wide by 4 inches high. The charts are stored in these lockers in sturdy plastic garbage bags labeled to show the area covered. Charts should always be stored flat, never rolled up. I keep a list of all charts carried in a small note book. In the same book is a list of courtesy flags that will be needed.

Numerous publications are always needed—sight reduction tables, tide tables, the annual almanac, list of radio aids, pilots, and so on. In the past few years I have tried electronic charts, but I find they are great for approaching a harbor or anchorage, but useless for route planning and ocean passages. Without question, GPS has greatly simplified safe navigation, but attention must still be paid to a good lookout, watching the depth-finder, and looking ahead for changes in the weather or wind.

A boat is always falling apart. Gear and equipment failures should be rectified as soon as possible. You need a good stock of spare parts, tools, and the equipment manuals. Routine maintenance must include engine oil changes on schedule (every 100 hours of running on my boat), changing the external and internal zincs, lubricating winches, checking battery water, checking the fuel filters, and so on. On a passage I walk along the deck every day, I look at everything with an eye for loose screws, chafe, tears in the sails, or anything amiss.

Meals and Food

A plentiful supply of tasty, hot food is essential for good well-being on the boat. To provide this I do the cooking, and there are several reasons. The first is that I don't get sea-sick. The second reason is that food supplies are scattered throughout the boat in various lockers, and neophyte cooks could waste a lot of time finding the right thing, whereas I know where it's all stored. Thirdly, cooking at sea is an acquired art, as the stove on the boat is not gimbaled, and the pans are kept in place by adjustable fiddles.

I serve meals as closely as practical at set times, so that off-watch crew can count a given sleep period. But breakfast is a self-serve affair, people are coming off or on watch around 8 am, and can help themselves to porridge, cereal, fruit, bread, or eggs, with tea or coffee. If it is calm or we are at anchor, I often make pancakes, but I don't like to have a frying pan with hot oil on the stove if the boat is rolling or heeled. Crew can make a hot drink at any time, but I like to serve tea or coffee with a couple of cookies in the mid-morning, if anyone is awake. Lunch is served at noon. There is usually tea, coffee, and cookies in mid-afternoon, followed by happy hour at 5 pm. Supper is at 7 pm, and as mentioned, I like the galley completely cleaned up and everything stored before the night watches begin. If this is not done, then too often a gybe in the middle of the night is accompanied by the crash of crockery as plates, pots, and mugs slide out of the dish-rack.

Lunch usually consists of soup and a sandwich, along with a beer or soda. I try to find out from the crew what their preference is while we are shopping, so that the right numbers of cans are stored away. Happy hour consists of a small snack, cheese on crackers for example, served with rum and apple juice and a slice of lemon. A small percentage of crew prefers the juice without the rum, and that's okay, as there is more for me in the long run. For supper, I serve one of six or seven entrees, served with one of four carbohydrates. These are served each day so that the full cycle covers a week, and the food does not seem too repetitious.

I usually buy eight or ten loaves of whole wheat bread at the start of a long cruise. These are stored in the freezer, which is set to about 35°F. When the bread runs out, I bake a loaf every day in a Swedish oven—a 7-inch-diameter pan with a small flue in the center. The flue is placed over a burner which is set to a very low flame. This uses much less propane than heating up the entire oven.

For the entrees I used canned meat—corned beef, Spam, Werlings 14-ounce cans of beef, chicken, pork and turkey. Corned beef makes an excellent spaghetti sauce with a jar of Ragu. Chicken makes a good curry with commercial paste or powder. I serve pork or turkey with mushroom soup as a casserole. Chili is good with diced Spam, onions, tomato paste and chili powder. Baked beans are also good with diced Spam or pork, and I add diced and paste tomato, and use plenty of crushed red pepper.

Loaf of bread made in Fiona's Swedish *oven.*

I try to use onions and garlic in every dish, as these vegetables keep well. Citrus fruit and leafy green things do not last very long on a boat, depending on the temperature. Canned beef goes well with onions, along with canned mixed veggies and gravy browning as a stew. Useful canned veggies include green and red beans, lima beans and peas, mushrooms, diced tomatoes, and tomato paste. Carbohydrates used on the boat are rice, macaroni and cheese, spaghetti, and fresh or instant potatoes.

We have trailed a line for fish at times and indeed caught a few and eaten them. But there are disadvantages—they are messy to clean and usually provide so much flesh you are eating fish for days. There is also the problem in tropical waters of fish carrying a toxin called "ciguatera," a terrible affliction you may experience when eating an affected fish, and the symptoms may last for years. To satisfy a yearning for fish I try to serve canned tuna at least once a week in the lunch-time sandwich. Canned sardines or smoked oysters are also a tasty option for happy hour snacks.

Dessert is fresh fruit, if any is left, or canned fruit. If anyone gets hungry during a long night watch there is a snack locker with dried fruit, chocolate, granola bars, and other items like that.

For hot drinks I stock tea and coffee, both regular and decaffeinated, and sometimes cocoa. I lay in several cases of long-life milk, as throughout most of the world except developed countries, this is the kind of milk people drink. It is only used with hot drinks and cereal; it is not practical to carry enough to drink directly. I generally use about a quart a day at sea. I try to have an extra beer or soda for each person at supper. I poll the crew for their preferences in regard to soda and beer, aiming for at least two cans per person per day. How much I carry depends, of course, on the expected time to the next port and reasonable re-supply facilities. I usually carry rum by the case, bought hopefully in the Caribbean for about one-third the New York price. I also carry juice, especially apple juice for the *Fiona* cocktail.

The boat carries 200 gallons of fresh water in three tanks, and I carry an emergency supply of five gallons in two plastic jugs for use with the life-raft or if the water becomes contaminated, which has happened. I generally keep the beer and soda for a day in the refrigerator, along with a quart of fresh water which I ask users to replenish when they pour some out. That doesn't always happen. Some crews, presumably with very sensitive palates, have complained about the taste of water from the tanks. I add about a tablespoon of bleach to each 50 gallons when filling the tank. To me, it is not detectable, but I rarely drink water directly; I prefer tea or coffee. I subscribe to W.C. Field's observation when he tasted water for the first time after many years, "I don't know what it is, but it won't sell!" I also carry a Brita filter which can be used when water from the tank is added to the fresh water container in the refrigerator. Bottled water is a problem on a boat because of the need to store the plastic containers. Plastic must never be dumped at sea. The deal I make with crew who must have bottled water is that the water and the empties are to be stored in their own personal locker space, which is quite limited.

For the circumnavigation in 1995 to 1997, I fitted a water-maker. It did provide a useful source of water between Australia and the Mediterranean, a region where good water was hard to find. But it was fairly heavy on the battery, and the problem of keeping the filters free of algae if it was not used every day became too onerous. When we got home, I scrapped it and I have never used or needed one since.

Cleanliness is not strongly encouraged; on long legs we usually rig the shower in the forward head once a week. Typically, I find we use about a gallon a day of water per person for all purposes, including cooking.

Safety Survival

I always have a safety briefing with a new crew at the start of a voyage. I stress that safety is very much an individual matter, that they should not do anything stupid, and that they should remember the square rigger maxim—one hand for the ship and one hand for yourself. *Fiona* has all the modern safety apparatus—good lifelines, jacklines for safety harnesses, life jackets, life rings with flashers, and man-over-board poles and life-sling. The U.S. Coast Guard mandates that emergency flares are renewed every three years, but based on what I read of actual sinkings, a hand-held VHF radio is much more likely to summon help from a passing ship. We carry a four-man life raft, EPIRB, and ditching bags.

It is important in the briefing to discuss how to use this stuff, for example if someone falls overboard. The drill is different by day or night. I show the crew how to use the GPS, AIS, and radios. As mentioned previously, I ask the crew not to leave the cockpit unless another crew member is watching out. Wearing a harness is something I leave to individuals most of the time. If they feel more comfortable with a harness on, that is their choice. But if I decide conditions are a little fraught, reefing the mainsail in heavy weather for example, I ask everyone to buckle up.

Keeping Warm

Fiona has two heating systems. The first is a commercially-made space heater, which operates on diesel fuel, with a heat exchanger to dry circulating air. This small unit provides about 8,000 BTUs of heat and has air ducts to the aft and main cabins. It does not raise the cabin temperature much above 50 F in Arctic conditions, but it dries the air and is greatly appreciated when one is in high latitudes. The pump and fan draw about 4 amps, so this space heater's use is limited to a few hours a day when sailing.

The other heating system is a heat exchanger with circulating engine cooling waters, similar to a car engine heater. This warms the main cabin and keeps us toasty when the engine is running in cold climates.

Morale

Many factors influence the morale on board. Maintaining good morale is primarily the responsibility of the skipper. Never act like Captain Bligh, do not yell at the crew—but sometimes that's easier said than done. Try to match the tasks you assign to individuals to their skill level. If they do well, say so. If they screw up, as often happens, discuss it in a reasonable way. Do not use the possessive pronoun "my" or "mine." It is "our" boat, "our" problem, and so on.

On long trips, I often assign areas of responsibility to crew members. Some like rigging, so I get them to overhaul all the lines, or replace chafed ropes. Those who are used to navigation I encourage to plot routes, position fixes, and enter waypoints into the GPS. On many trips, I have given a simple course in celestial navigation, and within a week some can plot position lines using the sun.

I have e-mail on the boat using Sailmail, and so encourage crew to send the occasional message home or to friends. Good food on time is essential for morale, and in all my years, I can count on the fingers of one hand the times when conditions were too rough to cook, and usually no one feels like eating at times like that.

In colder climes, make sure all the wet clothing and foul weather gear is dried. I often hang stuff in the engine room to dry, but not everyone likes that, as clothes acquire that indefinable, yachtie smell of diesel, mold, and oily seawater.

On pleasant evenings about once a week, I usually screen a movie, starting about happy hour. In the early days, I used a small TV set with a video camera as a VCR. Nowadays, laptop computers can play color movies on DVDs. Younger crew members use an MP3 player, but I do have a radio in the main cabin with a CD player. The speakers can be switched off and headphones plugged in for listening without disturbing sleeping crew.

I carry many books, split between sailing classics and paperback trash that we trade with other boats in port. I like to carry back copies of the *Guardian Weeklies*, which my daughter collects while I am away and mails to intermediate ports or sends to crew joining the boat.

In tropical waters on calm days, we often stop the boat for a swim over the side. The point of the whole trip is to make sure everyone is enjoying the experience.

13 | Reflections

O ver the years I have met hundreds of live-aboard sailors, and we have exchanged many stories over rum in *Fiona*'s cockpit at happy hour. These social interactions with other cruisers are always great fun. I have also read many books written by amateur long-distance sailors, and I have to say that we are all different and we all have a variety of objectives and motivations, some of them quite inexplicable.

Before adopting the cruising life-style it is important to have a very clear picture of just what it is you want. This affects every aspect of the experience, from the type of boat and gear that you carry, to how the trip will be financed, and the level of skill that must be developed. Spending a winter in the Caribbean is rather different than sailing round the world, and sailing to high latitudes is another ratchet on the learning curve. As I aged, I realized that I personally preferred the journey rather than the destination. Many try to get into the culture of remote places that are open to those with a stout, sea-worthy boat. A sailboat is a nearly ideal way to do this—you are self-sufficient and can stay for long periods, needing only basic supplies. And yet this has never appealed to me. I am not an anthropologist.

Of course, I have spent a lot of time observing local life in the vast number places I've visited as I have traveled the world by sea. Many cultures I've run into are making an uneasy transition from their traditional life-style to one which is adopting many western methods and ideas. In countries which are considered to be "developing," the cult of the automobile is all-powerful. Countries I have visited occasionally over the years have seen incredible changes, going from donkeys and horse-drawn carts to mass ownership of motorbikes and cars, with semis roaring along multi-lane highways. Even cultures I had not visited previously but had read about are changing beyond recognition.

The Inuit of northern Canada and Alaska come to mind. It was only in 1905 that Amundsen wrote of spending two years with a people that were living in the Stone Age. But when we visited the same village he founded, only a little over a hundred years later during the 2009-2010 cruise, the inhabitants lived in centrally-heated, prefabricated houses, and traveled mostly by snowmobile or all-terrain vehicle. I don't blame them in the slightest; the old ways resulted in a life that was cruel, brutish, and short. I know some of them try to retain some old skills—they harness huskies to sleds, but when they hunt for seals, it is with a modern rifle mounting a telescopic sight. The food they carry on the expedition often came from a supermarket, which was restocked by air. Every northern settlement I saw, from Greenland to Alaska, had a tank farm, or oil depot.

An oil tank farm, Dutch Harbor, Alaska, 2009

On my first visit to French Polynesia in 1990, we anchored at a small, remote village in the Marquesas Islands, where a man approached us as we walked through the luxuriant jungle and asked us into his bamboo hut. His kids were in an adjacent room, screened off by a thin curtain. Intrigued by the noise, I peeped in, and found that they were watching a violent, shoot-em-up movie on a VHS cassette. He swapped a Tapa cloth for some five-minute epoxy. Almost no culture can survive cars and TV, let alone the internet. Personally, I am not critical of these changes, as they seem inevitable, and for many, the western way of life is more comfortable than the way people lived before. But slowly, I have begun to have serious doubts about the viability of what is happening.

These doubts began in a small way during the 2004-2005 cruise as we ploughed our way through the South Atlantic to the Falkland Islands. A British woman sailor was racing a maxi (an out-and-out speed sailboat), in the Global Vendee, a very tough solo circumnavigation. Her name was Ellen MacArthur, and she was passing the Falkland Islands from the west as we approached from the north. The local radio news broadcasts were full of her exploits, as it looked like she would set a record for a non-stop circumnavigation. And indeed she did, and the British awarded her the distinction of Dame of the British Empire, the female equivalent of a knighthood, for the feat. We must have passed each other somewhere before we arrived. We didn't see her, but what caught my attention was a short news item that reported she had been burned by falling against the hot diesel engine on her boat. Although the engine did not propel the boat, it powered many auxiliary services.

I began to ponder on the idea that a true sailboat race would not use auxiliary power. And after a few calculations, I concluded that a boat could race across an ocean without using any fossil fuel, deriving all energy needed for on-board services, such as lights, radios, and cooking from the wind, the sunlight, and the motion of the boat through the water. This wasn't exactly theoretical; for years aboard *Fiona*, I had generated power to charge the battery under sail from an alternator running off the propeller shaft. Although it was not enough to make the boat independent of charging from the engine, it provided experimental data that showed scaling up was feasible.

As I mentioned in Chapter 6, this grew into the idea of the Green Ocean Race—a sailboat race across an ocean for boats dependent entirely on energy they generated themselves. The analogy with our own planet, Earth, was overwhelming. Those boats, alone on a vast ocean making their energy, directly or indirectly from the sun, were like Earth spinning through space at some time in the future when the human race has used up the fossil fuel. I have already been working to get organizations with a stake in alternative forms of energy production to sponsor a race, and hope that it will become a reality one of these days.

Slowly, my interest and attention has shifted to encompass not only the race itself, but to the analogy I have drawn, the earth itself. Where would alternative energy come from if we humans consume our inheritance of fossil fuel? That will not happen soon, but it is clear that the oil, gas, and coal companies are very good at extracting every last barrel, cubic foot, and ton from the earth. More and more it seems as if that unhappy event—the depletion of fossil fuel on Earth—is inevitable.

The more I read about this subject, the more perturbed I have become about the immense effort and treasure that is being expended to combat global warming. I have begun to feel that all these well-meaning folk have been concentrating on the wrong problem. Much of the efforts to combat global warming will simply extend the period we use fossil fuel. Virtually all the carbon in the remaining reserves will be released anyway. Does anyone really believe that we will not pump the last remaining gallon of oil or mine the last ton of coal? The human race does not seem to work that way. If fossil fuels *are* left in the ground to combat global warming this will only hasten the need for alternatives.

In my own sailing career, I have seen the Grand Banks fished out; not a single cod is left to sustain commercial fishing. Surely this is a guide to what will happen to energy. Probably very little of the carbon which is released when a hydrocarbon is burned will be captured at the source, and thus all the carbon bonded in fossil fuels since the carboniferous period some hundreds of millions of years ago will again enter the atmosphere. How much warming this will cause is almost impossible to figure out with any precision. Many mechanisms absorb carbon naturally—the oceans, trees, and plant life. But what will be the effect of the surplus carbon? It is rather like trying to calculate the level of water in a bath tub fed by a hundred faucets. The flows are varying all the time, and emptied by a thousand drains, all of them clogging or unclogging.

I thought about these things as *Fiona* sailed tens of thousands of ocean miles, in calms and storms. I concluded that we must deal with next phase, which is how society will function without fossil fuel. With regard to the problems created by a carbon surplus and global warming, we have already soiled our own nest, so to speak. Signs of the pollution caused by the massive use of fossil petro carbons are everywhere at sea. On calm days, when the sea is really flat, the surface can be seen to be covered by countless tiny particles of pulverized polystyrene, the remains of millions of coffee cups and packaging materials. On the trip to Tahiti in 1990, Shoel and I sailed past a vast plastic "gyre"—a huge area in the Pacific which was full of oily plastic debris. A large sea turtle was tangled up with some polypropylene rope.

Islands in the tropics which lie in the trade wind belts frequently have beaches on the windward side which are littered with every kind of plastic trash—flip-flops, cartons, rope, netting, balloons, you name it. On both trips in which I succeeded in landing on the Antarctic continent (Chapters 3 and 7), I was able to compare snow and ice conditions for the same month, eight years apart. Of course, two samples do not constitute a scientific survey, but on the second cruise there was definitely much less snow and ice. And the fact *Fiona* made it through the Northwest Passage on the first try (Chapter 9) shows that for the long term, it must be getting warmer up there. It took Amundsen three years to complete the Northwest Passage.

Some of the palliatives promoted to combat global warming will alleviate the energy supply problem in the future, but they will not solve it. Wind generation and solar power may ultimately produce about 30 percent to 50 percent of the electric power we use at present. But to reach this level will take many years, and vast investment in power transmission and energy storage.

Many human activities, such as travel by air and sea, and the activities of humans in remote habitats well off the power grids, will still need the convenience of portable energy sources. The population in the U.S. is rising about one percent a year, and it is rising even faster in developing parts of the world. These extra humans will add to the demand for energy, so the faster we get to work figuring out how to provide it, the better.

Alternative energy sources are quite evident everywhere. In the Baltic literally hundreds of giant wind generators stand on coastal plains in Denmark and Germany. In Brazil the fuel for the teen-ager's scooter is likely to be alcohol, distilled from sugar. On lonely Fernando de Noronha a vast wind generator turned slowly in the southeast trade winds—until destroyed by a bolt of lightning! The motive for these developments is usually given as a response to global warming and the initiative comes from governments, either directly or by tax breaks. Norway has huge installations of hydroelectricity, and in Iceland I was intrigued to find geothermal plants generating their electricity. But many countries generate most of their electricity using fossil fuel, and transportation depends almost entirely on oil or its derivatives.

The span of recorded human history is only about 8,000 years, give or take. Almost the entire consumption of fossil fuel has occurred in the last 200 years. It will probably fall to zero in another hundred years, simply a spike in the historical record. But the effect of this spike has been to produce the most astounding change in history; the quality of life for millions, if not billions, of people has been lifted to an astonishing level. Many of us in the developed, and even developing, world lead lives of such luxury, diversity of choice, and comfort that would have seemed impossible even for a king a couple of centuries ago.

But the bill has to be paid, and what do you do when you have spent your inheritance? Well, I guess you buckle down to work, if you want to keep what you have. Discussing the inevitable depletion of fossil fuel is not popular. Nobody wants to think about the day when they press the switch and the lights don't come on. We live in an age of symbols and sound bites, but the solution to the energy problem is a rational, hard-headed mix of technology, economics, and politics.

I have often wondered which societies that I have visited by boat would be able to survive in a post-fossil fuel age. My conclusion is that very few would. Certainly, the Kuna Indians in the San Blas, the Polynesians in the Gambiers, and many other small groups could survive by fishing and rudimentary farming. But would they be allowed to? Desperate people in the vast megalopolitan areas would probably attack them for their resources. When societies like the Kuna Indians lived their self-sufficient way a century or two ago, the world population was much smaller and far less energy intensive. In other words, there is a strong chance society will break down if we enter the post-fossil fuel era without adequate preparation. Possibly a few island societies would survive, if they are far from land, like St. Helena, Pitcairn, and even Tristan da Cunha, but I am not sure I would like to live there.

To avoid this terrible possibility, we must find not only practical energy sources but also alternative models for our society to replace what has developed since the industrial revolution began. It is easy to say this, and yet speaking as an engineer, I have no idea how it can be accomplished unless we scale back our energy usage drastically from the levels we have become accustomed to.

My hope is that I can help raise public awareness about the prospect of a post-fossil fuel society, and at the same time strike a positive tone about change. This is what I hope can be accomplished with the Green Ocean Race, which will focus attention on the development of alternative sources of energy. I hope the challenge of designing a boat to be self-sufficient will excite the imagination of many young people with an interest in the sea. It is in their lifetime that the energy problem will become acute.

14 | Acknowledgements

Organizing a long cruise like the kind you have just read about takes an enormous amount of support, both at sea and on land. At sea the crew is particularly important, and by and large the nearly two hundred guys and gals that signed up to sail with me worked out wonderfully and contributed to my enjoyment of the sail. Only a few gave me real problems, so in the book I have changed their names. Only two crew stayed with me for the complete trip, Long Island to Long island—Walter Van Vleck sailed round the world and Mike Demont circumnavigated South America and sailed to Antarctica. Bob Bennett and David Pontieri circumnavigated the world on a rough passage round the southern capes.

Keeping the boat functional often required help from a friend who shipped vital spares and equipment to remote, obscure, ports when the boat fetched up on land. My old friend 'Red' Harting looked after this until he passed away; after that my son Colin ably kept me sailing. The boat's medical kit, ignored until a crisis, was upgraded after the end of each cruise by my friend Dr. Bob Chernaik. It is impossible to separate oneself when at sea from the trivia of the life left on land; bills, taxes, subscriptions, etc.—all have to be dealt with; I can't thank my daughter Brenda enough for insulating me from these time-consuming details.

When *Fiona* returns to port she is well looked after by Kevin and the gang at Weeks Yacht Yard in Patchogue. The sails, which are usually fairly battered, are cared for, or replaced, by Mark at Doyle Sails. Tricky mechanical repairs get the attention of Bob Berg who has a superbly equipped machine shop. While I am away Holly Allen moves into my house in Brookhaven, she keeps it clean and deals with the inevitable maintenance chores.

The popular website www.yachtfiona.com was run initially by Rich Hollander, but in recent years my daughter Brenda has assumed this task. Lew Schatzer has edited the videos made on each major trip—a thankless chore—squeezing many hours of rough footage into polished movies.

In writing this book, dredging up memories of decades of incident-filled sailing, I am indebted to Peg Daisley who kept me steering a firm course towards the goal of actually publishing it. Peg dealt patiently and capably with the task of editing hundreds, if not thousands, of errors, suggestions and corrections into the first draft text. Jay Pizer brought an artistic flair to the layout and managed to avoid the repetitive conformity which plagues many travel books.

During the time this book was being pulled together, 2015 and 2016, I sailed *Fiona* on a ten-month, 14,000-mile cruise, to Canada, Scotland, the Baltic, and the Caribbean, and later, on a month-long cruise to Maine. There's life in the old sea-dog yet!

Acknowledgements

Index

Index

Index

Index

Index

Index

Index

Index

Index

Index

Index

Index

Index

CPSIA information can be obtained
at www.ICGtesting.com
Printed in the USA
BVOW09s0728250717

490002BV00005B/17/P